Measuring Psychological Constructs

Measuring Psychological Constructs

Advances in Model-Based Approaches

Edited By
Susan E. Embretson, PhD

American Psychological Association
Washington, DC

Copyright © 2010 by the American Psychological Association. All rights reserved. Except as permitted under the United States Copyright Act of 1976, no part of this publication may be reproduced or distributed in any form or by any means, including, but not limited to, the process of scanning and digitization, or stored in a database or retrieval system, without the prior written permission of the publisher.

Published by
American Psychological Association
750 First Street, NE
Washington, DC 20002
www.apa.org

To order
APA Order Department
P.O. Box 92984
Washington, DC 20090-2984
Tel: (800) 374-2721;
Direct: (202) 336-5510
Fax: (202) 336-5502;
TDD/TTY: (202) 336-6123
Online: www.apa.org/books/
E-mail: order@apa.org

In the U.K., Europe, Africa, and the Middle East,
copies may be ordered from
American Psychological Association
3 Henrietta Street
Covent Garden, London
WC2E 8LU England

Typeset in New Century Schoolbook by Circle Graphics, Inc., Columbia, MD

Printer: Edwards Brothers, Ann Arbor, MI
Cover Designer: Minker Design, Bethesda, MD

The opinions and statements published are the responsibility of the authors, and such opinions and statements do not necessarily represent the policies of the American Psychological Association.

Library of Congress Cataloging-in-Publication Data

Measuring psychological constructs : advances in model-based approaches / Susan E. Embretson, editor. — 1st ed.
  p. cm.
 Based on presentations at a conference held in Feb. 2006 at the Georgia Institute of Technology in Atlanta, Georgia.
 Includes bibliographical references and index.
 ISBN-13: 978-1-4338-0691-9
 ISBN-10: 1-4338-0691-6
 1. Psychological tests. I. Embretson, Susan E.
 BF176.M43 2010
 150.28'7—dc22

2009022368

British Library Cataloguing-in-Publication Data
A CIP record is available from the British Library.

Printed in the United States of America
First Edition

APA Science Volumes

Attribution and Social Interaction: The Legacy of Edward E. Jones

Best Methods for the Analysis of Change: Recent Advances, Unanswered Questions, Future Directions

Cardiovascular Reactivity to Psychological Stress and Disease

The Challenge in Mathematics and Science Education: Psychology's Response

Changing Employment Relations: Behavioral and Social Perspectives

Children Exposed to Marital Violence: Theory, Research, and Applied Issues

Cognition: Conceptual and Methodological Issues

Cognitive Bases of Musical Communication

Cognitive Dissonance: Progress on a Pivotal Theory in Social Psychology

Conceptualization and Measurement of Organism–Environment Interaction

Converging Operations in the Study of Visual Selective Attention

Creative Thought: An Investigation of Conceptual Structures and Processes

Developmental Psychoacoustics

Diversity in Work Teams: Research Paradigms for a Changing Workplace

Emotion and Culture: Empirical Studies of Mutual Influence

Emotion, Disclosure, and Health

Evolving Explanations of Development: Ecological Approaches to Organism–Environment Systems

Examining Lives in Context: Perspectives on the Ecology of Human Development

Global Prospects for Education: Development, Culture, and Schooling

Hostility, Coping, and Health

Measuring Patient Changes in Mood, Anxiety, and Personality Disorders: Toward a Core Battery

Occasion Setting: Associative Learning and Cognition in Animals

Organ Donation and Transplantation: Psychological and Behavioral Factors

Origins and Development of Schizophrenia: Advances in Experimental Psychopathology

The Perception of Structure

Perspectives on Socially Shared Cognition

Psychological Testing of Hispanics

Psychology of Women's Health: Progress and Challenges in Research and Application

Researching Community Psychology: Issues of Theory and Methods

The Rising Curve: Long-Term Gains in IQ and Related Measures

Sexism and Stereotypes in Modern Society: The Gender Science of Janet Taylor Spence

Sleep and Cognition

Sleep Onset: Normal and Abnormal Processes

Stereotype Accuracy: Toward Appreciating Group Differences

Stereotyped Movements: Brain and Behavior Relationships

Studying Lives Through Time: Personality and Development

The Suggestibility of Children's Recollections: Implications for Eyewitness Testimony

Taste, Experience, and Feeding: Development and Learning

Temperament: Individual Differences at the Interface of Biology and Behavior

Through the Looking Glass: Issues of Psychological Well-Being in Captive Nonhuman Primates

Uniting Psychology and Biology: Integrative Perspectives on Human Development

Viewing Psychology as a Whole: The Integrative Science of William N. Dember

APA Decade of Behavior Volumes

Acculturation: Advances in Theory, Measurement, and Applied Research

Aging and Cognition: Research Methodologies and Empirical Advances

Animal Research and Human Health: Advancing Human Welfare Through Behavioral Science

Behavior Genetics Principles: Perspectives in Development, Personality, and Psychopathology

Categorization Inside and Outside the Laboratory: Essays in Honor of Douglas L. Medin

Chaos and Its Influence on Children's Development: An Ecological Perspective

Child Development and Social Policy: Knowledge for Action

Children's Peer Relations: From Development to Intervention

Commemorating Brown: The Social Psychology of Racism and Discrimination

Computational Modeling of Behavior in Organizations: The Third Scientific Discipline

Couples Coping With Stress: Emerging Perspectives on Dyadic Coping

Developing Individuality in the Human Brain: A Tribute to Michael I. Posner

Emerging Adults in America: Coming of Age in the 21st Century

Experimental Cognitive Psychology and Its Applications

Family Psychology: Science-Based Interventions

Inhibition and Cognition

Measuring Psychological Constructs: Advances in Model-Based Approaches

Medical Illness and Positive Life Change: Can Crisis Lead to Personal Transformation?

Memory Consolidation: Essays in Honor of James L. McGaugh

Models of Intelligence: International Perspectives

The Nature of Remembering: Essays in Honor of Robert G. Crowder

New Methods for the Analysis of Change

On the Consequences of Meaning Selection: Perspectives on Resolving Lexical Ambiguity

Participatory Community Research: Theories and Methods in Action

Personality Psychology in the Workplace

Perspectivism in Social Psychology: The Yin and Yang of Scientific Progress

Primate Perspectives on Behavior and Cognition

Principles of Experimental Psychopathology: Essays in Honor of Brendan A. Maher

Psychosocial Interventions for Cancer

Racial Identity in Context: The Legacy of Kenneth B. Clark

The Social Psychology of Group Identity and Social Conflict: Theory, Application, and Practice

Strengthening Couple Relationships for Optimal Child Development: Lessons From Research and Intervention

Strengthening Research Methodology: Psychological Measurement and Evaluation

Transcending Self-Interest: Psychological Explorations of the Quiet Ego

Unraveling the Complexities of Social Life: A Festschrift in Honor of Robert B. Zajonc

Visual Perception: The Influence of H. W. Leibowitz

Contents

Contributors xi

Foreword xiii

Preface xv

    1. Measuring Psychological Constructs With Model-Based
        Approaches: An Introduction 1
        Susan E. Embretson

Part I. Model-Based Approaches to Measuring Qualitative Differences Between Individuals 9

    2. Mixture Distribution Item Response Theory, Latent Class
        Analysis, and Diagnostic Mixture Models 11
        Matthias von Davier

    3. Skills Diagnosis for Education and Psychology With
        IRT-Based Parametric Latent Class Models 35
        Louis A. Roussos, Louis V. DiBello, Robert A. Henson,
        Eunice Jang, and Jonathan L. Templin

    4. Cognitive Psychometrics: Using Multinomial
        Processing Tree Models as Measurement Tools 71
        William H. Batchelder

Part II. Model-Based Approaches to Isolating Entangled Constructs 95

    5. Unidimensionality and Interpretability of
        Psychological Instruments 97
        Jan-Eric Gustafsson and Lisbeth Åberg-Bengtsson

    6. Using Item Response Theory to Disentangle Constructs
        at Different Levels of Generality 123
        David Thissen and Lynne Steinberg

Part III. Model-Based Approaches for Measuring Personality, Psychopathology, and Attitudes From Self-Reports 145

    7. Measuring Psychopathology With Nonstandard Item Response Theory Models: Fitting the Four-Parameter Model to the Minnesota Multiphasic Personality Inventory 147
Niels G. Waller and Steven P. Reise

    8. MIXUM: An Unfolding Mixture Model to Explore the Latitude of Acceptance Concept in Attitude Measurement 175
James S. Roberts, Jürgen Rost, and George B. Macready

Part IV. Cognitive Psychometric Models for Interactive Item Generation 199

    9. Recent Development and Prospects in Item Generation 201
Isaac I. Bejar

    10. Modeling the Effect of Item Designs Within the Rasch Model 227
Rianne Janssen

    11. Cognitive Design Systems: A Structural Modeling Approach Applied to Developing a Spatial Ability Test 247
Susan E. Embretson

Index 275

About the Editor 285

Contributors

Lisbeth Åberg-Bengtsson, PhD, Department of Education, University of Gothenburg, Gothenburg, Sweden
William H. Batchelder, PhD, School of Social Sciences, University of California, Irvine
Isaac I. Bejar, PhD, Educational Testing Service, Princeton, NJ
Louis V. DiBello, PhD, Learning Sciences Research Institute, University of Illinois, Chicago
Susan E. Embretson, PhD, Department of Psychology, Georgia Institute of Technology, Atlanta, GA
Jan-Eric Gustafsson, PhD, Department of Education, University of Gothenburg, Gothenburg, Sweden
Robert A. Henson, PhD, Educational Research Methodology Department, The University of North Carolina at Greensboro
Eunice Jang, PhD, Department of Curriculum, Teaching, and Learning, University of Toronto, Toronto, Ontario, Canada
Rianne Janssen, PhD, Department of Educational Sciences, University of Leuven, Leuven, Belgium
George B. Macready, PhD, College of Education, University of Maryland, College Park
Steven P. Reise, PhD, Department of Psychology, University of California, Los Angeles
James S. Roberts, PhD, School of Psychology, Georgia Institute of Technology, Atlanta
Jürgen Rost, PhD, IPN Institute for Science Education, University of Kiel, Kiel, Germany
Louis A. Roussos, PhD, Measured Progress, Dover, NH
Lynne Steinberg, PhD, Department of Psychology, University of Houston, Houston, TX
Jonathan L. Templin, PhD, Department of Educational Psychology and Instructional Technology, University of Georgia, Athens
David Thissen, PhD, L. L. Thurstone Psychometric Laboratory, University of North Carolina, Chapel Hill
Matthias von Davier, PsyD, Educational Testing Service, Princeton, NJ
Niels G. Waller, PhD, Department of Psychology, University of Minnesota, Minneapolis

Foreword

In early 1988, the American Psychological Association (APA) Science Directorate began its sponsorship of what would become an exceptionally successful activity in support of psychological science—the APA Scientific Conferences program. This program has showcased some of the most important topics in psychological science and has provided a forum for collaboration among many leading figures in the field.

The program has inspired a series of books that have presented cutting-edge work in all areas of psychology. At the turn of the millennium, the series was renamed the Decade of Behavior Series to help advance the goals of this important initiative. The Decade of Behavior is a major interdisciplinary campaign designed to promote the contributions of the behavioral and social sciences to our most important societal challenges in the decade leading up to 2010. Although a key goal has been to inform the public about these scientific contributions, other activities have been designed to encourage and further collaboration among scientists. Hence, the series that was the "APA Science Series" has continued as the "Decade of Behavior Series." This represents one element in APA's efforts to promote the Decade of Behavior initiative as one of its endorsing organizations. For additional information about the Decade of Behavior, please visit http://www.decadeofbehavior.org.

Over the course of the past years, the Science Conference and Decade of Behavior Series has allowed psychological scientists to share and explore cutting-edge findings in psychology. The APA Science Directorate looks forward to continuing this successful program and to sponsoring other conferences and books in the years ahead. This series has been so successful that we have chosen to extend it to include books that, although they do not arise from conferences, report with the same high quality of scholarship on the latest research.

We are pleased that this important contribution to the literature was supported in part by the Decade of Behavior program. Congratulations to the editors and contributors of this volume on their sterling effort.

Steven J. Breckler, PhD
Executive Director for Science

Virginia E. Holt
Assistant Executive Director for Science

Preface

This book highlights several explanatory approaches to model-based measurement. These approaches not only extend rigorous psychometric methods to a variety of important psychological constructs but, more important, also have the potential to fundamentally change the nature of the constructs that are measured. The models in the exploratory approaches have special parameters or features that can represent important aspects of constructs that are not represented in standard item response theory models.

The chapters in this volume are based on presentations that were given at a conference, "New Directions in Measuring Psychological Constructs With Model-Based Approaches." The conference was held in February 2006 at the Georgia Institute of Technology in Atlanta. The conference was jointly sponsored by the American Psychological Association and the Georgia Institute of Technology. The book features chapters by 11 internationally distinguished authors, who have varying perspectives on how measurement constructs are impacted by modern psychometric modeling approaches.

Special recognition must be given to individuals who contributed their time and effort to the conference and to the production of this volume. Dr. James Roberts assisted not only with managing the conference but also with reviewing chapters for this volume. Several graduate students in the Quantitative Psychology Program at the Georgia Institute of Technology also contributed to both the conference and the editing of the book. These students are Robert Daniel, Heather McIntyre, Hi Shin Shim, and Vanessa Thompson.

Finally, Marshall Picow, my husband, had a vital role in supporting me throughout the period of the conference and the preparation of the book. This volume probably would not have been possible without his unfailing and devoted support during my recovery from a serious accident that occurred during the week after the conference.

Measuring Psychological Constructs

1

Measuring Psychological Constructs With Model-Based Approaches: An Introduction

Susan E. Embretson

More than a half century has passed since Cronbach (1957) made his well-known distinction between the correlational and the experimental disciplines in psychology. The disciplines were characterized not only by distinct methods but also by different kinds of constructs. Psychological measurement is almost entirely within the correlational discipline, which has individual differences as a primary focus. Certainly substantial changes have occurred within the two scientific disciplines and within psychological measurement over the past 50 years. But have the constructs that are measured using contemporary psychometric methods become better integrated with constructs that arise from the experimental discipline of psychology?

Within the measurement field over the past half century, item response theory (IRT) models and methods have replaced classical test theory (CTT) as the basis for developing many psychological and educational tests. IRT is model-based measurement, in that the individual item responses are modeled. Thus, IRT models include not only one or more estimates to represent the persons but also estimates to represent the psychometric properties of items. This contrasts sharply with CTT, in which the main target is total score, not item responses. Hence, item properties are not represented directly in the model.

The many practical, technical, and statistical advantages of IRT for developing psychological and educational tests have been published widely in both methodological and substantive journals. Further, IRT has been a major focus in numerous conferences and workshops, and these gatherings have resulted in many edited books. The properties of IRT models have also been given considerable attention. For example, *Rasch Models: Foundations, Recent Developments and Applications* (Fischer & Molenaar, 1995) especially highlights the formal quantitative aspects of the models. *Objective Measurement: Theory Into Practice, Volume 5* (Wilson & Engelhard, 2000) is an example of a series that contains a broad sampling of new applications and extensions of IRT models. Other books, such as *Computerized Adaptive Testing* (Wainer, 1990), focus specifically on a major practical advantage of IRT-based tests. Collectively, the many available edited volumes have made substantial contributions to psychometric methods and have further extended IRT into measurement in many substantive areas.

However, the integration of model-based approaches of IRT with substantive research on psychological constructs has received less attention. An edited book, *Test Validity* (Wainer & Braun, 1988), contains chapters that are focused on new approaches to explicating validity, which includes IRT model-based approaches. Although contemporary psychological theory is represented by a couple of articles in this book, the vast majority of articles concern methodological developments arising from within the correlational discipline. Another edited book that arose from a measurement-oriented conference focuses more directly on construct issues. A conference honoring Samuel Messick was held at Educational Testing Service in 1997. Although the papers from this conference (see Braun, Jackson, & Wiley, 2002) raised several issues about psychological constructs, they were not related to specific model-based measurement approaches. Furthermore, many papers at the conference could be characterized as primarily based on correlational methods of theory development.

The topics of two edited books are more directly relevant to interfacing measurement methods with contemporary psychological constructs. *Test Theory for a New Generation of Tests* (Frederiksen, Mislevy, & Bejar, 1993) introduced model-based measurement as providing new approaches to testing and new ways to interface with substantive theory. Few applications have yet been realized, even though the book preceded the present volume by more than 15 years. Unfortunately, such delays are not atypical in the slowly evolving world of psychological testing. Some important recent developments in model-based measurement are covered in *Explanatory Item Response Models* (De Boeck & Wilson, 2004), along with many interesting illustrative applications. A major goal of De Boeck and Wilson was to provide an integrated presentation of several recent IRT models that could be specified with common statistical framework (i.e., as nonlinear mixed models). Hence, the scope of their book was necessarily limited.

Thus, despite many important developments in psychological measurement in the past half century, there is little evidence that the integration between measurement and the constructs that stem from psychological theory has progressed much since Cronbach (1957) noted the two separate disciplines of psychology. Perhaps the areas are fundamentally incompatible. This would be especially true if individual differences were never of interest in experimentally based theories. However, another possibility is that typical applications of IRT, like its predecessor CTT, may introduce constraints that have limited the applicability of psychometric methods to constructs of interest in contemporary psychology. That is, the most widely used psychometric methods are most appropriately applied when a single source of impact (i.e., underlying dimension) influences both persons and items.

The purpose of this volume, in part, is to present a broad spectrum of model-based measurement approaches that remove some of the constraints. Typical test development practices under both CTT and IRT require several assumptions that do not necessarily interface well with psychological constructs as conceptualized theoretically. That is, the test developer must assume that (a) the same construct can characterize responses of all persons, (b) items have identical psychometric properties when administered to different persons, (c) items are fixed entities with known stimulus content, (d) items are calibrated prior to test scoring, (e) item response probabilities are monotonically related to the trait to be measured, and (f) internal consistency between items on a test indicates adequate assessment of a trait.

Although these assumptions seem fundamental to developing psychometrically rigorous tests, they have also functioned to define a narrow set of tasks and conditions that are deemed appropriate for measurement. One obvious consequence has been the popularity of multiple-choice tasks and related objective item formats because they more readily meet the constraints than do other tasks, such as constructed responses. Yet constructed response tasks and performance assessment are often regarded as more authentic measures that better represent conceptualizations of the domain or construct. The constraints also impact test content in other ways than item format. For example, empirical tryout of items involves evaluation and selection in terms of the constraints noted above. Item attrition is often quite high; a rate of 50% attrition is not atypical. With such high item attrition, the surviving items may not represent very well the original conceptualization of the task domain.

Several developments in model-based measurement have the potential to impact the nature of constructs that can be measured in psychology. Some of these developments remove one or more constraints, as described earlier, whereas other developments, such as explanatory psychometric models, permit a new level of integration of measurement and psychological theory. Many of these models (e.g., De Boeck & Wilson, 2004; Embretson, 1999; Glas & Van der Linden, 2003; Mislevy, Steinberg, & Almond, 2003; Roberts, Donoghue, & Laughlin, 2000; Rost, 1990, 1991; von Davier & Rost, 1995) have appeared in the psychometric literature but have not yet been available to the broader audience of psychologists.

The purpose of this volume is to highlight several explanatory approaches to model-based measurement that can impact the nature of the psychological constructs that can be measured with rigorous psychometric methods. In this book, model-based measurement approaches that are more appropriate for the constructs of interest in many substantive areas of psychology are explicated and illustrated with applications. New developments of model-based measurement in four different areas are included as follows: (a) model-based approaches to measuring qualitative differences between individuals; (b) model-based approaches to isolating entangled constructs; (c) model-based approaches for measuring personality, psychopathology, and attitudes from self-reports; and (d) cognitive psychometric models for interactive item generation during testing.

In Part I, Model-Based Approaches to Measuring Qualitative Differences Between Individuals, several different types of explanatory models are represented. Qualitative differences between persons in the nature of a construct may occur either in cognitive measurement or in personality and attitude measurement. A well-studied source of qualitative differences between groups is differential item functioning (DIF), which is a violation of the traditional psychometric constraint that items have identical properties for all examinees. A common psychometric procedure is to eliminate items showing DIF, which consequently narrows measurement of the construct. Another approach is to use model-based approaches with DIF items included but with group-specific parameters. Although the item domain is not narrowed by using this approach, it is nonetheless controversial because an individual's estimated score will be impacted by demographic variables, such as gender or ethnicity.

In contrast, a model-based solution has broad potential to identify classes of individuals who differ qualitatively on the construct. These classes are based not on demographics but on the pattern of item responses. Mixture IRT models (e.g., Rost, 1991; von Davier & Rost, 1995) can be applied when the test scores do not represent the same construct for different examinees. Such a test probably would have poor fit to a traditional IRT model because the assumption of unidimensionality is violated. The mixture IRT models identify latent classes of examinees for whom the construct differs qualitatively. Thus, both the score levels and the latent class memberships of the persons can provide important information about individual differences. To give an example, success in solving spatial tasks does not necessarily involve spatial analogue processing. Some spatial tasks may be solved by either analogue or verbal-analytic processes, which can have implications for the external correlates of test scores (Embretson, 2007). Of course, tasks that can be solved by more than one method could be eliminated from spatial ability measurement; however, the remaining tasks may be sufficiently restricted so as to adversely impact the theoretical scope of the construct. In chapter 2, Matthias von Davier presents an overview of mixture distribution IRT models. His chapter shows a progression of models, from unidimensional IRT models and latent class models to the mixture distribution IRT models, to handle varying assumptions about the nature of the construct.

Items that measure the same dominant trait can also differ qualitatively. Diagnostic IRT-based models, such as the fusion model (Roussos et al., 2007), can be used to relate qualitative features of items to item solving. In mathematics achievement, for example, qualitative information about the specific skills that an examinee has mastered, as well as overall competency level, may be obtained. The diagnostic IRT models relate scored attribute requirements in the items to performance. In chapter 3, Louis A. Roussos and his coauthors present an overview of diagnosing skills through diagnostic IRT models.

Another approach to model-based measurement of cognitive skills is based on multinomial processing tree (MPT) models. MPT models were initially developed to study normal cognition in specific experimental paradigms in cognitive psychology, but more recently MPT models have been applied to understand and measure how special populations differ in latent cognitive skills. In chapter 4, William Batchelder reviews the methodological issues that arise when MPT models are used for psychological assessment. He also describes recent applications to special populations.

In Part II, Model-Based Approaches to Isolating Entangled Constructs, two approaches are presented that have an interesting relationship to the traditional psychometric principle of internal consistency. Selecting items by internal consistency can lead to measuring either constructs at the wrong level of generality (Gustafsson, 2002) or trivial constructs (see Steinberg & Thissen, 1996). Model-based measurement approaches can aid in untangling the trivial or inappropriate constructs from the theoretically targeted construct. In chapter 5, Jan-Eric Gustafsson and Lisbeth Åberg-Bengtsson describe how model-based results reveal that the intended construct of a psychological test in itself can be understood in terms of both more general and more specific constructs. Such results have important implications for distinguishing between constructs because tests that fit unidimensional measurement models, in fact, typically reflect multiple constructs. Furthermore, broad constructs typically cannot be measured with a single item type because the specific constructs would confound the measurement. In chapter 6, David Thissen and Lynne Steinberg describe how explicit or implicit internal structure in many self-report measures, such as clusters of questions based on some common stimulus or questions that are too similar, adds extraneous covariation among the item responses. Internal consistency consequently becomes inflated by these trivial sources of item covariation. They describe methods to use IRT models so as to remove these trivial sources of covariation that become entangled with the construct of interest.

In Part III, Model-Based Approaches for Measuring Personality, Psychopathology, and Attitudes From Self-Reports, models that are especially applicable to self-report measures are described. For constructs in the psychopathology or personality domain, standard IRT models do not fit many measures. The two-parameter and the three-parameter logistic models, which are often applied, predict that the probability of item endorsement increases to 1.0 for extreme trait levels. Yet, some extreme behaviors are not highly likely to be endorsed even by individuals with extreme pathology. In chapter 7, Niels G. Waller and Steven P. Reise present a study on a test for psychopathology in which the four-parameter logistic model is estimated to add an upper asymptote for item responses. They explore how the construct is impacted by the choice of a model.

For some psychological constructs, particularly in attitude measurement, a particular behavior or item endorsement is not increasingly likely for persons at higher levels of the construct. That is, a particular behavior (or attitude) may be likely at a moderate level of the trait but not at higher levels, as other behaviors replace it. If the traditional monotonic psychometric models are applied, such items will be eliminated as inappropriate, and the construct will be consequently narrowed. Recent developments in nonmonotonic models (Roberts et al., 2000) have brought unfolding models into the domain of IRT. In chapter 8, James Roberts and his coauthors describe an extension of nonmonotonic models to include mixtures that can be used to model DIF or to decrease the impact of unconscientiously responding examinees from the measurement process. The latter application will increase the validity of the central construct under study in a given application.

In Part IV, Cognitive Psychometric Models for Interactive Item Generation During Testing, model-based approaches are interfaced with computer algorithms to develop items with targeted psychometric properties. In these approaches, test items are developed "on demand" or even "on the fly" without empirical tryout. Thus, the traditional constraint of requiring that test items that are fixed entities with previously obtained calibrations will not be met because the items are generated anew. The model-based IRT approaches for item-generation interface prior research on the items with test calibration. Models for two different item-generation approaches, the item-model approach (Bejar, 2002) and the item-structure approach (Embretson, 1999), have been developed. In chapter 9, Isaac Bejar presents a broad overview of the substantive basis of item generation methods and their implications for psychometric models. Item difficulties in contemporary item generation are predictable from prior research findings using special IRT models. However, in the modeling sense, it is important to view the items as having a random element because prediction is not perfect. New developments in item-response theory models (De Boeck & Wilson, 2004; Janssen, Schepers, & Peres, 2004) include both random and fixed effects, so that the degree of item differences may be rigorously assessed in the course of measurement. The random element is particularly appropriate when items are not fixed entities. In chapter 10, Rianne Janssen develops a random effects version of the linear logistic test model (LLTM; Fischer, 1973) and discusses several types of applications. In chapter 11, I present the structural modeling approach to developing a test with predictable item difficulties based on a cognitive model. An additional benefit of the structural modeling approach is that items may be banked by levels and sources of cognitive complexity using a cognitive IRT model, such as the LLTM or the 2-PL Constrained model. An application to measuring spatial ability using an item generator is given to illustrate the structural modeling principles.

As a collection, the chapters in this book present several new options for the researcher and the test developer. Because IRT is a rapidly developing field, many other new models may also be developed in the next few years. Of course, only time will tell whether applications of these models will broaden the scope of measurement to include constructs that are more related to other areas of psychological theory. Testing practices evolve slowly, unfortunately. However, the possibility of applying rigorous psychometric methods to very different kinds of psychological constructs is exciting.

References

Bejar, I. I. (2002). Generative testing: From conception to implementation. In S. H. Irvine & P. C. Kyllonen (Eds.), *Item generation for test development* (pp. 199–218). Mahwah, NJ: Erlbaum.

Braun, H., Jackson, D. N., & Wiley, D. E. (Eds.). (2002). *The role of constructs in psychological and educational measurement*. Hillsdale, NJ: Erlbaum.

Cronbach, L. J. (1957). The two disciplines of scientific psychology. *American Psychologist, 12*, 671–684.

De Boeck, P., & Wilson, M. (2004). *Explanatory item response models*. New York: Springer.

Embretson, S. E. (1999). Generating items during testing: Psychometric issues and models. *Psychometrika, 64*, 407–433.

Embretson, S. E. (2007). Mixed Rasch model for measurement in cognitive psychology. In M. von Davier & C. H. Carstensen (Eds.), *Multivariate and mixture distribution Rasch models: Extensions and applications* (pp. 235–254). Amsterdam: Springer-Verlag.

Fischer, G. H. (1973). Linear logistic test model as an instrument in educational research. *Acta Psychologica, 37*, 359–374.

Fischer, G. H., & Molenaar, I. V. (Eds.). (1995). *Rasch models: Foundations, recent developments and applications*. New York: Springer-Verlag.

Frederiksen, N. A., Mislevy, R. J., & Bejar, I. I. (1993). *Test theory for a new generation of tests*. Hillsdale, NJ: Erlbaum.

Glas, C. A. W., & Van der Linden, W. (2003). Computerized adaptive testing with item cloning. *Applied Psychological Measurement, 27*, 247–261.

Gustafsson, J. E. (2002). Measurement from a hierarchical point of view. In H. I. Braun, D. N. Jackson, & D. E. Wiley (Eds.), *The role of constructs in psychological and educational measurement* (pp. 73–95). London: Erlbaum.

Janssen, R., Schepers, J., & Peres, D. (2004). Models with item and item group predictors. In P. De Boeck & M. Wilson (Eds.), *Explanatory item response models*. New York: Springer.

Mislevy, R. J., Steinberg, L. S., & Almond, R. G. (2003). On the structure of educational assessments. *Measurement: Interdisciplinary Research and Perspectives, 1*, 3–62.

Roberts, J. S., Donoghue, J. R., & Laughlin, J. E. (2000). A general item response theory model for unfolding unidimensional polytomous responses. *Applied Psychological Measurement, 24,* 3–32.

Rost, J. (1990). Rasch models in latent classes: An integration of two approaches to item analysis. *Applied Psychological Measurement, 14,* 271–282.

Rost, J. (1991). A logistic mixture distribution model for polychotomous item responses. *The British Journal of Mathematical and Statistical Psychology, 44,* 75–92.

Roussos, L. A., DiBello, L. V., Stout, W., Hartz, S. M., Henson, R. A., & Templin, J. L. (2007). The fusion model skills diagnosis system. In J. P. Leighton & M. J. Gierl (Eds.), *Cognitive diagnostic assessment for education: Theory and applications* (pp. 275–318). Cambridge, England: Cambridge University Press.

Steinberg, L., & Thissen, D. (1996). Uses of item response theory and the testlet concept in the measurement of psychopathology, *Psychological Methods, 1,* 81–97.

von Davier, M., & Rost, J. (1995). Polytomous mixed Rasch models. In G. Fischer & I. Molenaar (Eds.), *Rasch models: Foundations, recent developments and applications* (pp. 371–379). New York: Springer.

Wainer, H. (1990). *Computerized adaptive testing: A primer.* Hillsdale, NJ: Erlbaum.

Wainer, H., & Braun, H. (1988). *Test validity.* Hillsdale, NJ: Erlbaum.

Wilson, M., & Engelhard, G. (2000). *Objective measurement: Theory into practice* (Vol. 5). Stanford, CT: Ablex.

Part I

Model-Based Approaches to Measuring Qualitative Differences Between Individuals

2

Mixture Distribution Item Response Theory, Latent Class Analysis, and Diagnostic Mixture Models

Matthias von Davier

Different people may use different strategies when solving an item in a proficiency test or when responding to items on a questionnaire. Some of the strategies chosen may work well for all items in a given test, and some strategies may be appropriate only for a subset of the items. An example is *mixed number subtraction,* a class of problems similar to the ones studied by Tatsuoka and colleagues (Tatsuoka, 1987). Consider the following two items:

1. Solve: $2\frac{3}{8} - 1\frac{1}{8} = ?$ and   2. Solve $2\frac{1}{4} - 1\frac{1}{8} = ?$

Assume that students who use Strategy A solve these items by subtracting the integer parts and the numerator parts separately while disregarding potential differences in the denominator. This strategy would most probably lead to a correct answer to Item 1 and an incorrect answer to Item 2, because disregarding the denominators will lead to mistakes.

People who apply Strategy B solve the items in a completely different way: All mixed numbers are converted to fractions, and then the difference is calculated. Finally, the result is converted back into a mixed number. For example, Item 2 is solved using Strategy B as follows:

2. Solution: $2\frac{1}{4} - 1\frac{1}{8} = \frac{9}{4} - \frac{9}{8} = \frac{18}{8} - \frac{9}{8} = \frac{9}{8} = 1\frac{1}{8}.$

Strategy B involves, in comparison with Strategy A, more calculations, and using this strategy may take longer than using Strategy A. However, if correctly executed, Strategy B will generally result in correct responses.

Obviously, if only the solutions are recorded, as is often the case in psychological testing and educational measurement, one can only judge whether students were able to solve the item and perhaps derive some hypotheses regarding where they went wrong if samples of incorrect solutions can be examined. The application of a certain strategy or thinking process is often not observable, although there is indication that students differ in how they approach problems as well as in how well they perform once an approach is chosen. More generally, many different strategies may be present, and particular types of strategies may be assumed if students switch between different approaches to solving a problem, depending on the items presented to them.

Tatsuoka (1987) studied strategy differences in students solving mixed number additions. Other types of tasks that are often hypothesized to be prone to strategy differences are spatial tasks that involve mentally rotating a three-dimensional structure that is depicted in a test in two dimensions. Kelderman and Macready (1990), Mislevy and Verhelst (1990), Rost (1990), and Rost and von Davier (1993) referenced these types of strategy differences and used a particular approach to analyze data in search of the assumed strategy groups of test takers. These authors found that such questions can be suitably analyzed using methods involving mixture distributions (see also Embretson, 2007). The mixture components represent the different strategies or approaches students take to solve the tasks administered in an assessment.

More formally, mixture distributions are composite distributions, describing populations composed of two or more subtypes or subpopulations. In most cases, the component distributions are of a simple parametric form but with different parameters (such as means or variances) describing the differences between subpopulations. The parametric families commonly found in mixtures are distributions such as the normal distribution for real-valued random variables, the Poisson distribution for count data, or the binomial distribution for sums of binary random variables. In social sciences, psychometrics, and educational measurement, some commonly used mixture distribution models are latent class analysis models, the mixed Rasch model, as well as mixture item response theory models and mixture growth curve models. Recently, diagnostic models for skill profile reporting have been extended to mixture distribution models.

This chapter gives an overview of mixture distribution models used in psychometrics and educational measurement and provides references to developments and applications of this flexible class of models.

Mixture Distribution Models

For illustration purposes, I start with an example of an early attempt to measure certain features of human beings with the goal of coming up with an average representing a given sample. This example involved the length of the human left foot in a settlement in medieval Europe. For illustration, let us refer to foot length as a random variable denoted by x. Assume we want to model the distribution of this variable x in a medieval settlement (see Figure 2.1).

Let's say we have available data on this variable from two historic samples. Assume that one dataset is based on people selected at a farmers marketplace, whereas another was drawn at the cloth-maker's store. The tabulation of results for foot-length x in these two samples is provided in Table 2.1. Sample 1 has data based on 16 people from the farmers marketplace; Sample 2 has data from 14 people assessed in front of the cloth-maker's store.

The first question that comes to mind is whether there is a simple, well-known, tractable model for this type of data—for example, whether we may assume a normal distribution for the combined sample. However, if we look at

Figure 2.1. Wood-print depicting the determination of an average of foot lengths. From *Geometrie* by J. Koelbel, 1575, Frankfurt, Germany. Image in public domain.

our "made-up" data file, given in Table 2.1, we may suspect that there is more to the data, so that a simple normal density may not be sufficient to model these data appropriately.

One may argue that it is obvious that the two samples come from two quite different distributions. One could test for mean differences, assuming that the two samples drawn are from two unknown populations. However there are a few measures above 10.0 in Sample 1, and there are also measures somewhat below 10.0 in Sample 2. Alternatively, one could try and see whether the measures taken can be predicted in some fashion on the basis of other knowledge we have about the people measured. However our made-up medieval samples

Table 2.1. Results of Foot-Length Measures From Two Samples, Raw Measures, Means, and Standard Deviations

	Sample 1: Marketplace	Sample 2: Cloth maker
Raw data	9.1, 9.2, 8.9, 9.4, 9.8, 10.2, 8.8, 9.3, 9.5, 10.0, 9.3, 8.8, 9.0, 9.1, 10.1, 9.3	10.5, 10.7, 10.8, 10.4, 9.9, 10.0, 10.5, 10.4, 10.3, 9.8, 10.9, 10.8, 10.1, 9.7
Sample mean	9.3625	10.343
S.D.	0.448	0.392

do not contain other variables such as gender or age. Let us assume that the historic source tells us that only adults participated in the measurements.

In that case, we may assume that our observations were drawn from both genders, and the observed difference between samples may simply stem from the possibility that there were more females than males in one place, and more males than females in the other place. The difference between means of the two samples drawn in locations may be an underestimate of the "true" gender difference between the foot lengths of males and females because we cannot be sure that there were only males in one sample and only females in the other sample.

It would be nice to have a way to sort this out without exactly knowing the gender of each person contributing a measure in each case. As it turns out, there were researchers who thought so as early as 1886 (Newcomb, 1886; cited in McLachlan & Peel, 2000), even though Pearson (1894) is often given credit for the first application of a mixture of normal distributions to major data analysis. The question these (and other) researchers asked was: How can we represent the fact that observations in a sample may come from groups with different properties, without knowing which group each observation was coming from?

The mathematical modeling of this problem takes the form of a weighted sum of terms, with the weights representing the probability of observing a member of each gender in a given sample. As an example, the expectation μ_{market} of the sample mean $\hat{\mu}_{market}$ is

$$\mu_{market} = \left[\pi_{female|market} \times \mu_{female}\right] + \left[\pi_{male|market} \times \mu_{male}\right] \quad (1)$$

where μ_{female} represents the mean of measures in the female part of the population, and μ_{male} represents the mean of the measures in the male part of the population. The $\pi_{female|market}$ represents the (unknown) proportion of females in the sample collected at the marketplace, and $\pi_{male|market} = 1 - \pi_{female|market}$ is the proportion of males in this sample. Once we know the values for μ_{male} and μ_{female}, we are able to calculate the estimated proportion of females (and males) for a given sample mean $\hat{\mu}_{market}$.

If not a simple sample statistic like the average, but the full distribution of a random variable is of interest, the weighted sum is taken across the different distributions of the unknown sample components. In that case, the generic discrete mixture of two distributions becomes $f(x) = \pi_1 f(x|g=1) + \pi_2 f(x|g=2)$ with mixing components $\pi_1 = p(g=1)$ and $\pi_2 = p(g=2) = 1 - \pi_1$. If more than two mixing components are involved, we have

$$f(x) = \sum_{g=1}^{G} \pi_g f(x|g) \quad (2)$$

with mixing proportions π_g and the constraint $\sum_g \pi_g = 1$. The general form of a discrete mixture distribution is suitable for various types of random variables and has been used in various fields of research (see McLachlan & Peel, 2000). In the next section, an important special case, the mixture of normal distributions, is introduced. Then, a variety of mixture models for discrete random variables is introduced, such as scored responses of examinees to questionnaires or tests. This form of discrete mixture models is suitable for analyses of multi-dimensional discrete data such as item response data, which is often found in psychometrics, educational measurement, and other social sciences.

Mixtures of Continuous Random Variables

Recall the univariate normal distribution, which has the density

$$\phi(x;\mu,\sigma) = \frac{1}{\sqrt{2\pi}\sigma} \exp\left(-\frac{(x-\mu)^2}{2\sigma^2}\right) \quad (3)$$

with mean μ and standard deviation σ. The sample mean $M(x) = \frac{1}{n}\sum x_i$ is an unbiased estimate of μ and the sample variance $s^2(x) = \frac{1}{n-1}\sum(x_i - M(x))^2$ is an unbiased estimate of σ^2. Figure 2.2 shows densities for different values of μ and σ.

Mixtures of normal distributions are a statistical tool used in many areas. One of these areas is quantitative genetics, in which normal mixtures are used to detect heterogeneity of observations based on hidden structure (e.g., Gianola, Heringstad, & Odegaard, 2006). The term *hidden structure* from quantitative genetics is obviously related to the term *latent* in connection with *variable* or *structure,* which is commonly used in social science models.

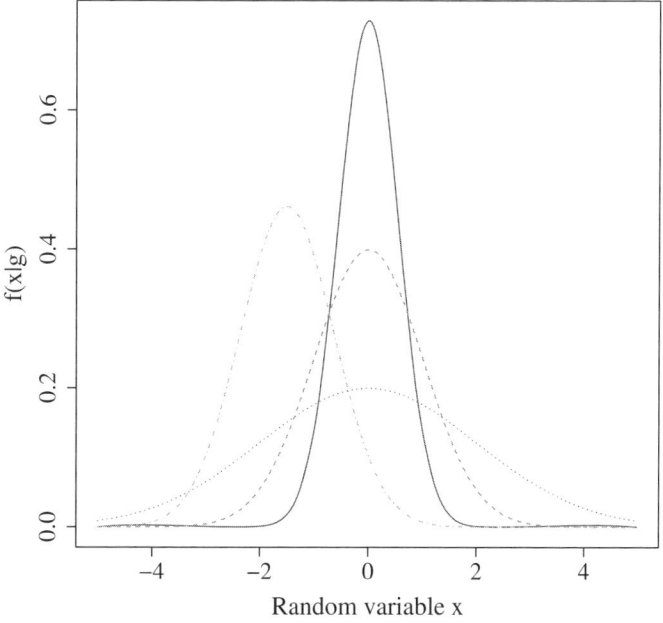

Figure 2.2. The normal density for different values of μ and σ.

Mixtures of Normal Distributions

The general form of a discrete mixture of G normal distributions is

$$f(x) = \sum_{g=1}^{G} \pi_g f(x|g) = \sum_{g=1}^{G} \pi_g \frac{1}{\sqrt{2\pi}\sigma_g} \exp\left(-\frac{(x-\mu_g)^2}{2\sigma_g^2}\right), \quad (4)$$

with group-specific mean μ_g, standard deviation σ_g, and mixing proportions π_g. Figure 2.3 provides examples of marginal densities based on a mixture of only two normals. The different shapes are the result of a variation of the mixing proportions $\pi_1 = p(g1) = 1 - p(g2) = 1 - \pi_2$. This small set of examples shows that discrete mixtures of normal distributions are quite flexible in adopting different shapes, even when only two mixture components are involved.

Discrete mixture distributions can easily be specified for multidimensional random variables, that is, for a variable $\vec{x} = (x_1, \ldots, x_d)$ with d real valued components. In that case,

$$f(\vec{x}) = \sum_{g}^{G} \pi_g \frac{1}{(2\pi)^{d/2}|\Sigma|^{1/2}} \exp\left(-\frac{1}{2}(\vec{x}-\vec{\mu}_g)^T \Sigma_g^{-1}(\vec{x}-\vec{\mu}_g)\right) \quad (5)$$

is the d-dimensional mixture density of $\vec{x}$. As before, the π_g denote the mixing proportions, and $\vec{\mu}_g$ is the mean vector, and Σ_g is the variance-covariance matrix of mixing component g. Figure 2.4 shows a sample from a mixture of two bivariate normal distributions.

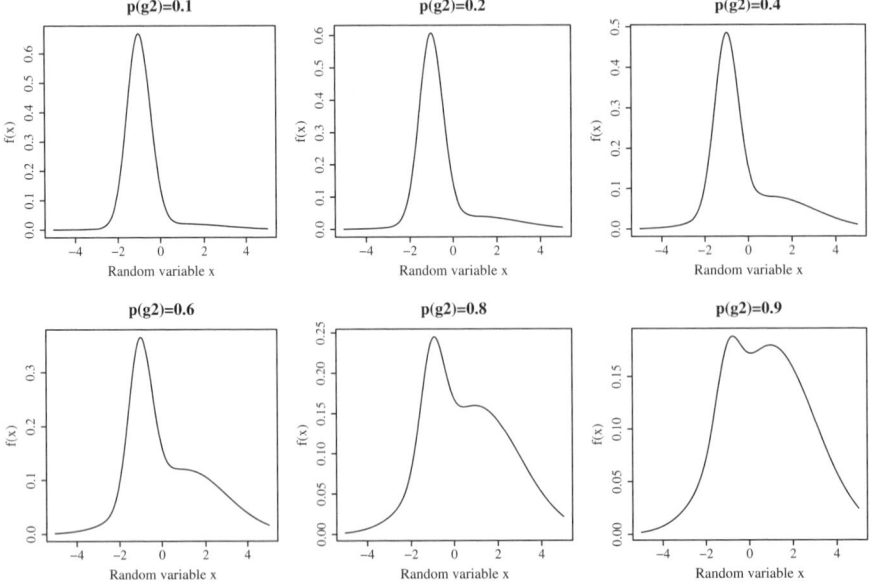

Figure 2.3. Marginal densities of mixtures of two normal densities with varying mixing proportions for two groups, $g1$ and $g2$, with $p(g1) = 1 - p(g2)$.

Mixture of bivariate normals

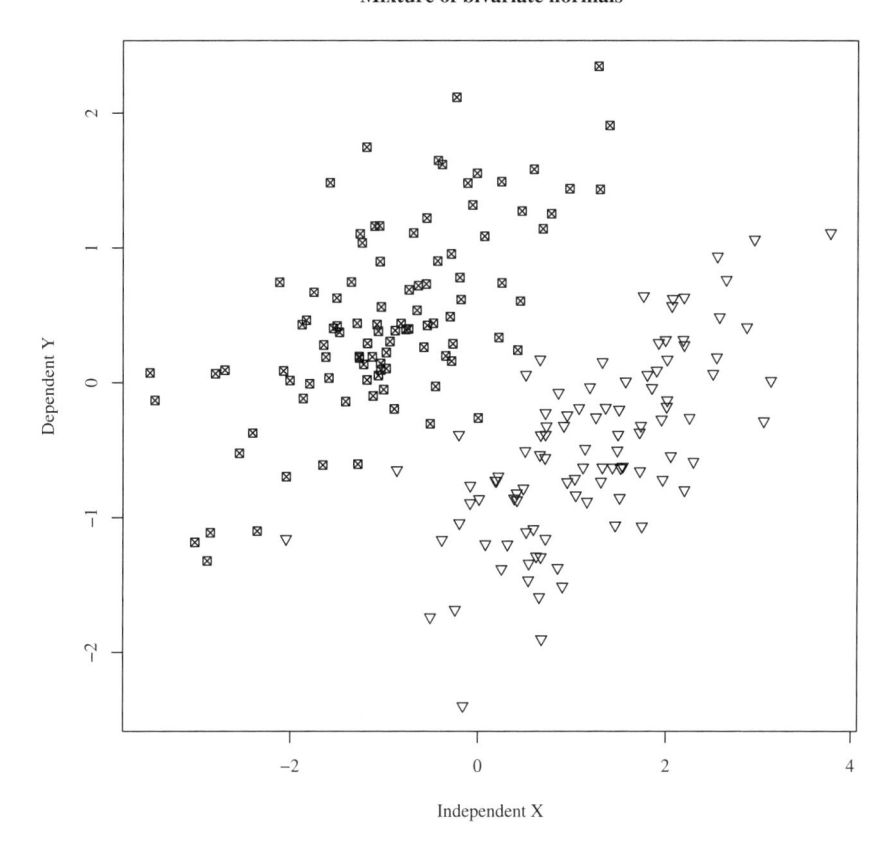

Figure 2.4. Mixture of two bivariate normal samples.

The *x*-axis represents an independent variable, say, for example, the length of some micro-organism, and the *y*-axis represents a dependent variable, for example, the CO_2 consumption of these microorganisms. It can be seen that there are two subsamples identified, in which the two variables show some obvious relationship. The correlation between the independent and the dependent variable is about 0.69 in both subsamples but is only –0.05 for the joint sample across the two mixture components. The two identified subsamples could, for example, represent microorganisms from different strains or something similar. Unmixing the two subsamples is crucial to understanding the data, because there is an almost linear relationship between the observed variables if calculated for the separate(d) samples.

Wolfe (1970) described a method for estimating the parameters of multivariate normal mixture models. Unfortunately, the fact that mixture distributions are easily defined does not imply easy estimation of the model parameters $(\pi_g, \vec{\mu}_g, \sum_g)_{g=1\ldots G}$ (e.g., Marin, Mengersen, & Robert, 2005; McLachlan & Peel, 2000). Real data rarely are as clearly identified as belonging to several separable populations; neither the location and dispersion of subpopulations nor the number of mixture components is known beforehand in most cases.

The estimation of parameters using mixture models, therefore, involves making decisions about the assumed structure of the mixture components as well as estimating a sequence of models and choosing between these candidate models based on considerations of parsimony and model-data fit.

Estimation of Normal Mixture Models

Mixture distribution models assume that the observations collected in a sample come from a finite number of different populations, whereas the information about each observation's parent population is missing because it was either not collected or it is not directly observable. The estimation of models that include unobserved variables is not straightforward because the collected data are missing a central piece of information, namely, information about the population from which each observation was drawn.

Several algorithms for the estimation of model parameters can handle incomplete data, among these the expectation-maximization (EM) algorithm (Dempster, Laird, & Rubin, 1977) and related methods. The EM algorithm seems to be the method of choice for most large-scale applications of mixture or latent variable models (McLachlan & Peel, 2000). These algorithms greatly profit from the availability of fast computers because parameter estimates have to be updated over the course of many iterative steps. Bayesian approaches to estimation, such as Markov chain Monte Carlo (MCMC) methods, have also been discussed and applied to the estimation of discrete mixture models (Marin et al., 2005). However, the computational burden is even greater for MCMC methods, which are based on chains containing thousands of systematic draws from conditional distributions given data and preliminary estimates.

The central building blocks of the EM algorithm are outlined in the following paragraphs. Assume that the d-dimensional random variable $\vec{x}$ is distributed according to the mixture normal density $f(\vec{x})$ as given in Equation 2. Assume that this random variable was collected based on a sample of size N, and that the observations are enumerated, so that they may be referred to as observation $\vec{x}_1$ to observation $\vec{x}_N$. If the data were completely observed, an additional variable would be available for each observation, which I denote by c in this chapter. If the c were observed, the vector $(c_1, \ldots, c_N)$ would contain the observed membership of each observation to one of the $g = 1 \ldots G$ mixing components of Equation 2. The EM algorithm is based on an iterative method that maximizes the likelihood function of the complete (or better "completed") data, using each observed record that has been proportionally placed into each (unobserved) population based on preliminary parameter estimates.

Mixtures of Distributions for Discrete Observed Variables

In social sciences, education, and psychology, observed variables are often discrete, so that the possible outcomes can be enumerated and represented as a finite set of numbers or symbols. Examples are responses to math problems that are either correct or incorrect or, in some cases, are responses that receive partial credit, so that a response scored as zero represents the least favorable solution (incorrect), a score of 1 represents a partially correct solution, and a score of 2 represents the completely correct solution.

Models for discrete data exist in abundance. However, in their basic formulation, they often do not provide means to detect hidden structure. Most models for discrete data were originally formulated in terms of probabilities modeled by functional families using transformations of the counts observed on the set of discrete dependent variables. These probabilistic models often contain only observed variables but can be extended to include hidden structure, or better, in the language of social sciences, to include *latent variables* (Goodman, 1974; Haberman, 1977; Lazarsfeld & Henry, 1968). These early developments have spurred research in different disciplines in the past 3 decades, with an increased level of research since 1990 on discrete mixture models in psychometrics and educational measurement (Kelderman & Macready, 1990; Mislevy & Verhelst, 1990; Rost, 1990).

Item Response Data as Evidence of Underlying Skills

Item response data are collected in standardized assessment situations in which a sample of examinees respond to a set (or to different but overlapping sets) of tasks, often referred to as *items*. Examinees respond by producing a recorded reaction to these items. A response can be bubbled in an answer sheet; by selecting one of a fixed number of response options; or by writing a number, a word, a sentence, or longer text. Then, responses are typically scored, that is, classified into correct, incorrect, or partially correct (partial credit) scoring categories.

The set of observed responses from an examinee is viewed as evidence that relates to some underlying, not directly observable, attribute. For example, a student's response to a series of 20 mixed number addition problems is considered a behavioral sample that can be used to draw inferences about the student's general skill in adding fractions and mixed numbers. Therefore, responses are viewed as indicators of indirectly observed skills or latent variables, rather than being directly identified with the ability to be measured. The theoretical advantage of this is well known: Latent variable models such as item response theory (IRT) state the probability of a response by an examinee to a given item in explicit, and therefore falsifiable terms, whereas the classical test theory (CTT) model, which operates on sums of scored responses, does not make explicit assumptions about the response process. CTT assumes that the sum of scored responses is a meaningful summary of student responses, whereas (parametric) IRT makes explicit mathematical assumptions relating the likelihood of item responses to examinee ability. This reliance of IRT models on a specific functional form may seem like an advantage for CTT (e.g., Hambleton & Jones, 1993); however, not making explicit assumptions does not imply the absence of implicit assumptions. For example, let the score X_v of examinee v on a test be defined as

$$X_v = \sum_{i=1}^{I} x_{vi} \quad (6)$$

where $x_{vi} = 1$ if examinee v responds correctly to item i and zero otherwise. If we assume that this is a meaningful summary of student ability, as it relates to responding to items $(x_1, \ldots x_I)$, then what follows for the response to a new item x_{I+1} belonging to the same domain? Let us say we tested an examinee on 19 mixed number additions and we want to express our subjective probability how the student will perform on mixed number addition Item 20. Should we assume that the observed frequency of students responding correctly to Item 20 depends in some systematic way on the sum of the first 19 items $X_{v|19} = \sum_{i=1}^{19} x_{vi}$? An implicit assumption used in test construction is that the response to any item of the test and the total score should be positively correlated. We often use the point bi-serial correlation to assess this relationship, and we discard or eliminate items from a scale if they do not correlate sufficiently with the overall score. Behind this stands the implicit assumption that the expected response $E(x_{vi})$ and the total score X_v should be positively related.

A slightly stronger assumption is that the probability of a positive response (recall that $E(x_{vi}) = P(x_{vi} = 1)$ for binary, that is, $x \in \{0,1\}$, response variables) increases strictly with the total score X_v or even the remainder score $X_v - x_{vi}$. With this, we are just one assumption away from the Rasch model (Rasch, 1980), namely, the assumption that the score X_v is sufficient to estimate the examinee's ability (Molenaar, 1995). The Rasch model defines the probability of an observed vector of responses as

$$P(x_1,\ldots,x_I|\theta,\vec{\beta}) = \prod_{i=1}^{I} P(x_i|\theta,\beta_i) = \prod_{i=1}^{I} \frac{\exp(x_i(\theta-\beta_i))}{1+\exp(\theta-\beta_i)}. \quad (7)$$

The θ_v represents examinee v's outcome on a real-valued skill variable in the Rasch model, the β_i represent the item difficulties in the Rasch model. The marginal probability of the responses is then

$$P(x_1,\ldots x_I) = \int_\theta \prod_i P_i(x_i|\theta,\beta_i) \phi(\theta;\vec{\eta}) d\theta, \quad (8)$$

where $\phi(\theta;\vec{\eta})$ denotes the distribution (with parameters $\vec{\eta}$) of the ability variable θ. The sufficiency of the unweighted score X yields $P(x_1, \ldots, x_I | X, \theta, \vec{\beta}) = P(x_1, \ldots, x_I | X, \vec{\beta})$, or,

$$\prod_i P(x_i|\theta,\beta_i) = \prod_i P(x_i|X,\beta_i) P(X|\theta) \quad (9)$$

for the Rasch model (e.g., von Davier, Rost & Carstensen, 2007). Thus, integrating over θ eliminates this parameter and we have

$$P(x_1,\ldots x_I;\vec{\beta}) = \int_\theta \prod_i P(x_i|X,\beta_i) P(X|\theta) \phi(\theta;\vec{\eta}) d\theta = \prod_i P(x_i|X,\beta_i) P(X). \quad (10)$$

The sufficiency of the total score X in the Rasch model shows that the probabilities of responses $P(x_i|X, \beta_i)$ fall into a set of $I + 1$ equivalency classes for this model, because $X \in \{0,1,2,\ldots,I\}$ and for each of these X, there are different $P_i(x|X)$. Equation 4 shows that the marginal probability of a response pattern can be written without the latent ability variable θ. This is frequently used for estimating item parameters in the Rasch model and is referred to as conditional maximum likelihood estimation. Conditional estimation uses (9) and maximizes the likelihood function

$$L(\vec{\beta}) = \sum_{v=1}^{N} \ln P(x_1,\ldots x_I; \vec{\beta}). \quad (11)$$

This is particularly useful because it avoids systematic bias that occurs when estimating ability θ and item parameters $\vec{\beta}$ jointly (Haberman, 1977; Kiefer & Wolfowitz, 1956), and it yields consistent estimates without assuming a specific ability distribution $\phi(\theta; \vec{\eta})$. If the test score X is defined as a weighted sum

$$X_v = \sum_{i=1}^{I} \alpha_i x_{vi} \quad (12)$$

we arrive at a model that is commonly known as the two-parameter logistic (2PL) IRT model (Lord & Novick, 1968). Then, we have

$$P(x_{v1},\ldots,x_{vI}|\theta_v) = \prod_{i=1}^{I} P_i(x_{vi}|\theta_v) = \prod_{i=1}^{I} \frac{\exp(x_{vi}\alpha_i(\theta_v - \beta_i))}{1 + \exp(\alpha_i(\theta_v - \beta_i))} \quad (13)$$

with θ_v and β_i as defined above and with an additional discrimination parameter α_i. If the α_i represent a limited number of prespecified integer (or rational weights) weights, conditional estimation is still possible (Verhelst & Glas, 1995). If the α_i are estimated model parameters, conditional estimation can no longer be used. In this case, an ability distribution $\phi(\theta; \vec{\eta})$ (either continuous or discrete) for θ is often assumed for estimation. Joint estimation is also possible, but it leads to the abovementioned bias and should therefore not be considered further. Therefore, using (10) to maximize

$$L(\vec{\beta},\vec{\alpha},\vec{\eta}) = \sum_{v=1}^{N} \ln P(x_{v1},\ldots,x_{vI};\vec{\beta},\vec{\alpha},\vec{\eta}) \quad (14)$$

with respect to item parameters $\vec{\beta}$, $\vec{\alpha}$ and with respect to distribution parameters $\vec{\eta}$ is the method of choice (marginal maximum likelihood, MML; Bock & Aitkin, 1981) utilized in a number of modern implementations of IRT estimation.

The arguments about sufficiency and monotonicity can be easily generalized to response variables $x_i \in \{0,1,2,\ldots,m_i\}$, that is, response variables with more than two ordinal categories (Andrich, 1982; Masters, 1982; Rost, 1988) arriving at a Rasch model for polytomous ordinal data or the generalized partial credit model (Muraki, 1992).

One may ask why we should make these stronger assumptions and use the Rasch model or more general IRT models instead of modeling based on sums of item responses. Some of the advantages of using a model-based approach for item response data are as follows:

- Testable assumptions are a good thing; for example, if items do not work as expected given model assumptions, it may mean that responding correctly to an item may not be indicative of a high value on the underlying skill.
- A model-based approach for responses to individual items allows for much more complex test designs, including multiple blocks of items and linkages across multiple test forms, than do designs supported by CTT and score-based equating methods.
- Models that assume a set of variables underlying item responses can easily be extended to approaches in which each response is indicative of more than one skill variable, that is, each observed indicator may be indicative of one or more underlying skills. A similar approach based on sums of item scores would reuse the same item score in multiple subscores and would therefore lead to artifacts.
- Models that assume one underlying skill dimension can be compared with more complex, as well as less complex, models in terms of statistical checks of model-data fit. As an example, specific model diagnostics (Glas; 2007; Molenaar, 1983) can be designed that are indicative of items or groups of items that perform poorly with respect to discriminating between high- and low-skilled examinees.

The last two bulleted points address extensions found in discrete mixture models, some of which are presented in this chapter. This section introduced the Rasch model and the 2PL model as examples of item response models for discrete observed data. In the next section, I introduce a different model for this type of data, the *latent class analysis* (LCA; Lazarsfeld & Henry, 1968), which can be viewed as the basic framework for all mixture models for discrete item response data. Most, if not all, discrete mixture models for item response data can be understood in terms of extending the basic model used in LCA.

Latent Class Analysis

Latent class models, like IRT models, relate a set of item responses to an unobserved variable. Unlike IRT models, the LCA does not assume a real-valued continuous latent variable. Instead, latent class models assume that the observed item responses are independent given a latent nominal variable. This also produces equivalency classes, much like the Rasch model and some other IRT models do. A typical setup includes, as before, $\vec{x}_v = (x_{v1}, \ldots, x_{vI})$, the observed item responses, whereas c_v is the unobserved class membership of examinee v. In contrast to the discrete c_v used in LCA, the IRT models presented in the previous section specify a continuous θ_v that represents the unobserved skill or proficiency. The basic latent class model follows from a set of three assumptions, some of which match assumptions commonly used in IRT:

1. Response probabilities depend on class membership c: $P_i(x|c_v)$ and $P_i(x|c_w)$ can, and will commonly, be different if $c_v \neq c_w$. This assumption is weaker than in IRT, because IRT assumes a real-valued θ and monotonicity in θ.
2. Local independence given class membership $c: P(x_1,\ldots,x_I|c) = \prod_{i=1}^{I} P_i(x_i|c)$. This is identical to the assumption used in IRT.
3. Class memberships are mutually exclusive and exhaustive, that is, each examinee v falls into one, and only one, latent class $c = c(v) \in \{1, \ldots, C\}$. Similarly, in IRT each examinee is characterized by exactly one real-valued $\theta = \theta(v)$.

These assumptions make the LCA a discrete mixture distribution model because it follows from this set of three assumptions that the marginal probability of a response pattern is given by

$$P(x_1,\ldots,x_I) = \sum_c \pi_c \prod_i^I P_i(x_i|c) \qquad (15)$$

with unknown class sizes (or mixing proportions) $\pi_c = p(c)$ (see Formann, 1992).

As an illustration, Figure 2.5 shows three class-specific profiles of conditional response probabilities $P_i(x = 1|c)$ for classes $c = 1, 2, 3$. Let us assume that each class is of size $p(c) = 1/3$, and each item has a different probability in each class, so all classes have different profiles of conditional response probabilities.

The LCA is a very flexible model because the number of classes C is not specified a priori and is often determined by some measure of model-data fit used to compare the fit of LCA models with increasing numbers of classes. This, however, is also a weakness of the LCA. With the addition of classes to the model, the

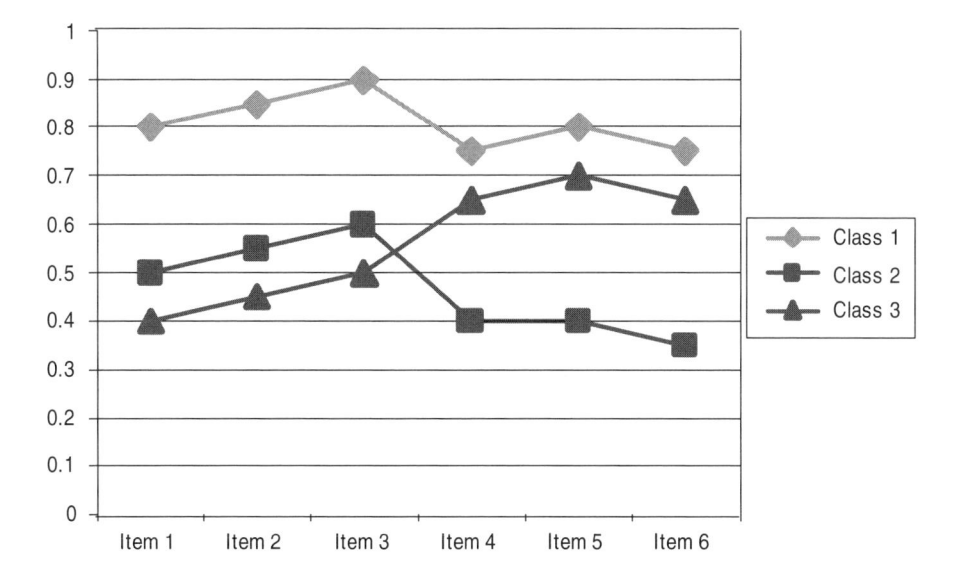

Figure 2.5. Class profiles of item difficulties for three latent classes and six items.

fit between model predictions and observed data will always improve, which may result in an LCA solution that is not well suited to describe the observed variables dependencies in a succinct way. In addition, the increase in number of classes leads to a substantial increase in the number of parameters to be estimated. For more details about applications of LCA, see the volumes by Langeheine and Rost (1988), Rost and Langeheine (1997), and Hagenaars and McCutcheon (2002), as well as the chapter by Dayton and Macready (2007). Often, confirmatory approaches to LCA, that is, approaches constraining the number of classes and/or prescribing class-specific patterns of response probabilities, seem more adequate than unconstrained LCA. Theories about the assessed domain coupled with construct-driven rational test construction will lead to hypotheses about how groups or latent classes of examinees should differ in their responses to the observed variables. These theories can then be translated in an expectation about the number of classes and the expected profile of response probabilities within classes. Some of these more structured approaches based on LCA can be viewed as models including latent structures. These latent structure models share some interesting similarities with IRT models, and an important special case of constrained LCA is discussed in the next section.

Located Latent Class Models

The LCA model in its original form does not constrain conditional response probabilities. However, there might be good reason to assume that latent classes are ordered with respect to the $P_i(x|c)$. More specifically, that the class indices or labels can be rearranged so that for all pairs $c > k \in 1 \ldots C$ we have

$$P_i(x=1|c) > P_i(x=1|k) \text{ for all } i \in \{1,\ldots,I\}. \quad (16)$$

This condition implies that one may compare classes in terms of their likelihood of endorsing the items, or may choose higher rather than lower response categories on the set of items if ordinal, polytomous items are considered. Ordered latent classes imply something that comes strikingly close to the monotonicity assumption in IRT. Moreover, ordered latent class models are often conveniently written as located latent class models (Formann, 1992; Uebersax, 1993). In the located latent class model, a finite number of different (ability) levels, the locations in the model, β_c, and item threshold difficulties $\vec{\alpha}_i = (\alpha_{i1}, \ldots, \alpha_{im})$ are used to define the conditional probabilities given latent class. If a logistic form is used, this can be written as

$$P_i(X=x|c) = \frac{\exp(x\beta_c - \alpha_{ix})}{1 + \sum_{y=1}^{m} \exp(y\beta_c - \alpha_{iy})}. \quad (17)$$

Equation 17 is suitable for both dichotomous (0, 1) response variables x as well as for polytomous, ordered response variables $x \in \{0, \ldots, m\}$. Located latent class models and IRT models may yield identical parameter estimates while the necessary number of ordered ability levels is rather small (De Leeuw & Verhelst, 1986; Lindsay, Clogg, & Grego, 1991). For such an application in which a located latent class model is used to mimic an IRT model, the spacing of ability levels ($\beta_1, \ldots, \beta_C$) and the class sizes ($\pi_1, \ldots, \pi_C$) can both be viewed as model parameters (see Heinen, 1996), even though it is often convenient to estimate only one type of parameter. If the β_c are constants and the π_c are estimated, this approach to estimating latent variable models is commonly referred to as *seminonparametric estimation* (Heinen, 1996) because the β_c are not considered model parameters but a priori specified constants.

Many common IRT estimation methods based on the implementation of marginal maximum likelihood (MML) methods use seminonparametric estimation routinely for approximating the continuous marginal ability distribution with discrete ability levels. Using real data, Haberman (2005), as well as Formann (2007), have shown that IRT-type located latent class models can be quite competitive in terms of model-data fit. Schmitt, Metha, Aggen, Kubarych, and Neale (2006) presented a simulation study to demonstrate how to detect nonnormal ability distributions using semi-nonparametric methods with located latent class models.

Mixture Distribution IRT Models

IRT models assume that the same item parameter set and the same ability distribution hold for all examinees. What if that is not plausible? An example in which different groups may show tendencies to respond in different ways to the test items is vertical linking across grades, because students in different grades may differ more than just in terms of ability levels. Opportunities to learn and repeat the material covered in the following grade may put more emphasis on some topics than others. Assessments administered across different school types, or assessments given to students from different training programs, may show that some areas covered by certain training programs lead to systematically different tendencies to respond positively to these programs. Test-taking training may change the performance of students on certain item types or the performance on items that can be solved using trainable strategies.

Rost (1990), Mislevy and Verhelst (1990), and Kelderman and Macready (1990) have studied situations like the ones listed previously using mixture distribution generalizations of IRT models. In *mixture IRT*, the conditional response probabilities depend on the population (observed group or latent class) an examinee belongs to in addition to the latent proficiency variable. In this case, the marginal probability of a response vector is

$$P(x_1, \ldots x_I) = \sum_{c=1}^{C} \pi_c \int_\theta \prod P_i(x_i|\theta,c)\phi_c(\theta)d\theta \quad (18)$$

with class-dependent ability distribution $\phi_c(\theta) = \phi(\theta; \vec{\eta}_c)$—$\phi$ is often chosen to represent a general family of distributions, of which the same or different instantiations are chosen to hold in the different mixture components—and class-dependent conditional response probabilities $P_i(x_i|\theta, c) = P(x_i|\theta, \beta_{ic})$. The latter class dependency indicates that the items may have different parameters β_{ic} in different classes, and therefore function differently in different classes. If class dependency is found for all items, Rost and von Davier (1993) pointed out that different skills are measured in the different populations with (seemingly) the same set of items. However, linking subsets of items across subpopulations is feasible. Moreover, linking is required if a common scale across subpopulations is to be established (von Davier & Rost, 2007; von Davier & Yamamoto, 2004a).

Applications of Mixture IRT

In cognitive psychology, mixture IRT models have found application in a variety of settings (Embretson, 2007). Work on the identification of strategy groups dates back to the origins of mixture IRT (Kelderman & Macready, 1990; Mislevy & Verhelst, 1990; Rost, 1990). The consequences of differential validity, moderated by latent class membership, can already be found in work in which a mixture of an independence class (no ability variation) and a class that follows common IRT assumptions has been developed (Yamamoto, 1989). In Yamamoto's HYBRID model, the class specific ability distributions ϕ differ substantially: Whereas in the IRT class a normal distribution may be assumed to hold, the independence class may be represented as a class with a degenerate ability distribution, in which the variance has been set to zero.

In noncognitive assessment, work on coping styles (von Davier & Rost, 1996), the faking of responses by job applicants (Eid & Rauber, 2000; Eid & Zickar, 2007; Zickar, Gibby, & Robie, 2004), and differences between response sets of examinees on personality questionnaires (Rost, Carstensen, & von Davier, 1999) have used mixture IRT models.

A test-speededness condition often leads to a change in response strategy when examinees run out of time while responding to items on a test. Mixture models for analyzing speeded tests have been developed by Yamamoto and Everson (1997) and applied to different testing programs by Yamamoto and Everson (1997), Boughton and Yamamoto (2007), and Bolt, Cohen, and Wollack (2002).

Developmental processes are often conceptualized in terms of distinguishable stages, characterized by what learners can or cannot do at these different stages. Wilson (1989) and Draney and Wilson (2007) have described the *Saltus model,* a model that can be used to implement these stage-like developmental assumptions. Technically, the Saltus model is a constrained mixture distribution Rasch model and, in this sense, a special case of the mixed Rasch model (Rost, 1990). The Saltus model imposes a structure on the overall differences between latent class dependent item difficulties. More specifically, it adds the Saltus parameter τ_c to each of the class independent item parameters, that is,

$$\alpha_{ic} = \tau_c + \tilde{\alpha}_i. \quad (19)$$

The class-dependent item difficulty for item i in class c in the Saltus model is additive in the Saltus parameter τ_c and the cross class item difficulty $\tilde{\alpha}_i$.

The assessment of whether tests are unidimensional or multidimensional represents another field in which mixture IRT has been applied. Rost and von

Davier (1995) suggested using the mixed Rasch model for assessing the fit of the Rasch model. The assessment of multidimensionality using mixture IRT is a topic covered by Rijmen and De Boeck (2003). The basic question is whether a test is unidimensional or whether there are additional latent student variables to be considered. As Rijmen and De Boeck (2003) pointed out, if additional variables beyond the main ability need to be modeled to fit the observed data, should those additional student variables be conceptualized as discrete (latent class) variables or as continuous (latent trait) variables? This question can be addressed by comparing the model-data fit of a (confirmatory) multidimensional IRT model assuming multiple ability factors with a mixture IRT model that assumes one continuous ability and multiple classes with class-specific item parameters. The next two sections present an approach in which comparisons of this sort—for example, between mixture IRT models and confirmatory, multidimensional IRT—can be made.

Diagnostic Models and Mixture IRT Models

Diagnostic modeling of student responses aims at reporting skill profiles of students or groups of students. Skill profiles consist of several, often discrete, skill variables, which are conceptualized as discrete latent variables in diagnostic models. Multidimensional IRT (MIRT; Reckase, 1985) models and diagnostic models are both used to analyze data assuming multiple student variables. MIRT assumes continuous latent variables and is an extension of unidimensional IRT, whereas diagnostic models may be viewed as an extension of located latent class models. In this sense, diagnostic models can be understood as multiple classification latent class models (e.g., Haberman, 1977; Haertel, 1989; Maris, 1999), as well as multidimensional discrete IRT models (e.g., Heinen, 1996; Kelderman & Rijkes, 1994). The rule space approach (Tatsuoka, 1983) can be seen as another base of diagnostic modeling. However, rule space is not a probabilistic approach, unlike LCA and related methods. Rule space determines ideal response patterns of students with certain skill profiles in an expert-guided and prescriptive way, and then classifies students according to these ideal patterns.

Diagnostic models usually contain a design matrix, commonly referred to as a Q-*matrix,* relating items to (multiple) skills. The idea behind using design matrices is confirmatory; a model of student skills and how these skills relate to students' observed item responses is developed and then put to the test. A test of the diagnostic model usually consists of comparing the fit of the diagnostic model with a more parsimonious model (e.g., a unidimensional IRT model) and checking whether model predictions based on the multidimensional diagnostic models improve on the predictions of the unidimensional approach.

Table 2.2 provides two examples of Q-matrices with two skills and seven items, which should be considered a textbook example as the number of items tapping into each of the skills is rather small and should be at least two to three times larger for any real application. Model 1 assumes simple structure (or between-item multidimensionality; see Adams & Wu, 2007), and Model 2 assumes within-

Table 2.2. Examples of Between Item and Within Item Multidimensionality as Represented in Different Q-Matrices

	Q-matrix 1		Q-matrix 2	
	Skill 1	Skill 2	Skill 1	Skill 2
Item 1	1	0	1	0
Item 2	1	0	1	0
Item 3	1	0	1	1
Item 4	0	1	0	1
Item 5	0	1	0	1
Item 6	0	1	0	1
Item 7	0	1	1	1

item multidimensionality for Items 3 and 7. The Q-matrix entries are either zero or one; $q_{ik} = 0$ denotes that skill k is not required for item i and $q_{ik} = 1$ denotes that skill k is required for item i.

Junker and Sijtsma (2001) described a framework of disjunctive and conjunctive diagnostic models and discussed the relationship of this approach to nonparametric IRT models. DiBello, Roussos, and Stout (2007) gave an overview of some of the models commonly referred to as *diagnostic models*. DiBello et al. (2007) listed the linear logistic test model (LLTM; Fischer, 1973), a constrained version of the Rasch model, as a diagnostic model. Note, however, that the LLTM does not contain multiple student skill variables but contains design matrices that prescribe how item difficulties relate to a set of underlying item component parameters. In contrast to componential IRT models (Embretson, 1990) and other multidimensional IRT models, the LLTM does not decompose person ability variables into multiple components. Haberman and von Davier (2007) discussed some important cautionary considerations when using diagnostic models. Some limitations, such as the relationship between the number of items and the number of distinguishable skills, as well as the ability to distinguish between highly correlated skills, are often neglected. Von Davier, DiBello, and Yamamoto (2006) gave an overview of selected diagnostic models for reporting profiles of skills. The extension of the general diagnostic model (GDM) to a mixture distribution IRT type model is covered in the next section.

A Mixture General Diagnostic Model

Von Davier and Yamamoto (2004b) and von Davier (2005) presented a framework for a GDM. Von Davier (2005) developed the partial credit version of the GDM and conducted a parameter recovery study based on this model. The GDM was extended to a mixture GDM (M-GDM; von Davier, 2007; von Davier & Rost, 2007; von Davier & Yamamoto, 2007) and contains 2PL and generalized partial credit model (GPCM; Muraki, 1992) IRT as well as multidimensional versions of these IRT models (2PL and GPCM MIRT models), (multiple classification) latent class models, located latent class models, and a compensatory version of the reparameterized unified model as special cases. Hence, it shares (depending on what types of latent skill variables are used) many important features with MIRT and with multiple classification latent class models. The GDM provides a common framework for several types of models, and the general form of the GDM can be adapted to what is needed: IRT, latent class, mixture IRT, MIRT, and diagnostic models with dichotomous mastery/nonmastery skills or ordinal skills. Model-data fit diagnostics are readily available using tools from IRT and categorical data analysis. The mixture and nonmixture GDM is estimated using the EM algorithm in the software package *mdltm*[1] (von Davier, 2005). In contrast, many previous implementations of diagnostic models used computationally much more costly MCMC methods. More important, the common framework of discrete and continuous latent traits used in the GDM family of models facilitates comparisons between models from seemingly distinct families of latent trait models.

The mixture GDM is defined using the following setup: Assume K discrete skills, and a K–dimensional latent skill variable $a = (a_1, \ldots a_K)$ with components $a_k \in \{s_0, \ldots, s_{l(k)}\}_k$. The s_l are real-valued skill levels and are chosen by the user. Common choices for estimating an IRT model within the GDM framework are $K = 1$ and $l(1) = 40$ and equally spaced skill levels with $s_0 = -4.0$ and $s_{40} = +4.0$. A common choice for diagnostic modeling is $1 < k < K$, with K between 2 and 10, and $a_k \in \{-1.0, +1.0\}$ for mastery/nonmastery skills or $a_k \in \{-1.0, 0.0, +1.0\}$ for skills with three levels. Extensions to four or more levels are straightforward. The probability of a response x to a polytomous, ordinal item i in class c for an examinee with skill pattern $(a_1, \ldots, a_K)$ is then

$$P_i(x|c,a_1,\ldots,a_K) = \frac{\exp\left(\sum_{z=1}^{x}\beta_{izc} + x\sum_{k}q_{ik}\gamma_{ikc}a_k\right)}{1 + \sum_{y=1}^{m_i}\exp\left(\sum_{z=1}^{y}\beta_{izc} + y\sum_{k}q_{ik}\gamma_{ikc}a_k\right)} \quad (20)$$

with $x \in \{0, \ldots, m_i\}$, and with slope parameters γ_{ik} and threshold parameters β_{ix}. The q_{ik} represent the Q-matrix entries and usually will take on only the values zero or one, that is, $q_{ik} \in \{0,1\}$. The mixture GDM assumes local independence, like IRT and LCA do, and mutually exclusive and exhaustive classes. Thus, the marginal probability of a response pattern is

$$P(x_1,\ldots x_I) = \sum_{c}\pi_c \sum_{a_1}\cdots\sum_{a_K} p(a_1\ldots a_K|c)\prod_{i=1}^{I}P_i(x_i|c,a_1,\ldots,a_K) \quad (21)$$

where $p(a_1, \ldots a_K|c)$ is the probability of skill pattern $(a_1, \ldots, a_K)$ in class c, and the π_c are the class sizes as defined above. Von Davier (2005; 2007) reported on a successful parameter recovery study and an application of the GDM to language testing using data from a computer-based English language test. Xu and

---

[1] For availability and licensing of the *mdltm* software for research purposes, please contact mvondavier@ets.org or dlembeck@ets.org.

von Davier (2006) described successful parameter recovery when estimating the GDM using sparse samples of item responses with conditions containing up to 50% missing data. For common IRT models, the GDM provided a means to generate MML estimates using semi non-parametric estimation (Heinen, 1996). Parameters estimated were found to be virtually identical to those obtained from BILOG for the 2PL, and those obtained using conditional maximum likelihood estimates when estimating the dichotomous or polytomous Rasch model. Xu and von Davier (2006) described application of the GDM and a multiple group version of the GDM to data from the National Assessment of Educational Progress. Xu and von Davier (2007) developed a log-linear model for the latent skill profile distribution $p(a_1, \ldots, a_k)$, and von Davier and Rost (2007), von Davier (2007), as well as von Davier and Yamamoto (2007) described the M-GDM.

Outlook and Summary

Discrete mixture distribution models for item response data are a common staple of categorical data analysis. They come in many forms—for example, LCA, latent structure model, discrete latent trait models, mixture IRT and mixed Rasch models, and multidimensional extensions of these. In their edited volume, von Davier and Carstensen (2007) collected 22 contributions by an international group of researchers on model extensions and applications that grew out of mixture distribution Rasch models, multidimensional Rasch models, and related approaches. Mixture distribution models for item response data can be used to estimate and test IRT models and allow for the extension of IRT models by means of effects of unobserved and observed grouping variables and covariates. The edited volume by De Boeck and Wilson (2004), as well as the one by Rao and Sinharay (2006), contains several chapters about these types of discrete mixture models. The GDM (von Davier, 2005, 2007) places diagnostic skill profile approaches into a modeling framework that allows for direct comparisons between diagnostic models expressed as mixture models of the latent class type to models with continuous ability variables such as IRT-based mixture and nonmixture models. Haberman (2005), Schmitt et al. (2006), Formann (2007), and Vermunt (2001) have provided examples in which latent class type IRT models are quite competitive in terms of model-data fit when compared with models with continuous latent variables.

This chapter provided a short survey of mixture models for continuous variables and discrete item response data. Given the vast amount of research over more than a century, this chapter can only deliver coverage in certain areas. If this chapter was successful in an attempt to raise interest in this important area of psychometric modeling, then the reader is further encouraged to pick up some of the books on the topic, such as the one on mixture models for continuous data by McLachlan and Peel (2000), or the edited volumes on mixture and multivariate Rasch models (von Davier & Carstensen, 2007), or the conference proceedings on "Mixture Models in Latent Variable Research" (Hancock & Samuelsen, 2007). The study and application of mixture distribution models for item response data can lead to interesting discoveries of hidden structure in data from educational and psychological assessments.

References

Adams, R., & Wu, M. (2007). The mixed-coefficients multinomial logit model: A generalized form of the Rasch model. In M. von Davier & C. H. Carstensen (Eds.), *Multivariate and mixture distribution Rasch models* (pp. 57–75). [New York: Springer.

Andrich, D. (1982). An extension of the Rasch model for ratings providing both location and dispersion parameters. *Psychometrika, 47,* 105–113.

Bock, R. D., & Aitkin, M. (1981). Marginal maximum likelihood estimation of item parameters: Application of an EM algorithm. *Psychometrika, 46,* 443–459.

Bolt, D. M., Cohen, A. S., & Wollack, J. A. (2002). Item parameter estimation under conditions of test speededness: Application of a mixture Rasch model with ordinal constraints. *Journal of Educational Measurement, 39,* 331–348.

Boughton, K., & Yamamoto, K. (2007). A HYBRID model for test speededness. In M. von Davier and C. H. Carstensen (Eds.), *Multivariate and mixture distribution Rasch models.* (pp. 147–156). New York: Springer.

Brandt, S. (1998). *Data analysis* (3rd ed.). Berlin, Germany: Springer-Verlag.

Dayton, C. M., & Macready, G. B. (2007). Latent class analysis in psychometrics. In C. R. Rao & S. Sinharay (Eds.), *Handbook of statistics (Vol 26, Psychometrics,* pp. 421–446). Amsterdam: Elsevier.

De Boeck, P., & Wilson, M. R. (2004). *Explanatory item response models: A generalized linear and nonlinear approach.* New York: Springer-Verlag.

De Leeuw, J., & Verhelst, N. D. (1986). Maximum likelihood estimation in generalized Rasch models. *Journal of Educational Statistics, 11,* 183–196.

Dempster, A. P., Laird, N. M., & Rubin, D. B. (1977). Maximum likelihood from incomplete data via the EM algorithm. *Journal of the Royal Statistical Society, Series B, 39,* 1–38.

DiBello, L. V., Roussos, L., & Stout, W. (2007). Review of cognitively diagnostic assessment and a summary of psychometric models. In C. R. Rao & S. Sinharay (Eds.), *Handbook of statistics (Vol. 26: Psychometrics*, (pp. 979–1027). Amsterdam: Elsevier.

Draney, K., & Wilson, M. (2007). Application of the Saltus model to stage-like data: Some applications and current developments. In M. von Davier & C. H. Carstensen (Eds.), *Multivariate and mixture distribution Rasch models* (pp. 119–130). New York: Springer.

Eid, M., & Rauber, M. (2000). Detecting measurement invariance in organizational surveys. *European Journal of Psychological Assessment, 16,* 20–30.

Eid, M., & Zickar, M. (2007). Detecting response styles and faking in personality and organizational assessments by mixed Rasch models. In M. von Davier & C. H. Carstensen (Eds.), *Multivariate and mixture distribution Rasch models* (pp. 255–270). New York: Springer.

Embretson, S. (1990). Diagnostic testing by measuring learning processes: Psychometric considerations for dynamic testing. In N. Frederiksen, R. L. Glasser, A. M. Lesgold, & M. G. Shafto (Eds.), *Diagnostic monitoring of skills and knowledge acquisition* (pp. 453–486). Hillsdale, NJ: Erlbaum.

Embretson, S. (2007). Mixed Rasch models for measurement in cognitive psychology. In M. von Davier & C. H. Carstensen (Eds.), *Multivariate and mixture distribution Rasch models* (pp. 235–253). New York: Springer.

Fischer, G. H. (1973). The linear logistic model as an instrument in educational research. *Acta Psychologica, 37,* 359–374.

Formann, A. K. (1992). Linear logistic latent class analysis for polytomous data. *Journal of the American Statistical Association, 87,* 476–486.

Formann, A. K. (2007). (Almost) equivalence between conditional and mixture maximum likelihood estimates for some models of the Rasch type. In M. von Davier & C. H. Carstensen (Eds.), *Multivariate and mixture distribution Rasch models* (pp. 177–189). New York: Springer.

Gianola, D., Heringstad, B., & Odegaard, J. (2006). On the quantitative genetics of mixture characters. *Genetics, 173,* 2247–2255.

Glas, C. A. W. (2007). Testing generalized Rasch models. In M. von Davier & C. H. Carstensen (Eds.), *Multivariate and mixture distribution Rasch models* (pp. 37–55). New York: Springer.

Goodman, L. (1974). Exploratory latent structure analysis using both identifiable and unidentifiable models. *Biometrika, 61,* 215–231.

Haberman, S. J. (1977). Maximum likelihood estimates in exponential response models. *The Annals of Statistics, 5,* 815–841.
Haberman, S. J. (2005). *Latent-class item response models* (ETS Research Report RR-05-28). Princeton, NJ: Educational Testing Service.
Haberman, S. J., & von Davier, M. (2007). Some notes on models for cognitively based skills diagnosis. In C. R. Rao & S. Sinharay (Eds.), *Handbook of statistics (Vol. 26: Psychometrics,* pp. 1031–1038). Amsterdam: Elsevier.
Haertel, E. H. (1989). Using restricted latent class models to map the skill structure of achievement items. *Journal of Educational Measurement, 26,* 301–321.
Hagenaars, J. A., & McCutcheon, A. L. (Eds.). (2002). *Applied latent class analysis models.* Cambridge, England: Cambridge University Press.
Hambleton, R. K., & Jones, R. W. (1993). Comparison of classical test theory and item response theory and their applications to test development. *Educational Measurement: Issues and Practice, 12*(3), 38–47.
Hancock, G., & Samuelsen, K. M. (Eds.). (2007). *Mixture models in latent variable research.* Charlotte, NC: Information Age Publishing.
Heinen, T. (1996). *Latent class and discrete latent trait models: Similarities and differences.* Thousand Oaks, CA: Sage.
Junker, B. W., & Sijtsma, K. (2001). Cognitive assessment models with few assumptions and connections with nonparametric item response theory. *Applied Psychological Measurement, 25,* 258–272.
Kelderman, H., & Macready, G. B. (1990). The use of loglinear models for assessing differential item functioning across manifest and latent examinee groups. *Journal of Educational Measurement, 27,* 307–327.
Kelderman, H., & Rijkes, C. M. P. (1994). Loglinear multidimensional IRT models for polytomously scored items. *Psychometrika, 59,* 149–176.
Kiefer, J., & Wolfowitz, J. (1956). Consistency of maximum likelihood estimates in the presence of infinitely many incidental parameters. *Annals of Mathematical Statistics. 27,* 887–906.
Koelbel, J. (1575). *Geometrie.* Frankfurt, Germany.
Langeheine, R., & Rost, J. (Eds.). (1988). *Latent trait and latent class models.* New York: Plenum Press.
Lazarsfeld, P. F., & Henry, N. W. (1968). *Latent structure analysis.* Boston: Houghton Mifflin.
Lindsay, B., Clogg, C. C., & Grego, J. (1991). Semiparametric estimation in the Rasch model and related exponential response models, including a simple latent class model for item analysis. *Journal of the American Statistical Association. 86,* 96–107.
Lord, F. M., & Novick, M. R. (1968). *Statistical theories of mental test scores.* Reading, MA: Addison-Wesley.
Marin, J. M., Mengersen, K., & Robert, C. P. (2005). Bayesian modelling and inference on mixture of distributions. In D. K. Rey & C. R. Rao (Eds.), *Handbook of statistics. Bayesian thinking: Modeling and computation* (Vol. 25, pp. 459–508). New York: North Holland
Maris, E. (1999). Estimating multiple classification latent class models. *Psychometrika, 64,* 187–212.
Masters, G. N. (1982). A Rasch model for partial credit scoring. *Psychometrika, 47,* 149–174.
McLachlan, G., & Peel, D. (2000). *Finite mixture models.* New York: Wiley.
Mislevy, R. J., & Verhelst, N. D. (1990). Modeling item responses when different subjects employ different solution strategies. *Psychometrika, 55,* 195–215.
Molenaar, I. W. (1983). Some improved diagnostics for failure of the Rasch model. *Psychometrika, 48,* 49–72.
Molenaar I. W. (1995). Estimation of item parameters. In G. H. Fischer & I. W. Molenaar (Eds.), *Rasch models: Foundations, recent developments and applications* (pp. 39–52). New York: Springer-Verlag.
Muraki, E. (1992). A generalized partial credit model: Application of an EM algorithm. *Applied Psychological Measurement, 16,* 159–176.
Newcomb, S. (1886). A generalized theory of the combination of observations so as to obtain the best result. *American Journal of Mathematics, 8,* 343–366.
Pearson, K. (1894). Contributions to the theory of mathematical evolution. *Philosophical Transactions of the Royal Society of London, A, 185,* 71–110.

Rao, C. R., & Sinharay, S. (Eds.). (2006). *Handbook of statistics (Vol. 26: Psychometrics)*. Amsterdam: Elsevier.

Rasch, G. (1980). *Probabilistic models for some intelligence and attainment tests*. Chicago: University of Chicago Press.

Reckase, M. D. (1985). The difficulty of test items that measure more than one ability. *Applied Psychological Measurement, 9,* 401–412.

Rijmen, F., & De Boeck, P. (2003). A latent class model for individual differences in the interpretation of conditionals. *Psychological Research, 67,* 219–231.

Rost, J. (1988). Test theory with qualitative and quantitative latent variables. In R. Langeheine & J. Rost (Eds.), *Latent trait and latent class models*. (pp. 147–171). New York: Plenum Press.

Rost, J. (1990). Rasch models in latent classes: An integration of two approaches to item analysis. *Applied Psychological Measurement, 14,* 271–282.

Rost, J., Carstensen, C. H., & von Davier, M. (1999). Sind die Big Five Rasch-Skalierbar? [Is the Big Five personality inventory Rasch scalable?]. *Diagnostica, 45,* 3, 119–127.

Rost J., & Langeheine R. (Eds.). (1997). *Applications of latent trait and latent class models in the social sciences.* Muenster, Germany: Waxmann.

Rost, J., & von Davier, M. (1993). Measuring different traits in different populations with the same items. In R. Steyer, K. F. Wender, & K. F. Widaman (Eds.), *Psychometric methodology: Proceedings of the 7th European meeting of the Psychometric Society in Trier*. Stuttgart, Germany: Gustav Fischer Verlag.

Rost, J., & von Davier, M. (1995). Mixture distribution Rasch models. In G. H. Fischer & I. W. Molenaar (Eds.), *Rasch models: Foundations, recent developments and applications* (pp. 257–268). New York: Springer.

Schmitt, J. E., Mehta, P. D., Aggen, S. H., Kubarych, T. S., & Neale, M. C. (2006). Seminonparametric methods for detecting latent non-normality: A fusion of latent trait and ordered latent class modeling. *Multivariate Behavioral Research, 41,* 427–443.

Tatsuoka, K. K. (1983). Rule space: An approach for dealing with misconceptions based on item response theory. *Journal of Educational Measurement, 20,* 345–354.

Tatsuoka K. K. (1987). Validation of cognitive sensitivity for item response curves. *Journal of Educational Measurement, 24,* 233–245.

Uebersax, J. S. (1993). Statistical modeling of expert ratings on medical treatment appropriateness. *Journal of the American Statistical Association, 88,* 421–427.

Verhelst, N. D., & Glas, C. A. W. (1995). The one parameter logistic model. In G. H. Fischer & I. W. Molenaar (Eds.), *Rasch models: Foundations, recent developments and applications* (pp. 215–238). New York: Springer.

Vermunt, J. K. (2001). The use of restricted latent class models for defining and testing nonparametric and parametric item response theory models. *Applied Psychological Measurement, 25,* 283–294.

von Davier, M. (2005). *A general diagnostic model applied to language testing data* (ETS Research Report RR-05-16). Princeton, NJ: Educational Testing Service.

von Davier, M. (2007). *The mixture general diagnostic model* (ETS Research Report RR-07-32). Princeton, NJ: Educational Testing Service.

von Davier, M., & Carstensen, C. H. (Eds.). (2007). *Multivariate and mixture distribution Rasch Models*. New York: Springer.

von Davier, M., DiBello, L. V., & Yamamoto, K. (2006). *Reporting test outcomes using models for cognitive diagnosis* (ETS Research Report 06-28). Princeton, NJ: Educational Testing Service.

von Davier, M., & Rost, J. (1996). Die Erfassung transsituativer Copingstile durch Stimulus-Response Inventare [The assessment of coping styles across situations using stimulus response inventories]. *Diagnostica, 42,* 313–332.

von Davier, M., & Rost, J (2007). Mixture distribution item response models. In C. R. Rao & S. Sinharay (Eds.), *Handbook of statistics (Vol. 26, Psychometrics,* pp. 643–659). Amsterdam: Elsevier.

von Davier, M., Rost, J., & Carstensen, C. H. (2007). Extending the Rasch model. In M. von Davier & C. H. Carstensen (Eds.), *Multivariate and mixture distribution Rasch models* (pp. 1–12). New York: Springer.

von Davier, M., & Yamamoto, K. (2004a). Partially observed mixtures of IRT models: An extension of the generalized partial credit model. *Applied Psychological Measurement, 28,* 389–406.

von Davier, M., & Yamamoto, K. (2004b, October). *A class of models for cognitive diagnosis.* Paper presented at the fourth Spearman Conference, Philadelphia, PA.

von Davier, M., & Yamamoto, K. (2007). Mixture distribution and HYBRID Rasch models. In M. von Davier & C. H. Carstensen (Eds.), *Multivariate and mixture distribution Rasch models* (pp. 99–115). New York: Springer.

Wilson, M. R. (1989). Saltus: A psychometric model of discontinuity in cognitive development. *Psychological Bulletin, 105,* 276–289.

Wolfe, J. H. (1970). Pattern clustering by multivariate mixture analysis. *Multivariate Behavioral Research, 5,* 329–350.

Xu, X., & von Davier, M. (2006). *Cognitive diagnosis for NAEP proficiency data* (ETS Research Report RR-06-08). Princeton, NJ: Educational Testing Service.

Xu, X., & von Davier, M. (2007, April). *Estimating structured diagnostic models.* Paper presented at the annual meeting of the National Council on Measurement in Education, Chicago.

Yamamoto, K. (1989). *A Hybrid model of IRT and latent class models* (ETS Research Report No. RR-89-41). Princeton, NJ: Educational Testing Service.

Yamamoto, K. Y., & Everson, H. T. (1997). Modeling the effects of test length and test time on parameter estimation using the HYBRID model. In J. Rost & R. Langeheine (Eds.), *Applications of latent trait and latent class models in the social sciences* (pp. 89–98). Muenster, Germany: Waxmann.

Zickar, M. J., Gibby, R. E., & Robie, C. (2004). Uncovering faking samples in applicant, incumbent, and experimental data sets: An application of mixed model item response theory. *Organizational Research Methods, 7,* 168–190.

3

Skills Diagnosis for Education and Psychology With IRT-Based Parametric Latent Class Models

Louis A. Roussos, Louis V. DiBello, Robert A. Henson, Eunice Jang, and Jonathan L. Templin

Diagnostic assessments have long been used in education and psychology, and recent advances in latent class modeling could result in significant improvements in their statistical performance and, not coincidentally, in their availability to a wider range of applications in terms of both practitioners and subjects. This chapter presents the theory and practice of these new psychometric models with an emphasis on practical implementation. To this end, a broadly conceived implementation framework is presented with detailed practical advice and two detailed example applications from psychology and education.

The implementation of any assessment program is a complicated affair; if new psychometric modeling advances are to have a positive effect, it is important for practitioners to see how these new models integrate into the entire implementation process. Although these new models present new challenges and obstacles for practical implementation, they also offer the potential for many significant advantages that have brought this research to the precipice of practical implementation in operational assessment programs.

In this chapter, we first present the psychometric terminology relevant to parametric latent class models based on item response theory (IRT). Next, we present a general organizing scheme for the diagnostic assessment implementation process, which we conceive as involving six components: the assessment purpose, the nature of the skills, the assessment tasks, the psychometric model, model estimation, and score reporting. We describe each component separately, noting that the separate delineations mainly provide a convenient, coherent vehicle for discussion. In practice the process is not really compartmentalized—different components naturally overlap and interact with each other. Following the general description of the implementation process, we present its application to two very different examples in education and psychology. Finally, we offer concluding remarks, pointing out advantages and disadvantages of using these new models and describing what we see as the next steps on the road to operational implementation.

Terminology

We use the term *skill* to refer to an unobservable characteristic or attribute of an individual, and we assume there are several such skills of interest for a given diagnostic setting. The term *skill* is used with the understanding that the unobservable attribute of interest could also refer to other characteristics, such as acquired knowledge or the presence of a personality trait. We also assume that it is desired to classify or diagnose each individual into two or more ordered categories on each skill or attribute—for example, whether a student exceeds, meets, or is below state standards on an inferencing skill in English language arts. The term *skill profile* is used to refer to the vector that presents an individual's skill category for each of the skills. For example, for a diagnosis of mastery versus nonmastery on each of two skills, there are four possible skill profiles: nonmaster of first, nonmaster of second; nonmaster of first, master of second; master of first, nonmaster of second; and master of first, master of second. For convenience, we use the term *examinees* to refer to individuals who are to be assessed, although the setting need not be an examination.

Diagnosing examinees by classifying them into ordered categories on a (generally unordered) set of skills can be accomplished by using latent class models while introducing skill-based restrictions through parametric item response functions (IRFs), similar to those used in IRT for continuous latent traits. Thus, we refer to these models as *IRT-based parametric latent class models*. These models allow the advantages of latent class models to be integrated with those of parametric IRT. When the diagnostic goal is to classify examinees into skill-based categories (as contrasted with placing examinees on a continuous scale for each skill), latent class models have the advantage of directly addressing the classification goal. Moreover, for latent class models that use skill-based parametric IRFs, each latent class is intrinsically linked to a specific examinee skill profile, estimable parameters describe the quality of the diagnostic instrument and that of the skill-based classifications, and a variety of model-checking approaches exist for parametric IRT models. In this chapter, these advantages are discussed in more detail and demonstrated with two applications.

To make the scope manageable, the rest of the chapter is restricted to latent class models with two classes, as well as to instruments composed of dichotomously scored items. However, the general principles presented here are equally applicable to polytomously scored items (or other such tasks) and to latent class models with more than two classes, as well as to continuous latent trait models (e.g., DiBello, Roussos, & Stout, 2007).

General Framework for the Diagnostic Assessment Implementation Process

As noted by Junker (1999), the challenges of designing a diagnostic assessment are "how one wants to frame inferences about students, what data one needs to see, how one arranges situations to get the pertinent data, and how one justifies reasoning from the data to inferences about the student" (p. 4). This recognition of assessment design as a process of reasoning from evidence was summarized by Pellegrino, Chudowsky, and Glaser (2001) as the *assessment triangle:* cognition, observation, and interpretation. The *evidence-centered design (ECD) paradigm,* developed by Mislevy, Almond, and their colleagues (e.g., Mislevy, Steinberg, & Almond, 2003), frames that recognition into a systematic and practical approach to assessment design. In this section, we adapt and augment the ECD paradigm to describe a framework for the entire implementation process for diagnostic assessment, elaborating on practical aspects of cognitively based assessment design and also going beyond design to illuminate practical issues in regard to estimation and score reporting.

The diagnostic assessment implementation process is conceptualized as involving six components:

1. description of assessment purpose;
2. description of latent attributes of diagnostic interest (skills space);
3. development and analysis of assessment tasks (dichotomous items);
4. specification of a psychometric model linking performance to latent skills;
5. estimation of model parameters and evaluation of the results; and
6. development of systems for reporting assessment results to examinees, teachers, and others.

As we detail next, the components of a successful implementation process are not necessarily as sequential and compartmentalized as idealized in the previous section. Although the idealization is useful as an organizing framework, it is important to note that a successful implementation process generally requires considerable interaction and feedback between the components and demands close collaboration among all who are involved in the process, such as, users, test designers, content experts, cognitive psychologists, and psychometricians.

Assessment Purpose

The purpose of the assessment should be clearly delineated, and this purpose has strong implications for Component 1, the description of the latent attribute space. For example, if the diagnostic purpose is to classify examinees in terms of discrete ordered categories of competency on a selected set of multiple skills, a substantive explication of what this "competency" means would seem to be required. A specific example of this is the typical standard setting process that is conducted for state testing programs in the United States (Cizek, Bunch, & Koons, 2004), in which there are only a small number of discrete classification levels on each skill. However, if the purpose of the assessment is a more traditional ranking of examinees along a broad general competency scale, then an appropriate skill space selection would seem to be a single continuous scale. In this chapter, our focus is on latent class models, so we are concerned with settings like state standards testing, in which the diagnostic goal is classification to a small number of ordered discrete levels on each skill.

The determination of assessment purpose also interacts with Component 3, choosing tasks that provide appropriate information about skills. In particular, the diagnostic purpose may be targeted to making predictions about real-life settings that involve solving problems requiring complex combinations of skills. In such cases, it may be helpful to use assessment tasks that individually involve two or more skills, an advantage of the models that are the focus here. Also, the number and type of skill mastery categories can affect the types of tasks. It may be helpful to have tasks directed not only to particular skills but also to particular difficulty levels of the skills as appropriate for the prescribed categories in the assessment purpose.

In designing an effective diagnostic assessment, satisfying the assessment purpose is the prime motivation and, thus, should be accomplished with care. However, in many applications of complex diagnostic models in the literature, skills diagnosis is conducted as a post-hoc analysis (called *retrofitting*), usually as a demonstration of a new statistical model or method or as an attempt to extract richer information than called for by the original assessment design. In such cases, skills diagnosis essentially becomes a new additional purpose for the assessment instrument. Though the instrument has already been designed in such cases, delineating the assessment purpose is still important because it affects the selection of the skills space, choice of the psychometric model, analysis of the given tasks, choice of model fit evaluation method, and the nature of the score reports.

Thus, there are two kinds of practical skills diagnostic settings: (a) analysis of existing assessment data using more complex models to extract richer information than provided by unidimensional analyses and (b) designing a test from the start for a skills diagnostic purpose. One good example of a study in which the consideration of assessment purpose preceded and motivated the discussion of the development of a skills diagnosis implementation procedure is that of Klein, Birenbaum, Standiford, and Tatsuoka (1981), who investigated the diagnosis of student errors in math problems involving the addition and subtraction of fractions. However, most of the extant examples are of the first type, as are both of the examples we elaborate on in the following sections.

Description of Attribute Space

As mentioned earlier, the assessment purpose leads naturally to the question of what is to be assessed about the test takers—what proficiencies are involved and what types of inferences are desired. The second component in our implementation process thus requires a detailed formulation of the skills and other attributes that will be measured to accomplish the test purpose. In this step, a detailed representation of the skills or attributes space is developed in light of the purpose and based on cognitive science, educational psychology, measurement, and relevant substantive literature. Often such literature will lead to multiple representations to be considered before a selection is made. In general this component of the implementation process considers how many and what kinds of skills or attributes are involved, at what level(s) of difficulty, and in what form of interaction. All of these issues will typically become more refined on the basis of a detailed analysis of the tasks, so a detailed discussion of each is deferred until the next section.

It is also important to keep in mind how the skills interact with each other in terms of correlational or ordinal relationships. For example, mastery of one skill might be known to occur only when another skill has first been mastered. Also, some skill pairs may tend to be more positively correlated than others. Delineating this information is clearly helpful for more effective implementation of the task development and analysis component of the implementation process, as discussed next.

Development and Analysis of Assessment Tasks

Logically, considering assessments as systems for reasoning about mental capabilities according to evidence from tasks administered to examinees, the choice of tasks should be based primarily on a consideration of the amount and kinds of evidence needed to support desired inferences about examinee attributes. Ideally, test developers should consider a wide variety of possible tasks, choosing feasible ones that best match the purpose of the assessment. It is especially important when using IRT-based latent class models to consider tasks involving multiple skills because these models are especially made for such tasks and because the inclusion of multiple-skill tasks generally enhances the correspondence between the assessment tasks and the real-life tasks they are attempting to predict examinee mastery about.

Task development not only involves casting a wide net for tasks that show promise for measuring the skills of interest but also requires a detailed analysis of such tasks to provide an in-depth delineation of the skills involved, the difficulty of applying the skills, and how the skills interact in the task solution behavior. Even when skills diagnosis is to be applied to an assessment instrument that already exists, a detailed task analysis must still be carried out even though the choice of tasks is moot. In this case, the process is not necessarily easier. The task analysis may actually be more difficult when the tasks are already chosen because of the constraint on finding a good match between the tasks and the specified skills to be diagnosed.

The analysis of the task-solving behavior and skills or cognitive processes clearly plays a critical role in implementing skills diagnosis. A number of important outcomes result from this stage of the implementation process. The most important are (a) the list of tasks to be used on the assessment instrument and (b) a refined description of the skills and how they interact. Some skills from the initial representation may have no tasks readily available that measure them (e.g., if multiple-choice items are the only available tasks, certain types of skills cannot be measured). The number of skills may also need to be adjusted upward or downward. Some skills may turn out to be so closely related that they need to be combined to form a new higher order skill. By contrast, sometimes practitioners may find they need to break down a skill into two or more subskills because the task analysis reveals important distinctions not previously considered.

The refined skill descriptions also must be sufficiently rich in detail so that independent raters have a high degree of agreement in deciding which skills are associated with each task. In particular, an indicator matrix is developed that specifies which skills are associated with each task. The development of the list of skills and the indicator matrix are nontrivial exercises that can be very time consuming and costly to conduct. But if these exercises are not done well, the skills diagnosis will not yield productive results.

This indicator matrix is referred to as the Q-matrix in the skills diagnosis literature. The elements of Q are denoted by q_{ik}, such that $q_{ik} = 1$ when skill k is associated with item i, and $q_{ik} = 0$ otherwise. In other words, the rows represent tasks, the columns represent skills, and the entries are 1s and 0s, indicating, respectively, whether a specific skill is or is not intended to be measured by a particular task. In general, the number of items per skill must be sufficient to enable accurate measurement of each skill. However, if the number of skills per item is too large, then too many parameters are introduced than can be well estimated. This is especially important when tasks are dichotomously scored, as the 0 to 1 probability range can be divided up to distinguish only a limited number of different latent classes. On the other hand, if the number of skills is reduced too much by deleting or combining, the remaining skills may lack diagnostic utility or interpretability. Making this compromise between too many or too few skills is a vital aspect of carrying out a successful skills diagnostic analysis. This is discussed in more detail in our first example.

A key consideration in the development of the Q-matrix and the associated detailed skill descriptions is the match between task difficulty and the difficulty of the skills involved. Easy tasks cannot yield usable information about mastery of difficult skills. Similarly, care must be taken in associating easy-to-apply skills to difficult tasks. For tasks involving two or more skills, an important distinction is whether the skills interact in a conjunctive or compensatory manner (or a complex mixture of the two). A conjunctive interaction is when successful performance on the task as a whole requires successful application of every component skill. Lack of success on any one skill causes a sharp reduction in successful performance on the task. A compensatory interaction is when lack of success on applying one skill can be compensated for by successful application of another. An extreme compensatory model is a disjunctive model in which successful application of any one skill is sufficient to yield a high likelihood of success on the task as a whole.

Specification of Psychometric Model

The psychometric model includes two parts, the model for the skills space (the *ability* model) and the IRF model, which links the ability model with the possible scored item responses.

ABILITY MODEL. For simplicity in this chapter, we generally use the term *skills* to refer to the latent attributes being measured. We recognize that the latent examinee characteristics of interest do not always fit well with this term (e.g., in diagnosing the amount of knowledge an examinee has or in diagnosing the presence of an illness). Specifically, when IRT-based latent class models are used, ordered categories represent ordered levels of skill proficiency. Letting α stand for this categorical examinee ability variable, then, for example, in a simple mastery/nonmastery assessment setting, $\alpha = 1$ represents mastery on a skill, whereas $\alpha = 0$ represents nonmastery. For convenience, we assume α is dichotomous, but IRT-based latent class models are equally applicable to settings in which skill mastery is defined at more than two levels. We also assume for convenience that the assessment tasks are scored dichotomously (e.g., correct vs. incorrect), although these latent class models can be (and in some cases, have already been) easily extended to polytomously scored tasks.

Let K stand for the number of skills measured by an assessment instrument and let k index be a particular skill (thus, k takes on a value between 1 and K). Similarly, we use I for the number of items with item index i and J for the number of examinees with examinee index j. Next, we define for the jth examinee a vector $\underline{\alpha}_j = (\alpha_{j1}, \alpha_{j2}, \ldots, \alpha_{jK})$ denoting the state of mastery or proficiency of the examinee on each of the K skills. In the latent-class-model approach, α_{jK} is a categorical variable, such that

$$\alpha_{jk} = \begin{cases} 1 & \text{if Examinee } j \text{ has mastered Skill } k \\ 0 & \text{otherwise} \end{cases} \quad (1)$$

In addition to the $\underline{\alpha}$ (α_K, $k = 1, \ldots, K$) ability vector, the ability model should also model the relationships between the K skills. The simplest approach is to model the correlations among the skills. To adjust for the dichotomous nature of the α_K variables, tetrachoric correlations can be used. If an ordered relationship occurs between two skills in the sense that an examinee cannot attain mastery on one skill until some other skill is first mastered, it is advantageous for either the model or the estimation procedure to be modified to include such relationships. If needed, the relationships among the K components of the ability vector can be modeled using more complex methods, such as log-linear or hierarchical models.

IRF MODELS. The goal of an IRF model is to represent the performance of an examinee on an item based on the skills required in responding to the item and examinee proficiency on these skills. The general idea behind all the IRT-based latent class models is that the higher the proficiency of an examinee on the item's required skills, the higher the probability that the examinee will get the item right. Specifically, an IRF tells the probability of an examinee giving a correct item response, conditional on an examinee's mastery standing on each of the skills required for the item, as indicated by the Q-matrix. The most important distinction to consider in selecting the IRF is the type of skill interaction that is believed to occur in solving the items as indicated by the task analysis. As described previously, this interaction is either conjunctive or compensatory.

The most popular models used in the IRT-based latent class approach have been conjunctive models, probably because the skill interactions in these applications have generally been viewed as better fitting a conjunctive interaction compared with a compensatory one. For example, the early applications of skills diagnosis have focused more on assessment of skills in mathematics, in which the solution of a task is broken down into a series of steps, all of which must be successfully performed to have a correct response on the task. Viewed in this way, the task analysis naturally leads to a preference for a conjunctive model. Conjunctive models include the DINA ("deterministic input; noisy 'and' gate") model of Haertel (1989), NIDA ("noisy input; deterministic 'and' gate") model of Junker and Sijtsma (2001), the reparameterized unified model (RUM) of Hartz (2002) and Hartz and Roussos (2008), and the conjunctive multiple classification latent class models (MCLCMs) of Maris (1999).

The use of compensatory IRT-based latent class models has become popular more recently (as compared with conjunctive models). As IRT-based latent class models are applied in a greater variety of diagnostic settings, the use of compensatory models will certainly increase as well. For example, medical and psychological diagnosis is an area in which compensatory models seem particularly relevant because such diagnoses are typically made based on the presence of only some of the possible symptoms; that is, the absence of certain symptoms can be compensated by the presence of others—the presence of all symptoms is not required. Compensatory models include the disjunctive MCLCM and compensatory MCLCM (Maris, 1999), DINO (Templin & Henson, 2006), and NIDO (Templin, Henson, & Douglas, 2009).

Regardless of whether a model is conjunctive or compensatory, another important consideration is model complexity. Generally, the greater the number of parameters in the IRF, the greater the noise in the parameter estimation, and the greater the chance of nonidentifiability (i.e., more than one set of parameter estimates that fit the data equally well). For example, if k_i is the number of skills specified for the ith task, the RUM has $k_i + 2$ parameters per item; but a reduced version with $k_i + 1$ parameters per item can be introduced, if necessary. The NIDA model is the simplest conjunctive model. It has two parameters per skill, and these parameters do not change values across the items. This severe restriction may be helpful for data sets having small sample sizes that do not support estimation of more complex models. The DINA model has just two parameters per item. Because the number of items always exceeds the number of skills, DINA has more parameters than does NIDA and is, thus, a more flexible model. However, DINA has a strong restriction in that it assumes that the probability of a correct response, given nonmastery on at least one skill, does not depend on the number and type of skills that are not mastered. Similar types of flexibility and restrictions also exist for the compensatory models. For example, the NIDO and DINO models are the counterparts to NIDA and DINA previously mentioned. Practitioners who desire more IRF flexibility should study the general diagnostic model (GDM) of von Davier (2005), a generalized modeling framework that has the capability of containing most (if not all) of the above models in addition to accommodating new variations of them. However, when developing new models, practitioners must be careful to avoid nonidentifiability and conduct reliability and validity studies with real and simulated data. (See DiBello, Roussos and Stout, 2007, for a review of a wide variety of conjunctive and compensatory models, including latent trait models as well as latent class models.)

Estimation of Model Parameters and Evaluation of Results

The next step in the implementation process is fitting the model to data via a selected estimation method evaluating these results, including the use of model-checking statistical procedures. The estimation and evaluation are usually implemented in an iterative fashion because the evaluation typically leads to changes in either the specification of the psychometric model or in the estimation procedure. First, we briefly review the selection of an estimation method, and then we review in detail methods for evaluating the results.

METHODS OF ESTIMATION. The preferred estimation method has been marginal maximum likelihood estimation (MMLE; e.g., see Bock & Aitkin, 1981), in which item parameters and ability distribution parameters are estimated based on a likelihood function integrated over the distribution of examinee ability as represented by the vector of α_K ability variables ($k = 1, \ldots, K$). This distribution is often approximated by the population proportion of masters on each skill and tetrachoric correlations between the K skills. To do this estimation, expectation maximization (EM) or Markov chain Monte Carlo (MCMC) algorithms are used. Because both the examples we describe below used MCMC estimation, we provide a brief conceptual description of MCMC.

First, a probabilistically based computational method is used to generate Markov chains of simulated values to estimate all the parameters. Each time point (or step) in the chain corresponds to one set of simulated values (a simulated value for each parameter). MCMC theory states that after a large enough number of steps (called the *burn-in* phase of the chain), the remaining simulated values will closely approximate the desired Bayesian posterior distribution of the parameters. Thus, MCMC estimation is accomplished by running suitably long chains, simulating all parameters at each time point of the long chain, discarding the burn-in steps, and finally using the remaining steps in each chain as posterior distributions to estimate the parameter values and their standard errors. The practitioner must carefully choose the number of chains to be used, the total length of the chain, and the amount to be used for the burn-in. The post-burn-in chains are estimates of the posterior distributions of the parameters. For more information on the use of MCMC in skills diagnosis, see Roussos et al. (2007).

In addition to item parameter estimation, methods must also be used for estimating the examinee ability vector, $\underline{\alpha}$. Maximum likelihood and Bayesian techniques have been developed in this regard. MCMC studies (see above) for RUM, DINO, DINA, NIDA, and compensatory MCLCM have included some evaluation of ability estimation. As mentioned earlier, in implementing an estimation method, constraints can sometimes be introduced so that appropriate model restrictions are included. The available flexibility depends on the particular software used or on access to the source code and programming expertise.

EVALUATION OF RESULTS. Evaluation of the results of the estimation algorithm is another critical component of the skills diagnosis implementation process. A wide variety of methods can and should be applied at this stage, including convergence checking; interpreting the item parameter estimates; and calculating and interpreting statistics for model fit, reliability, and validity.

Convergence checking. Iterative item parameter estimation methods, such as EM algorithm and MCMC, require checking for convergence before further analysis is done—either convergence to within some specified tolerance as in an EM algorithm or convergence to a posterior distribution in the case of MCMC. Because the statistical information one obtains from MCMC estimation (a full posterior distribution) is richer than that obtained from an EM algorithm (an estimate and its standard error), the evaluation of whether convergence has occurred is more complete, yet also more difficult, in the MCMC case. In skills diagnosis applications, convergence may be difficult to obtain, depending on model complexity and how well the design and assumptions of the model correspond to the reality of the data. In some cases, complex models may be statistically nonidentifiable. In other cases, identifiable models may be difficult to estimate well because of ill-conditioned likelihood functions.

Although much has been written in the literature regarding the convergence of Markov chains in MCMC estimation, there is no simple statistic that reliably evaluates whether the Markov chain for each model parameter has converged. Four methods have been frequently used: chain plots (i.e., plots that display the estimate of a parameter for each step in a chain), estimated posterior distribution, autocorrelations of the chain estimates, and calculating Gelman and Rubin $\hat{R}$ (Gelman, Carlin, Stern, & Rubin, 1995) for multiple chains. If convergence has occurred after the burn-in phase of the chain, the plotted data will look like random noise with no discernible trends, the posterior distribution of these values will focus on a limited segment of the estimation scale, the autocorrelations will reduce as distance between the chain steps increases, and the $\hat{R}$ value for multiple chains will be less than 1.2. In our experience, inspecting the chain plots and the posterior distributions has been very helpful, whereas inspecting autocorrelations and $\hat{R}$ values has been less helpful.

If nonconvergence occurs, the first thing to check is whether the burn-in phase of the MCMC chain was long enough to reach the posterior distribution phase. This can be checked by running an extremely long chain. If the longer chain still does not result in convergence, one can probably rule out chain length as the problem. In this case, one can revisit the model-building steps and reconsider the Q-matrix and the selected model to see where changes may be warranted. For example, if a skill is assigned to items having a large range of difficulty, the MCMC algorithm may not converge to a single level of difficulty for the skill. For more about MCMC convergence, the reader is referred to Sinharay (2004).

Interpretation of model parameters. The estimates for the ability distribution and item parameters should be evaluated for internal consistency, reasonability, and concurrence with substantive expectations. For example, a key issue for mastery/nonmastery diagnostic models is whether the proportion of examinees estimated as masters on each skill is relatively congruent with substantive theoretical expectations. If a skill turned out much harder (or easier) than expected (e.g., from a standard-setting perspective), the Q-matrix should be revisited and the item difficulty levels investigated for the items to which the skill has been assigned. In addition, the choice of tasks for that skill can be revisited to see whether more appropriate tasks can be found (e.g., if the proportion of masters for a skill is too low, one could try replacing the harder tasks for that skill with easier ones). Ultimately, the definition of the skill may need to be adjusted, for example, by suitable modification of Q or in a more basic way leading to a new set of tasks. The relationships among the different skills can also be investigated—for example, estimates of the tetrachoric correlations.

Next, the item parameters should be closely inspected because they are a key determinant of success in the diagnosis. All IRT-based latent class models have item parameters indicating how the items performed for diagnostic purposes. Item parameters may indicate, for example, how well an item discriminates between masters and nonmasters for each skill assigned to it by the Q-matrix. This may result in the test developer changing the corresponding Q-matrix entry to 0, resulting in one less item parameter being estimated.

Model fit statistics. When a Bayesian approach to parameter estimation (e.g., MCMC) has been used, posterior predictive model (PPM) statistics are a relatively straightforward and easily interpretable approach to evaluating model fit that compares observed and model-predicted statistics. Specifically, the fitted Bayesian model produces posterior distributions for the model parameters, and one then simulates from these posterior distributions and estimates the predicted distribution of a statistic or discrepancy measure based on the simulated data. Then one compares the observed statistic with its predicted distribution. Sinharay (2006) gave an example of applying PPM fit statistics to data in a skills diagnosis setting that uses the DINA model. Henson, Roussos, and Templin (2005) have also developed and applied PPM-based statistics, including checks on both item difficulties and item pair correlations. A more traditional fit statistic is the log-likelihood statistic, which compares the fit of competing models, especially nested models. This statistic was used by von Davier (2005) in an analysis of Test of English as a Foreign Language (TOEFL) data from Educational Testing Service (ETS), in which the predicted log likelihood of the manifest distribution for the compensatory MCLCM is compared with that of a unidimensional two-parameter logistic model.

Reliability. As with all measurement instruments, estimation of reliability is another important aspect for skills diagnosis applications. As noted by DiBello, Roussos, and Stout (2007), although standard reliability coefficients as estimated for assessments modeled with a continuous unidimensional latent trait do not translate directly to assessments modeled with IRT-based latent class models, conceptions of reliability from first principles do still apply. Diagnostic skills classification reliability can be conceptualized in terms of the twin notions of (a) the correspondence between inferred and true skill mastery state and (b) the consistency of classification if the same assessment were administered to the same examinee twice.

In particular, to estimate classification reliability, the method of Henson, Roussos, Douglas, and He (2008) can be used. This method can be thought of as comprising two steps. In the first step, the method generates parallel sets of simulated data (based on the calibrated model) and estimates mastery or nonmastery for each simulated examinee on each set. In the second step, the method uses the results of the first step to calculate (a) the proportion of times that an examinee is classified correctly according to the known true attribute state (the correct classification rate for the attribute/skill) and (b) the proportion of times an examinee is classified the same for that skill on two parallel tests (estimated test–retest consistency rate). The calculated rates can also be adjusted for agreement by chance, for example, with the Cohen kappa statistics.

Validity. Before any diagnostic instrument can be fully implemented into an operational testing program, statistical evidence must be gathered to demonstrate with real data the validity of the inferences drawn from the instrument. Educational and psychological testing has a long tradition of validity research, and this research needs to be extended to IRT-based latent class diagnostic models. Although only a limited amount of such research has been conducted so far, its importance will undoubtedly rise greatly given that the gathering of validity evidence appears to be the last major hurdle to overcome before operational implementation can be seriously considered. The development of appropriate models, estimation methods, and model-checking methods has progressed to a sophisticated level, but validity research, until now, has lagged behind.

We divide our discussion of validity into two parts, internal validity and external validity. By *internal validity* we mean using data from the test itself to evaluate the validity of the estimated skill mastery classifications of the examinees. By *external validity* we mean using data external to the test (not necessarily item response data) to evaluate the mastery classifications. Two internal validity statistics are IMstats and EMstats (Hartz and Roussos, 2008), which define an examinee to be an *item master* if he or she is classified as a master of every skill required by that item. For each item, examinees are thus separated into two subsets: item masters and item nonmasters. The IMstats procedure compares the average observed score on the item between the item masters and the item nonmasters. If these two scores are close, the inferred skill classification has little effect on performance on that item. This indicates that the Q-matrix coding for the item should be investigated, including perhaps the skill description. EMstats does a similar comparison for the individual examinees. Using IMstats and EMstats as starting points, other similar internal validity statistics could be derived to better fit the purposes of specific settings.

In terms of external validity, very little realistic research has been completed with IRT-based latent class models. However, there is a rich literature on validity analyses that can be adapted to skills diagnosis (Messick, 1989). In one example of skills diagnosis application, Tatsuoka and Tatsuoka (1997) conducted skills diagnosis in a classroom setting (more than 300 students in all), performing diagnosis at a pretest stage, providing remediation instruction based on the estimated mastery states of the diagnosis, and then evaluating the effectiveness of the diagnosis-based instruction with a posttest diagnosis. The results were investigated by looking at how student mastery states changed from before to after the diagnosis-based instruction. In our education example that follows, we also discuss a study by Jang (2005).

Validity studies, especially external validity, are needed on a larger scale for IRT-based latent class models—studies that directly investigate whether the estimated mastery states make sense in terms of relevant real-life consequences.

Development of Systems for Scoring and Reporting

The last critical component to be discussed here is how to translate the model ability estimates to understandable scores embedded in readable informative reports. There are many obstacles to be overcome in this step. The solution will certainly vary according to the obstacles across different settings.

STANDARD SETTING. One issue that naturally arises is that of how to interpret the classification label *master* for a skill. Such an interpretation is typically used as a basis for *standard setting,* which is the process used to determine what observed score on an assessment instrument is to be the cutoff between a master and a nonmaster. IRT-based latent class models were originally intended to be used to determine masters and nonmasters solely on the basis of the statistical behavior of the item responses. The substantive interpretation of what it means to be a master (as would be fleshed out in a standard setting) has only an indirect influence on mastery estimation through the test design and is not explicitly used in the mastery estimation. Of course, as mentioned earlier, if the likelihood-based mastery estimation resulted in a skill being easier or harder than intended, practitioners should appropriately modify the assessment tasks or the definition of the skill.

However, in some settings the use of observed subscores is preferred over likelihood-based methods for determining skill mastery. In such cases, the standard setting-process can be implemented in its usual manner and result in the determination of an observed score that functions as the cutoff between mastery and nonmastery. (For a didactic description of standard setting in education, see Cizek, Bunch, & Koons, 2004.)

EQUATING. In some settings, it is important to ensure that the mastery estimation for alternate forms, including comparisons across different testing times (e.g., from one year to the next), is comparable, that is, the same mastery classification given on different forms has the same interpretation. In theory, if the IRT-based latent class model fits the data perfectly, equating occurs automatically (Roussos & Xu, 2003). But models never fit data perfectly, so analyses should be carried out to evaluate the equating. Studies of equating using the RUM by Roussos and Templin (2004, 2005) have used data deliberately simulated with misfit to the assumed model. By using overlapping test forms across different test administrations, these researchers demonstrated successful linking using standard estimation practices.

PROFICIENCY SCALING OF SKILL SCORES. In some settings, skills diagnosis may be conducted on a test that reports a single score while also providing diagnostic classification information for several skills. By *proficiency scaling* we mean relating examinee classification on the individual skills to their score on the test as a whole. In such settings, test takers and users may need statistics that illuminate the relationship between skill mastery and the observed total test scores—the scores being something they are more familiar with and can easily observe for themselves.

One example in this regard is the work of Templin and Henson (2008), who developed estimators of the relationship between all possible test scores and all possible skill mastery patterns (all possible values of the vector of α_K mastery parameters for the $k = 1, \ldots, K$ skills). The estimation method is based on simulating 100,000 examinee item responses from the fitted model. To make these results more interpretable, two sets of summary statistics are produced. The first set of statistics summarizes the distribution of skill mastery patterns given a test score, and the second summarizes the distribution of test scores for each possible skill mastery pattern.

ESTIMATION OF SKILL MASTERIES USING SUBSCORES. Sometimes practitioners may need to use simple subtest scores to determine examinee mastery. IRT-based latent class models can be used to help determine the optimal cut-points for a subscoring approach by conducting simulations based on the fitted model. For details, see Henson, Templin, and Douglas (2007).

DEVELOPMENT OF SCORE REPORTS. Translation of skills diagnosis results into readable and informative score reports is a challenge that must be eventually confronted by every approach to skills diagnosis, and different settings have different challenges. IRT-based latent class models produce mastery classifications; different levels of sophistication may be used in translating them into a score report, depending on the nature of the assessment. The higher the stakes of the diagnosis, the more supporting evidence and transparency there should be in explaining the scores and relating them to future consequences.

For example, the College Board currently provides a Score Report Plus that is sent to each student who takes the PSAT/NMSQT (Preliminary SAT/National Merit Scholarship Qualifying Test). This is the first nationally standardized test to give some limited diagnostic skills-based feedback using an approach based on the diagnostic methodology of Tatsuoka (1983) that results in mastery classification on a set of skills (similar to results produced by IRT-based latent class models). This score report is limited to skills for which an examinee shows strong signs of weakness, only to a maximum of three skills per major content area, and does not attempt to assign a score to these skills. Even with these limitations, this application was a major advancement in the operability of skills diagnosis. (Interested readers are encouraged to visit http://professionals.collegeboard.com/testing/psat/scores/student, which includes detailed information about the Score Report Plus, as well as a link to a sample student score report.)

In the first example in the next section, we present details from a study by Jang (2005) in which she developed more extensive score reports, separately for students and teachers, that give information on each skill, including a formal statistical measure of proficiency. Jang's work is the most complete example we know of a user-friendly diagnostic report and makes a good starting point for much-needed further research in this area.

Example Applications

Up to this point, the chapter has focused on general descriptions of practical procedures associated with the implementation of IRT-based latent class models in skills diagnosis applications. We now present two example applications to demonstrate the instantiation of the implementation procedure, pointing out how each example addresses each step of the implementation process.

Educational Measurement

Jang (2005) conducted a validity study of the fusion model skills diagnosis system (Roussos et al., 2007), which uses the RUM IRT-based latent class model. Students in a classroom setting were given a pretest and a posttest using two test forms designed to be approximately parallel forms. For convenience, the forms used for the pretest and posttest are referred to as Form 1 and Form 2, respectively. The specific setting was a summer English language program for nonnative speakers conducted at a large midwestern university. The two test forms were from the LanguEdge English Language Learning (ELL) assessment developed by ETS. Each form had 39 multiple-choice items (constructed response items were not included in Jang's study), and ETS provided data for about 1,350 examinees per form, with no one identified as having taken both forms.

PURPOSE OF THE ASSESSMENT APPLICATION. ETS developed the LanguEdge as a prototype for the latest version of TOEFL (e.g., see Eignor, Taylor, Kirsch, & Jamieson, 1998), but Jang defined a new classroom formative assessment purpose for the test: to extract diagnostic information to be used by teachers and learners in a university-based summer ELL program. This was a low-stakes setting—the diagnostic assessment was not used in grading the students. A total of 27 students were enrolled in two course sections with a different teacher for each section. Diagnostic feedback was offered as an estimation of mastery versus nonmastery for each student for a set of skills to be agreed upon by Jang and the course teachers. It was important that the skills be both understandable to the teachers and theoretically defensible from the perspective of second-language (L2) learning theory.

DESCRIPTION OF THE SKILLS SPACE. Jang (2005, 2006) conducted a detailed literature investigation as she considered how to represent reading comprehension in L2 learning. Jang reported great controversy as to whether reading comprehension was decomposable into skills. Moreover, among the many researchers who supported a skills representation, there was still further controversy about the nature of those skills. The representations varied greatly from one setting to another, depending on the theoretical framework used, the purpose of the representation, and the specific tasks being analyzed. In other words, Jang reported finding much support for a skills-based approach to L2 reading comprehension but little agreement on the specific representation of those skills. So, the next step was to analyze the specific tasks at hand to obtain a firmer handle on possible skills space representations.

TASK ANALYSIS. Because in this example the tasks already existed, the next step in the implementation process was to carefully analyze the given tasks (i.e., the multiple-choice items on the two test forms) to develop the set of skills with detailed descriptions, including judging the relative difficulty of the skills; describing how the skills interact in solving the tasks; and developing detailed and replicable coding procedures to be used in constructing the Q-matrix, which indicates which skills are associated with which tasks.

Development of Q-matrix. Jang (2005, 2006) first conducted a series of preliminary analyses: analysis of the solution process and possible strategies for solving each item; analyzing task textual features, such as the word count for each task stimulus and difficulty of the vocabulary in the item stems or reading passages; consulting the ETS test specification codes and accompanying descriptors from the original test developers; and performing nonparametric latent dimensionality analyses. She then conducted in-depth, think-aloud verbal protocol analyses, which alone identified 18 processes as possible skill candidates. Through the combination of all these analyses, she initially identified 32 distinct processes or features that could have been used as skills or attributes, a number she knew was not statistically supportable. After reducing the number of skills to 16, she found that there were still some skills that had too few items associated with them. She finally reduced the number of skills to nine, a number she found was both statistically and substantively supportable. Indeed, the statistical dimensionality analyses identified three clusters of items that corresponded to three of the skills that had larger numbers of items associated with them (statistical analyses tend to identify fairly large dimensions; see Jang & Roussos, 2007). She noted that further reductions by combining or eliminating skills, although possibly resulting in still increased mastery estimation reliability, would have not been supported either substantively or statistically. Specifically, either skills that were too distinct would have been combined or skills would have been eliminated, resulting in some items having no assigned skills.

Using all the above analyses together, Jang developed a final skills space simultaneously satisfying the new teaching and learning purpose of her assessment and theoretically defensible based on existing linguistic literature. The final Q-matrix averaged about two skills per item (which translated to about eight items per skill).

Skill interaction. As mentioned previously, in developing the skills space, it is also important to investigate how the skills interact in the task-solution process. An important distinction for within-task interaction is one we have referred to as *conjunctive versus compensatory*. Recall that by *conjunctive* skill interaction we mean that successful application of all the required skills for a task seems necessary for successful performance on the task as a whole; and by *compensatory* we mean that a higher level of competence on one skill can compensate for a lower level of competence on another skill to result in successful task performance. Jang (2005, 2006) noted that, depending on the skill representation she chose, she could have been led to either a conjunctive model, a compensatory model, or a mixture of the two models. She decided that a conjunctive skill representation was adequate for her particular setting because, based on her task analyses and her reading of the literature, some of the inter-skill relationships appeared to conform to a conjunctive model to some extent;

the skills that did not interact conjunctively were mostly amenable to being combined into higher order skills that did seem to behave conjunctively with the remaining skills.

Q-matrix skill descriptions. Another important outcome of the task analysis process is the development of specific skill descriptors that are used for an initial substantive assignment of skills to tasks. The skill descriptions need to be sufficiently clear that independent raters can reliably agree on these assignments. To give an idea of the amount of detail required, we present the nine skill descriptions as follows:

- Skill 1: Deduce word meaning from context (CDV). Deducing the meaning of a word or a phrase by searching and analyzing text and by using contextual clues appearing in the text.
- Skill 2: Determine word meaning out of context (CIV). Determine word meaning out of context with recourse to background knowledge.
- Skill 3: Comprehend text through syntactic and semantic links (SSL). Comprehend relations between parts of text through lexical and grammatical cohesion devices within and across successive sentences without logical problems.
- Skill 4: Comprehend text-explicit information (TEI). Read expeditiously across sentences within a paragraph for literal meaning of portions of text.
- Skill 5: Comprehend text-implicit information at global level (TIM). Read selectively a paragraph or across paragraphs to recognize salient ideas paraphrased based on implicit information in text.
- Skill 6: Infer major arguments or a writer's purpose (INF). Skim through paragraphs and make propositional inferences about arguments or a writer's purpose, with recourse to implicitly stated information or prior knowledge.
- Skill 7: Comprehend negatively stated information (NEG). Read carefully or expeditiously to locate relevant information in text and to determine which information is true or not true.
- Skill 8: Summarize major ideas from minor details (SUM). Analyze and evaluate the relative importance of information in the text by distinguishing major ideas from supporting details.
- Skill 9: Determine contrasting ideas through diagrammatic display (MCF). Recognize major contrasts and arguments in the text whose rhetorical structure contains the relationships such as compare/contrast, cause/effect, or alternative arguments, and map them into mental framework.

Skill difficulty and item difficulty. Before a diagnostic model is fit to the data, practitioners often have a rough idea of the relative difficulty of each skill and of the individual items. Once data are available, but before a diagnostic model is fit to the data, simple item difficulty statistics can be computed, such as the proportion-correct score or the estimated difficulty parameter from unidimensional IRT. Because ETS data were available, Jang conducted a unidimensional IRT analysis of the LanguEdge forms and compared the IRT item difficulty parameters with skill difficulty based on the complexity of the processing involved. The results showed excellent correspondence between the order based on skill difficulty and that based on the IRT analysis, except for one skill, SUM, "summarizing major ideas from minor details," which the IRT analysis indicated to be much easier than Jang believed it would be based on her process analysis.

SPECIFICATION OF PSYCHOMETRIC MODEL. For Jang's research, an IRF was needed that was applicable to dichotomously scored items and dichotomous mastery (i.e., mastery versus nonmastery). Furthermore, as reported in the task analysis results, Jang determined that some skills seemed to interact in a conjunctive manner, whereas the remaining skills seemed like they could be combined to form higher order skills that also seemed conjunctive. Of the available conjunctive-model IRFs, she chose the RUM in the form, which assumes the Q-matrix is "complete"; that is, it assumes the Q-specified skills are sufficient for modeling the item responses so that the ability and item parameter for representing missing skills in the Q-matrix could be dropped from the model.

The resulting modified RUM IRF is given as follows:

$$P(X_{ij} = 1 | \underline{\alpha}_j) = \pi_i^* \prod_{k=1}^{K} r_{ik}^{*(1-\alpha_{jk})q_{ik}} \qquad (2)$$

where X_{ij} represents the dichotomously scored item response of examinee j to item i, $\underline{\alpha}_j$ is the vector of K dichotomous mastery variables for examinee j, π_i^* is the probability of a correct response on item i for an examinee who has mastered all the required skills for the item, and r_{ik}^* is the ratio for item i of the expected performance on skill k of a nonmaster to the expected performance of a master of the skill. For examinees who have not mastered a required skill, the item response probability will be multiplicatively reduced by an r_{ik}^* for each nonmastered skill, where $0 < r_{ik}^* < 1$. The more strongly the item depends on mastery of a skill, the lower the item response probability should be for a nonmaster of the skill, which translates to a lower r_{ik}^* for that skill on that item. Thus, r_{ik}^* functions like a reverse indicator of the strength of evidence provided by item i about mastery of skill k. The closer r_{ik}^* is to 0, the more discriminating item i is said to be for skill k.

The RUM IRF was implemented within a Bayesian framework called the *fusion model system*. The fusion model uses a vector of parameters (p_k, $k = 1 \ldots K$) to model the proportion of the population who has mastered each of the K skills, and it uses tetrachoric correlations to model the correlations between the dichotomous skills. Furthermore, the ability parameter is an estimate of the probability that an examinee is a master of each skill. In Bayesian language this is called the *posterior probability of mastery (ppom)* on each skill. The ppom can be rounded to the nearest integer (0 or 1) to estimate skill mastery, but the ppom itself is an indication of the statistical strength of that estimate. In this particular example, Jang estimated that an examinee was a skill master if the ppom was greater than 0.6 or a nonmaster if ppom was less than 0.4. Examinee mastery status on a skill was estimated as "indeterminate" if the ppom was between 0.4 and 0.6.

ESTIMATION OF MODEL PARAMETERS AND EVALUATION OF RESULTS. Next Jang proceeded to fit the model to the data using MCMC estimation. Jang then evaluated the results of the estimation using a variety of methods, including standard model fit statistics, as well as analyses targeted to the particular methods, data, and objectives of interest in her study. All these analyses are discussed in more detail below.

Estimation. The fusion model system (Roussos et al., 2007) was used to estimate the model parameters and conduct evaluative statistical analyses. The estimation software within this system is called *Arpeggio* (Russos et al, 2007), which provides MCMC estimation. The first step was to use Arpeggio to conduct a joint calibration of the two forms using the ETS data along with one Q matrix for both forms together.

Convergence checking. Convergence was evaluated for the π_i^*, r_{ik}^*, and p_k parameters by studying graphs of the posterior distributions, chain plots, and autocorrelation functions for chain lengths of 5,000, 15,000, and 30,000. Examples of these graphs are shown in Figure 3.1 for one of the r^* parameters from Form 1. The chain plots show every 10th term in the chain to simplify the plots and reduce the sizes of the output files. In this particular example, it seems evident from the chain plots that the first 1,000 steps can adequately serve as the burn-in. The plots clearly indicate that the chains have settled into a stable distribution. Convergence was seen to occur for all the item parameters as well as for the population ability distribution parameters (the p_k values). The graphs of the posterior distributions supported the inference from the chain plots that convergence has occurred, as there was little change in the posterior distributions after the first 1,000 chain steps, and the mass of each distribution was confined to a limited range of values.

The figure also shows the autocorrelation function, which can be used to determine the degree of independence between two groups of data separated by a specified number of steps in the chain. If autocorrelation is relatively high, the chains must be run longer to estimate the posterior distribution with reasonable accuracy. Figure 3.1 indicates there is little autocorrelation between chain estimates that are spaced 500 or more steps apart. This example illustrates good convergence results and is no doubt due to the careful model development that Jang conducted.

Interpretation of model parameters. Once convergence was confidently attained, Jang next looked at the proportion of examinees who were estimated as masters, nonmasters, and indeterminate on each of the skills. The results for Form 1 are presented in the top half of Table 3.1. Note that the results show no obvious anomalies, such as values close to zero or one. Indeed, these results showed strong agreement with the expectations of Jang and the unidimensional IRT results that were reported previously; that is, the results indicate that the SUM skill appeared to be easier for the examinees than was expected

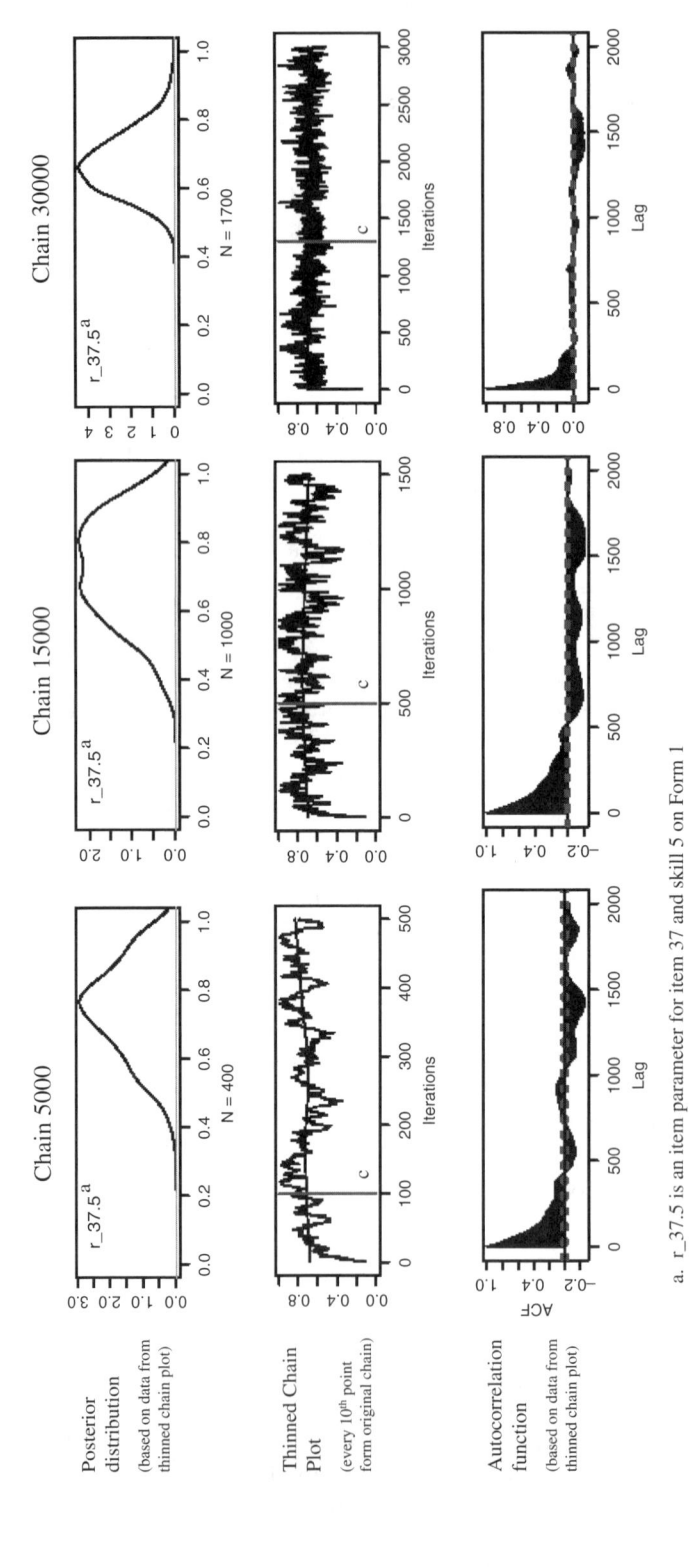

Figure 3.1. Effect of chain length on item parameter estimation convergence.

a. r_37.5 is an item parameter for item 37 and skill 5 on Form 1
b. N=number of post-burn-in points in thinned chain plot
c. vertical line denotes burn-in

Table 3.1. Mastery Classification Statistics

	Classification proportions for Form 1		
Skill	Masters	Non-masters	Indeterminate
CDV	.56	.31	.13
CIV	.54	.37	.08
SSL	.49	.39	.12
TEI	.50	.43	.07
TIM	.45	.46	.09
INF	.46	.44	.10
NEG	.38	.47	.15
SUM	.58	.32	.11
MCF	.43	.51	.06

	Model-predicted correct classification rates					
	Form 1			Form 2		
Skill	Overall	Masters	Non-masters	Overall	Masters	Non-masters
CDV	.87	.88	.85	.92	.94	.88
CIV	.93	.94	.92	.84	.86	.80
SSL	.89	.89	.89	.89	.90	.88
TEI	.94	.94	.94	.88	.88	.87
TIM	.91	.90	.91	.95	.96	.94
INF	.91	.91	.91	.91	.91	.90
NEG	.84	.83	.84	.81	.83	.78
SUM	.90	.90	.88	.89	.90	.87
MCF	.95	.94	.95	.85	.87	.83
Mean	.90	.90	.90	.88	.90	.86

from Jang's substantive process analysis. In this case, Jang did not feel a need to consider any further modifications for purposes of her study, but she recommended further work to investigate this particular skill.

The item parameters, π_i^* and r_{ik}^*, were then inspected in detail because they indicate how well the items performed for diagnostic purposes. The π_i^* parameter (i.e., probability of correct response conditional on mastery of all skills required by an item) is desired to be close to unity (1.0). The smallest π^* value for Form 1 was 0.46, and it was the only one below 0.50. For Form 2, the four smallest π^* values were 0.42, 0.43, 0.44, and 0.46, and were again the only ones below 0.50 for that form. Jang considered adding new skills to the Q-matrix to help with the low π^* values, but such skills would have had insufficient items to justify keeping them.

The r_{ik}^* parameter indicates how well each item discriminates between masters and nonmasters for each of the skills assigned to the item, with larger r^* values indicating poorer discrimination. After identifying 13 r^* values greater than 0.9 (about 9% of the total), Jang eliminated the corresponding Q-matrix entries (i.e., changed the entry from a 1 to a 0) for these item-skill combinations because the r^* values indicated the items had poor discrimination power for these skills. The 0.9 criterion was arbitrarily chosen on the basis of the needs of this particular application (Jang wanted to err more on the side of keeping initial Q-matrix entries intact, rather than eliminating them), and other criteria may be more appropriate in other settings.

Model fit statistics. Using the MCMC posterior distributions, Jang conducted PPM checking by comparing model-predicted statistics with statistics from the observed data, in particular, the item-pair correlations, the item proportion-correct scores, and the observed score distribution. She reported that the mean absolute difference (MAD) between predicted and observed item proportion-correct scores was 0.002 and the MAD for the correlations was 0.049. Both results supported the claim of good fit of the model to the data. Shown in Figure 3.2 is a comparison between the observed and predicted score distributions for Form 1. The misfit at the very lowest and highest parts of the distribution were expected as the mastery/nonmastery examinee model overestimated the scores of the lowest scoring examinees and underestimated the scores of the highest scoring examinees. The goal of the analysis was to estimate mastery/nonmastery rather than to scale examinees, and this misfit actually had no effect on the mastery/nonmastery classification. Specifically, all the high-scoring examinees whose scores were underestimated were all classified as masters of all the skills, in spite of the underestimation; all the low-scoring examinees whose scores were overestimated were still classified as nonmasters on all the skills, in spite of the overestimation.

Reliability. Jang estimated classification reliability using the method of Henson et al. (2008) in which parallel sets of simulated data are generated on the basis of the calibrated model. Mastery/nonmastery for each simulated examinee on each skill is estimated for each generated data set, and the proportion of

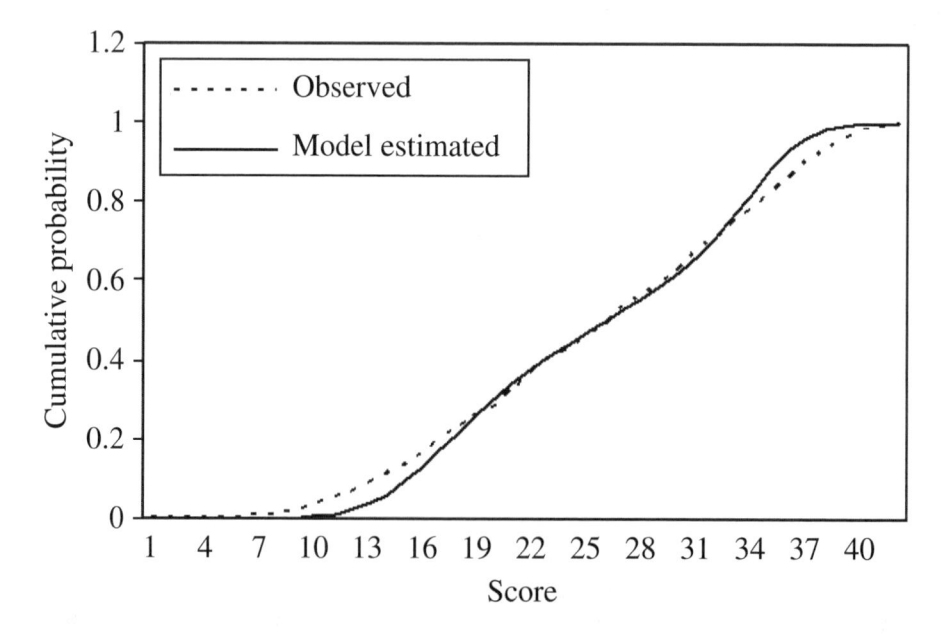

Figure 3.2. Comparison of observed and model estimated score distributions for Form 1.

times an examinee is classified correctly according to the simulated true mastery state is calculated, thus producing an estimate of correct classification rate for the skill. The results are shown in the bottom half of Table 3.1. Jang concluded that the correct classification rates for the test forms were sufficiently reliable for her application. Form 1 was slightly more reliable ($M = 90\%$) than Form 2 ($M = 88\%$). No skill had a correct classification rate below 80%.

Internal validity. Jang conducted an IMstats analysis as provided for in the fusion model system. Recall that for each item, IMstats divides the examinees into groups according to how many of the particular skills required by the item each examinee has been estimated as having mastered. Examinees who have mastered all the skills required by an item are called *item masters,* and those who are nonmasters on at least one of the skills required for an item are called *item nonmasters.* We remind the reader that this use of the terms *master* and *nonmaster* is different from our usual usage with respect to mastery of individual skills. Here mastery is discussed relative to all the skills required for an item, not mastery relative to a single skill. IMstats computes the observed proportion-right score on each item for the examinees falling into each of the specified groups for that item. The results are examined to see whether the item masters have performed decidedly better than item nonmasters. Figure 3.3 presents Jang's IMstats results for Form 1.

The results seem to indicate a high degree of internal validity for the skills diagnosis, as the mean score differences between item masters and item nonmasters are quite large for the vast majority of the items. The results also point to certain problematic items. Jang noted that the worst of the problematic items

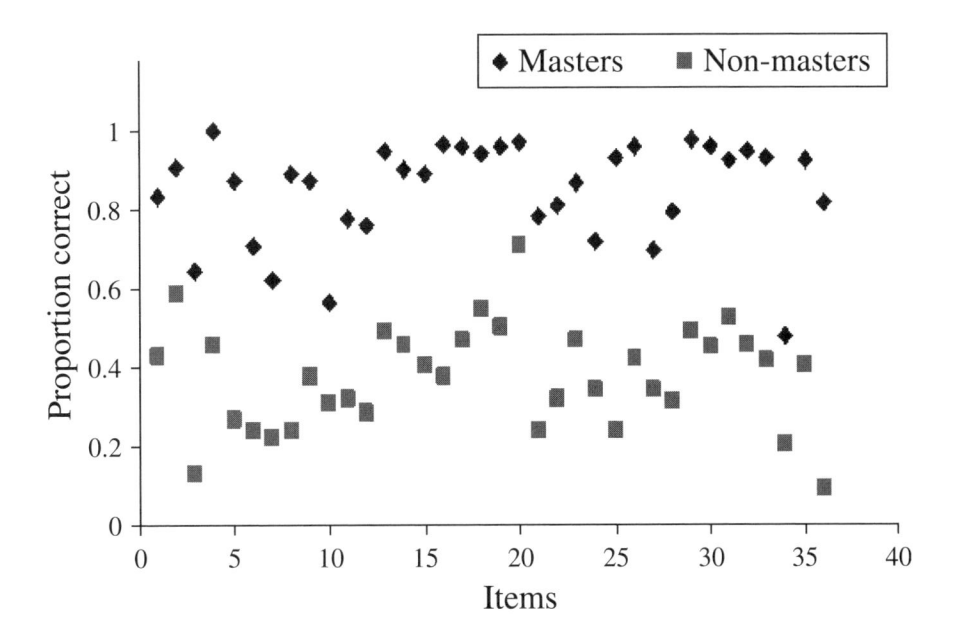

Figure 3.3. IMstats internal validity check comparing performance difference between item masters and item nonmasters.

were almost all very hard, but there was also one that was very easy. The hard items included all the items that were found above to have low π^* values. As noted by Jang, the test she used had been originally intended as a norm-referenced test for which items are needed that cover a wide range of difficulty over many skills, whereas diagnostic mastery testing is optimal when the difficulty level of a skill is held as nearly constant as possible at the level at which mastery is desired to be evaluated. Given that the test had not been originally designed for skills diagnosis, the number of problematic items seems comparatively small and indicates that the Q-matrix was carefully designed in regard to this issue.

Pretest/posttest validity analysis. The diagnostic results indicated that on average, the students improved their reading skills. This was as expected because the students received instruction directly related to the construct of the assessment instrument, and the new diagnostic purpose seemed to be well implemented in the instrument (as evidenced by the above statistical evaluation). However, Jang was also interested in whether the use of the diagnostic assessment had improved the instruction and learning. The use of a control group would be the ideal way to answer this question, but such was not available for her study. To gain additional external validity information in regard to this issue, Jang conducted surveys and interviews with the students and teachers after the pretest scores and the posttest scores had been reported. At both time points, the overall feedback of the students was very positive, indicating they generally found the diagnostic information both accurate and helpful; however, the feedback also indicated that most of the students actually used the information to guide their study either only "a little bit" or "not at all." Interviews with the teachers showed that one teacher used little of the diagnostic information to guide her instruction, whereas the other explicitly used skills-based instruction and used the pretest results to help her. Readers are referred to Jang (2005) for more detailed analyses of her results.

SCORE REPORTING. The results of the pretest and posttest skills diagnoses were reported back to the students and teachers in the form of descriptive reports detailing each student's strengths and weaknesses. The design of the reports was based on interviews with the students and teachers to ascertain their opinions about the sort of information they would find useful in a diagnostic score report. Jang also reviewed the score report used by the College Board in regard to the PSAT/NMSQT (http://professionals.collegeboard.com/testing/psat/scores/student).

An example of one of Jang's student reports for the pretest results is given in Figure 3.4. To help one understand the classifications, she reported an elaborated written description of each skill, a probabilistic measure of the skill classification ("skill mastery standing") so that the user has a measure of the strength of the evidence, and a list of the items ("Example Questions") involving the skill ordered from the highest discriminating item to the lowest so the user can better understand the relationship of their scored item performance to their skill classification. The flags on the left side of the second page indicate skills that need improvement. A question mark indicates that the skill mastery is indeterminate. As mentioned earlier, Jang's work is the most complete example

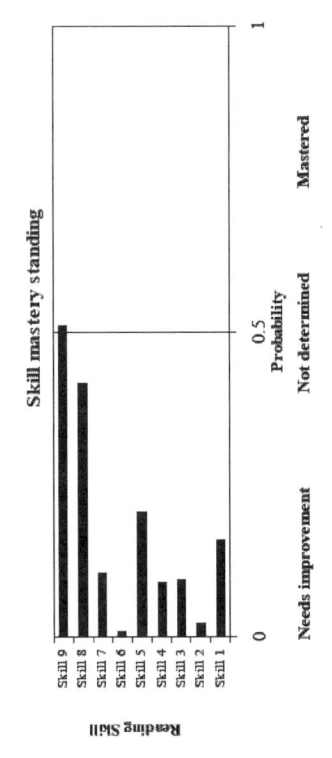

Figure 3.4. Student diagnostic score report for pre-instruction test.

we know of a user-friendly diagnostic report. The reader is referred to Jang (2005) for more examples of her teacher and student score reports.

Psychological Assessment Example

The *Diagnostic and Statistical Manual of Mental Disorders* (4th ed., text rev.; *DSM–IV–TR;* American Psychiatric Association, 2000) defines most psychological disorders using a set of criteria that are either met or not met. Individuals are classified as having a disorder if a specific number of the criteria are satisfied. Although IRT-based latent class models have been typically used in education applications to determine mastery of skills, they easily generalize to psychological assessment applications to determine those criteria that have been met in questionnaires developed to measure disorders based on their *DSM–IV–TR* defined criteria. In our psychological assessment example, Templin and Henson (2006) developed a new IRT-based latent class model and applied it to an existing instrument for measuring pathological gambling. They defined a new diagnostic purpose for the instrument and fit their new model to a new sample of 593 undergraduates.

PURPOSE OF THE ASSESSMENT APPLICATION. The *DSM–IV–TR* defines pathological gambling based on 10 dichotomous (met/not met) criteria. An individual who meets any 5 of the 10 criteria is classified as a pathological gambler. One of the most common scales used to assess pathological gambling is the South Oaks Gambling Screen (SOGS; Lesieur & Blume, 1987). SOGS classifies individuals as either probable or nonprobable pathological gamblers; however, SOGS was not developed to measure each criterion, and so the specific criteria that have been met by any individual cannot be assessed. As noted by Templin and Henson (2006), knowing which criteria cause a particular case of pathological gambling could have substantial impact on the method of treatment for the disorder.

As an alternative to SOGS, Feasel, Henson, and Jones (2004) developed the Gambling Research Instrument (GRI), a 41-item questionnaire designed to measure each of the 10 *DSM* criteria with a subscore for each criterion. The GRI could not be directly used as a subscore-based diagnostic instrument, as no subscore cut-points were developed for the individual criteria. Because a criterion-based diagnosis could provide substantial advantages and the GRI provides one possible foundation for such diagnosis, Templin and Henson (2006) designated this new purpose for the GRI and used IRT-based latent class models to achieve their objective.

DESCRIPTION OF ATTRIBUTE SPACE. The latent attributes that are the object of the "skills" diagnosis are not skills but, rather, the 10 *DSM* criteria. These criteria are dichotomous latent traits—that is, an individual either does or does not meet each individual criterion. The criteria are already well defined, and their descriptions are as follows:

- Criterion 1: PREO. Is preoccupied with gambling; for example, preoccupied with reliving past gambling experiences, planning the next venture, or thinking of ways to get money with which to gamble.

- Criterion 2: INCR. Needs to gamble with increasing amounts of money to achieve the desired excitement.
- Criterion 3: CONT. Has repeated unsuccessful efforts to control, cut back, or stop gambling.
- Criterion 4: IRRI. Is restless or irritable when attempting to cut down or stop gambling.
- Criterion 5: ESCA. Gambles as a way of escaping from problems or of relieving dysphoric mood (e.g., feelings of helplessness, guilt, anxiety, depression).
- Criterion 6: RETU. After losing money gambling, often returns another day to get even.
- Criterion 7: LIES. Lies to family members, therapist, or others to conceal extent of gambling involvement.
- Criterion 8: CRIM. Has committed crimes (e.g., forgery, fraud, theft, embezzlement) to finance gambling.
- Criterion 9: LOSS. Has jeopardized or lost a significant relationship, job, educational, or career opportunity because of gambling.
- Criterion 10: MONY. Relies on others for money to relieve desperate financial situation caused by gambling.

TASK ANALYSIS. Because the assessment tasks already existed (the GRI survey questions), the next step in the implementation process was to carefully analyze the tasks to determine the Q-matrix (which criteria go with which tasks) and to describe how examinee standing on each criterion interacts in the process of task endorsement. The tasks were statements about activities or behaviors that relate to the 10 pathological gambling criteria. A 0–5-point Likert-type scale was originally developed for the GRI tasks, but Templin and Henson (2006) dichotomized the scoring because they found that for the subjects they were targeting (college undergraduates), most of the task responses were either 0 or 1. Thus, a score of 0 meant the examinee did not endorse the item, and a 1 or more was scored as merely a 1, indicating the examinee did endorse the item.

Development of Q-matrix. Although each item on the GRI was originally assigned to one particular criterion, a reanalysis by two raters experienced in measurement of pathological gambling revealed a substantial number of items for which both raters agreed that more than one criteria should be assigned. In other words, for some items, endorsement seemed related to more than one criterion. One example Templin and Henson (2006) cited was an item that stated, "I worry that I am spending too much gambling." Endorsement of this statement could be related to Criterion 2 (INCR), Criterion 3 (CONT), and/or Criterion 6 (RETU). This substantive reanalysis of the GRI items resulted in a Q matrix having an average of 1.3 criteria per item, which translated to about 5.5 items per criterion.

Skill interaction. In this case, *skill interaction* refers to how a subject's meeting or not meeting the 10 criteria theoretically interact to lead to either endorsing or not endorsing an item. As in the education example, the major distinction to be made is between conjunctive and compensatory interaction. In the above example of an item with three criteria, Templin and Henson (2006) considered whether it was necessary that all three criteria be met for a subject to have a high probability of endorsing the item statement, as would be true for a conjunctive model. They noted it seems clear that a high probability of endorsing the item would likely result if even just one of the three criteria were met. This is a type of compensatory interaction called *disjunctive* because it is the direct opposite of conjunctive. Placing the two types side by side makes this clear: For conjunctive, not meeting just one of the three criteria causes a low probability of endorsement; but for disjunctive, meeting just one of the three criteria causes a high probability of endorsement.

SPECIFICATION OF PSYCHOMETRIC MODEL. To accommodate the disjunctive interaction of the criteria, Templin and Henson (2006) naturally wanted a disjunctive model. The only such model available was one by Maris (1999), which has nonidentifiable item parameters. The Maris disjunctive model could be reparameterized in a way similar to the RUM (Roussos et al., 2007), but the number of parameters per item is higher than they desired, given their relatively small sample size of 593 subjects. Instead, they wanted a disjunctive version of the conjunctive DINA model, which has only two parameters per item; but such a model did not exist. Thus, Templin and Henson developed a new model that is the disjunctive counterpart of DINA. Appropriately, they called their new model DINO, which stands for "deterministic input; noisy 'or' gate." Ability is modeled with a K-dimensional vector $\underline{\alpha}$ of 0s and 1s, where $\alpha_{jk} = 1$ indicates that subject j meets criterion k, and 0 means the criterion has not been met. The DINO item parameters can be expressed, as follows:

$$\pi_i = \text{Probability subjects endorse item } i, \text{ given they have met at least one criterion.} \quad (3)$$

$$r_i = \text{Probability subjects endorse item } i, \text{ given they have met none of the item's criteria.} \quad (4)$$

If we let X_{ij} represent the dichotomously scored response of subject j to item i, such that $X_{ij} = 1$ indicates endorsement of the item statement, then the IRF for DINO can be written as

$$P(X_{ij} = 1 | \underline{\alpha}_j) = \pi_i^{\left[1 - \prod_{k=1}^{K}(1-\alpha_{jk})^{q_{ik}}\right]} r_i^{\prod_{k=1}^{K}(1-\alpha_{jk})^{q_{ik}}}. \quad (5)$$

If a subject has met at least one of the criteria associated with item i, as specified by the Q-matrix, the exponent for π_i will be 1 and the exponent for r_i will be 0. Conversely, if a subject has not met any of the criteria for item i, the exponent for π_i will be 0, whereas that for r_i will be 1. DINO thus represents the disjunctive counterpart of the conjunctive DINA model for dichotomously scored items.

Templin and Henson (2006) implemented their DINO IRF within a Bayesian model framework, which facilitates direct estimation of ability distribution parameters. They used a vector of parameters $(p_k, k = 1 \ldots K)$ to model the proportion of the population meeting each of the K criteria, and they used tetrachoric correlations to model the correlations between the dichotomous criteria. From their Bayesian approach, for each individual, they were able to estimate not only the probability that each criterion is met but also the probability that at least 5 of the 10 criteria have been met—each individual's probability of pathological gambling (PPG). The specific classification rule they used was as follows: If a subject's PPG is 0.5 or more, the individual is classified as a pathological gambler. Different decision rules may be more appropriate for other settings.

A significant advantage of diagnostic modeling can be highlighted here. Specifically, Templin and Henson (2006) pointed out that because individuals can be given a criteria profile instead of only being labeled as either pathological or nonpathological gamblers, differential treatments could be formulated that focus on those particular criteria that are most likely met. In addition, high-risk individuals (e.g. those meeting three or four of the criteria) could be easily identified so that potentially preventative actions could be taken.

ESTIMATION OF MODEL PARAMETERS AND EVALUATION OF RESULTS. Next, Templin and Henson (2006) used MCMC to estimate their model parameters, and then they used a variety of analyses to evaluate the results of the estimation. The following sections briefly describe the estimation procedure and each of their evaluation analyses.

Estimation. On the basis of their data from 593 college students who responded to all 41 of the GRI items, Templin and Henson (2006) estimated the DINO model parameters using an MCMC algorithm that had uniform priors on all item and ability distribution parameters. They used an MCMC chain that had a total length of 50,000 steps, of which the first 40,000 were used for the burn-in period.

Convergence checking. Convergence was evaluated for the π_i, r_i, and p_k parameters by calculating the Geweke (1992) index and by visual inspection of the MCMC chain plots. The results indicated that the chains for the model parameters had converged to stable posterior distributions.

Interpretation of model parameters. Given convergence, mean estimates of all the ability distribution and item parameters were obtained. The ability distribution parameters, the proportion of the students who were estimated as having met each of the 10 criteria, are presented in the top part of Table 3.2.

As expected from a sample of undergraduate students, the proportion of individuals meeting any given criterion was generally low, with all values being below 50%. The highest p_k's were 49%, 48%, and 47% for Criteria 2 (INCR), 7 (LIES), and 5 (ESCA), respectively, as contrasted with the lowest p_k of 8% (CRIM). These indicate that individuals often gamble for excitement or escapism and may gamble deceptively, but seldom do they commit crimes to finance their gambling. Templin and Henson (2006) were satisfied that these estimates were realistic and that they do not indicate any obvious statistical problems, such as floor or ceiling effects.

The item parameters, π_i and r_i for each item, were then inspected in detail to see how well the items performed for diagnostic purposes. They wanted large values of π_i (probability of endorsing the statement for item i, given that at least one Q-specified criterion was met) and low values of r_i (probability of endorsing

Table 3.2. Ability Distribution and Example Ability Estimation Statistics for Pathological Gambling Criteria

Ability distribution

Proportion	PREO	INCR	CONT	IRRI	ESCA	RETU	LIES	CRIM	LOSS	MONY
	.44	.49	.35	.34	.47	.42	.48	.08	.17	.15

Ability estimation statistics for three individuals

Individual	PREO	INCR	CONT	IRRI	ESCA	RETU	LIES	CRIM	LOSS	MONY	PPG
A	.00	.01	.00	.00	.00	.77	.11	.00	.00	.00	.00
B	.99	.99	.29	.99	1.00	.02	.06	.00	.01	.00	.33
C	1.00	1.00	.16	.99	1.00	.05	.73	.00	.02	.00	.75

item i, given that no criteria were met). To aid in their interpretation of the π_i and r_i estimates, Templin and Henson (2006) developed an item diagnostic index (IDI_{DINO}) that combines the two item parameters, as follows:

$$IDI_{DINO} = \frac{\pi_i/(1-\pi_i)}{\pi_i/(1-r_i)}. \quad (6)$$

Technically, this index is the ratio of the odds of endorsing the item for someone who meets any of the criteria for the item to the odds of endorsement for someone who meets none of the criteria. If the index = 1, then the probability of endorsing the item for those who meet none of the criteria is no different than for those who have met one or more of the criteria—clearly indicative of an item with poor diagnostic power for its corresponding criteria. The bigger the index, the better; a value of 2 or more means the odds of endorsing the item for someone who meets one criterion are at least twice the odds for those who meet none of the criteria. The results of Templin and Henson (2006) revealed only three problematic items, 4, 12, and 20, which had index values of 1.21, 1.10, and 1.10, respectively. For the remaining items, the lowest index was 2.80. Overall, the mean was 62.3, the median was 54.2, and the standard deviation was 57.0.

Investigating the three items with low index values, Templin and Henson (2006) concluded that they performed poorly because they were poorly written or they should have been keyed for different criteria, or the items were inappropriate for their college-age population. For example, Item 4 was "I enjoy talking with my family and friends about my past gambling experiences," and Criterion 1 (PREO, "Is preoccupied with gambling") was assigned to it. The sentence focuses on whether subjects "enjoy" talking with friends and family—an activity a college student would endorse even if he or she were not a pathological gambler. Such information about item quality provides valuable feedback for modifying and improving the assessment instrument.

Model fit statistics. Using MCMC posterior distributions, Templin and Henson (2006) conducted a PPM check comparing model-predicted statistics with observed data statistics. In particular, for each item-pair they calculated the Pearson correlation and Cohen's κ. The RMS difference between observed and predicted was 0.042 for the correlations and 0.038 for the Cohen's κ values, both of which indicate good fit to the data.

External validity. In a separate study not reported in Templin and Henson (2006), the researchers collected complete data on 112 experienced gamblers who filled out the GRI and SOGS. As mentioned previously, SOGS is one of the most commonly used instruments for studying pathological gambling. It consists of 20 dichotomous (yes/no) items, and an affirmative response to any 5 items indicates an individual is probably a pathological gambler. Lesieur and Blume (1987) validated the instrument by comparing its results with clinical diagnoses for a large number of individuals. Templin and Henson (2006) estimated the DINO diagnostic model parameters for these data, again using MCMC with a total chain length of 50,000 and a burn-in of 40,000. Inspection of the chain plots indicated convergence occurred for all the model parameter estimates, and the posterior standard deviations were surprisingly small (typically 0.01–0.05 for item parameter estimates of 0.10–0.60, respectively) given the relatively small sample size.

The fitted model was then used to estimate the probabilities of meeting each of the 10 criteria for each of the 112 gamblers, and those probabilities were then used to estimate each gambler's PPG (i.e., probability of pathological gambling, as described previously). If PPG was 0.5 or more, an individual was classified as a pathological gambler. They then compared the SOGS pathological gambling classification results with those of their diagnostic model and found that 89.2% of the classifications from their DINO analysis of the GRI data were consistent with classifications made by SOGS. Correcting for agreement by chance, a Cohen's κ value of 0.69 ($p < .001$) was calculated indicating substantial agreement beyond chance (0 indicates chance agreement, and 1 indicates perfect agreement).

SCORE REPORTING. Although Templin and Henson (2006) did not develop formal score reports, they did present, as mentioned above, two types of scoring statistics. The first type was a profile of each individual's standing on the 10 criteria in terms of his or her estimated probability of meeting each criterion. The second statistic was each individual's PPG. Specifically, Templin and Henson (2006) presented detailed results for three individuals to highlight the advantages of diagnosing the individual criteria in addition to the overall diagnosis of pathological gambling. These results are presented in bottom part of Table 3.2. Individuals A and B were both diagnosed as not being pathological gamblers. However, although Individual A had a high probability (0.77) of meeting one criterion (RETU) and very low probabilities (less than 0.15) on all the others, Individual B had very high probabilities (0.99 or more) of meeting four criteria (PREO, INCR, IRRI, and ESCA) and low probabilities (less than 0.30) on the others. Thus, Subjects A and B are much different from each other in terms of their gambling behaviors and activities and, seemingly, in terms of their risk of becoming pathological gamblers; but the overall classification (not being pathological gamblers) gives no indication of these differences. Such differences may be helpful in some cases for treatment purposes, especially in regard to identifying those at risk of becoming pathological gamblers and taking preventative measures in that regard.

Concluding Remarks

This chapter has focused on the practical challenges of developing and carrying out the diagnosis of examinee attributes using IRT-based parametric latent class models. To facilitate the discussion, a general organizing scheme was presented for the diagnostic assessment implementation process consisting of six general steps: (a) description of the assessment purpose, (b) description of a model for the latent attributes, (c) development and analysis of the assessment tasks, (d) specification of a psychometric model, (e) estimation of model parameters and evaluation of the results, and (f) development of systems for scoring and reporting.

As discussed in the chapter, the steps of a successful implementation process are not strictly sequential but require considerable interaction and feedback between them. In particular, because of the diversity of expertise demanded by the different steps, close collaboration is required among users, test designers, cognitive psychologists, and psychometricians. Research supporting the components of the implementation process was shown to be well developed in terms of models, estimation techniques, and model-checking statistics. It is hoped that the broadly conceived implementation framework presented here provides a useful starting point for helping practitioners think more clearly and thoroughly about diagnostic assessment, especially in regard to IRT-based latent class models. The implementation framework presented here is certainly not intended to be the definitive word on how to construe diagnostic assessment—practitioners are strongly encouraged to think of it as only a starting point and to adapt and make changes as needed to better fit their own specific settings.

To demonstrate the implementation process for conducting diagnostic analyses with IRT-based latent class models, this chapter presented two real-data examples, one in an educational setting and the other in a psychological setting. All six components of the implementation process were discussed for each example so that readers could get a more concrete understanding of the abstract descriptions given earlier in the chapter and also so that they could begin to imagine how such analyses might be carried out in their own assessment settings.

In summary, the overarching theme of the chapter is that successful implementation of diagnostic assessment, from design to scoring, requires a team effort among a variety of professionals. Compared with traditional applications of unidimensional (single scale) IRT models to single-score tests, multidimensional (multiple skills) diagnostic assessment requires significantly increased complexity while also yielding significantly richer results about the subjects and the assessment tasks. The next step in the development of IRT-based latent class diagnostic assessment appears to be in its application to actual operational settings, in particular in terms of validity studies. Given the advanced state of statistical tools for IRT-based latent class skills diagnosis, such studies could take place in the context of pilot studies in operational testing programs, thereby advancing skills diagnosis to the threshold of operational status. In particular, in educational assessment settings there is a great need for standardized tests that provide formative assessment to help instruction and learning. Furthermore, given the advanced state of diagnostic testing in detecting and treating psychological disorders, IRT-based latent class models seem propitiously positioned to have, perhaps, an even more immediate and positive impact in this area of application.

References

American Psychiatric Association. (2000). *Diagnostic and statistical manual of mental disorders* (4th ed., text rev.). Washington, DC: Author.

Bock, R. D., & Aitkin, M. (1981). Marginal maximum likelihood estimation of item parameters: Application of an EM algorithm. *Psychometrika, 46,* 443–459.

Cizek, G. J., Bunch, M. B., & Koons, H. (2004). Setting performance standards: Contemporary methods. *Educational Measurement: Issues and Practice, 23,* 31–50.

DiBello, L. V., Roussos, L. A., & Stout, W. (2007). Review of cognitively diagnostic assessment and a summary of psychometric models. In C. R. Rao & S. Sinharay (Eds.), *Handbook of Statistics (Vol. 26, Psychometrics,* pp. 979–1030). Amsterdam: Elsevier.

Eignor, D., Taylor, C., Kirsch, I., & Jamieson, J. (1998). *Development of a scale for assessing the level of computer familiarity of TOEFL examinees* (TOEFL Research Report No. 60). Princeton, NJ: Educational Testing Service.

Feasel, K., Henson, R., & Jones, L. (2004). *Analysis of the Gambling Research Instrument (GRI).* Unpublished manuscript.

Gelman, A., Carlin, J. B., Stern, H. S., & Rubin, D. R. (1995). *Bayesian data analysis.* London: Chapman & Hall.

Geweke, J. (1992). Evaluating the accuracy of sampling-based approaches to calculating posterior moments. In J. M. Bernardo, J. O. Berger, A. P. Dawid, & A. F. M. Smith (Eds.), *Bayesian statistics 4: Proceedings of the Fourth Valencia International Meeting* (pp. 169–194). Oxford, England: Clarendon Press.

Haertel, E. H. (1989). Using restricted latent class models to map the skill structure of achievement items. *Journal of Educational Measurement, 26,* 333–352.

Hartz, S. M. (2002). *A Bayesian framework for the unified model for assessing cognitive abilities: Blending theory with practicality.* Unpublished doctoral dissertation. Champaign: University of Illinois.

Hartz, S. M., & Roussos, L. A. (2008). *The fusion model for skills diagnosis: Blending theory with practice* (ETS Research Rep. No. RR-08-71). Princeton, NJ: Educational Testing Service.

Henson, R. A., Roussos, L. A., Douglas, J. A., & He, X. (2008). Cognitive diagnostic attribute-level discrimination indices. *Applied Psychological Measurement, 32,* 275–288.

Henson, R. A., Roussos, L., & Templin, J. L. (2005). *Fusion model "fit" indices.* Unpublished ETS Project Report.

Henson, R. A., Templin, J. L., & Douglas, J. (2007). Using efficient model based sum-scores for conducting skills diagnoses. *Journal of Educational Measurement, 44,* 361–376.

Jang, E. E. (2005). *A Validity narrative: Effects of reading skills diagnosis on teaching and learning in the context of NG TOEFL.* Unpublished doctoral dissertation. Champaign: University of Illinois.

Jang, E. E. (2006, April). *Pedagogical implications of cognitive skills diagnostic assessment for teaching and learning.* Paper presented at the annual meeting of the American Educational Research Association, San Francisco, California.

Jang, E. E., & Roussos, L. A. (2007). An investigation into the dimensionality of TOEFL using conditional covariance-based nonparametric approach. *Journal of Educational Measurement, 44,* 1–21.

Junker, B. (1999, November). *Some statistical models and computational methods that may be useful for cognitively-relevant assessment.* Prepared for the Committee on the Foundations of Assessment, National Research Council.

Junker, B., & Sijtsma, K. (2001). Cognitive assessment models with few assumptions, and connections with nonparametric item response theory. *Applied Psychological Measurement, 25,* 258–272.

Klein, M., Birenbaum, M., Standiford, S., & Tatsuoka K. K. (1981). *Logical error analysis and construction of tests to diagnose student 'bugs' in addition and subtraction of fractions* (Tech. Rep. 81-6-NIE). Urbana: University of Illinois, CERL.

Lesieur, H. R., & Blume, S. B. (1987). The South Oaks Gambling Screen (SOGS): A new instrument for the identification of pathological gamblers. *American Journal of Psychiatry, 144,* 1184–1188.

Maris, E. (1999). Estimating multiple classification latent class models. *Psychometrika, 64,* 187–212.

Messick, S. (1989). Validity. In R. L. Linn (Ed.), *Educational measurement* (3rd. ed., pp. 13–103). New York: Macmillan.

Mislevy, R. J., Steinberg, L. S., & Almond R. G. (2003). On the structure of educational assessments. *Measurement: Interdisciplinary Research and Perspectives, 1,* 3–67.

Pellegrino, J. W., Chudowsky, N., & Glaser, R. (2001). *Knowing what students know: The science and design of educational assessment.* Washington, DC: National Academy Press.

Roussos, L. A., DiBello, L. V., Stout, W., Hartz, S. M., Henson, R. A., & Templin, J. L. (2007). The fusion model skills diagnosis system. In J. P. Leighton & M. J. Gierl (Eds.), *Cognitive diagnostic assessment for education: Theory and applications* (pp. 275–318). Cambridge, England: Cambridge University Press.

Roussos, L. A., & Templin, J. L. (2004). *Effect of skill heterogeneity on fusion model equating: A comparison of two methods.* Unpublished ETS Project Report.

Roussos, L. A., & Templin, J. L. (2005). *Theoretically grounded linking and equating for mastery/non-mastery skills diagnosis models.* Unpublished ETS Project Report.

Roussos, L. A., & Xu, X. (2003). *Equating with the fusion model using item parameter invariance.* Unpublished ETS Project Report.

Sinharay, S. (2004). Experiences with Markov chain Monte Carlo convergence assessment in two psychometric examples. *Journal of Educational and Behavioral Statistics, 29,* 461–488.

Sinharay, S. (2006). Model diagnostics for Bayesian networks. *Journal of Educational and Behavioral Statistics, 31,* 1–33.

Tatsuoka, K. K. (1983). Rule space: An approach for dealing with misconceptions based on item response theory. *Journal of Educational Measurement, 20,* 345–354.

Tatsuoka, K. K., & Tatsuoka, M. M. (1997). Computerized cognitive diagnostic adaptive testing: Effect on remedial instruction as empirical validation. *Journal of Educational Measurement, 34,* 3–20.

Templin, J. L., & Henson, R. A. (2006). Measurement of psychological disorders using cognitive diagnosis models. *Psychological Methods, 11,* 287–305.

Templin, J. L., & Henson, R. A. (2008, March). *Understanding the impact of skill acquisition: Relating diagnostic assessments to measurable outcomes.* Paper presented at the annual meeting of the American Educational Research Association, New York.

Templin, J. L., Henson, R. A., & Douglas, J. (2009). *General theory and estimation of cognitive diagnosis models as constrained latent class models.* Manuscript submitted for publication.

Von Davier, M. (2005). *A general diagnostic model applied to language testing data* (ETS Research Rep. No. RR-05-16). Princeton, NJ: Educational Testing Service.

4

Cognitive Psychometrics: Using Multinomial Processing Tree Models as Measurement Tools

William H. Batchelder

The main goal of this chapter is to describe an increasingly popular approach to model-based measurement of latent cognitive processing capacities such as memory storage, memory retrieval, stimulus discrimination, and logical inference. The approach uses a family of graphic tree models for categorical data called *multinomial processing tree (MPT) models*. MPT models were initially developed as a family of information processing models to study normal cognition in specific experimental paradigms in cognitive psychology (Batchelder & Riefer, 1986, 1990, 1999; Riefer & Batchelder, 1988). More recently, MPT models have been used as psychological assessment tools to measure how special populations differ in specific cognitive processing capacities (e.g., Batchelder, 1998; Batchelder & Riefer, 2007). Riefer, Knapp, Batchelder, Bamber, and Manifold (2002) provided a good example of this approach, and it is discussed in some detail later in this chapter. Because the use of MPT models for model-based measurement departs from the usual way that cognitive models are used, our research group calls this approach *cognitive psychometrics*. Cognitive modeling has been a popular theoretical approach in experimental psychology since the 1950s, and by now there are several hundred cognitive models that qualify as parametric statistical models. Typically, cognitive models are theoretically based and designed for data collected in tightly constrained experimental paradigms, and as such they have limited applicability outside of their intended domains. This property differentiates cognitive models from data analysis models such as analysis of variance, linear regression, and log-linear models, in which the models are used across a wide range of scientific problem areas. Normally, cognitive models are used as theoretical tools to understand basic cognitive processes rather than as measurement tools. There are several exceptions to this norm; for example, there are a wide range of measurement applications of signal detection models (e.g., MacMillan & Creelman, 2005), paired-comparison scaling

---

This chapter was written with support from National Science Foundation grants to A. K. Romney and W. H. Batchelder (Co-PIs, SES-0136115) and X. Hu and W. H. Batchelder (Co-Principal Investigators [Co-PIs], SES-0616657), and a grant from the Alzheimer's Association to W. H. Batchelder and E. Batchelder (Co-PIs, IIRG-03-6262).

models (e.g., David, 1988), and models for analyzing confusion matrices (e.g., Takane & Shibayama, 1992). Our development of MPT models as assessment tools discussed in this chapter is also a departure from the normal use of cognitive models.

The other chapters in this volume are examples of psychometric models from the areas of item response theory (IRT) and structural equation models that are primarily used to model differences in individuals and groups rather than as basic tools to understand normal cognition. This difference motivates a secondary goal of the chapter, which is to compare and contrast cognitive and psychometric modeling. This discussion includes information on the early history of academic psychology to help facilitate an understanding of some of the differences between cognitive and psychometric modeling, especially in how the parameters are defined and how the models are analyzed. Nevertheless, it is shown that parametric statistical models in both areas share many properties, especially the basic data structure that they apply to.

The chapter is divided into two main sections. The first section describes the class of MPT models as a natural way to model information processing behavior and is divided into four subsections. The first subsection presents a detailed example of an MPT model that can separately measure memory storage and memory retrieval capacities in a free-recall task. In the second subsection, an application of the example MPT model to the assessment of storage and retrieval capacities in individuals with schizophrenia and organic alcoholics is presented. The third subsection formally defines the class of binary MPT models and discusses the standard approach to statistical inference for these models as well as some of their additional statistical and mathematical properties. The final subsection reviews some of the applications of MPT models to explain processing deficits in special populations.

The second section of the chapter compares and contrasts cognitive and psychometric modeling. It is divided into three subsections. In the first, a review of the early history of psychology explains the origin of the division of labor between the study of normal cognition and the study of individual differences in cognition. Then the next subsection focuses on some of the similarities and differences between cognitive models and IRT models. The final subsection provides some ways that ideas from IRT models might be incorporated productively into MPT models. In particular, it describes some recent work that develops random effects and hierarchical versions of MPT models.

The Nature of MPT Models

The idea for formalizing the class of MPT models came originally from categorical data modeling in statistical genetics (e.g., Elandt-Johnson, 1971). Many models in statistical genetics have a graphic tree structure because the genes of offspring depend on the genes of their parents, and this property iterates across several generations. The tree structure of these models is suggestive of the typical situation in cognitive information processing because a given manifest cognitive act may be viewed as following from a conditional sequence of latent cognitive microacts. For example, a correct recognition response to an event from the past may occur because there is attention to the original event, then storage and maintenance of a memory trace of the event, and finally subsequent recognition of the event given the trace. The failure of any of these microacts leads to an alternate processing sequence and quite possibly to a different recognition response. This view suggests that the likelihood of a particular cognitive microact is conditional on the previous sequence of microacts. This conditional branching structure is difficult to represent in the language of general linear models or log-linear models because such models most naturally represent a manifest response as the result of the simultaneous occurrences of various main effects and interactions of underlying latent variables. Thus probabilistic tree models were viewed as a natural way to capture the temporal branching character of information processing sequences. Riefer and Batchelder (1988) first described MPT models as a special class of parametric models for product multinomial data structures, and Hu and Batchelder (1994) formalized the class of models and provided a classical approach to inference at the class level. Batchelder and Riefer (1999) provided a review of MPT modeling, including a discussion of over 80 applications of MPT models, and additional applications are discussed in Batchelder and Riefer (2007). Before describing in general the properties of MPT models, I provide in the following section an example of an MPT model along with its use to measure differences in information processing capacities between special populations.

An MPT Model for Clustering in Free-Recall Memory

An example of an MPT model is one that was designed to disentangle cluster storage from cluster retrieval in a standard free-recall memory paradigm (Batchelder & Riefer, 1980, 1986). The experimental paradigm involves a study list consisting of clusterable pairs of words (e.g., lawyer, teacher; daisy, rose) and singletons (i.e., items without a category partner). The participants study each word in the list one at a time and are later given a memory test in which they are asked to recall the studied items in any order. Recall of each pair is scored into the following four mutually exclusive categories: (a) C_1, both items recalled consecutively; (b) C_2, both items recalled nonconsecutively; (c) C_3, one and only one item recalled; and (d) C_4, neither item recalled. The model postulates two processing trees, one for the pairs and one for the singletons; however, in the example discussed, the list used did not have any singletons, so Figure 4.1 presents just the processing tree for the clusterable pairs.

The model postulates three parameters, c, r, and u, each designed to measure a different latent cognitive process. The parameter c measures the probability that the members of a pair are clustered during study and stored in memory. Parameter r is the conditional probability that a stored cluster is retrieved from memory during the recall test, and parameter u is the conditional probability that a word in a pair that was not clustered is recalled as a singleton. Because all three parameters are interpreted as probabilities, they must satisfy $0 < c, r, u < 1$. Notice in Figure 4.1 that the parameter u appears several times in the tree. Here it reflects the assumption that conditional on cluster failure, with probability $1 - c$, each item acts independently as a singleton.

```
              r ────────── C₁
         c <
       /      1-r ──────── C₄
      /
     /                u ── C₂
    /            u <
   <                  1-u ─ C₃
    \       
     \  1-c
      \            u ── C₃
       \      1-u <
                    1-u ─ C₄
```

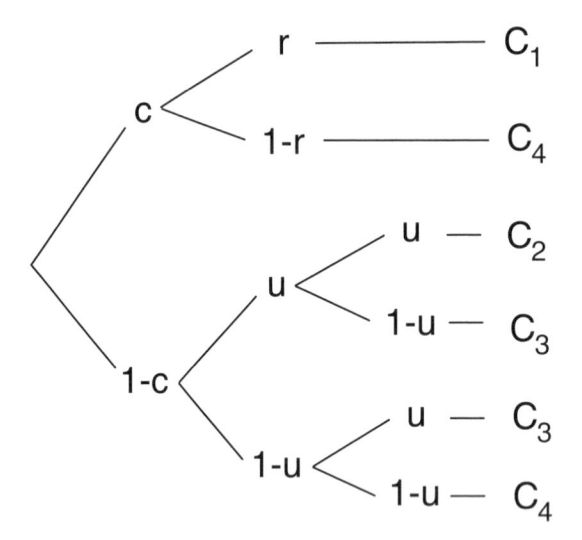

Figure 4.1. The processing tree for the pair-clustering model.

The assignment of categories to branches is motivated by psychological considerations and simplifying assumptions. The top branch in Figure 4.1 has a probability cr, which is the probability of both storing and then retrieving the cluster. The model assigns this branch to category C_1 on the assumption that items in retrieved clusters are recalled consecutively. The next branch has probability $c(1-r)$, representing successful cluster storage but unsuccessful retrieval. This branch is assigned to category C_4, indicating recall of neither item in the pair. Notice that this is one of two branches that lead to category C_4, the other being the lowest branch of the tree representing unsuccessful cluster storage coupled with recall failure on both items in a pair. In this case, $\Pr(C_4) = c(1-r) + (1-c)(1-u)^2$. A simplifying assumption in the model concerns the recall of nonclustered pairs. Notice that with probability $(1-c)u^2$, items in a pair are not clustered, but both are independently recalled. This branch is assigned to category C_2, reflecting nonconsecutive recall of the two items in a pair. This assumption is an approximation because there is a small chance for two nonclustered items to be recalled consecutively; however, it greatly simplifies the analysis of the model while maintaining the main processing stages in the task.

The pair-clustering model is like many other MPT models in that it postulates parameters that tap latent processing capacities that combine to yield manifest categorical responses. In this case, the processes are cluster storage, cluster retrieval, and the recall of nonclustered items. In a typical MPT model, there is a many–one relationship between processing branches and response categories; however, a necessary condition for model identifiability (different model parameters generate different probability distributions) is that there are fewer parameters than response categories. The pair-clustering model in Figure 4.1 has six branches, four response categories, and three parameters, and model identifiability is easily established (see Batchelder & Riefer, 1986).

To justify the use of an MPT model to interpret the effects of experimental manipulations on latent cognitive capacities, it is important to validate the substantive interpretations of the parameters. Usually validation is argued by showing face validity of the model, namely, that the parameters change in predictable ways when standard, well-understood experimental manipulations are conducted. For example in the pair-clustering model, a manipulation such as additional study time or a short spacing (lag) between the items in a clusterable pair should facilitate clustering and therefore should result in an increase in estimates of the parameter c. On the other hand, presenting retrieval cues after study but during recall should increase cluster retrieval r but should not affect cluster storage c. The validity of the pair-clustering model has been established through its successful application to these as well as several other experimental manipulations that on their face should have predictable effects on storage and retrieval processes in human memory (see Riefer et al., 2002). Once the model has been validated it can be used as a tool to measure the separate effects of experimental variables on cluster storage as measured by c and cluster retrieval as measured by r.

The pair-clustering model was first used to understand the role of lag between clusterable items in free recall (Batchelder & Riefer, 1980). The *lag* is defined as the number of unrelated words that appear between the presentations of the members of a clusterable pair in the study list. It was known that when a word is repeated in a free-recall study list, item recall probability often increases with increasing lag between the repetitions. This is a version of the well-known advantage in recall performance of spaced versus massed practice. However, a number of studies on the lag for clusterable pairs failed to create a clear relationship between item recall and lag. In some experiments short lags created better item recall, and in other studies long lags created better item recall. Notice that from the model, the probability of item recall (R) is given by $\Pr(R) = \Pr(C_1) + \Pr(C_2) + \Pr(C_3)/2 = cr + (1-c)u$. It is easy to see that this expression involves the parameters for all three latent processes in the model, and if the effects of lag are different on each parameter, various relationships between lag and item recall probability are possible.

Batchelder and Riefer (1980) showed in several experiments that controlled the spacing variable that estimates of the cluster storage parameter (c) decreased with lag, and estimates of the cluster retrieval parameter (r) increased with lag. The result that cluster storage decreased with lag was attributed to the well-known importance of instance contiguity in forming associations. The increase of cluster retrieval with spacing was attributed to the advantage of nonoverlapping retrieval contexts, namely that the retrieval cues for each item in a pair have less redundant overlap as the spacing between the items becomes greater. This is one of the explanations for the advantage of spaced practice in the repeated-word example discussed earlier. The application of the pair-clustering model to understand lag effects illustrates a general advantage of MPT models in that they provide model-based methods for the separate measurement of latent cognitive capacities that combine to produce manifest category responses.

A variety of validated MPT models have been invented for different cognitive paradigms, and they have been used in a number of experimental studies reviewed in Batchelder and Riefer (1999). The psychological research areas in which these models have appeared include proactive and retroactive interference in memory, the effects of bizarre imagery on memory, memory for the source of information (source monitoring), information pooling, the process dissociation procedure, eyewitness memory, hindsight bias, object perception, speech perception, letter identification, propositional reasoning, the confirmation bias, social cognition, and social networks. Also, there have been a number of recent applications of MPT models to assess cognitive capacities in special populations; these are discussed at the end of this main section.

An Application of MPT Modeling to Special Populations

Riefer et al. (2002) used the pair-clustering model to examine storage and retrieval deficits in two well-studied clinical populations: people with schizophrenia and alcoholics with organic brain damage. They matched male groups of schizophrenic individuals and organic alcoholics, respectively, with appropriate control groups, equating the comparison groups on age and education. A great deal of research on both schizophrenic individuals and organic alcoholics has shown that both groups suffer episodic memory problems compared with normal controls. One issue addressed by theorists in these areas is whether these deficits are mainly due to problems with storage or with retrieval. But as Riefer et al. pointed out, research and theorizing on this issue is mixed and inconclusive in both areas, with some theorists in each area concluding that the problem is mainly one of storage and others concluding that the problem lies with retrieval. It is under these circumstances that formal modeling can help clarify these theoretical issues by providing a model-based measure of the underlying cognitive processes in question.

Each group in the Riefer et al. (2002) study memorized a list of 20 category pairs over six study-test trials in which the lag between members of a category pair was large. The pair-clustering model was used to obtain maximum likelihood estimates (MLEs) for the storage and retrieval parameters for both groups on each of the six trials (the next subsection describes estimation theory for MPT models). These estimates are displayed in Figure 4.2 for the schizophrenic study and in Figure 4.3 for the organic alcoholic study.

The MLEs of the cluster storage parameter c are displayed in the left graphs of the two figures, and the MLEs of the corresponding estimates of the cluster retrieval parameter r are displayed in the right graphs. The two figures show that the MLEs are nondecreasing over trials. One would expect that the parameters for both cognitive capacities would increase with repeated study trials, and in fact the MLEs were estimated under this order restriction (for details on order-restricted inference for MPT models, see Knapp & Batchelder, 2004). For the schizophrenic group, Riefer et al. (2002), using likelihood ratio hypotheses tests, concluded that there were both storage and retrieval deficits compared with the control group. However, the deficit was stronger for retrieval, occurring after the first trial and continuing throughout the later trials as well. In contrast, the differences in storage between the schizophrenic individuals and the controls were not as pronounced, and they only became statistically significant on the later trials when fatigue might have set in.

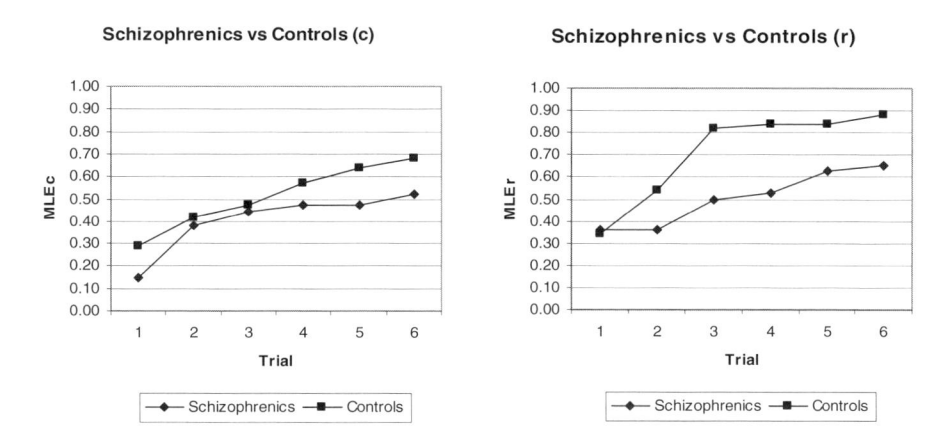

Figure 4.2. Maximum likelihood estimates of c (left panel) and r (right panel) for the schizophrenics and their controls under the assumed order constrains.

A similar pattern to that found in the schizophrenic study occurred for the organic alcoholics, with retrieval deficits being stronger than storage deficits and occurring on earlier trials. What was particularly striking about the organic alcoholics was their performance across the six study-test trials. Prior research has shown that alcoholics with organic brain damage often exhibit minimal improvement in their recall of a list of words even after multiple presentations of that list, and the modeling analysis suggests that this deficit is due to problems with retrieval and not storage. Although the organic alcoholics showed modest improvement in their storage of clusters over trials, their ability to retrieve clusters was basically low and lacked any evidence of improvement across the six list presentations.

In both studies in Riefer et al. (2002), the authors were concerned that individual differences between participants within a group may have biased the

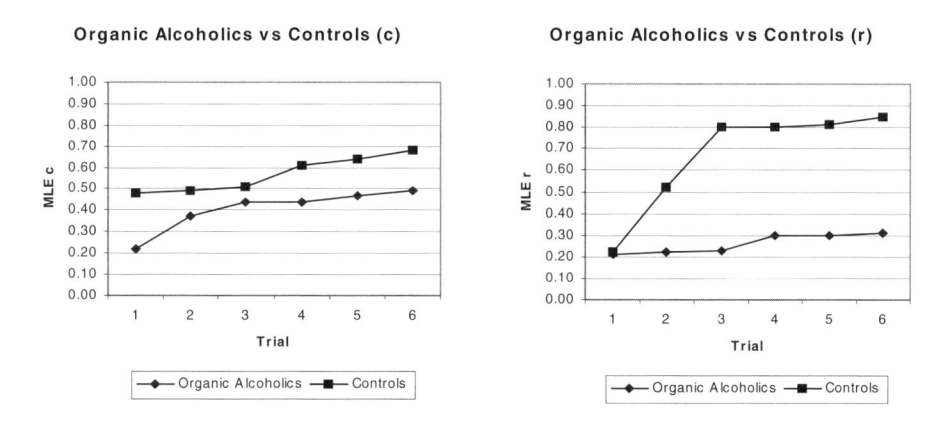

Figure 4.3. Estimates of c (left panel) and r (right panel) for the organic alcoholics and their controls.

conclusions because the primary analysis of the model leading to the estimates in Figures 4.2 and 4.3 treated the data within a group as a sample of independent and identically distributed (i.i.d.) observations from the model. The software package (see next subsection) that was used to obtain the MLEs and test hypotheses about the parameters includes an option to simulate and analyze data from the model under the assumption that the parameters c and r vary independently from participant to participant with beta distributions (see Equation 10). Although Riefer et al. (2002) showed that the hypothesis tests and MLEs in the studies were changed somewhat under simulations that injected modest amounts of variability in the parameters, none of the major conclusions presented in the article were changed by this fact. The simulation work followed the logic of an extensive simulation study of the pair-clustering model under various sample sizes and amounts of parameter heterogeneity in Riefer and Batchelder (1991b). In the final part of this chapter, several approaches to incorporating participant heterogeneity into MPT models as random effects are described.

Formal Definitions and Statistical Inference

In this subsection, MPT models are defined. First, the class of binary MPT (BMPT) models for a single category system is described in detail. Then some of the other types of tree structures that have appeared in the MPT literature are informally presented. Any BMPT model has four aspects: (a) observable categories, (b) latent parameters, (c) tree architecture, and (d) computational rules. These are described as follows:

- *Observable categories.* The data structure for a BMPT model consists of observations that fall into K mutually exclusive and exhaustive observable response categories, $C = \{C_1, \ldots, C_K\}$. The categories correspond to ways that a participant's response to some experimental event is scored.
- *Latent parameters.* A BMPT model has S parameters $\{\theta_1, \ldots, \theta_S\}$. The parameters are functionally independent, and each is free to vary in the open interval $(0,1)$. Thus, the parameter space for the model is $\theta = (\theta_1, \ldots, \theta_S) \in \Omega = (0,1)^S$. Each parameter θ_S is interpreted as the probability of the successful execution of some latent cognitive microact, and $(1 - \theta_S)$ is the probability of its failure. Some examples are storing an item in memory, accessing a certain fact from semantic memory, making a particular logical inference, discriminating the source of a particular memory, or guessing a specific response to a question. In contrast to IRT models, the parameters are not person parameters but parameters that tap various cognitive capacities involved in the task that is being modeled.
- *Tree architecture.* The tree architecture is a full binary tree with a single initial node (the root), intermediate nodes, and terminal nodes (leaves). Each nonterminal node is associated with a single parameter θ_S and a binary branching into two nodes (children) that represent, respectively, the success, with probability, θ_S, and the failure, with probability $(1-\theta_S)$,

of the latent cognitive microact represented by the parameter. Nonterminal nodes also can be associated with fixed numerical values in the unit interval instead of parameters. Each leaf corresponds to one of the categories in C. Categories and parameters can occur several times in the tree (e.g., the model in Figure 4.1).
- *Computational rules.* The final aspect of a BMPT is the computational rules that enable one to compute category probabilities in terms of the parameters. Because of the binary architecture of the tree, each BMPT consists of exactly (A + 1) branches, where A is the number of nonterminal nodes in the tree. Each branch is made up of a sequence of one or more parameterized or numerical links terminating in a particular category. The model assumes that on each trial (observation), one of the branches is probabilistically selected, and the category at the end node of that branch is the observed category for that trial. The chosen branch for a trial depends on a sequence of binary choices at nonterminal nodes starting with the initial node. Each choice probability is given by the parameter or number associated with the corresponding node. This probability rule follows standard Markovian assumptions in decision trees and probabilistic automata.

Given the above assumptions, it is easy to see that the probability of the *i*th branch terminating in category C_k denoted by B_{ik} is a function of the parameter vector given by

$$\Pr(B_{ik}|\theta) = r_{ik} \cdot \prod_{s=1}^{S} \theta_s^{a_{iks}} (1-\theta_s)^{b_{iks}}, \qquad (1)$$

where a_{iks} and b_{iks} are nonnegative integers representing the number of times θ_S and $(1 - \theta_S)$, respectively, govern the probabilities associated with the links that comprise branch B_{ik}, and r_{ik} is the product of the numbers on the links of B_{ik}, or set to one if there are no numerical links on B_{ik}.

Let I_k be the number of branches in the model tree that terminate in category C_k, then manifest category probabilities are given for all $k = 1, \ldots, K$ by

$$\Pr(C_k|\theta) = \sum_{i=1}^{I_k} \Pr(B_k|\theta). \qquad (2)$$

The sum/product form of Equation 2 coupled with Equation 1 implies that category probabilities are finite degree polynomials in the parameters of the model. Further, it is clear from the form of Equations 1 and 2 that although branch probabilities are linear in the log of the probabilities, category probabilities are not. So BMPT models are not a special case of the class of log-linear models. Given their structure, it is easy to see that for any well-formed BMPT, $\sum_{k=1}^{K}\Pr(C_k|\tilde{\theta}) = 1$, for all $\tilde{\theta} \in \Omega$. Thus, any BMPT defines a parameterized subset of all possible probability distributions over the K categories.

There are two main generalizations of BMPTs that have been developed in the MPT literature. The first involves allowing more than two links at some internal nodes of the tree. These multilink MPT models are designed to handle the case where more than two latent cognitive microacts are possible at some internal nodes, for example, in which there are several ways to store an item in memory or in which there are several possible guesses to be made with imperfect memory. Another important generalization of BMPTs allows the data structure to include two or more disjoint systems of categories. In this formulation, each disjoint category system is modeled by a separate tree but all link probabilities are specified in terms of a single common parameter set. Multitree MPTs arise in many cognitive experiments involving within-participant designs, in which a participant is required to respond to items from several experimentally defined types. For example, the pair-clustering model discussed earlier falls into this class when the recall study list has singletons as well as clusterable pairs. Other examples come from recognition memory paradigms; for example, in yes/no recognition memory experiments there are two types of items, namely, old items and new distracters. Multitree MPTs also arise in between-group experimental designs, in which each group has the same tree structure, and a theorist wants to test hypotheses about parameter equality across groups to examine group differences. If one has a sample (under i.i.d. conditions) from each of the corresponding category systems and if the systems are independent, then the data structure in this case is a product multinomial structure, and multitree MPT models become parametric product-multinomial models. Hu and Batchelder (1994) provided the details for these two generalizations of BMPT models.

The main purpose of defining classes of MPT models is that their inference can be developed at the class level rather than at the specific model level. Thus, a scientist is free to construct a substantively interpretable model and utilize the general inference machinery to analyze it. This is in sharp contrast to many of the more complex cognitive models that have been published, in which the modelers have developed special ways to analyze their own particular model that do not transfer in a natural way to others' models. The main work on inference for MPT models assumes that one has access to a sample of size $N > 1$ from the model (a sequence of categorical observations of N i.i.d. random variables). In this case, the data structure for a BMPT is a parameterized multinomial distribution. Given the category count random variables N_k, for $k = 1, \ldots, K$, the BMPT model from Equations 1 and 2 defines the parametric family of distributions

$$\Pr(<N_k>_{k=1}^{K} = <n_k>_{k=1}^{K} | \theta) = N! \prod_{k=1}^{K} \frac{\left(\sum_{i=1}^{I_k} r_{ik} \prod_{s=1}^{S} \theta_s^{a_{iks}} \cdot (1-\theta_s)^{b_{iks}}\right)^{n_k}}{n_k!}, \quad (3)$$

for all nonnegative integer vectors $<n_k>_{k=1}^{K}$ with $\sum_{k=1}^{K} n_k = N$ and $\theta \in (0,1)^S$. Notice that the tree representation of a BMPT will specify the other values that occur in Equation 3, namely, K, S, and the I_k, r_{ik}, a_{iks}, and b_{iks}, for $k = 1, \ldots, K$, $s = 1, \ldots, S$, and $i = 1, \ldots, I_k$.

The key to the statistical analysis of MPT models is the fact that if the latent counts that occur for each branch are known in addition to the manifest category counts, then the MLEs of all the parameters can be written in a simple closed-form expression. Hu and Batchelder (1994) showed this in general for a variety of MPT models, including the MPT models discussed in this chapter. To illustrate the idea, suppose that each branch of a BMPT model leads to a unique category, that is, $I_k = 1$ for all $k = 1, \ldots, K$, and thus the branch frequencies are the category counts, n_k. Then it is easy to see that the MLE of each θ_S is given by

$$\hat{\theta}_s = \frac{\sum_{k=1}^{K} n_k \cdot a_{1ks}}{\sum_{k=1}^{K} n_k \cdot (a_{1ks} + b_{1ks})}. \quad (4)$$

Equation 4 represents the number of times a link with probability θ_s is taken, divided by the number of times a node corresponding to parameter θ_s is encountered. Both these quantities are easy to determine from the category counts. In other words, Equation 4 is just a version of the well-known fact that for a Bernoulli process the proportion of "successes" is the MLE for the probability of a success.

The structural and parametric requirements of MPT models, especially those that pertain to Equations 1 and 2, are sufficiently restrictive to yield many consequences that are described in detail in Hu and Batchelder (1994). Most importantly, for members of the model family employing the EM (expectation-maximization) algorithm (e.g., Dempster, Laird, & Rubin, 1977), statistical inference, including goodness-of-fit, point and interval parameter estimation, and hypothesis testing, is computationally straightforward to conduct. The EM algorithm is a well-known iterative method for obtaining MLEs for certain statistical models, in which some of the data can be regarded as missing. In this case the missing data are taken to be the latent branch frequencies, subject to constraint by the observed category frequencies. The EM algorithm starts by selecting initial estimates for the branch frequencies and computes estimated MLEs, $\hat{\theta} = (\hat{\theta}_1, \ldots, \hat{\theta}_S)$, of the parameters from Equation 4 using the estimated branch frequencies. Then the branch frequencies are reestimated by their expectations using the estimated MLEs by the equation

$$\tilde{n}_{ik} = \frac{n_k \cdot \Pr(B_{ik} | \hat{\theta})}{\Pr(C_k | \hat{\theta})}. \quad (5)$$

Equation 4 with the current estimates of the branch frequencies and Equation 5 are alternated until a stable fixed point is achieved. Under fairly general conditions for MPT models, this algorithm is guaranteed to converge to a parameter vector $\hat{\theta}$ that corresponds to a local minimum of the log likelihood measure G^2, the quantity whose global minimization yields the MLEs (Hu & Batchelder, 1994, Observation 4).

The EM algorithm has a number of statistical advantages in working with MPT models. First, it is not necessary to specify step size when using the EM algorithm. Second, the simple structure of MPT models allows one to obtain closed-form expressions for the observed Fisher information matrix, and they can be used to provide asymptotic approximations to the variance-covariance matrix of the parameter estimators at the end of the search. Most important, use of the EM algorithm for estimation, goodness-of-fit, and hypothesis testing enables statistical inference for the entire class of MPT models to be accomplished within a single programmable framework. In Hu and Batchelder (1994), the EM algorithm was extended for MPT models to the entire Read and Cressie family of goodness-of-fit statistics for categorical models (Batchelder, 1991; Read & Cressie, 1988). This family includes not only G^2 but other traditional fit methods like minimum chi-square and modified minimum chi-square.

There are several sources of software for analyzing MPT models that are free and Web-accessible (e.g., Hu & Phillips, 1999; see http://irvin.psyc.memphis.edu/gpt/). The software enables an investigator to represent the model as a specific set of equations like Equations 1 and 2 of this chapter. Then one can enter one or more sets of categorical data for the model and perform point estimation and confidence interval estimation of the parameters, conduct goodness-of-fit tests, and test hypotheses about the model's parameters both within one group and between groups. The software also enables the investigator to simulate data from a model, in which the possibility that different participants may have different parameter values is allowed. These simulations allow one to obtain point and confidence interval estimates when the sample size is not large enough to use asymptotic methods based on the likelihood function.

There have been a number of statistical and mathematical results for BMPT models that hold at the class level. One result is that the class of BMPTs is "closed" under a variety of dimension-reducing and/or order-constraining restrictions on the parameter space. By *closed* I mean that if the parameters of a BMPT are restricted in certain ways, one can construct a new BMPT (without parameter restrictions) that is statistically equivalent to the original model with the restrictions on its parameters. Such results are important because when the parameter space of a BMPT is constrained, it is no longer a BMPT because the requirement of functional independence of the parameters is violated, thus the general class-level software is no longer applicable. However, because of the closure properties, an equivalent BMPT can be constructed, and it can be analyzed with the general software. Many of these closure properties are discussed in Knapp and Batchelder (2004) and Hu and Batchelder (1994).

Application of MPT Models for Psychological Assessment

The Riefer et al. (2002) study is just one of several applications of the pair-clustering model to analyze differences in storage and retrieval processes in special populations. In an earlier study, Riefer and Batchelder (1991a) used the pair-clustering model to compare college students and elderly participants on storage and retrieval. In that study, the elderly population performed more poorly in recall memory because of retrieval deficits, not storage deficits. Also there have been a number of recent applications of other BMPT models to measure other cognitive capacities in special populations. Batchelder (1998) discussed a number of methodological issues that arise when MPT models are used for psychological assessment instead of experimentally designed studies, and Batchelder and Riefer (2007) provided a review of some of these applications. The review included an MPT model for measuring storage and retrieval by Chechile (2004). Chechile's model has been used to explore the storage-retrieval bases behind a variety of memory phenomena in special populations, most notably in children with developmental dyslexia (Chechile, 2007).

One large area of applications of MPT models is the study of memory for the source of information in clinical populations, including individuals with schizophrenia. In these studies, participants received a list of items from two sources (male vs. female voice or presented auditorily vs. visually); later, they received old and new items and were required to discriminate the source of old items. These studies used the MPT models of source monitoring developed by Batchelder and Riefer (1990) and Bayen, Murname, and Erdfelder (1996). In addition, there are several studies that used MPT models to analyze data from tests in standard neuropsychological test batteries. For example, Batchelder, Chosak-Reiter, Shankle, and Dick (1997) developed a BMPT model for the free recall subtest of the neuropsychological test battery of the Consortium to Establish a Registry for Alzheimer's Disease (Morris et al., 1989), and Chosak-Reiter (2000) developed a BMPT model for the Boston Naming Test (Kaplan, Goodglass, & Weintraub, 1983). One of the goals of modeling standard tests in diagnostic batteries is to better utilize the data that are collected. Standard scoring schemes for neuropsychological test batteries base their performance scores on selective aspects of the data, and a lot of potentially useful information for diagnosis is ignored. Another large area of application of MPT models is the process dissociation procedure (Jacoby, 1991, 1998). This task is related to the source monitoring task and is used to separate explicit recollection from feelings of general familiarity for the item. The process dissociation task has proven to be an important tool in studying amnesia among other memory phenomena.

Comparing Cognitive and Psychometric Modeling

Cognitive psychologists and psychometricians are quite active in inventing probabilistic models and developing their statistical inference, and most psychologists with advanced knowledge of modern statistics work in these areas. Both cognitive models and models in test theory are developed to assess and understand aspects of cognitive performance. For these reasons, it might seem natural that there would be a great deal of collaboration between workers in these fields, but in my experience such collaborations are rare, and workers in these areas are relatively isolated from and unfamiliar with each others work. These observations motivate the secondary goal of this chapter, which is to explore the different approaches used in cognitive and psychometric modeling and to understand the bases behind the relative separation of these two groups of modelers.

I will base my analysis on the working hypothesis that cognitive modelers and test theory modelers are relative disjoint groups of scholars. By this I mean that they do not often attend the same conferences, publish in the same journals, read and cite modeling work in each others' areas or collaborate on modeling projects. Most cognitive modelers identify with the Society for Mathematical Psychology and a variety of experimental psychology societies, and most psychometric test theorists identify with the Psychometric Society and a variety of applied statistics societies. Only a small fraction of these modelers attend the same annual meetings or have publications in both the *Journal of Mathematical Psychology* and *Psychometrika,* the flagship journals of the Society for Mathematical Psychology and the Psychometric Society, respectively. Of course, there are exceptions to the working hypothesis at both the individual level and the society level, but in my experience the exceptions are not many. Further, I believe that the hypothesis well represents the "received view" of modelers in these two areas. A full scholarly analysis of the working hypothesis would require much empirical work comparing coauthorships, citation indices, and conference participation.

Insights From the Early History of Psychology

To an outsider, the fact that probabilistic modelers in psychology fall into two largely disjoint groups might seem puzzling. However, a brief inspection of the early history of psychology as a research and academic discipline provides one of the clues to this puzzle (for a similar view, see Cronbach, 1957). Academic psychology started in the late 1800s, and its roots can be traced to scientific developments mostly in Germany and England. Most historians of psychology select Wilhelm Wundt and the establishment of his experimental psychology laboratory at Leipzig Germany in 1879 as the start of academic psychology (e.g., Boring, 1957; Hergenhahn, 2008). Before Wundt's laboratory, the German tradition was established with the scientific work of Johann Müller, Hermann von Helmholtz, Ernst Weber, Gustav Fechner, Franciscus Donders, as well as Wundt and many others. This work provided the main underpinnings of the field of experimental psychology. The key characteristic of this work that provides part of the clue for the current puzzle is that it was almost entirely concerned with understanding how basic human processes function in such areas as sensation, perception, attention, and memory. In particular, German experimental psychology produced relatively little research on how humans differed from one another.

On the other hand, the psychological tradition in England was fairly separate from the German tradition, and it is the English tradition that concerned itself with individual differences. The English tradition in psychology can be traced to the work of Charles Darwin and especially to the work that followed in the spirit of Darwin's work. Darwin's theory of evolution (1859, 1871) was grounded on several principles, not the least of which was the fact that individuals differ in their physical traits. His most psychological book was *The Expression of Emotions in Man and Animals* (Darwin, 1872), and in this work he attempted to explain the differences between and within species on the nature of emotional responses. Although Darwin's book concerning emotions was not that influential in the psychological movement in England, the work of Darwin's cousin, Sir Francis Galton, set the stage for the emergence of English psychology. Edwin Boring (1957), in his major early history of experimental psychology, wrote,

> There can be no doubt that Sir Francis Galton (1822–1911) was the pioneer of a "new" psychology in Great Britton, that is to say, of an experimental psychology that was primarily, though not entirely, concerned with the problem of human individual differences. (p. 482)

Galton's psychological concerns were mostly centered on measuring individual differences between people on a variety of physical, personality, and cognitive traits. Galton's interests in individual differences led him to study differences in both physical and psychological traits in over 9,000 individuals. This work required Galton to develop statistical measurement tools like correlation, the quintrix, and models for analyzing twin studies. In addition, Galton is a principal figure behind England's emergence as a center for the development of statistical theory as well as the related field of psychometrics. From this analysis, it should be clear why the psychometric approach to modeling has a historical tie to early English psychology and thus is heavily invested in the measurement of individual differences. Psychometrics as a field developed with close connections to the historical development of the field of statistics; for example, statisticians who followed Galton, such as Karl Pearson, Charles Spearman, Roland Fisher, and William Gosset, contributed in major ways to both statistics and psychometrics. Indeed, efforts to solve statistical problems that arose within psychology are a major reason why the history of the field of statistics from the late 1800s on is so strongly tied to England (e.g., Porter, 1986; Stigler, 1986).

What is missing so far in the solution to the puzzle of the relative separation of the cognitive and psychometric modeling groups is the nature of cognitive modeling itself. In the early German tradition in experimental psychology, serious mathematical modeling was confined to the areas of sensation, perception, and psychophysics, in which there were direct ties to the natural sciences, especially physics and physiology. Cognitive modeling came onto the scene much later in the 1950s with the origin of the field of mathematical psychology (see Batchelder, 2000). During the 1940s and 1950s, the information sciences developed many approaches that cognitive psychologists could use as the basis for constructing formal models of human cognition. These include automata theory, game theory, information theory, operations research, and many results in stochastic processes. A number of experimental psychologists became aware of these approaches, and workers in the information sciences began to do collaborative work with psychologists. Since the stochastic learning models of Estes (1950) and Bush and Mosteller (1951), all subfields of cognitive psychology have many formal models, and a large number of these can be classified as parametric statistical models. Almost all of the applications of these models have the same properties, namely, that fairly homogeneous groups of participants are exposed to experimental manipulations in an effort to study the effect of the manipulations on the workings of normal cognition. Often there are interesting experimental phenomena that a cognitive model can explain given certain settings of its parameters, and discovering and explaining these phenomena rather than measuring individual differences is the main driving force in cognitive modeling.

Contrasting Cognitive Memory Modeling and Item Response Theory

In this subsection, two active areas of modeling are compared, one from cognitive psychology and the other from psychometric test theory. One of the most active areas in cognitive modeling is human memory, and there are many parametric stochastic models in this area. Although the focus is on memory models, models in other areas of cognition like categorization and choice are often similar in character. In test-theory modeling, the most active area is IRT, and most models in this area are also parametric stochastic models (e.g., Embretson & Reise, 2000). As explained later in this chapter, the data structures for these two kinds of models are very similar; however, the nature of the models and their associated statistical inference are quite different.

Cognitive memory models are developed for list memory experiments, and models in IRT are developed mostly for tests of knowledge and ability. It turns out that the statistical structure of a typical list memory experiment in cognitive psychology and a typical psychometric ability test are quite similar. The data structure for a list memory experiment is a participant by item-event random matrix, $\mathbf{X} = (X_{ij})_{N \times M}$, where X_{ij} is a random variable representing participant i's response to item-event j, $i = 1, 2, \ldots, N$ and $j = 1, 2, \ldots, M$. The item-events (hereafter items) can refer to such things as to-be-remembered items (in which each participant is given the same list of items), particular types of items (e.g., studied items and new distracter items in recognition memory), serial positions (e.g., in a free-recall study list), or a group of related items (e.g., clusterable items in free recall). The response of the participant to an item is characterized by one or more behavioral indices such as a simple dichotomous score like "old/new," a response in a category describing memory retrieval, a confidence rating on an ordered category scale, or a response time on a continuous scale.

In the case of IRT models, the usual data structure is also generally of the form, $\mathbf{X} = (X_{ij})_{N \times M}$, where X_{ij} is a random variable representing the performance of participant i on test item j. In this case, test items vary in difficulty, but each participant usually receives the same or an equivalent set of items, though there may be alternate test forms or the items may be ordered differently from participant to participant. The performance measure may be a simple dichotomy such as "pass/fail," a more elaborate categorization as in ordered and unordered polytomous models, or a continuous grade as in the scoring of essay items. Although it is usually the case that only a single performance measure is collected for each item, sometimes response latencies are also collected, and in the case of grading essay type questions, the scores of several judges may constitute the scoring of an item (e.g., Johnson & Albert, 1999). From the point of view of statistical theory, there is very little difference between the standard data structure in cognitive modeling and IRT (of course in adaptive testing participants may not receive comparable items and the analogy breaks down); however, as explained later in this chapter, there are very substantial differences in the types of models that are developed for the data structure.

Many cognitive memory modelers and item response theorists postulate parametric stochastic models to describe the data structure $\mathbf{X}$. However, it is at this point that the two approaches differ quite dramatically. A cognitive memory model generally specifies parameters $\theta = (\theta_1, \ldots, \theta_S) \in \Omega \subseteq \mathrm{Re}^S$. Corresponding to each $\tilde{\theta} \in \Omega$, the model specifies a mechanism that leads to a marginal distribution of each X_{ij}. The BMPT model in Figure 4.1 is one example; however, most cognitive memory models have much more complex latent architecture and probability mechanisms than BMPT models (e.g., Clark & Grondlund, 1996; Rumelhart & McClelland, 1986; Shiffrin & Steyvers, 1997).

The parameters of a memory model have to do with both the architecture of the memory system (e.g., the size of a memory buffer, the number of features that encode an item, and the structure of memory search mechanisms), and the cognitive processes that take place within the architecture (e.g., matching items, priming items, retrieval, guessing). Typically, parameters in memory models do not refer to individual participants, and individual items are reflected in the parameters only by allowing them to be different across sets of experimentally different item types (e.g., primacy items, old studied items, or new distracter items). Once the marginal distributions of the X_{ij} have been specified for each item type, data are pooled over subsets of items of the same type and usually over participants as well, and these data are treated as a "sample" from the cognitive model. In the case of categorical data, if the N participants are regarded as homogeneous and the M items are of the same type, then the model for the data matrix $\mathbf{X} = (X_{ij})_{NxM}$ is technically a parameterized multinomial model like that in Equation 3. However, as mentioned, many of the memory models are much more complex than BMPT models, and the complexity of the processes that lead from the parameters to the marginal distributions of the data may be too complicated to express in closed form and hence to conduct inference in the usual ways with parametric models. In these cases, modelers may derive some properties of the model to test without working with the likelihood function of the data, or they may simulate data from the model in an effort to find parameters that capture complex patterns of data across conditions and stimulus types.

In almost all cases of cognitive modeling, researchers have to be aware of the possibility that unmodeled inhomogeneities in participants and/or items may violate the assumption of identically distributed marginal distributions, and if this happens it may flaw the statistical analysis of their data. Explicit discussions of the impact of the policy of aggregating data over participants that differ in their parameters trace back to the seminal article of Estes (1956). In that article, Estes demonstrated that individual participant differences can lead to group mean learning curves that obscure the shapes of the individual learning curves. Since Estes's article, many papers have appeared describing possible unfortunate consequences of individual differences in aggregated data (e.g., Batchelder, 1975; Heathcote, Brown, & Mewhort, 2000; Hintzman, 1980), but until recently very little work of a statistical nature has appeared in the cognitive modeling literature that provides positive statistical solutions to the problem of parameter inhomogeneity in aggregated data. Only in the past decade or so have some of the technical approaches to random effects modeling appeared in cognitive modeling papers (e.g., Karabatsos & Batchelder, 2003; Klauer, 2006; Lee & Webb, 2005; Rouder & Lu, 2005; Smith & Batchelder, 2008), and this is addressed later in this chapter.

The nature of IRT models is quite different from that of cognitive models despite the similarity in the data structure. There is some controversy over what exactly counts as an IRT model, and indeed the same can be said about stochastic memory models. For my discussion, I adopt what might be viewed as a narrow representation of IRT models, and in particular I suppress their representation as item characteristic curves (e.g., Lord & Novick, 1968). Almost all the parameters of an IRT model refer to specific participants (respondents) or specific items and can be written as $\varphi_{ij} = (\theta_i, \alpha_j)$, where the two component vectors refer, respectively, to participant i's and item j's parameters, $i = 1, \ldots, N$ and $j = 1, \ldots, M$. The $\boldsymbol{\theta}_i$ specify properties of the participants' abilities, and the $\boldsymbol{\alpha}_i$ specify properties of the items' difficulty with respect to a selected body of knowledge. Measuring individual differences in such things as participant ability, item difficulty, and item discriminability parameters is the main goal of IRT. Generally IRT models, unlike cognitive models, are not specified in terms of explicit cognitive processing steps that lead a participant to retrieve information from memory and process the information to produce a particular response to a test item.

In IRT models, each X_{ij} has its own marginal distribution, and there is only a single observation of each X_{ij} in $\mathbf{X}$ to work with. Although the random variables do not satisfy the independence assumption, they usually satisfy the assumption of conditional independence given the parameters. For example, if the data are dichotomous pass (1)/fail (0), the probability function of the data matrix is given by

$$\Pr\left[\mathbf{X} = (x_{ij})_{N \times M} \mid \varphi = <(\boldsymbol{\theta}_i)_{i=1}^{N}, (\boldsymbol{\alpha}_j)_{j=1}^{M}>\right] = \prod_{i=1}^{N}\prod_{j=1}^{M} \Pr[X_{ij} = x_{ij} \mid (\boldsymbol{\theta}_i, \boldsymbol{\alpha}_j)] \quad (6)$$

for all possible 1-0 matrices $(x_{ij})_{N \times M}$. Unlike the case of cognitive modeling, analysis of an IRT model is not plagued with possible inhomogeneities in participants and items because the model is explicitly designed to specify and measure them.

It is possible to examine the contrast in approaches to modeling more completely by considering one of the simplest IRT models, known as the two-parameter Rasch model (e.g., Fischer & Molenaar, 1995). That model assumes a single ability parameter θ_i for each participant and a single item difficulty parameter α_j for each item, where $-\infty < \theta_i, \alpha_j < \infty$. Then the component of the right-hand term of Equation 6 is written as

$$\Pr(X_{ij} = 1 \mid \theta_i, \alpha_j) = [1 + \exp-(\theta_i - \alpha_j)]^{-1}. \quad (7)$$

It is well known that Equation 7 is a simple additive model in log-odds with no interaction between participants and items, that is

$$\text{logit}[\Pr(X_{ij} = 1 \mid \theta_i, \alpha_j)] = \theta_i - \alpha_j. \quad (8)$$

This model has essentially the same additive logit structure as several popular models in the cognitive area, such as Luce's (1959) paired comparison model (also known as the Bradley–Terry–Luce model), where the indices refer to choice objects, and Massaro's (1987) fuzzy logic model of perception (FLMP) for a two-factor, two-response perception experiment (e.g., Crowther, Batchelder, & Hu, 1995). For example, the FLMP is developed for factorial perception experiments in which an item is made up of a combination of levels from each of two factors, for example, $I_{ij} = (f_i, g_j), f_i \in F, g_j \in G$. The participant must classify each item into one of two perceptual categories C_1 and C_2 (e.g., one of two words in a speech recognition experiment). The model associates parameters with the factor levels, for example, $\vartheta_i \in (0,1)$ for $f_i \in F$ and $\beta_j \in (0,1)$ for $g_j \in G$. The response equation for the model takes the form

$$\Pr[C_1|(f_i,g_j)] = \frac{\vartheta_i \cdot \beta_j}{\vartheta_i \cdot \beta_j + (1-\vartheta_i) \cdot (1-\beta_j)}, \quad (9)$$

for all $(f_i, g_j) \in F \times G$. Equation 9 is a reparameterization of Equation 7, where $\theta_i = \ln\left(\frac{\vartheta_i}{1-\vartheta_i}\right)$ and $\alpha_j = \ln\left(\frac{1-\beta_j}{\beta_j}\right)$, and it is statistically equivalent to the two parameter Rasch model, with participants corresponding to the factor levels in F and items corresponding to the factor levels in G.

Despite their formal similarity, statistical inference for the Rasch model differs from the paired comparison model and the FLMP model. Typically Luce's choice model and the FLMP are analyzed with data assumed to consist of independent samples for each combination of i and j, which is the same way that most other cognitive models discussed earlier are analyzed. On the other hand, statistical inference for the Rasch model is much more challenging because there is only one observation for each of the NxM random variables. This extra complexity in inference characterizes the more complicated IRT models as well. Although there are ways to estimate all the parameters of the Rasch model separately as fixed effects, the more usual approach is to introduce random effects in the participants, and sometimes even for the items (e.g., De Boeck, 2008). Thus hierarchical modeling has been a part of the statistical inference for IRT models for almost a half century; however, it is rarely used in paired-comparison models and never in FLMP modeling. In fact, as mentioned, only in the past few years has hierarchical modeling been used in the cognitive area.

Incorporating Ideas From Psychometric Modeling Into MPT Models

Unlike most cognitive models, BMPT models are sufficiently simple that ideas used in IRT modeling may aid in their analysis. In particular, the main drawback in the way that MPT models have been used as measurement tools concerns the lack of appropriate tools for handling individual differences. One approach proposed in Batchelder and Riefer (2007) assumes that the parameters of a BMPT are jointly distributed over participants at the hierarchical level as independent beta distributions. To illustrate, let θ_s be one of the parameters in a BMPT model and assume that participants' values of θ_s are drawn i.i.d. from the beta distribution given by

$$g(\theta_s|\tau_{1,s}, \tau_{2,s}) = \frac{\Gamma(\tau_{1,s} + \tau_{2,s})}{\Gamma(\tau_{1,s})\,\Gamma(\tau_{2,s})} \theta_s^{\tau_{1,s}-1}(1-\theta_s)^{\tau_{2,s}-1}, \quad (10)$$

where the two parameters of the beta distribution, $\tau_{1,s}$ and $\tau_{2,s}$, are in a parameter space Φ consisting of pairs of positive numbers, that is, $(\tau_{1,s}, \tau_{2,s}) \in \Phi = (0,\infty)^2$, and $\Gamma(\cdot)$ is the well-known gamma function (e.g., Evans, Hastings, & Peacock, 2000). Then, assuming the parameters are independent, the joint distribution of the BMPT parameter is given by

$$g[\theta = (\theta_1, \ldots, \theta_S)|\tau = <\tau_{1,s}, \tau_{2,s}>_{s=1}^{S}] = \prod_{s=1}^{S} g(\theta_s|\tau_{1,s}, \tau_{2,s}). \quad (11)$$

Such a formulation leads to a new class of models called *beta-BMPTs* because they bear a resemblance to the well known beta-binomial distribution (e.g., Evans, et al., 2000). Beta-BMPTs were already formulated as a simulation option in the software package by Hu and Phillips (1999), and Smith and Batchelder (in press) formulated them as Bayesian hierarchical models and developed their statistical theory using Markov Chain Monte Carlo methods.

There are two drawbacks to the beta-BMPT approach to handling individual differences. First, beta-BMPT models do not specify any correlations over participants between the cognitive parameters. This is an unfortunate consequence of the approach because many of the parameters in a BMPT are designed to measure cognitive capacities, and one would naturally expect such capacities to show a pattern of positive correlations. A second drawback of beta-BMPT models is that although they can handle participant heterogeneity, they assume item homogeneity within each participant.

Klauer (2006) provided a general statistical approach to hierarchical latent class BMPT models that can specify parameter correlations. His approach was to create finite mixtures (see Titterington, Smith, & Makov, 1985) of BMPT models, where each component model is characterized by a fixed parameter vector. Stahl and Klauer (2007) presented software that can apply to hierarchical latent class BMPT models in general, which they called *HMMTree models*. Klauer's (2006) approach of using latent class BMPTs can specify correlations between parameters because if the data come from a mixture of a few BMPTs, there will be correlations between parameters depending on the locations of the parameter vectors for each component of the mixture. However, in applications to special populations in which one expects parameter variation to come from continuous distributions with uni-modal marginals, the Klauer approach may not be completely satisfactory.

Our group has been implementing a principled approach to the two limitations of beta-BMPTs, both of which are motivated by ideas from psychometric test theory. The first idea involves introducing participant-item subscripts on the MPT parameters, that is, the parameters are written as $\theta_{ij} = <\theta_{ij,s}>_{s=1}^{S}$. Of course, without additional specification, this approach introduces too many parameters, namely, $NxMxS$ parameters for only NxM data points. However, the number of parameters can be greatly reduced by applying the simple two-parameter Rasch model in the form of Equation 9 to each latent parameter, namely,

$$\theta_{ij,s} = \frac{\vartheta_{i,s}\beta_{j,s}}{\vartheta_{i,s}\beta_{j,s} + (1-\vartheta_{i,s})(1-\beta_{j,s})} \qquad (12)$$

where $\forall i, j, s, 0 < \vartheta_{i,s}, \beta_{j,s} < 1$. Our group calls these models *Rasch-BMPT models*, and in applying them one would not aggregate the data over either participants or items but would analyze them by using some of the approaches used to analyze IRT models. Karabatsos and Batchelder (2003) used this approach for a particular BMPT model called the *general Condorcet model* (see also Batchelder & Romney, 1988). Jared Smith of our group has been investigating Bayesian hierarchical approaches to Rasch BMPTs. In his work, the four types of component parameters in Equation 12 have independent beta hyperdistributions. Another approach under investigation is to model the probits of the component parameters with a multivariate Gaussian. Some of this work was presented in Batchelder and Smith (2006).

The second idea is motivated by the fact that Rasch-BMPT models lack a natural correlation structure between the cognitive parameters. One approach to handle the correlation structure on the cognitive parameters is to implement an idea due to Spearman's (1904) analysis of the structure of intelligence. Spearman's idea was that there was a single general factor in intelligence that was operative across different subtests of intelligence. In this view, the true correlation between different intelligence subtests is zero if general intelligence is partialled out. One way to incorporate this idea into Equation 12 is to specify a cognitive ability g_i for each participant and specific factor t_s for each parameter, and apply again the Rasch model in Equation 9 by specifying

$$\vartheta_{i,s} = \frac{g_i t_s}{g_i t_s + (1 - g_i)(1 - t_s)}, \quad (13)$$

where $0 < g_i, t_s < 1$. Viewed as a fixed effects model, when Equation 13 is incorporated into Equation 12, there are a total of $N + S(M + 1)$ parameters, which is still less than the $N \times M$ data points.

Early results with a Bayesian hierarchical implementation of the Spearman idea were reported in Batchelder and Smith (2006), but the jury is still out on the most productive computational approaches to analyze the specifications of participant and item heterogeneity in BMPT models in Equations 12 and 13. There is a lot of work remaining to be done, and I am hopeful that psychometric researchers with experience in IRT modeling will join in our efforts to develop sound methods for model-based measurement of cognitive skills in special populations using MPT and other cognitive models.

References

Batchelder, W. H. (1975). Individual differences and the all-or-none vs. incremental learning controversy. *Journal of Mathematical Psychology, 12*, 53–74.

Batchelder, W. H. (1991). Getting wise about minimum distance measures. *Journal of Mathematical Psychology, 35*, 267–273.

Batchelder, W. H. (1998). Multinomial processing tree models and psychological assessment. *Psychological Assessment, 10*, 331–344.

Batchelder, W. H. (2000). Mathematical psychology. In A. E. Kazdin (Ed.), *Encyclopedia of psychology* (Vol. 5, pp.120–123). Washington, DC: American Psychological Association.

Batchelder, W. H., Chosak-Reiter, J., Shankle, W. R., & Dick, M. B. (1997). A multinomial modeling analysis of memory deficits in Alzheimer's and vascular dementia. *Journal of Gerontology: Psychological Sciences, 52B*, 206–215.

Batchelder, W. H., & Riefer, D. M. (1980). Separation of storage and retrieval factors in free recall of clusterable pairs. *Psychological Review, 87*, 375–397.

Batchelder, W. H., & Riefer, D. M. (1986). The statistical analysis of a model for storage and retrieval processes in human memory. *British Journal of Mathematical & Statistical Psychology, 39*, 120–149.

Batchelder, W. H., & Riefer, D. M. (1990). Multinomial processing models of source monitoring. *Psychological Review, 97*, 548–564.

Batchelder, W. H., & Riefer, D. M. (1999). Theoretical and empirical review of multinomial process tree modeling. *Psychonomic Bulletin & Review, 6*, 57–86.

Batchelder, W. H., & Riefer, D. M. (2007). Using multinomial processing tree models to measure cognitive deficits in clinical populations. In R. W. J. Neufeld (Ed.), *Advances in clinical cognitive sciences: Formal models and assessment of processes and symptoms* (pp. 19–50). Washington, DC: American Psychological Association.

Batchelder, W. H., & Romney, A. K. (1988). Test theory without an answer key. *Psychometrika, 53,* 71–92.

Batchelder, W. H., & Smith, J. B. (2006, June). *Modeling subject and item differences in multinomial processing tree models.* Paper presented at the International Meeting of the Psychometric Society, Montreal, Canada.

Bayen, U. J., Murname, K., & Erdfelder, E. (1996). Source discrimination, item detection, and multinomial models of source monitoring. *Journal of Experimental Psychology: Learning, Memory, & Cognition, 22,* 197–215.

Boring, E. G. (1957). *A history of experimental psychology* (2nd ed.). New York: Appleton-Century-Crofts.

Bush, R. R., & Mosteller, F. (1951). A mathematical model for simple learning. *Psychological Review, 58,* 313–323.

Chechile, R. A. (2004). New multinomial models for the Chechile-Meyer task. *Journal of Mathematical Psychology, 48,* 364–384.

Chechile, R. A. (2007). A model-based storage retrieval analysis of developmental dyslexia. In W. J. J. Neufeld (Ed.), *Advances in clinical cognitive sciences: Formal models and assessment of processes and Symptoms* (pp. 51–80). Washington, DC: American Psychological Association.

Chosak-Reiter, J. (2000). Measuring cognitive processes underlying picture naming in Alzheimer's and cerebrovascular dementia: A general processing tree approach. *Journal of Clinical and Experimental Neuropsychology, 22,* 351–369.

Clark, S. E., & Grondlund, S. D. (1996). Global matching models of recognition memory: How the models match the data. *Psychonomic Bulletin & Review, 3,* 37–60.

Cronbach, L. J. (1957). The two disciplines of scientific psychology. *American Psychologist, 12,* 671–684.

Crowther, C. S., Batchelder, W. H., & Hu, X. (1995). A measurement-theoretic analysis of the fuzzy logic model of perception. *Psychological Review, 102,* 396–408.

Darwin, C. (1859). *On the origin of the species by means of natural selection.* London: John Murray.

Darwin, C. (1871). *The descent of man.* London: John Murray.

Darwin, C. (1872). *The expressions of emotions in man and animals.* London: John Murray

David, H. A. (1988). *The method of paired-comparisons.* New York: Oxford University Press.

De Boeck, P. (2008). Random item IRT models. *Psychometrika, 73,* 533–559.

Dempster, A. P., Laird, N. M., & Rubin, D. B. (1977). Maximum likelihood from incomplete data via the EM algorithm. *Journal of the Royal Statistical Society: Series B, 39,* 1–38.

Elandt-Johnson, R. C. (1971). *Probability models and statistical methods in genetics.* New York: Wiley.

Embretson, S., and Reise, S. (2000). *Item response theory for psychologists.* Mahwah, NJ: Erlbaum.

Estes, W. K. (1950). Toward a statistical theory of learning. *Psychological Review, 57,* 94–107.

Estes, W. K. (1956). The problem of inference from curves based on group data. *Psychological Bulletin, 53,* 134–140.

Evans, M., Hastings, N., & Peacock, B. (2000). *Statistical distributions.* Wiley: New York.

Fischer, G. H., & Molenaar, I. W. (1995). *Rasch models: Foundations, recent developments, and applications.* New York: Springer-Verlag.

Heathcote, A., Brown, S., & Mewhort, D. J. (2000). *Psychonomic Bulletin & Review, 7,* 185–207.

Hergenhahn, B. R. (2008). *An introduction to the history of psychology* (6th ed.). Belmont, CA: Wadsworth, Cengage Learning.

Hintzman, D. L. (1980). Simpson's paradox and the analysis of memory retrieval. *Psychological Review, 87,* 398–410.

Hu, X., & Batchelder, W. H. (1994). The statistical analysis of general processing tree models with the EM algorithm. *Psychometrika, 59,* 21–47.

Hu, X., & Phillips, G. A. (1999). GPT.EXE: A powerful tool for the visualization and analysis of general processing tree models. *Behavior Research Methods, Instruments, and Computers, 31,* 220–234.

Jacoby, L. L. (1991). A process dissociation framework: Separating automatic from intentional uses of memory. *Journal of Memory & Language, 30,* 513–541.

Jacoby, L. L. (1998). Invariance in automatic influences of memory: Toward a user's guide for the process-dissociation procedure. *Journal of Experimental Psychology: Learning, Memory and Cognition, 24,* 3–26.

Johnson, V. E., and Albert, J. H. (1999). *Ordinal data analysis.* New York: Springer-Verlag.

Kaplan, E., Goodglass, H., & Weintraub, S. (1983). *Boston naming test.* Philadelphia: Lea & Febiger.

Karabatsos, G., & Batchelder, W. H. (2003). Markov chain estimation methods for test theory without an answer key. *Psychometrika, 68,* 373–389.

Klauer, K. C. (2006). Hierarchical multinomial processing tree models: A latent-class approach. *Psychometrika, 71,* 7–31.

Knapp, B. R., & Batchelder, W. H. (2004). Representing parametric order constraints in multi-trial applications of multinomial processing tree models. *Journal of Mathematical Psychology, 48,* 215–229.

Lee, M. D., & Webb, M. R. (2005). Modeling individual differences in cognition. *Psychonomic Bulletin & Review, 12,* 605–621.

Lord, F. M., & Novick, M. R. (1968). *Statistical theories of mental test scores.* Reading, MA: Addison-Wesley.

Luce, R. D. (1959). *Individual choice behavior.* New York: Wiley.

MacMillan, N. A., & Creelman, C. D. (2005). *Detection theory: A user's guide* (2nd ed.). Mahwah, NJ: Erlbaum.

Massaro, D. W. (1987). *Speech perception by ear and eye: A paradigm for psychological inquiry.* Hillsdale, NJ: Erlbaum.

Morris, J. C., Heyman, A., Mohs, R. C., Hughes, J. P., van Belle, G., Fillenbaum, G., et al. (1989). The Consortium to Establish a Registry for Alzheimer's Disease (CERAD). Part I. Clinical and neuropsychological assessment of Alzheimer's disease. *Neurology, 39,* 1159–1165.

Porter, T. M. (1986). *The rise of statistical thinking, 1820–1900.* Princeton, NJ: Princeton University Press.

Read, T. R. C., & Cressie, N. A. C. (1988). *Goodness-of-fit statistics for discrete multivariate data.* New York: Springer-Verlag.

Riefer, D. M., & Batchelder, W. H. (1988). Multinomial modeling and the measurement of cognitive processes. *Psychological Review, 95,* 318–339.

Riefer, D. M., & Batchelder, W. H. (1991a). Age differences in storage and retrieval: A multinomial modeling analysis. *Bulletin of the Psychonomic Society, 29,* 415–418.

Riefer, D. M., & Batchelder, W. H. (1991b). Statistical inference for multinomial processing tree models. In J.-P. Doignon & G. Falmagne (Eds.), *Mathematical psychology: Current developments* (pp. 313–336). New York: Springer-Verlag.

Riefer, D. M., Knapp, B. R., Batchelder, W. H., Bamber, D., & Manifold, V. (2002). Cognitive psychometrics: Assessing storage and retrieval deficits in special populations with multinomial processing tree models. *Psychological Assessment, 14,* 184–201.

Rouder, J. N., & Lu, J. (2005). An introduction to Bayesian hierarchical models with an application in the theory of signal detection. *Psychonomic Bulletin & Review, 12,* 573–604.

Rumelhart, D. E., McClelland, J. L., & the PDP Research Group. (1986). *Parallel distributed processing: Explorations in the microstructure of cognition. Vol. 1: Foundations.* Cambridge, MA: MIT Press.

Shiffrin, R. M., & Steyvers, M. (1997). A model for recognition memory: REM-retrieving effectively from memory. *Psychonomic Bulletin & Review, 4,* 145–166.

Smith, J. B., & Batchelder, W. H. (2008). Assessing individual differences in categorical data. *Psychonomic Bulletin & Review, 15,* 713–730.

Smith, J. B., & Batchelder, W. H. (in press). Beta-MPT: Multinomial processing tree models for addressing individual differences. *Journal of Mathematical Psychology.*

Spearman, C. (1904). General intelligence objectively determined and measured. *American Journal of Psychology, 15,* 201–293.

Stahl, C., & Klauer, C. (2007). HMMTree: A computer program for latent-class hierarchical multinomial processing tree models. *Behavior Research Methods, 39,* 267–273.

Stigler, S. M. (1986). *The history of statistics: The measurement of uncertainty before 1900.* Cambridge, MA: Belknap Press of Harvard University Press.

Takane, Y., & Shibayama, T. (1992). Structures in stimulus identification data. In F. G. Ashby (Ed.), *Multidimensional models of perception and cognition* (pp. 335–362). Hillsdale, NJ: Erlbaum.

Titterington, D. M., Smith, A. F. M., & Makov, U. E. (1985). *Statistical analysis of finite mixture distributions.* New York: Wiley.

Part II

Model-Based Approaches to Isolating Entangled Constructs

5

Unidimensionality and Interpretability of Psychological Instruments

Jan-Eric Gustafsson and Lisbeth Åberg-Bengtsson

One of the fundamental ideas in the construction of psychological measurement instruments is that each instrument should be homogenous and measure one attribute only. The idea of unidimensionality is a central assumption of most models within both classical test theory and modern test theory (e.g., Gulliksen, 1950; Lord, 1980; McDonald, 1999). There are good statistical reasons for favoring one-dimensional models to solve measurement problems. Reasons of interpretation also speak in favor of a focus on unidimensionality, because if multiple attributes are measured, researchers will not know which attribute to invoke to account for a particular score.

However, many observations in the literature have suggested that the unidimensionality requirement may have negative effects on the interpretability and usefulness of the resulting measure. One problem is that this requirement causes measures to focus on narrow aspects of phenomena. For example, Humphreys (1962) observed that the principle of unidimensionality caused the construct of intelligence to splinter into a large set of measures of narrowly defined cognitive abilities, causing the broad construct of intelligence to fall out of focus for a long time.

Another indication that unidimensionality need not be a necessary characteristic of psychological instruments is that many instruments that have been proven to be highly useful for theoretical, diagnostic, and predictive purposes do not fulfill the unidimensionality requirement. For example, intelligence test batteries, such as the Wechsler series, are certainly not unidimensional but are considered to be extremely useful for purposes of diagnosis and prediction. In virtually any field of psychological measurement, there are numerous other examples of instruments that consist of different subtests aggregated into a composite score.

The emphasis on unidimensionality is based on the idea that a variable should be unitary and express one characteristic only. However, there are situations in which variables are not seen as unitary. In a multiple regression analysis, for example, the independent variables are typically regarded as unitary, but the dependent variable is not. Instead, the main aim of a multiple regression analysis is to decompose the dependent variable into different components of variance, with each accounted for by a different independent variable. Thus, in multiple regression analysis, the dependent variable is viewed as being complex, whereas the independent variables are viewed as being unitary. That researchers view the independent variables as unitary and the dependent variable as complex is an expression of their wish to find explanations of complex phenomena in simple terms. But in social and behavioral research, the distinction between independent and dependent variables is generally arbitrary, and often, as in path analysis and structural equation modeling, variables take on the roles of being both independent and dependent variables (e.g., Bollen, 1989). This indicates that the notion of the unitary variable is a simplification.

Lucke (2005) argued that heterogeneous instruments are necessary, because the phenomena under study in psychological research are only rarely unidimensional.

> The complexity of psychosocial behavior may require tests to be heterogeneous, perhaps irreducibly so, to maintain their reliability, validity and predictive utility.... A psychosocial entity such as social support, self-esteem, or depression is a contingently clustered set of attributes that covary under mutual causation or share underlying common causal mechanisms.... The number of attributes required to describe an entity is a problem of theory and discovery and cannot be determined a priori. The attempts to measure any single attribute in isolation from the others may distort the measurement results.... If a theory claims that an entity has multiple attributes, then the test measuring that entity should measure all the relevant attributes. Therefore, the test must be heterogeneous. The meaningfulness of a test lies not in a methodological prescription of homogeneity but in the test's ability to capture all relevant attributes of the entity it purports to measure. (p. 66)

These objections to the principle of instrument homogeneity indicate that this principle is neither a necessary nor a sufficient principle for achieving instruments that are practically and theoretically useful. Thus, Lucke's (2005) main point is that certain psychological phenomena may not be amenable to investigation under the unidimensionality assumption.

In a similar line of reasoning, within the framework of a discussion of psychological interpretations of factors, Coan (1964) introduced the term *referent generality* to refer to the scope of reference of a construct, or "the variety of behaviors or mental activities to which it relates and the degree to which it relates to them" (p. 138). The idea that constructs differ in degree of referent generality was introduced in relation to hierarchical models of intelligence and personality. For example, Burt's (1949) hierarchical model distinguishes four levels of factor generality: general, group, specific, and error.

At a theoretical level, distinctions between constructs of low- and high-referent generality are easy to make. It is not immediately obvious, however, how measurement of constructs of different referent generality should be accomplished. For example, the issue of how to best measure the high-referent generality construct, general cognitive ability, has been extensively discussed since the days of Binet and Simon (1916) and Spearman (1927). Furthermore, it may be noted that development of psychometric tools to support solution of these measurement problems has been sparse. Thus, there is a need for measurement concepts and techniques that make it possible to tackle complex measurement issues when the unidimensionality assumption cannot be relied on. In this chapter, these issues are approached and the same idea as was proposed by Coan (1964) and Lucke (2005) is relied on; namely, hierarchical factor models provide a useful frame of reference for issues of dimensionality.

Historical Perspective

Before we go into a more detailed discussion about psychometric problems, there may be reason to consider some historical aspects of the development of thought about measurement. With intervals of about 20 years, successive volumes of *Educational Measurement* have been published, with each volume containing chapters about different theoretical and practical aspects of measurement. The first edition of *Educational Measurement* was edited by Lindquist (1951). It included one chapter on reliability by Thorndike and one chapter on validity by Cureton.

In the reliability chapter, Thorndike centered his discussion of definitions of reliability on a classification of different sources of variance in test scores. He emphasized that any analysis of reliability needs to be based on a logical analysis, which for a given situation clarifies which sources of variance are to be regarded as systematic and which are to be regarded as error variance. Thorndike (1951) distinguished between six main categories of variance. Four of these categories were based on whether the source of variance is lasting or temporary and whether the source of variance is general or specific.

The first category of variance includes lasting and general characteristics of the individual and represents, among other sources of variance, level of ability on one or more general traits, which operate in a number of tests. Into this category, Thorndike (1951) also classified general test-taking skills and general ability to comprehend instructions. According to Thorndike, the factors in this category are sources of systematic variance, although this does not guarantee that they are also valid.

Thorndike (1951) labeled the second category of variance as lasting and specific characteristics of the individual. This category represents level of ability on traits required in a particular test. This may concern specific knowledge or skills as well as variance associated with the specific form and method of testing.

Thorndike (1951) described the third category of sources of variance in test scores as temporary but general characteristics of the individual. Examples of such factors are state of health, amount of sleep the night before the testing, and motivation to perform well. Thorndike observed that such factors vary both in their consistency over time and in their generality. He also observed that the specific purpose for which a test is used determines whether the sources of variance in this category are systematic variance or error variance.

The fourth category of sources of variance reflects temporary and specific characteristics of the individual. Examples of such factors are comprehension of a specific test task; levels of previous practice on a specific task; and short-time fluctuations of memory, attention, or effort. Thorndike argued that although short-time fluctuations must be regarded as sources of error variance, some factors that affect a test as a whole might, for certain purposes, be regarded as systematic factors.

Thorndike's classification of different sources of variance in test scores is based on the view that test scores reflect influence from attributes of different degrees of referent generality and temporal stability, and this is a powerful framework for discussing logical aspects of reliability. However, after Thorndike these distinctions have rarely been made.

In the chapter on validity, Cureton (1951) also discussed issues of dimensionality and referent generality at some length. He, too, observed that broad attributes may be of importance in several tests and that these attributes may combine in different ways in different test items.

> Suppose an arithmetic reasoning test draws upon three broad traits, say: a verbal trait, a number trait and a reasoning trait. The items of the test may be homogeneous in the sense that every item of the test measures whatever is measured by the entire test. This might be termed "three-factor" homogeneity. One-factor homogeneous tests are much harder to construct. (p. 648)

Thus, any test typically is factorially complex, but as long as the items are factorially complex in the same way, the test will be one-dimensional and will thus fulfill the main criterion of homogeneity.

Cureton (1951) proposed, however, an approach to deal with the factorial complexity of tests when he said,

> We may expect to find broad cognitive traits, interest traits, attitude traits, personality traits, achievement traits and various others. Having found them, we may assign trait scores to individuals and compute the intercorrelations among the trait scores. We can then factor-analyze the intercorrelations among the trait scores. If clearly defined factors are found, we may term them supertraits. If there is a general factor common to a number of broad cognitive factors, we may choose to call the corresponding supertrait "intelligence." There is evidence that such a supertrait "exists" in the sense defined. (p. 648)

Cureton (1951), thus, suggested a procedure that basically amounts to conducting a second-order factor analysis to understand the factorial composition of tests in terms of broad and narrow factors. He emphasized, however, that such an approach would not yield any interpretable results unless the measures analyzed were homogeneous.

> The term "trait," as used here, is a measurement concept, being defined by the operations which show that a set of item performances or test performances are to some degree homogeneous. If we want to learn about human traits in any scientific fashion, the only way we can do so is to construct homogeneous tests and use them in extensive factorial researches. (p. 649)

This recommendation has been followed in the sense that factor analysis of homogeneous instruments has been established as a main procedure in research on individual differences. But the recommendation to use higher order factor analysis has not been followed to any large extent, and it does not seem that

Cureton's advice has had much of an impact on the procedures used in the field of measurement.

In summary, both Thorndike (1951) and Cureton (1951) saw tests as measuring multiple abilities of different degrees of generality and both framed the study of reliability and validity in terms of determining which systematic factors are involved in test performance.

Basic Psychometric Concepts

There is reason to start the discussion by taking a somewhat closer look at how the dimensionality issue is dealt with in psychometric theory and how this relates to the two fundamental concepts in measurement theory, namely, reliability and validity. This discussion takes a starting point in the formulation of measurement theory by Bollen (1989), which may be described as linking structural equation modeling and classical test theory. This formulation makes explicit important ideas about the fundamental measurement concepts, and Bollen's (1989) text has had a strong influence on how issues of measurement have been handled within many fields of application. Finally, Bollen's (1989) formulation extends the very flexible congeneric measurement model proposed by Jöreskog (1971) into a more versatile multidimensional model.

Reliability

Bollen (1989) defined reliability as the consistency of measurement, or as freedom from random error. More formally, Bollen (1989) discussed the concept of reliability within the framework of a multidimensional latent variable model, as follows. Assume that we represent an $m \times 1$ vector of observed scores as x. The x scores depend on a $q \times 1$ vector, ξ, of latent variables; an $m \times 1$ vector, s, of specific variance components; and an $m \times 1$ vector, e, of errors of measurement, such that

$$x = \Lambda\xi + s + e. \quad (1)$$

Here Λ is an $m \times q$ matrix of coefficients (or factor loadings), and we assume $E(e) = 0$ and $E(s) = 0$. We also assume ξ, s and e to be uncorrelated.

The model in Equation 1 accounts for the observed variance in x in terms of systematic variance due to ξ, specific variance due to s, and random variation due to e. The specific variance component, s, is not easy to distinguish from the systematic ξ component. However, the s component may be understood as a systematic component that only influences a particular observed variable. In the reliability literature, the s component is also referred to as the unique component of x. Within the factor analytic framework, these unique components cannot easily be dealt with, and unless the model is set up in such a way that the s component can be explicitly identified, they will merge with e and be considered as sources of unreliability rather than as systematic sources of variance.

Traditionally, the reliability of an observed variable x_i is defined as the ratio of systematic variance (i.e., all components of variance except e_i) in x_i to the total variance of x_i. However, because of the problem of identifying the s_i contribution, Bollen (1989) proposed an alternative definition of the reliability of x_i, as "the magnitude of the direct relations that all [latent] variables have on x_i" (p. 221). This definition assumes that the contribution from the specific component s_i on x_i is zero. Should there be s_i variance, it must be explicitly represented in the model as ξ variance, because otherwise reliability will be systematically underestimated.

There are simple methods that may be applied when the amount of influence from an s_i component needs to be estimated. One approach is to split a measure, x_i, into subcomponents (e.g., half tests) and enter these subcomponents as observed variables connected to a latent variable, which represents all the nonrandom sources of variance in x_i. However, even though such a split-half technique can often and easily be implemented, it does make the model more complicated. Furthermore, in such a model there would be a set of latent variables, each of which would correspond to the nonrandom part of x_i. This may or may not be desirable, depending on the purpose of the model.

The definition of reliability discussed here pertains to a single indicator x_i. However, as shown by Bollen (1989), the reliability of an unweighted sum of indicators can easily be computed from the estimated factor loadings for all x, and this reliability estimate agrees with the basic definition of the reliability of a single indicator as the amount of variance accounted for by the latent variables.

Validity

A general definition of validity is the extent to which an operationalized variable effectively measures the variable it is supposed to measure. This issue cannot be approached unless there is a theoretically based definition of the intent of measurement. Bollen (1989) outlined four steps to take when setting up a measurement model. The first step involves formulation of a theoretical definition, which explains in as simple and precise terms as possible the meaning of a concept. According to Bollen, one important function of the theoretical definition is that it

> clarifies the dimensions of a concept. Dimensions are distinct aspects of a concept. They are components that cannot easily be subdivided into additional components. Since concepts have numerous possible dimensions, a definition is critical to set the limit on the dimensions a researcher selects. We need one latent variable per dimension. (p. 180)

Thus, the second step is to identify the different aspects, or dimensions, of the concept and the latent variables that may represent them. In the third step, measures are created as indicators of the latent variables, and in the fourth and final step, a measurement model is constructed in which the latent variables are connected to one or more measures. The measurement model takes the form specified in Equation 1.

Bollen (1989) discussed the several different proposed forms of validity, such as content validity, criterion validity, and construct validity. He argued that there are problems associated with all these forms of validity and proposed an alternative definition based on structural equation modeling: "The validity of a measure x_i of ξ_i is the magnitude of the direct structural relation between ξ_i and x_i" (p. 197). This simple and straightforward definition of validity resolves the problem that Bollen (1989) identified with the other forms of validity, although these details are beyond the scope of the following discussion.

Discussion

Bollen's (1989) definitions of the basic measurement concepts summarize much of the current psychometric thinking, and through taking advantage of the multidimensional structural equation model, the concepts of reliability and validity become more general and flexible than in the traditional formulations. Nevertheless, it seems that some basic problems remain to be sorted out that primarily involve the conceptualization of validity.

One basic problem with the approach to validity argued for by Bollen (1989) is that each concept is divided into sets of dimensions, each of which is represented with a single latent variable. This implies that a high-referent generality construct is represented as several low-referent generality constructs (Coan, 1964), whereas there is no latent variable that represents the common core of the construct. Suppose that several latent variables assumed to represent a single construct are entered as independent variables in a structural equation model. In such a model the estimated structural coefficients for the correlated latent variables would reflect the contribution of each dimension, whereas any effects of the variance that overlaps the latent variables would not be seen, because they would be concealed among the unanalyzed covariances among the latent variables. Thus, because there is no latent variable in the model that represents the common content of the construct over dimensions, the construct would become fragmented into several narrow constructs. One approach that could be used to solve this problem would be to introduce a second-order factor to represent the common variance of the different dimensions. However, according to Bollen (1989), there must be a direct link between the latent variable and the observed variable, which implies that the validity definition only covers relations between first-order factors and observed variables.

Another problem, which pertains both to reliability and to validity, is that no explicit allowance is made for the specific components of the measures. As has already been pointed out, this can easily be solved through extending the model with latent variables to capture the specific components. However, this would result in a set of latent variables with even lower referent generality, each latent variable corresponding to an observed variable. It certainly would be possible to analyze the structure among the latent variables through use of a higher order modeling approach, in which additional layers of latent variables are introduced in order to account for the covariances among lower order factors. Again, however, the restriction of the validity definition, which only allows for direct relations between first-order factors and the observed variable, prevents this. However, in such a model validity would get lost in the attempts to adequately represent reliability. Thus, even though Bollen's (1989) formulation of the basic ideas of measurement seems sound, there are problems that need to be attended to and the fundamental issue is how to represent broad aspects of constructs along with narrow aspects of constructs.

Hierarchical Modeling Approaches

We have already concluded that one possible approach that could be used to deal with the problem of representing aspects of constructs with different degrees of referent generality is hierarchical factor-analytic modeling. As has also been shown, this is not a new or an original idea, and several researchers have proposed hierarchical modeling as a method to come to grips with the problem of dealing with heterogeneous tests. Still, the impact on practical applications has been limited.

In a hierarchical factor model, some factors are broader than other factors. There are, however, different ways in which such models may be set up. One approach is through higher order factor analysis, which is closely related to Thurstone's multiple factor analysis. Thurstone (e.g., 1947) argued that factor models should have a "simple structure" in the sense that each factor is associated with a subset of the observed variables and that each observed variable is influenced by only one or a few factors. This allows an invariant determination and interpretation of factors, because when the simple structure criteria are satisfied, it becomes clear which observed variables a particular factor is related and to which variables it is not related. The best approximation to simple structure typically is obtained when the factors are allowed to be correlated in an oblique solution.

A higher order (HO) model may then be constructed through factoring the correlations among the factors, using the same factor analytic principles as when observed variables are analyzed. We may hypothesize, for example, that a single second-order factor accounts for the intercorrelations among the factors. If a single factor cannot account for the correlations among the factors, one or more additional second-order factors may be introduced. Should we end up with several second-order factors, these may be correlated. To account for these correlations, a third-order factor may be introduced and so on. Thus, with this approach, a hierarchy of factors is built up, starting from below with a large number of narrow first-order factors and ending at the top of the hierarchy with one, or a few, broad higher order factors.

An example of a simple HO model, which involves only six observed variables, three first-order (I, V, and S) and one second-order factor (G), is shown in Figure 5.1. In this model, the loading of I on G is assumed to be unity, so there is no residual variance in the first-order I factor. For the other two first-order factors, there are residuals, which are labeled V' and S', respectively. In an HO model, there are no direct relations between the observed variables and the higher order factors. It may also be noted that both the first-order factors and the second-order factor in this example satisfy the simple-structure criterion.

There has been, however, a considerable reluctance among researchers to fit HO models. One reason for this is that such models are technically more complicated to deal with than are factor models, which include only first-order

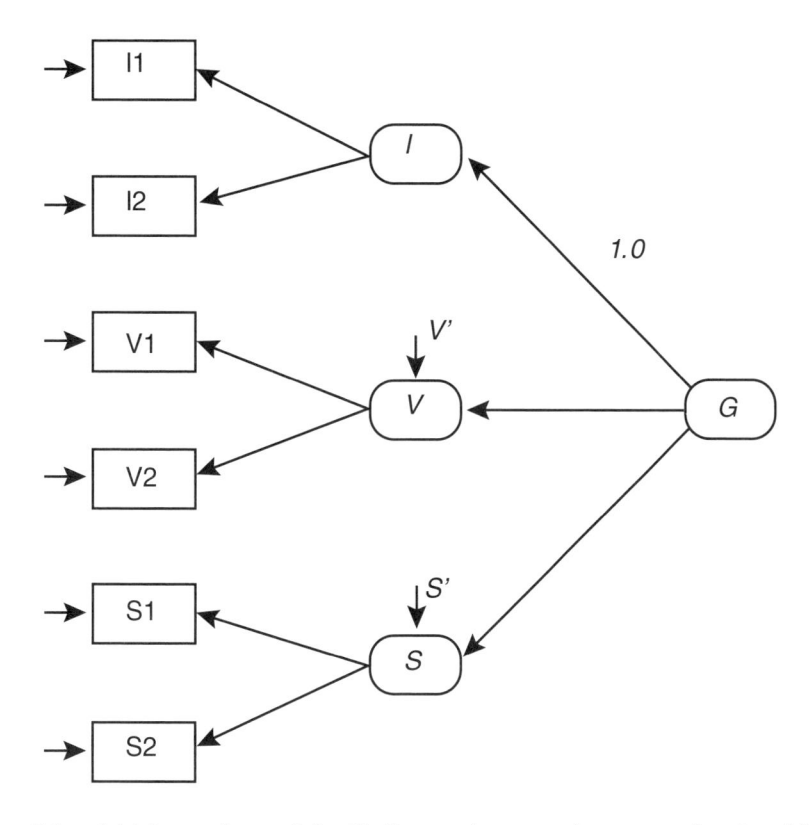

Figure 5.1. A higher order model with three primary and one second-order abilities.

factors. Another and perhaps more important reason is that higher order factors are difficult to interpret. Gorsuch (1983) pointed out that

> the understanding of primary factors is based upon interpretations of their relationships with the original variables. The interpretations are post hoc and subject to considerable error.... Interpretations of the second-order factors would need to be based upon the interpretations of the first-order factors.... Whereas it is hoped that the investigator knows the variables well enough to interpret them, the accuracy of interpretation will decrease with the first-order factors, will be less with the second-order factors and still less with the third-order factors. (p. 245)

Thus, the great perceived distance between the higher order factors and the manifest variables has been seen as a reason for avoiding higher order factors. It is possible, however, to transform a higher order model into a model in which all factors relate to the manifest variables, using the so-called Schmid and Leiman (1957) transformation (e.g., Yung, McLeod, & Thissen, 1999). After the transformation has been applied, the manifest variables relate to more than one factor, and if there is a general factor, it relates to all the manifest variables. Thus, such a model does not conform to the principles of simple structure, because each manifest variable is influenced by more than one latent variable.

It may be noted that the perception that higher order factors belong to a different category of factors, which is more distant from reality than first-order factors has been challenged by Humphreys (1962) and Coan (1964). They argue that the difference is a matter of breadth of influence, rather than due to the higher order factors being superordinate to the lower order factors. Thus, a higher order factor simply exerts influence on a greater number of manifest variables than does a lower order factor.

The transformed model with orthogonal factors is often referred to as the hierarchical factor model (Yung et al., 1999). However, terminology is not quite consistent. In keeping with the terminology established within the psychological literature (e.g., Coan, 1964), Gustafsson (1988) and Gustafsson and Balke (1993) used the label *hierarchical factor model* to refer to any type of model that includes both broad and narrow factors, whereas they referred to the orthogonal type of model as the nested factor (NF) model.

In an NF model, orthogonal factors are allowed to span a broader or a more narrow range of observed variables. A general factor typically is fitted first, after which successively more narrow factors are fitted to the residual correlations. In Figure 5.2, an NF model is shown for the same six observed variables as used to illustrate the HO model.

In this model, the ability factors are all directly related to the tests. Because the G factor accounts for variance in the tests to which V and S are related, the

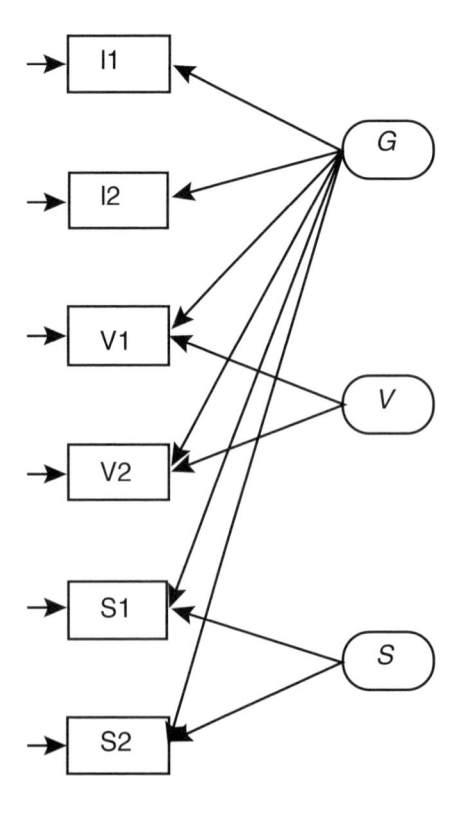

Figure 5.2. A nested-factor model with one broad and two narrow factors.

narrow factors are residual factors in this model, too. In this model, there is no I' (or I) factor because the G factor leaves no systematic variance unaccounted for in the two variables that measure the I factor.

The HO and NF models tend to carry the same substantive interpretations, and the numerical estimates of relations between observed variables and factors in an NF model and a Schmid and Leiman (1957) transformed HO model are typically highly similar. However, the HO model is more constrained than is the NF model (see Mulaik & Quartetti, 1997; Yung et al., 1999). It may also be noted that in the NF model in Figure 2, there are only three latent variables, whereas in the HO model in Figure 1, there are four latent variables. This is, of course, because of the equivalence between G and I, which in the top-down NF analysis causes the I factor to vanish, whereas it remains in the bottom-up HO analysis.

Implications of the Hierarchical Factor Model for Measurement

It has already been demonstrated that hierarchical factor models are useful for addressing measurement issues that involve heterogeneous tests. For example, Lucke (2005) proposed an extension of reliability theory to heterogeneous tests under the label *congeneric test theory*. Lucke's generalization of reliability and internal consistency to heterogeneous tests is based on a higher order factor-analytic modeling approach, and it shows, among other things, that reliability of a heterogeneous test is a function of the sum of the reliabilities of homogenous subtests plus the reliability of the correlations across subtests. McDonald (1999) also has made important contributions to measurement theory through taking a starting point in hierarchical modeling approaches. Still, however, there seems to be a need for further work along these lines.

Implications for Conceptions of Measurement

The hierarchical factor model in general, and the NF model in particular, have a number of interesting implications for conceptions of measurement. It may thus be noted that the NF model in a very concrete manner illustrates Humphrey's (1962) point that the broad factors are not at a greater distance from the observed variables than are the narrow factors. This impression is created by the way in which the HO model is presented, but from the NF model, it is immediately apparent that the broad factors simply exert an influence on a larger set of observed variables. Thus, breadth of influence on observed variables, rather than distance from observed variables, is what distinguishes broad and narrow factors.

In the discussion of Bollen's (1989) definition of validity, it was observed that the formulation did not easily accommodate the need to include latent variables of different degrees of generality because of the requirement that there may only be direct relations between latent and observed variables. However, in the NF model, all factors are basically first-order factors, and they all have direct relations with the observed variables. Thus, this type of model may be used to represent both broad and narrow latent variables in a multidimensional measurement model.

One of the consequences of adopting such a measurement model is that the simple structure idea, that each observed variable should only reflect one latent variable, must be replaced with the notion that observed variables are complex and typically measure several constructs of different degrees of referent generality. This is illustrated by Figure 2, in which it is seen that every observed variable is influenced by the general factor, along with a narrow factor. In addition, each variable has a specific factor, which is here confounded with the random error component. With a more elaborate hierarchical model it would, of course, be possible to identify more components of variance in the independent variables.

It must be emphasized, though, that adoption of a hierarchical measurement model is closely associated with adopting a particular theoretical model of the phenomenon under investigation. This is seen through the example of research on the structure of intelligence (Gustafsson, 2002). Thus, the question of whether general intelligence exists has been one of the most controversial questions in the history of psychological research. The hierarchical model explicitly introduces the general factor, so anyone who does not believe in the meaningfulness of such factor would be hesitant to adopt a hierarchical model for measuring cognitive abilities. However, all measurement models embody theoretical conceptions, so this is not a unique feature of hierarchical models.

On the basis of the implication of hierarchical measurement models, in which observed variables typically reflect a mixture of broad and narrow components of variance, Gustafsson (2002) formulated three propositions on measurement:

1. To measure constructs with high-referent generality, it is necessary to use heterogeneous measurement devices.
2. A homogenous test always measures several dimensions.
3. To measure constructs with low-referent generality, it is also necessary to measure constructs with high generality.

According to the first proposition, the best way and sometimes the only way to capture a construct with high-referent generality (e.g., general intelligence) is to use a heterogeneous test. Suppose that we want to measure a factor that is present in all the components in a battery. Such a general factor will, to some extent, be present in every test, even though the amount of variance accounted for in each component may be relatively small. However, the amount of variance accounted for by the different factors in the sum of the component scores not only depends on the mean factor loading, but also on the number of components in which the factor is involved (see Gustafsson, 2002). This is because the amount of variance associated with a latent variable is proportional to the square of the number of components to which it is related. For example, if there are 100 components in a test and a general factor is related to all of these, it would be weighted by a factor of 10,000. In contrast, a narrow latent variable that is involved in only five components would be weighted by a factor of 25. From this simple observation follows a principle of aggregation, which states that as the number of components in which a latent variable is involved increases, the variable will tend to dominate the variance in the sum of scores (see Humphreys, 1962).

Gustafsson (2002) used results from a reanalysis of data on a test battery initially analyzed by Holzinger and Swineford (1939) to demonstrate that this principle of aggregation caused a striking dominance of the G factor in the sum of scores and quite limited contributions from the other factors. Gustafsson (2002) also observed that these results explain the success of Binet's approach to measuring general ability with heterogeneous tests, as compared with the relatively modest amount of success met by Spearman's attempts to measure general intelligence with a single, highly G-loaded test.

The proposition that a homogeneous test measures several abilities follows directly from the fact that in the NF model, each observed variable is an indicator of several latent variables of different degrees of generality. As has already been pointed out, the principle of simple structure does not apply to NF models and there will typically be several sources of variance in each observed variable, unless the observed variable is heterogeneous and the principle of aggregation has caused the general factor to dominate the variance of the test. For example, a homogeneous test of spatial-visualization ability will measure a general factor of cognitive ability, a general visualization factor, and a narrow spatial-visualization factor.

The third proposition (i.e., that measurement of low generality constructs also requires measurement of high generality constructs) is closely related to the second one. It states that if our intention is to measure one or more narrow factors, it is necessary to partial out the influence of the more general factors that exert influence on the observed variable. This may, for example, be done through computing factor scores (Gustafsson & Snow, 1997), but this cannot be done unless information is available that allows estimation of the more general dimensions.

Measures of Reliability and Validity

One of the great advantages of the NF type of hierarchical model for measurement applications stems from the fact that it can easily be used to decompose the observed variance of a test in terms of contributions from the orthogonal latent factors. An NF model is fitted to the components of a test (e.g., items or subscales), and from the estimated factor loadings and factor variances, the proportions of variance in the sum of scores due to the different latent variables can be computed, as follows. Assuming the s vector in Equation 1 to be 0, this model generates, under the usual assumptions of independence of residuals and factors, the following covariance structure:

$$\Sigma = \Lambda \Psi \Lambda' + \Theta. \quad (2)$$

Ψ is the covariance matrix of the latent variables and Θ is the covariance matrix of the residuals in manifest variables. Assuming that we restrict attention to nested-factor models, Ψ is diagonal and Θ is also assumed to be orthogonal.

Here, our primary interest is on properties of functions of the observed variables. Let us assume that we construct a simple unit-weighted sum (T, for total) of the individuals' scores on the m variables. Because the variance of a sum of components is equal to the sum of all the elements of the covariance matrix for the components, it follows that

$$Var(T) = \sum_{j=1}^{k}\left(\sum_{i=1}^{m}\lambda_{ij}\right)^2 \psi_{jj} + \sum_{i=1}^{m}\theta_{ii} \qquad (3)$$

This formula, thus, achieves a decomposition of the total observed variance of T into different components due to the different latent variables and to the errors of measurement, which we can easily determine in terms of proportions of the total variance.

McDonald (1999) describes the coefficient Ω, which expresses the proportion of variance due to the general factor among a set of components and that can easily be computed from the estimated factor loadings, as shown above. For a unidimensional test, Ω is both a reliability coefficient and a validity coefficient (McDonald, 1999). For a multidimensional test, Ω expresses, according to McDonald (1999), the proportion of variance that the general factor accounts for in the sum of scores. Following Bollen (1989), this is a validity measure, even though the coefficient refers to the unweighted sum of scores rather than to the validity of a single component. We may also generalize McDonald's approach and compute a separate Ω for each of the other latent variables in an NF model. This measure expresses the proportion of total score variance accounted for by the latent variable.

We may also define a composite reliability coefficient, ρ_y, as the proportion of the total variance that is accounted for by all the latent variables. The composite reliability coefficient agrees with Bollen's (1989) definition of reliability, except that it refers to an unweighted sum of component scores rather than to the reliability of a single component.

It must be emphasized that, here, we are only focusing on characteristics of the variance of a unit-weighted sum of scores over the m components. Thus, we are still staying within the confines of classical test theory, and the approach taken is purely descriptive. Recently, interesting solutions to the problems of statistical inference concerning the reliability of scales within a latent variable framework have been developed and applied by several researchers (e.g., Hancock & Mueller, 2001; Raykov, 1997; 1998; Raykov & Shrout, 2002). It would, however, carry too far to discuss these here, and in the empirical demonstration to which we next turn, the simple descriptive technique is used.

Measurement Properties of the Swedish Scholastic Aptitude Test

The discussion so far has been quite general and abstract, and there is need to bring it down to a more concrete and applied level. This is accomplished through focusing on the Swedish Scholastic Aptitude Test (SweSAT) as an example. The SweSAT was developed as an additional instrument for gaining access to higher education in Sweden; when it was introduced in 1977, one of the aims was to rectify the uneven recruitment from different social groups. Originally, the test was taken only by small groups of applicants who did not have grades from upper secondary education. However, starting in the spring of 1991, everyone could take the test and make use of the results when applying for undergraduate studies. Thereby, the number of test takers increased from about 10,000 a year during the 1980s to more than 100,000 a year. This has made the SweSAT an important instrument for gaining access to those parts of the university systems in which there are more applicants than study places.

The SweSAT is designed to assess the general ability to successfully pass higher education courses. Reading skills, vocabulary, and skills of reasoning, primarily with quantitative information, are focused on in the test. However, the test lacks a theoretical basis for its construction, and little is known about what the total score computed from the subtests actually measures. However, during the last couple of decades, progress has been made in research on the hierarchical structure of cognitive abilities, which may be drawn on to achieve a better understanding of the measurement properties of the SweSAT.

Hierarchical models have proven extremely useful in research on cognitive abilities because they resolve the conflict between theorists who emphasize one general ability (e.g., Humphreys, 1985; Jensen, 1998; Spearman, 1927) and theorists who emphasize several specialized abilities (e.g., Guilford, 1967; Thurstone, 1938) by allowing for both categories of abilities in the model. The Carroll (1993) three-stratum model is an elaborate hierarchical model. The model is based upon reanalyses of a large number of correlation matrices collected throughout the 20th century. In the model, there are factors of three degrees of generality. At the first stratum, there are at least 60 narrow factors, many of which correspond to factors previously identified by Guilford, Thurstone, and other researchers working in the tradition of multiple factor analysis.

At the second stratum, some 10 broad factors are identified, most of which correspond to factors identified by Cattell (e.g., 1963), Horn and Cattell (1966), and other researchers using second-order factor analysis. Among the second-stratum factors, two are especially important. One is Fluid Intelligence (Gf), which is related to first-stratum factors representing induction, reasoning, problem solving, and visual perception. The other factor is Crystallized Intelligence (Gc), which is involved in language and reading tasks, as well as tests of declarative knowledge in wide areas. A third prominent factor is Broad Visual Perception (Gv), which involves manipulation of figural information, particularly when perception or mental manipulation is complex and difficult. At the top of the three-stratum model, Carroll (1993) identified the general factor (G). Among the second-order factors, Gf was found to have the highest correlation with G, and Gc was found to have the next highest correlation with G.

An alternative hierarchical model has been investigated in a series of empirical studies by Gustafsson and Undheim (Gustafsson, 1984, 1988; Gustafsson & Balke, 1993; Undheim, 1981; Undheim & Gustafsson, 1987). This model also identifies ability factors of three degrees of generality. However, the third-order G factor and the second-order Gf factor are regarded as one and the same factor in the model because several studies have shown that there is a perfect correlation between them (e.g., Gustafsson, 1984).

In order to study the dimensionality of the SweSAT, Gustafsson, Wedman, and Westerlund (1992) fitted CFA models to the six subtests that were included in the SweSAT up to 1991. Unlike the presently used SweSAT, these earlier versions included subtests of Study Techniques and General Information. The other four subtests were Data Sufficiency; Diagrams, Tables, and Maps; Swedish Reading Comprehension; and Vocabulary. Two factors were identified, one of which was a general factor on which all subtests had loadings and the other a verbal knowledge factor on which four subtests had loadings. The two subtests requiring logical reasoning and complex problem solving (Data Sufficiency and Diagrams, Tables, and Maps) had the highest loadings on the general factor, whereas they had no loadings on the verbal knowledge factor. The two factors were hypothesized to closely correspond to the G and Gc factors.

However, the Gustafsson et al. (1992) study was restricted by the limited number of subtests included in the SweSAT, and the authors argued that additional information would be needed to determine the measurement properties of the test. This is illustrated in an interesting study by Roberts et al. (2000), who investigated the construct validity of the Armed Services Vocational Aptitude Battery (ASVAB). This test serves as a screening test for military enlistees and as a guidance/counseling device in high schools in the United States. In two studies, Roberts et al. examined the factorial composition of the ASVAB by combining it with other tests of known factorial content. Their results showed that ASVAB primarily measured the Gc factor and not general intelligence, as it had been claimed. SweSAT is primarily composed of verbal tasks (i.e., vocabulary and reading comprehension in Swedish as well as English), and the two problem-solving subtests (i.e., Diagrams, Tables, and Maps; Data Sufficiency) have verbally formulated items. This makes it reasonable to believe that the Gc factor accounts for much of the individual differences in performance on the SweSAT, too.

In addition to the broad G and Gc factors, there is reason to believe that further, more narrow factors are involved in test performance in, for example, the domain of quantitative skills. Thus, these previous studies indicate that the SweSAT is multidimensional. However, it certainly would be desirable to achieve a better understanding of which sources of variance are reflected in the total SweSAT score and of how the measurement characteristics of the test determine the contributions from different factors. Following are results from three different studies that aim to answer these questions.

Study 1: Sources of Variance in the Diagrams, Tables, and Maps Test

The first issue to be addressed is the identification of the sources of variance through item-level analyses of a single subtest that has been constructed with the aim of being relatively homogeneous. Results are summarized from studies presented by Åberg-Bengtsson (1999), and some further analyses are made of the obtained results.

The Diagram, Tables, and Maps (DTM) test is a complex problem-solving test requiring responses to questions about information presented in tables, graphs, diagrams, and maps. Some items involve manipulation of numerical information, and Åberg-Bengtsson (1999) asked if these items require a quantitative ability over and above the ability measured by all the items. One reason for asking this question was the substantial male advantage in performance on DTM, and one hypothesis was that items requiring manipulation of numerical information were a main source of the gender difference in performance.

Åberg-Bengtsson (1999) conducted her analyses on a group of 19-year-old test takers (N = 14,431) who had taken the SweSAT in the spring of 1991. She fitted a series of CFA models to the item-level covariance matrix using maximum likelihood estimation techniques. Although the dichotomous item data violate the assumption of linearity of the regressions of items on latent variables, as well as the assumption of multivariate normality, this approach has the advantage that it models the simple summation of the item scores into a total score.

The modeling was done in several steps in which factors were successively added. In the first step, a general DTM factor (GenDTM)—presumed to measure a general ability to handle diagrams, tables, and maps—was first related to all items in the test. In the DTM subtest, the items are organized in a pairwise manner with each pair related to a particular theme on its own double page. Therefore, the residuals of items thus juxtaposed were stipulated to covary. Next, a nested "end of test factor" (End) was added to the model, which was significantly related to the last five items of the test, the loadings being successively higher for items closer to the end of the test. Third, a nested "quantitative" factor (Quant) was introduced. Items classified as *quantitative* involved more or less complicated arithmetic and calculations in addition to the reading of diagrams, tables, and maps. There were 13 items that had such characteristics. The standardized factor loadings are presented in Table 5.1. As has already been mentioned, 13 items had a significant loading on the Quant factor. For some items, the loadings were quite small, but eight had a loading larger than .1. For several items, the loading on the Quant factor was almost as large as the loading on the GenDTM factor.

In spite of the fact that the Quant factor was present in quite a few of the items, this factor only accounted for 6% of the variance in the unweighted sum of DTM item scores. Thus, the Ω coefficient for the Quant factor was .06, which may be compared with the Ω coefficient of the GenDTM factor, which was .57. Thus, the GenDTM factor accounted for almost 10 times as much variance in the sum of scores as did the Quant factor. One reason for this is that the GenDTM factor is present in each item and, according to the principle of aggregation, the amount of influence of a factor is proportional to the square of the number of items in which it is involved. Another reason for the higher Ω of the GenDTM factor is that the mean of the standardized item loadings was twice as high for GenDTM as for Quant (.28 and .14, respectively).

The model also included an End factor, defined by the last five items. For this factor, the item loadings increased as a function of the position of the item in the test. There is a time limit on the test, so this pattern of loadings may be an expression of the test being somewhat speeded. However, the End factor only accounted for 2% of the observed variance in the sum of scores.

In conclusion, the composite reliability of the DTM test was .65, and the main component contributing to the reliability of the test was the GenDTM factor. Thus, in spite of the fact that there were three identifiable sources of variance

Table 5.1. Nested-Factor Model for the DTM Test With One General and Two Specific Factors

Item	GenDTM	Quant	End	Residual
DTM Item01	0.04			1.00
DTM Item02	0.30	0.25		0.92
DTM Item03	0.17	0.04		0.98
DTM Item04	0.26	0.15		0.95
DTM Item05	0.32			0.95
DTM Item06	0.25	0.13		0.96
DTM Item07	0.16			0.99
DTM Item08	0.41			0.91
DTM Item09	0.20	0.14		0.97
DTM Item10	0.30			0.95
DTM Item11	0.19	0.09		0.98
DTM Item12	0.31	0.09		0.95
DTM Item13	0.23	0.14		0.96
DTM Item14	0.27	0.24		0.93
DTM Item15	0.34	0.23		0.91
DTM Item16	0.32	0.16	0.04	0.93
DTM Item17	0.34	0.05	0.10	0.93
DTM Item18	0.37		0.16	0.92
DTM Item19	0.45	0.05	0.27	0.85
DTM Item20	0.31		0.39	0.87
Proportion of variance in DTM sum	0.57	0.06	0.02	0.35

Note. DTM = Diagrams, Tables, and Maps; GenDTM = general DTM factor; Quant = quantitative factor; END = end of test factor.

in the DTM test, the test seemed fairly homogeneous. It should be observed, however, that the relatively small amount of variance accounted for by the Quant factor does not make it theoretically or practically unimportant. As was shown by Åberg-Bengtsson (1999), the Quant factor accounts for a considerable part of the gender difference in performance on the DTM test. Thus, the main conclusion of this analysis is that in a "microscopic" analysis (i.e., at the item level of a single test), it is possible to identify several narrow factors. However, in the sum of scores, these narrow factors contribute only marginal amounts of variance.

Study 2: Sources of Variance in the SweSAT Score

The next set of issues to be approached concerns which particular sources of variance may be identified in the total SweSAT score. Here, results from a study by Åberg-Bengtsson (2005) are summarized. The main aim of those analyses was to try to separate the Quant factor from a more general analytical factor, and through invoking the other subtests as well, more information was made available for the modeling. In the modeling, the DTM test was introduced at the item level, while the summed subtest scores were analyzed for the other five subtests. The model to be considered here was fitted to the same data as in Study 1 reported previously, and the same modeling techniques were used.

In the hypothesized model, a general factor (Gen) related to all manifest variables was introduced. Thus, with respect to the DTM subtest, the latent variable GenDTM was now exchanged for a broader general dimension. The two nested factors identified in the DTM-model, Quant and End (see Study 1), were also included in the model. The Data Sufficiency subtest (DS) was hypothesized to load on the Quant factor. Finally, the knowledge factor (Knowl), previously identified by Gustafsson et al. (1992), was brought into the model and related to the General Information (GI), Vocabulary (WORD), Reading Comprehension (READ), and Study Technique (STECH) tests. Even though this factor was tentatively labeled *knowledge,* it must be assumed that it is multidimensional and may, for example, include different verbal abilities as well as strategic performance. The hypothesized model is presented in Figure 5.3.

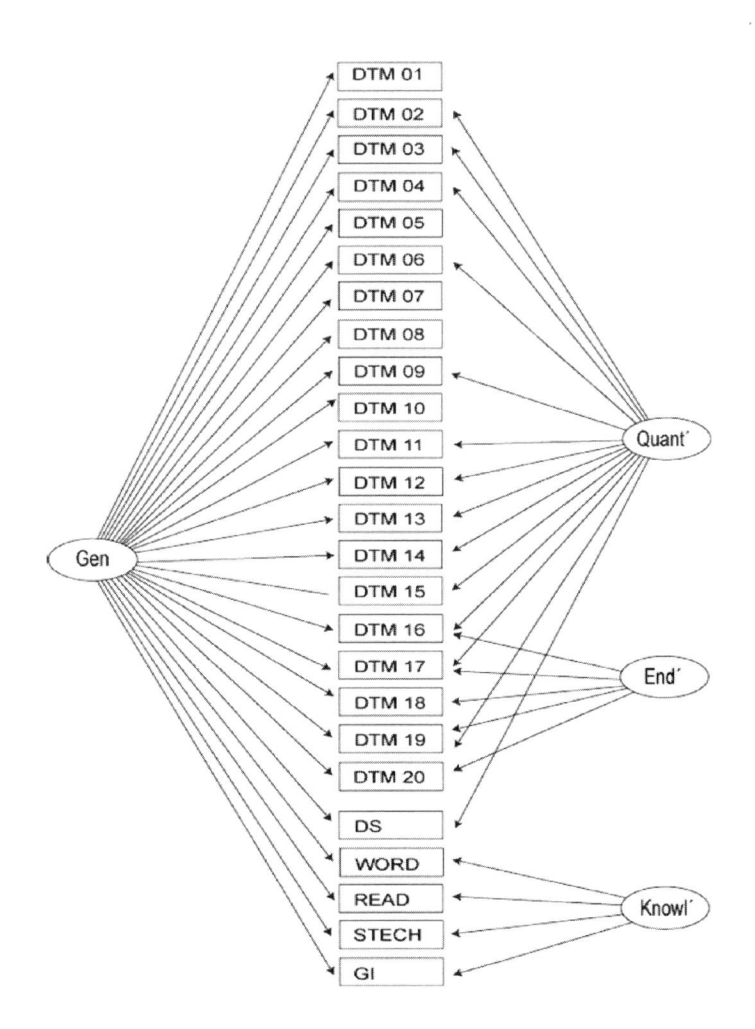

Figure 5.3. A nested-factor model for the SweSAT.

Table 5.2. Amount of Variance Due to the Different Factors in the Subtests

Factor	DTM	DS	WORD	READ	STECH	GI	SweSAT
Gen	0.57	0.48	0.21	0.35	0.40	0.30	0.66
Quant	0.06	0.09					0.01
End	0.02						0.00
Knowl			0.41	0.17	0.13	0.19	0.19
Residual	0.35	0.44	0.38	0.49	0.46	0.50	0.13

Note. DTM = Diagrams, Tables, and Maps; DS = Data Sufficiency; WORD = Vocabulary; STECH = Study Technique; GI = General Information; SweSAT = Swedish Scholastic Aptitude Test; Gen = general; Quant = quantitative factor; END = end of test factor; Knowl = knowledge.

Table 5.2 presents the estimated components of variance in each of the subtests, along with the computed proportions of variance in the total sum of scores that is due to each latent variable. It may first be observed that the Gen factor accounted for a larger proportion of variance in the total SweSAT score (.66) than in any of the subtests (.21–.57). This is, again, a consequence of the fact that the Gen factor influences each subtest, and the principle of aggregation causes it to dominate more in the total sum of scores than in any of the subtest scores. The Knowl factor was the second most important source of variance in the total SweSAT score (.19), and this factor was relatively important in the four verbal subtests, in which it accounted for between 13% and 41% of the variance. The Quant factor in this model was estimated to account for 9% of the variance in the DS subtest and for 6% of the variance in the DTM subtest. However, only 1% of the variance in the total SweSAT score was due to the Quant factor, which was only because a small proportion of the total number of items loaded on this factor.

Thus, the main conclusion from this study is that the total SweSAT score is dominated to a larger extent by the general factor than are any of the subtest scores. This is, again, due to the principle of aggregation, according to which the number of components in which a factor is involved determines the amount of variance contributed by the factor.

It may be asked how this general factor should be interpreted. The main question investigated in the Åberg-Bengtsson (2005) study was whether it is possible to separate the Quant factor from a general factor with the highest relation to the complex problem-solving tests. Such a result would lend support to the hypothesis that this general factor is close to the Gf factor, which is also close to the G factor (Gustafsson, 1984). This interpretation is supported by the fact that the two reasoning tests (DS and DTM) are, indeed, the ones most highly saturated by the general factor. The interpretation is also supported by the observation that the second most important factor was Knowl, with relations to the four verbal subtests. This factor, thus, seems to come close to Gc. However, to test these speculations it is necessary to combine the SweSAT with other tests that have known measurement properties.

Study 3: Combining the SweSAT With Other Measures

Carlstedt and Gustafsson (2005) reported a study in which SweSAT results were analyzed in combination with results achieved on the Swedish Enlistment Battery (SEB), which is used at conscription to military service. The main aim was to understand the meaning of the two dominant factors in the SweSAT through bringing in other measures with known properties.

The computer assisted test version of SEB (CAT-SEB) was developed to measure the theoretical constructs of G (or Gf), Gc, and Gv (Mårdberg & Carlstedt, 1998). The battery comprises 10 tests covering broad domains such as nonverbal problem solving, vocabulary, spatial tasks, and technical knowledge. Previous analyses of the test battery have confirmed the presence of the three ability factors (Carlstedt, 2001; Mårdberg & Carlstedt, 1998; Ullstadius, Gustafsson, & Carlstedt, 2002). The general factor influences all tests, but it exerts its strongest influence on the nonverbal problem-solving tests, indicating that the factor is close to Gf. The Gc and the Gv factors have also been found to replicate in different samples.

Six samples (N = 2,500–3,000) of 18-year-old males taking both the SweSAT and the SEB in 1997–1999 were used (Carlstedt & Gustafsson, 2005). Those who took the SweSAT in the autumn of the same year as they took the CAT-SEB (i.e., at 18 years), or in the following spring (i.e., at 19 years), were included.

The SEB included two Gf tests: Figure Series and Groups; five Gv tests: Dice 1 and Dice 2, Metal Folding Test, Block Rotation, and Technical Comprehension; and three Gc tests: Synonyms 1, Synonyms 2, and Antonyms. The SweSAT was revised in 1996 and the versions used included five subtests: WORD, READ, DTM, DS, and ERC.

A previously fitted model for the CAT-SEB (e.g., Carlstedt, 2001; Mårdberg & Carlstedt, 1998; Ullstadius, Gustafsson, & Carlstedt, 2002) formed the basis for the model, which included the G factor, under which the Gc and Gv factors were nested, along with a test specific (Di) factor. All the SweSAT tests were hypothesized to be influenced by the G factor. WORD, READ, and ERC were hypothesized to load upon Gc as well. The Quant factor was hypothesized to influence DTM, DS and Technical Comprehension.

The hypothesized NF model showed poor fit, but fit was improved by adding another residual factor on which all SweSAT tests had loadings. This factor was tentatively labeled Knowledge (Knowl). After introduction of this factor, the originally hypothesized Gc factor was reduced to a narrow vocabulary factor, and it was relabeled Voc. The broad Knowl factor accounted for somewhat more variance in the READ and ERC subtests than it did in the other subtests, but it also had an almost equally strong contribution to individual differences in performance in DTM and DS. This pattern suggests that the Knowl factor captures reading skills. Thus, in this model the Gc factor has been broken up into one factor representing reading skills and another factor representing vocabulary.

The model also included a Gf factor, which had relations to each and every subtest. For WORD, READ, and ERC, the Gf factor accounted for some 10% of the variance and for DTM and DS, it accounted for 31% and 36%, respectively.

Thus, the two problem-solving tests reflect considerably more Gf-variance than do the other three subtests. The Gf factor accounted for 33% of the variance in the total SweSAT score.

From Study 2, it was concluded that there is a relatively strong general factor in the SweSAT, which was tentatively interpreted as an analytic factor. However, the main result of the decomposition of the general SweSAT factor is that it represents a mixture of Gf and two different Gc components, the latter two being the strongest contributors of variance to the total SweSAT score (49%).

Discussion and Conclusions

The three studies briefly described here demonstrate some of the general principles that seem to be involved in heterogeneous tests. One basic principle is that a single score based on a heterogeneous test tends to reflect whatever is common among the items. However, one important lesson from Studies 2 and 3 is that care is needed when interpreting the nature of the factor common to a collection of subtests. Although it would make some sense to interpret the major source of variance in the total SweSAT score as being a factor of general cognitive ability, the results of Study 3 clearly demonstrated that the general factor of SweSAT is a mixture of Gf and Gc, the latter factor being the most important one. The reason for this is that almost all subtests pose quite heavy requirements for reading skills, and three subtests also measure knowledge of vocabulary. Thus, the bias towards Gc is explained by the fact that all the SweSAT subtests are verbally loaded.

It may, in contrast, be noted that in the considerably more heterogeneous SEB battery, the Gf factor accounted for no less than 75% of the variance, whereas Gc (or rather Voc) only contributed 10% of the variance in this test. Thus, in order to measure a construct with high-referent generality, it is an advantage to use a heterogeneous test battery. This observation is certainly not new; Messick (1989) argued that heterogeneity of tests may be necessary to avoid one of the two major threats to construct validity, namely, construct underrepresentation. As a hypothetical example, he discussed a complex construct involving three facets. Different aspects of the construct are measured by three measures that tap the three facets in different combinations. Messick (1989) observed the following:

> By virtue of the overlapping components, the three measures will intercorrelate positively and appear to converge in the measurement of "something," presumably the overall complex construct. Yet each measure is underrepresentative of some aspect of the construct. A composite of the three measures would cover all three aspects and, furthermore, the construct-relevant variance would contribute to the composite score while the irrelevant variance would not. (p. 35)

Thus, construction of heterogeneous measures is a way to avoid the problem of construct underrepresentation in the measurement of high-referent generality constructs.

The other major threat to construct validity—namely, construct-irrelevant variance—appears to be a potential problem when a more or less homogenous test is used to measure a high-generality construct. For example, the Raven Progressive Matrices Test is often used to measure the G factor, but as was observed by Gustafsson (2002), the variance of this test is not only affected by the G factor, but also by a substantial amount of test-specific variance. In a similar fashion, construct-irrelevant variance is a problem when a homogeneous instrument is used to measure a low-generality construct, but in this situation it is the more general sources of variance that form the irrelevant sources of variance. Even though Thorndike (1951) primarily discussed threats to reliability, he made a similar observation.

Finally, we would like to emphasize that the arguments about the nature of the measurement put forward in this chapter are valid only within the framework of a particular kind of structural model of the observed phenomena. Thus, if the hierarchical model is rejected in favor of a more traditional oblique measurement model, our lines of reasoning cease to make sense. The idea that sources of variance of different degrees of generality may be separated is based on adoption of a hierarchical structural model and this, in turn, is related to choice of particular theoretical positions. Although these choices could be challenged, any alternative model must also be defended on theoretical grounds. Thus, in this sense, psychological measurement is both model based and theory based.

References

Åberg-Bengtsson, L. (1999). Dimensions of performance in the interpretation of diagrams, tables and maps: Some gender differences in the Swedish Scholastic Aptitude Test. *Journal of Research in Science Teaching, 36,* 565–582.

Åberg-Bengtsson, L. (2005). Separating the quantitative and analytic dimensions of the Swedish Scholastic Aptitude Test (SweSAT). *Scandinavian Journal of Educational Research, 49,* 359–383.

Binet, A., & Simon, T. (1916). *The development of intelligence in children.* Baltimore: Williams & Wilkins.

Bollen, K. A. (1989). *Structural equations with latent variables.* New York: Wiley.

Burt, C. (1949). The structure of the mind: A review of the results of factor analysis. *British Journal of Educational Psychology, 19,* 100–111, 176–199.

Carlstedt, B. (2001). Differentiation of cognitive abilities as a function of level of general intelligence: A latent variable approach. *Multivariate Behavioral Research, 36*(4), 586–609.

Carlstedt, B., & Gustafsson, J. E. (2005). Construct validation of the Swedish Scholastic Aptitude Test by means of the Swedish Enlistment Battery. *Scandinavian Journal of Psychology, 46*(1), 31–42.

Carroll, J. B. (1993). *Human cognitive abilities.* Cambridge, England: Cambridge University Press.

Cattell, R. B. (1963). Theory of fluid and crystallized intelligence: A critical experiment. *Journal of Educational Psychology, 54,* 1–22.

Coan, R. W. (1964). Facts, factors and artifacts: The quest for psychological meaning. *Psychological Review, 71,* 123–140.

Cureton, E. E. (1951). Validity. In E. F. Lindquist (Ed.), *Educational measurement* (pp. 621–694). Washington, DC: American Council on Education.

Gorsuch, R. L. (1983). *Factor analysis* (2nd ed.). Hillsdale, NJ: Erlbaum.

Guilford, J. P. (1967). *The nature of human intelligence.* New York: McGraw-Hill.

Gulliksen, H. (1950). *Theory of mental tests.* New York: Wiley.

Gustafsson, J. E. (1984). A unifying model for the structure of intellectual abilities. *Intelligence, 8,* 179–203.
Gustafsson, J. E. (1988). Hierarchical models of individual differences in cognitive abilities. In R. J. Sternberg (Ed.), *Advances in the psychology of human intelligence* (Vol. 4; pp. 35–71). Hillsdale, NJ: Erlbaum.
Gustafsson, J. E. (2002). Measurement from a hierarchical point of view. In H. I. Braun, D. N. Jackson, & D. E. Wiley (Eds.), *The role of constructs in psychological and educational measurement* (pp. 73–95). London: Erlbaum.
Gustafsson, J. E., & Balke, G. (1993). General and specific abilities as predictors of school achievement. *Multivariate Behavioral Research, 28,* 407–434.
Gustafsson, J. E., & Snow, R. E. (1997). Ability profiles. In R. F. Dillon (Ed.), *Handbook on testing* (pp. 107–135). Westport, CT: Greenwood Press.
Gustafsson, J. E., Wedman, I., & Westerlund, A. (1992). The dimensionality of the Swedish Scholastic Aptitude Test. *Scandinavian Journal of Educational Research, 36,* 21–39.
Hancock, G. R., & Mueller, R. O. (2001). Rethinking construct reliability within latent variable systems. In R. Cudeck, S. du Toit, & D. Sörbom (Eds.), *Structural equation modeling: Present and future—A festschrift in honor of Karl Jöreskog* (pp. 195–216). Lincolnwood, IL: Scientific Software International.
Holzinger, K. J., & Swineford, F. (1939). A study in factor analysis: The stability of a bi-factor solution. *Supplementary Educational Monographs* (No. 48). Chicago: University of Chicago, Department of Education.
Horn, J. L., & Cattell, R. B. (1966). Refinement and test of the theory of fluid and crystallized intelligence. *Journal of Educational Psychology, 57,* 253–270.
Humphreys, L. G. (1962). The organization of human abilities. *American Psychologist, 17,* 475–483.
Humphreys, L. G. (1985). General intelligence: An integration of factor, test and simplex theory. In B. B. Wolman (Ed.), *Handbook of intelligence: Theories, measurements and applications* (pp. 201–224). New York: Wiley.
Jensen, A. R. (1998). *The g factor: The science of mental ability.* Westport, CT: Praeger.
Jöreskog, K. G. (1971). Statistical analysis of sets of congeneric tests. *Psychometrika, 36,* 109–133.
Lindquist, E. F. (Ed.). (1951). *Educational measurement.* Washington, DC: American Council on Education.
Lord, F. M. (1980). *Applications of item response theory to practical testing problems.* Hillsdale, NJ: Erlbaum.
Lucke, J. F. (2005). The α and the ω of congeneric test theory: An extension of reliability and internal consistency to heterogeneous tests. *Applied Psychological Measurement, 29*(1), 65–81.
Mårdberg, B., & Carlstedt, B. (1998). Swedish Enlistment Battery (SEB): Construct validity and latent variable estimation and profile prediction of cognitive abilities by the CAT-SEB. *International Journal of Selection and Assessment, 6*(2), 107–114.
Messick, S. (1989). Validity. In R. L. Linn (Ed.). *Educational measurement* (3rd ed.; pp. 13–103). New York: Macmillan.
McDonald, R. P. (1999). *Test theory: A unified treatment.* Mahwah, NJ: Erlbaum.
Mulaik, S. A., & Quartetti, D. A. (1997). First order or higher order general factor? *Structural Equation Modeling, 4*(3), 193–211.
Raykov, T. (1997). Estimation of composite reliability for congeneric measures. *Applied Psychological Measurement, 21,* 173–184.
Raykov, T. (1998). Coefficient alpha and composite reliability with interrelated nonhomogeneous items. *Applied Psychological Measurement, 22,* 375–385.
Raykov, T., & Shrout, P. E. (2002). Reliability of scales with general structure: Point and interval estimation using a structural equation modeling approach. *Structural Equation Modeling, 9,* 195–212.
Roberts, R. D., Goff, G. N., Anjoul, F., Kyllonen, P. C., Pallier, G., & Stankov, L. (2000). The Armed Services Vocational Aptitude Battery (ASVAB): Little more than acculturated learning (Gc)!? *Learning and Individual Differences, 12,* 81–103.
Schmid, J., & Leiman, J. (1957). The development of hierarchical factor solutions. *Psychometrika, 22,* 53–61.
Spearman, C. (1927). *The abilities of man.* London: MacMillan.

Thorndike, R. L. (1951). Reliability. In E. F. Lindquist (Ed.), *Educational measurement* (pp. 560–620). Washington, D.C: American Council on Education.
Thurstone, L. L. (1938). Primary mental abilities. *Psychometric Monographs* (No. 1). Chicago: The University of Chicago Press.
Thurstone, L. L. (1947). *Multiple factor analysis.* Chicago: The University of Chicago Press.
Ullstadius, E., Gustafsson, J. E., & Carlstedt, B. (2002). Influence of general and crystallized intelligence on vocabulary test performance. *European Journal of Psychological Assessment, 18,* 78–84.
Undheim, J. O. (1981). On intelligence II: A neo-Spearman model to replace Cattell's theory of fluid and crystallized intelligence. *Scandinavian Journal of Psychology, 22,* 181–187.
Undheim, J. O., & Gustafsson, J. E. (1987). The hierarchical organization of cognitive abilities: Restoring general intelligence through the use of linear structural relations (LISREL). *Multivariate Behavioral Research, 22,* 149–171.
Yung, Y. F., McLeod, L. D., & Thissen, D. (1999). On the relationship between the higher order factor model and the hierarchical factor model. *Psychometrika, 64,* 113–128.

6

Using Item Response Theory to Disentangle Constructs at Different Levels of Generality

David Thissen and Lynne Steinberg

The measurement of individual differences on constructs that are not directly observable is a cornerstone of research in personality, social, and health psychology, as well as in educational measurement and the study of cognitive ability. Psychological constructs, or *latent variables* as they are called in statistics, may have different scopes or levels of generality. Statistical latent variable models help define the generality of constructs; the models and methods of item response theory (IRT) serve that function for test and questionnaire data.

In what may be the earliest published work that clearly defines in modern statistical terms the nature of IRT as a latent variable model, Lazarsfeld (1950) wrote the following:

> The practice of testing can be roughly described as follows: The investigator assumes that a one-dimensional continuum exists, such as soldier morale, anti-Semitism or intelligence. People are assumed to be arranged on this continuum in an unknown way. The persons are exposed to a series of test items.... The scoring system developed for a test always implies certain assumptions, however vague, about the relations between performance on the items and the hypothetical continuum. Because the "response patterns" of the people are obtained from actual experiments, we shall call them *manifest data;* all information inferred as to the nature of the continuum or the position of the people thereon we shall call *latent.* (p. 363)

The vintage of Lazarsfeld's (1950) prose and his sociological perspective are clearly revealed in his choice of examples ("soldier morale, anti-Semitism or intelligence"); he was writing for a volume on data collected about American soldiers during World War II. However, substitution of any cognitive proficiency or personality trait or state would work as well, and as we shall see, Lazarsfeld's writing has been prophetic for IRT.

We are grateful to Michael Edwards for his MCMC item factor analysis software and his assistance with its use. We thank Susan Embretson and James Roberts for suggestions that improved the presentation. Any errors that remain are, of course, our own.

Lazarsfeld (1950) went on to select an exemplary latent variable ("ethnocentrism"; denoted x) for purposes of discussion and described three illustrative items. Then he began his statistical statement of what he called *latent structure analysis* but that subsequently came to be known as *latent trait theory* and finally *item response theory:* Lazarsfeld wrote, "We assume that the probability y, that respondents check the first alternative in the ith question, is a function $f_i(x)$ of their position on the continuum x. The graphical picture of our functions $f_i(x)$ we shall call the trace line of item i" (p. 364). Contemporary notation uses θ for the latent variable instead of x, and $T(\theta)$ for the trace line instead of $f_i(x)$, but we quote Lazarsfeld directly here.

After some expansion on this idea, Lazarsfeld (1950) wrote out a thoroughly modern definition of the nature of the latent variable model:

> All ... considerations can ... be reduced to an analysis of the interrelations between the items.... We shall now call a *pure test* of a continuum x an aggregate of items which has the following properties: *All interrelationships between the items should be accounted for by the way in which each item alone is related to the latent continuum.* (p. 367)

Lazarsfeld followed this clear (verbal) definition with a number of disclaimers, about the fact that it is not necessary to have "pure tests," some tests may be multidimensional, and so on.

Following that, Lazarsfeld (1950) gave "this idea a mathematical formulation" with a statement of local or conditional independence.

> If a group of people has the same x-value—i.e., the same degree of ethnocentricity—then with ethnocentricity held constant, nothing else "holds the two questions together." Thus, for all people with any specific x-value, x_c we have a fourfold table like the following:

	Item 1 Endorse	Item 1 Do not Endorse	
Item 2 Endorse			p_2
Item 2 Do not Endorse			$1-p_2$
	p_1	$1-p_1$	

In a pure test, there is no association between responses to the two items; therefore, the entry within the upper left-hand box ... is equal to $p_1 \times p_2$. In terms of the trace lines, for any $x = x_c$, the probability of a joint positive answer is the product of the independent probabilities for the two items....

$f_{12}(x_c) = f_1(x_c) f_2(x_c)$ ... So we come to the following definition of a pure test: It is an aggregate of items such that the trace line for a joint positive answer to several items $i, j, k, \ldots$ is the product of the trace lines of every item taken separately.

(1.1) $\quad f_{ijk\ldots}(x) = f_i(x) f_j(x) f_k(x)\ldots$

In actual experience, of course, it can easily happen that equation (1.1) is not fulfilled. There might be a little detail in the wording of two questions that "ties them together" beyond what can be accounted for by the underlying continuum. Thus for people who have the same x-value, we would find that $f_{12}(x)$ is greater or less than $f_1(x) f_2(x)$. In this case, we usually say that there has entered an additional factor, that we do not have a pure measurement of the continuum x. (pp. 367–368)

Thus, the ideas of local independence, and then local dependence (LD), something that " 'ties [the questions] together' beyond what can be accounted for by the underlying continuum," were clearly presented by Lazarsfeld over 50 years ago. Indeed, without close ties to the psychometric factor analytic tradition, Lazarsfeld attributed LD to "an additional factor"; he probably did not mean to use that term in the sense of factor analysis, but that is nonetheless correct.

The topics of this chapter are the use of IRT in the presence of LD and the use of IRT to distinguish between LD—covariation between item responses that does not reflect consistency based on the underlying trait that is the intended dimension of measurement—and the dependence of all of the items on the underlying continuum one intends to measure.

Local Dependence and Local Independence

In contemporary notation, the model assuming local independence is that the trace line for the joint response to two items is the product of the trace lines

$$T(u_1, u_2 | \theta) = T(u_1 | \theta) T(u_2 | \theta) \quad (1)$$

in which $T(u_k | \theta)$ is the trace line for response k to an item, and $T(u_j, u_k | \theta)$ traces the likelihood over θ of the response pattern $\{u_j, u_k\}$. For locally dependent items, there is inequality:

$$T(u_1, u_2 | \theta) \neq T(u_1 | \theta) T(u_2 | \theta). \quad (2)$$

For example, Thissen and Steinberg (1988) described a set of four items (originally presented by Bergan & Stone, 1985) from a test of preschool mathematics: (a) Identify the numeral "3," (b) identify the numeral "4," (c) match the numeral 3 with three blocks, and (d) match the numeral 4 with four blocks. Not surprisingly, Thissen and Steinberg (1988; and subsequently Hoskens & De Boeck, 1997) observed that the data suggest that responses to the two "identifying" items are more correlated than is explained with a single unidimensional mathematics proficiency construct across the four items, as are the responses to the two "matching" items.

As another example, Steinberg and Thissen (1996) discussed a set of three items comprising a Recent Victimization Scale from a larger study examining risk factors for violence in a sample of adult men admitted to acute-care inpatient units at a large urban mental health center (Klassen & O'Connor, 1994).

Those three items are as follows:

> In the past 6 months, has anyone . . .
> Push: . . . pushed, shoved, or slapped you in an unfriendly way?
> Hit: . . . hit you with a fist or object of some sort?
> Weapon: . . . threatened to hurt, or actually hurt you with a gun, knife, or weapon?

Again, not unexpectedly, and reminiscent of Lazarsfeld's (1950) remark about something that "'ties [the questions] together' beyond what can be accounted for by the underlying continuum," responses to the Push and Hit items are more correlated than is well explained by a single latent variable underlying all three items.

Thissen, Steinberg, and Mooney (1989) described the analysis of a set of reading comprehension items on a verbal proficiency test for graduate admissions. The 22 items were administered in blocks of 7, 4, 3, and 8 items following four passages. Thissen et al. (1989) presented evidence from item factor analysis that there was some degree of LD induced by the passages.

What can IRT do with such sets of items? To answer that question, this chapter has three sections. The chapter begins with a description of ideas of local independence and LD, treating the topic historically, mathematically, and with examples. The second section (to follow immediately) describes some approaches to the detection of LD. The third section discusses alternative approaches to modeling tests that may contain locally dependent items. This has been done by redefining the item responses, by constructing special IRT models with interaction parameters to explicitly parameterize LD, and with the use of item factor analysis; examples accompany the discussion of all three approaches.

Detection of Local Dependence

One might hope to use item factor analysis to detect LD, following Lazarsfeld's (1950) suggestion that LD reflects the effects of an additional factor. However, in practice that is difficult with contemporary implementations of item factor analysis (using widely available software).

As an illustration of both the potential for the detection of LD and the difficulties of using item factor analysis for this purpose, consider the factor loadings in Table 6.1, which is a partial summary of factor loadings for items on the Cook-Medley Hostility Scale of the Minnesota Multiphasic Personality Inventory (MMPI). Table 6.1 shows a subset of the results reported by Steinberg and Jorgensen (1996): Only 24 of the 27 items are included in the table, and only the largest loading for each item is shown. Steinberg and Jorgensen (1996) obtained this solution using full-information item factor analysis and full-information maximum likelihood estimation (FIML), as implemented in the computer soft-

Table 6.1. Partial Summary of Factor Loadings for Items on the Cook-Medley Hostility Scale of the MMPI

Item	Factor 1	2	3	4	5
1	.75				
2	.60				
3	.56				
4	.47				
5	.46				
6	.38				
7	.34				
8	.33				
9	.33				
10		.32			
11		**.85**			
12		**.78**			
13			.65		
14			.59		
15			.46		
16			.39		
17			.39		
18			.36		
19				.81	
20				.62	
21				.51	
22				.39	
23					**.81**
24					**.57**

Note. Shown is a subset of the FIML results reported by Steinberg and Jorgensen. Only 24 of the 27 items are included in the table, and only the largest loading for each item is shown. Data from "Uses of item response theory and the testlet concept in the measurement of psychopathology" by L. Steinberg & D. Thissen, 1996, *Psychological Methods, 1,* 81–97. Copyright 1996 by American Psychological Association. FIML = full-information item factor analysis and maximum likelihood estimation; MMPI = Minnesota Multiphasic Personality Inventory.

ware Testfact (Wilson, Wood, & Gibbons, 1998). This method of analysis takes into account the dichotomous nature of the true–false MMPI responses by using a multidimensional normal ogive IRT model to fit the data. The loadings (partially) shown in Table 6.1 represent a promax-rotated exploratory factor solution with five factors. The Cook-Medley scale had been expected to show multidimensionality as several researchers (e.g., Barefoot, Dodge, Peterson, Dahlstrom, & Williams, 1989) have suggested categorizations of the item set. The pattern of factor loadings suggests three "conceptual" factors and two additional factors due to LD.

For example, Items 11 and 12 (as numbered in Table 6.1), "Most people will use somewhat unfair means to gain profit or an advantage rather than to lose it" and "I think most people would lie to get ahead" are "tied together" (in

Lazarsfeld's words) by the phrase "most people" followed by words to the effect that they would do evil to gain advantage. Those items are the only two items with particularly large loadings on Factor 2, but a factor specific to those items, although comprehensible, is probably not one of the underlying constructs that the scale is intended to measure.

As another example, consider Items 23 and 24 (as numbered in Table 6.1), "I don't blame people for trying to grab everything they can get in this world" and "I do not blame a person for taking advantage of people who leave themselves open to it." Again, there is some wording in common—"I do not blame," followed by some kind of taking advantage—another comprehensible factor but not an intended one.

In principle, one might expect to be able to use item factor analysis to detect the presence of such LD item pairs in general. However, the blank space in Table 6.1 represents a problem: estimation of the smaller loadings for each item on each factor other than that on which this item has its largest loading. To detect LD with exploratory factor analysis, each LD pair of items creates its own factor. In an exploratory solution, all of the other items also have estimated loadings for that factor. The factor loadings for the other items are expected to be random deviations from zero; however, the presence of all of those additional parameters in the model makes estimation more difficult for the entire parameter set. Only large samples are amenable to this factor analytic approach; Steinberg and Jorgensen (1996) used a sample of 1,138 male respondents to obtain the results partially shown in Table 6.1. Even so, if there are many instances of LD, the number of factors rises beyond the comfortable scope of FIML exploratory factor analysis.

As alternatives to item factor analysis, residual-based statistics for IRT have been developed to detect LD; among them are Yen's (1984) Q_3 statistic, Chen and Thissen's (1997) *LD* indices, and others. These statistics are based on a process that involves fitting a unidimensional IRT model to the data and then examining the residual covariation between pairs of items, which should be zero if the unidimensional model fits. Steinberg and Thissen (1996) described the use of Chen and Thissen's (1997) G^2 *LD* index to identify locally dependent items among 16 dichotomous items on a scale measuring history of violent activity. Although this approach is more practical than the use of item factor analysis to detect LD, computation of the relevant statistics has not yet been implemented in widely available software. The statistics themselves have not been formally generalized to items with more than two response categories. Both of these facts have limited the use of such statistics in practice, although we expect that both limitations will be removed in future IRT software.

For tests or questionnaires with relatively few items and Likert-type response scales, the modification indices (MIs) of structural equation modeling (SEM) software may also serve as statistics to detect LD. When interitem polychoric correlations are fitted with a one-factor model, the result is a limited information parameter estimation scheme for the graded normal ogive model. The MIs for such a model are one degree of freedom chi-square scaled statistics that suggest unmodeled excess covariation between items—in the context of item factor analysis that is LD.

As an example, consider the MIs in Table 6.2 obtained from data described by Hill et al. (2007) for the PedsQL™ Social Functioning Scale items:

In the past ONE month, how much of a problem has this been for you ...

1. I have trouble getting along with other kids
2. Other kids do not want to be my friend
3. Other kids tease me
4. I cannot do things that other kids my age can do
5. It is hard to keep up when I play with other kids

Responses to these items are on a Likert-type 5-point response scale ranging from 0 (*never a problem*) to 4 (*almost always a problem*). The MIs in Table 6.2 were obtained with the computer software Lisrel 8 (Jöreskog and Sörbom, 1996) and an English-speaking sample of children, with data obtained by parent-proxy report. Fitting a one-factor model to the polychoric correlations among those five items yielded a model with an overall goodness of fit, $\chi^2(5, N = 1{,}289) = 131$, $p < .0001$, RMSEA = .14, and RMR = .12; in other words, a poor fit. Table 6.2 shows a large MI for the pair of Items 4 and 5: 70, which is very large for a statistic distributed as $\chi^2(1)$ under the null hypothesis of no LD. Those items both involve performance: doing what other kids can do and keeping up with other kids. The other items are more social in nature. Analysis of other samples (child self-reports as opposed to parent proxy reports, data from adolescents, data from Spanish speaking children) consistently yielded high MIs for the same item pair on this scale.

In the context of these five items, the pair of Items 4 and 5 exhibits LD. As a matter of fact, there may be a factor that could usefully be measured if there were more items. Social aspects of health-related quality of life may usefully be differentiated into the measurement of the quality of social interaction separately from the measurement of performance. In this case, LD in one context may be a suggestion of an important construct in a broader context.

Hill et al. (2007) described similar examples for other items of the PedsQL™ scales, illustrating the usefulness of this approach for Likert-type scales with small numbers of items. Unfortunately, the weighted least squares estimation of the confirmatory factor model on which these results are based does not work well for larger numbers of items, and other solutions will be required.

Table 6.2. Modification Indices for One-Factor Model Fitted to Interitem Polychoric Correlations Among Items of the PedsQL Social Functioning Scale, Used as Indices of Local Dependence

Item	Modification indices			
	1	2	3	4
2	11			
3	1	24		
4	39	3	4	
5	36	23	15	70

Hill et al. (2007) also described how the IRT analysis itself may give clues about LD. Excessively high values of the slope parameter for a pair or triplet of items may indicate LD: The high slope values may indicate that the trait has come to be defined as the latent variable that explains the high covariance between those two items. As an example, consider results obtained with the PedsQL™ Physical Functioning Scale:

> In the past ONE month, how much of a problem has this been for you...
> 1. It is hard for me to walk more than one block
> 2. It is hard for me to run
> 3. It is hard for me to do sports activity or exercise
> 4. It is hard for me to lift something heavy
> 5. It is hard for me to take a bath or shower by myself
> 6. It is hard for me to do chores around the house
> 7. I hurt or ache
> 8. I have low energy

The left panel of Figure 6.1 shows the trace lines for Samejima's (1969, 1997) graded model fitted to Item 3, when the scale comprises Items 1–4 and

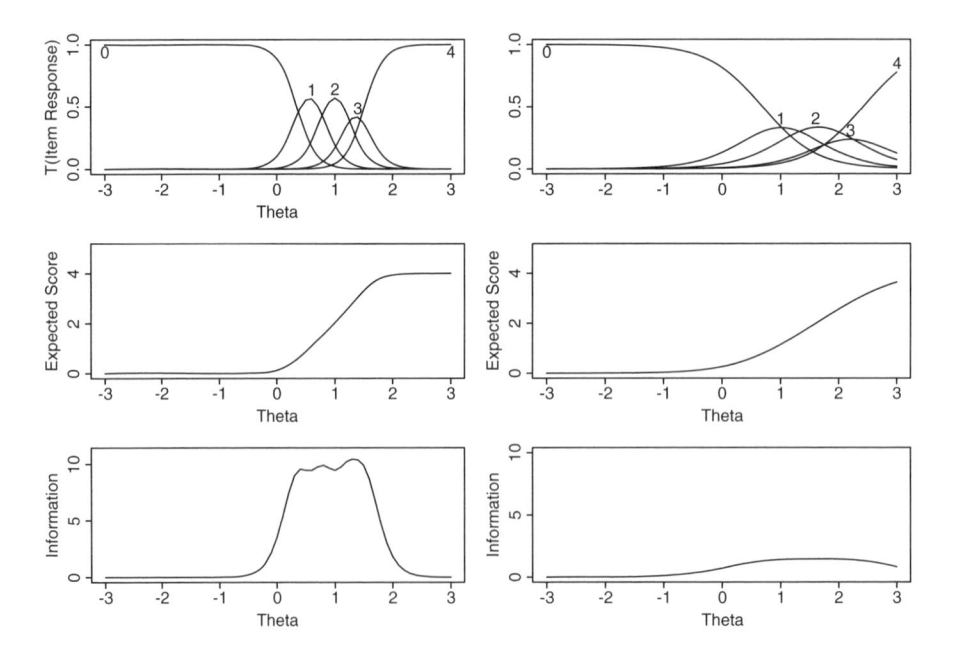

Figure 6.1. Top left: The trace lines for the graded model for Item 3 ("It is hard for me to do sports activity or exercise"; responses from 0 = *never a problem* to 4 = *almost always a problem*) of the PedsQL Physical Functioning Scale, when the scale comprises Items 1–4 and 6–8. Top right: The trace lines for Item 3 when the parameters of the model were estimated for the scale comprising Items 3-4-6-7-8. The expected score (0–4) and item information functions are in the center and lower panels, showing the consequences of higher (left) and lower (right) slope parameters.

6–8 (Item 5 was set aside because very few respondents indicated difficulty with bathing). As a matter of fact, Hill et al. (2007) noticed that Items 1, 2, and 3 all appeared to be very discriminating, whereas Items 4 and 6–had lower slope parameter estimates.

Suspecting that Items 1, 2, and 3 might be a locally dependent triplet on the basis of their very similar content, Hill et al. (2007) also estimated item parameters omitting each pair of those three items in turn, fitting reduced five-item scales as Items 1-4-6-7-8, 2-4-6-7-8, and 3-4-6-7-8. If the data had met the assumption of local independence, the result would have been essentially the same fitted trace lines for each item regardless of which of the other items are included in the analysis. However, the observed result was that when analyzed without the other two of the 1-2-3 triplet, each of the first three items was fitted with a much lower estimated slope, and the other four items were fitted with correspondingly higher slopes. The right panel of Figure 6.1 shows the fitted trace lines for Item 3 when the parameters of the model were estimated for the scale comprising Items 3-4-6-7-8, showing the much lower discrimination of Item 3 in that set.

The first analysis, yielding the trace lines shown in the left panel of Figure 6.1, is a classic example of "θ theft." Responses to the first three items (walking, running, and sports and exercise) are so highly related among themselves that when they are analyzed together θ becomes the latent variable that explains that covariance, and the other items' topics are relegated to second-class status. When only one of the first three items is included on the scale, θ becomes a latent variable that explains the covariation among a more varied set of physical activities, and the items are much more equally discriminating as indicators the respondent's position on that continuum.

After the fact, when data yield very high estimates of discrimination parameters for two or three items, LD (which means another factor for those items) may be suspected. However, it is not clear a priori how often LD may lead to high slope estimates, or θ theft. There is a limited literature that suggests that there can be any of a number of outcomes when unidimensional IRT models are fitted to multidimensional data. Reckase (1979) fitted the unidimensional three-parameter logistic model to a small number of multidimensional data sets and concluded that when there are several independent factors the model "picks one factor and discriminates among ability levels on it, while ignoring the other factors" (p. 226), whereas in situations that have a first factor that is large relative to the other factors, the model measures the first factor. Drasgow and Parsons (1983) and Harrison (1986) simulated multidimensional data using a second-order factor model with simple structure at the first level and found that when the contribution of the second-order general factor was large, that factor became θ for the IRT model; however, as the strength of the general factor decreased, the IRT model tended to measure the largest of the group factors. Working with multidimensional data from a model that involved items that measured more than one factor, Yen (1984) observed IRT analyses that made θ a composite of the underlying factors.

Because of the computational limitations of the 1970s and 1980s, the studies by Reckase (1979), Drasgow and Parsons (1983), Yen (1984), and Harrison (1986) used a very small number of example data sets with large numbers of items. They also obtained IRT parameter estimates obtained with the computer software LOGIST (Wingersky, Barton, & Lord, 1982), which implements an approach to estimation no longer in widespread use. Those studies did not establish clear general conditions under which an IRT analysis of multidimensional data might measure one general factor in the data, or one of the factors reflected by a subset of the items, or a composite of more than one factor. IRT analyses of smaller numbers of items using modern maximum marginal likelihood estimation, as was done with the PedsQL Physical Functioning Scale, has not been studied in simulation. So although there is anecdotal evidence, as previously described, that IRT analyses may reveal LD by exhibiting θ theft, it is not clear whether that happens often or rarely in the case of data with locally dependent item responses.

Modeling Tests With Local Dependence

At the end of the preceding section, we implicitly suggested omitting items from a scale as a method to deal with LD. That can always be done; if one item of an LD pair is omitted, the LD disappears, and if the scale is otherwise unidimensional, it becomes one for which local independence holds. However, in many situations, omitting items is not an attractive solution, and some strategy is desired that permits the use of standard unidimensional IRT models, with all of their attendant advantages and available software. One way to accomplish that goal is to combine pairs or triplets of items that exhibit LD into a single super item, or testlet, for purposes of item analysis and test scoring (Steinberg & Thissen, 1996; Thissen & Steinberg, 1988; Yen, 1993).

Redefining the "Item" Responses

As was mentioned in the introduction to this chapter, Thissen and Steinberg (1988) described a set of four items (originally presented by Bergan & Stone, 1985) from a test of preschool mathematics that exhibit LD in pairs. To fit data obtained with those items with an IRT model, we redefined the items as follows to construct two testlets:

- Redefined Item 1: Identify numerals 3 and 4
- Redefined Item 2: Match the correct numeral (again, 3 or 4) with a number of blocks.

For item analysis, the responses have been redefined: (a) correctly identify (match) neither 3 nor 4, (b) correctly identify (match) only 3, (c) correctly identify (match) only 4, and (d) correctly identify (match) both 3 and 4.

With the items so redefined, Thissen and Steinberg (1988) fitted the item response data with Bock's (1972, 1997) nominal model,

$$T(k) = \exp(a_k \theta + c_k) \bigg/ \sum_i \exp(a_i \theta + c_i) \qquad (3)$$

to obtain trace lines for each of the four response categories (k) for each (redefined) item, by estimating the sets of parameters denoted a_k and c_k. The estimated trace lines are shown in Figure 6.2. Note in the top panel of Figure 6.2, for the "identifying" item, the response categories are semiordered, with "identifying neither" and "identifying 3" both related to low levels of mathematics proficiency, "identifying 4" an intermediate response, and "identifying both" associated with high levels of mathematics proficiency. For the "matching" testlet, the patterns differ: "matching both" is associated with high levels of proficiency and all other responses indicate lower levels of knowledge.

The analysis of the "identify" and "match" items by Thissen and Steinberg (1988) previously described and the more theoretically elaborate investigation of these same data by Hoskens and De Boeck (1997) were intended to enhance our understanding of the latent structure underlying responses to those questions. However, in other contexts a testlet-based analysis of item sets with embedded LD may serve other purposes. There is a large literature on testlets, primarily in educational research, that addresses their use in test construction, especially for adaptive tests; their use to redefine items on measures of educational achievement so IRT can be used; and inaccuracies that may arise in the

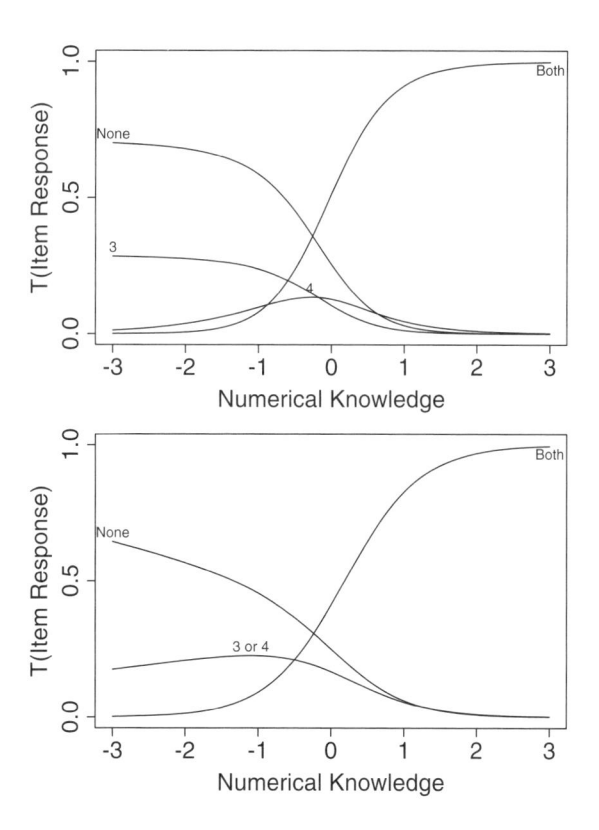

Figure 6.2. Nominal model trace lines for the response categories for redefined Item 1: Identify the numerals 3 and 4 (upper panel) and redefined Item 2: Match the correct numeral (again, 3 or 4) with a number of blocks (lower panel).

computation of reliability when LD is ignored and the "wrong" formulas for reliability are used (Lee, Brennan, & Frisbie, 2000; Sireci, Thissen, & Wainer, 1991; Wainer & Thissen, 1996). Testlet-based computations may correct the latter.

Figure 6.3 shows estimated trace lines (obtained with item parameters provided by Thissen et al., 1989) for the numbers of correct responses to multiple-choice items following reading passages on a reading comprehension test. The trace lines are those of Bock's (1972, 1997) nominal IRT model and show that larger numbers of correct responses are associated with higher levels of reading proficiency, and lower numbers of correct responses are associated with lower levels of proficiency, although less clearly in numerical order because of the effects of guessing on the number correct score. The primary motivation of the testlet-based analysis of the reading comprehension data was to obtain better estimates of the reliability of the test in the presence of LD induced by the passages.

With an example much more similar to the analysis of the "identifying" and "matching" items, Steinberg and Thissen (1996) described an analysis of three items composing a Recent Victimization Scale from a larger study examining risk factors for violence in a sample of adult men admitted to acute-care inpatient units at a large urban mental health center (Klassen & O'Connor, 1994):

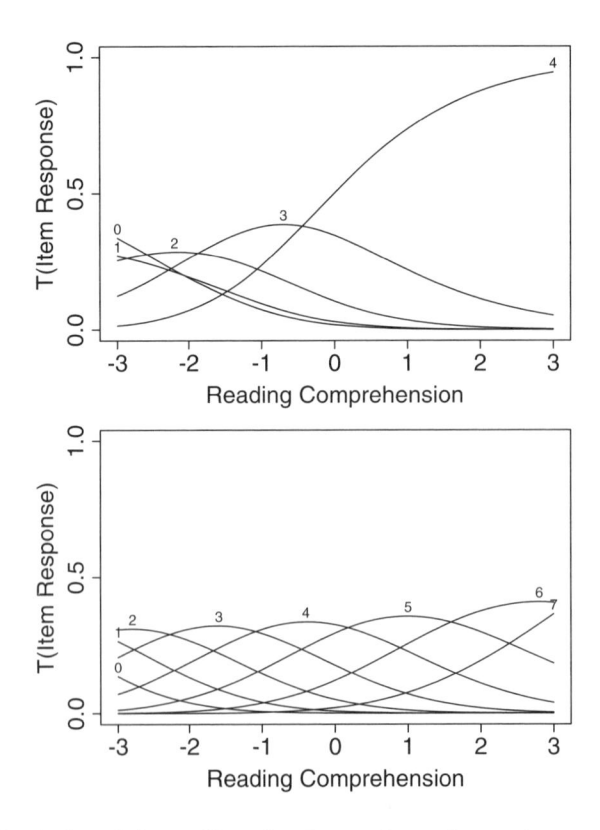

Figure 6.3. Nominal model trace lines for the numbers of correct responses to multiple-choice items following two reading passages on a reading comprehension test.

In the past 6 months, has anyone ... Push: ... pushed, shoved, or slapped you in an unfriendly way?
Hit: ... hit you with a fist or object of some sort?
Weapon: ... threatened to hurt, or actually hurt you with a gun, knife, or weapon?

Steinberg and Thissen (1996) combined the responses to the Push and Hit items into a new item with four response categories: "Neither Push nor Hit"; "Push but not Hit"; "Hit but not Push"; and "Both Push and Hit." Including the Weapon item, this creates a two-item test: The Weapon item remains dichotomous, and the combined Push–Hit testlet has four response categories.

When such a testlet is constructed, the main question for data analysis is: What is the scoring order of responses for the four-category item? Fitting the nominal IRT model serves to investigate the order of the four-response categories, in combination with the two-parameter logistic model for the Weapon item. Steinberg and Thissen (1996) described the investigation of category order and found that fitting with the nominal model suggested that the testlet's responses were approximately graded in the order that they are listed above. For simplicity, Steinberg and Thissen (1996) then fitted the data obtained with the testlet scoring with Samejima's (1969, 1997) graded model, which fits nearly as well as the nominal model.

Figure 6.4 shows that combining LD item responses into testlet scoring categories can have a good deal of effect on the implications that IRT suggests for a set of items. The upper left panel of Figure 6.4 shows the original two-parameter logistic trace lines for both positive and negative responses that were obtained fitting the three items, and the lower panel shows all eight (multiplicative) combinations of those trace lines (with the Gaussian population distribution) that are the "posterior densities" for each response pattern. The posterior densities are the theoretical distributions of respondents in the population who would select each response pattern, and the average of each of those densities is the expected a posteriori (EAP) IRT scale score for that response pattern. The densities in the left panel of Figure 6.4 are sharply divided between those for which the responses to the Push and Hit items are negative (00x) and those for which it is positive (11x); we note that combinations in which the responses are different for the Push and Hit items have relatively small posterior areas (proportions of the population, and so they are rare). The IRT analysis illustrated in the left panel of Figure 6.4 suggests "low versus high" scoring of the scale, with two fairly discrete groups.

In contrast, the right panel of Figure 6.4, showing the trace lines for the Weapon item as dichotomously scored and the Push and Hit items as a single graded testlet in the upper panel, has eight posterior densities in the lower panel that represent the same response patterns, in the approximately same proportions, as those in the left panel of Figure 6.4, but they are much different in shape. Instead of a near-dichotomy on the Push–Hit combination, as suggested by the analysis represented by the left panel, the results of the model shown in the right panel of Figure 6.4 suggest a much more continuously graded sequence of response patterns from low to high: Expressed as responses to the original {Push, Hit, Weapon} items the more popular response patterns are ordered {0,0,0}, {0,0,1}, {1,1,0} and {1,1,1} with posterior densities that overlap a good deal.

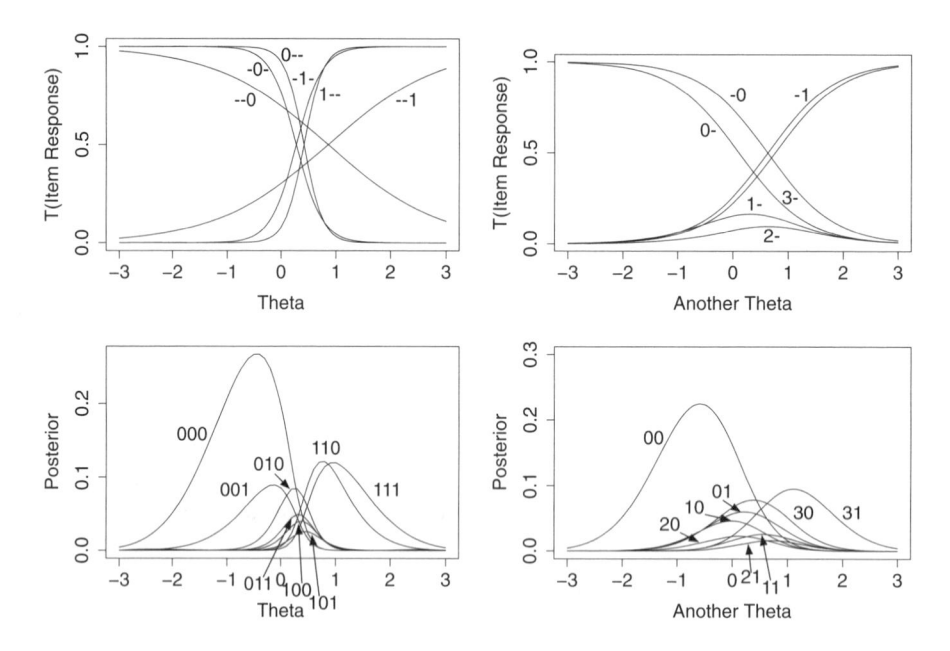

Figure 6.4. Left: The upper panel shows the two-parameter logistic trace lines for both positive and negative responses obtained fitting the three items: Push, Hit, and Weapon; the lower panel shows all eight (multiplicative) combinations of those trace lines (with the Gaussian population distribution) that are the posterior densities for each response pattern. Right: The upper panel shows the two-parameter logistic trace lines for both positive and negative responses the Weapon item with graded model trace lines for the response patterns for the Push and Hit items as a testlet; the lower panel shows all eight posterior densities. The first digit of each response pattern is 0–3 for the testlet response, and the second digit is 0–1 for the Weapon item response.

We conclude this section with the remarks that redefinition of the items into testlets can yield a conventional unidimensional IRT analysis that accommodates LD and that may provide more accurate estimates of measurement precision than may be obtained if LD is ignored. Scores obtained with the redefined items and the testlet model may be less distorted than scores that would be obtained fitting an IRT model that assumes local independence. What redefinition of the items does not do by itself is produce an item analysis at the individual item level. In the following section, we discuss models that can do that.

IRT Models With Interaction Parameters

Hoskens and De Boeck (1997) described a very flexible class of parametric models for LD that may arise from different response processes. They began their explanation with reference to the one-parameter logistic model, parameterized as

$$T(u_i|\theta) = \frac{\exp[u_i(\alpha\theta - \beta_i)]}{1 + \exp[(\alpha\theta - \beta_i)]} \quad (4)$$

in which u is the item response to item I; α and β are the discrimination parameter (equal for all items) and the difficulty parameter, respectively; and θ is the latent variable being measured.

Proceeding with their analysis, Hoskens and De Boeck (1997) described a class of models for a pair of items exhibiting LD; for their models, Table 6.3 shows the log odds of each pair of responses to {0,0}, for one-parameter logistic trace lines with "interaction?" appended for two of the response patterns, to stand in for additional terms that are included for LD induced by different processes. Hoskens and De Boeck distinguished between *order* and *combination* dependencies, where order dependencies arise when an item's response is influenced by the response to an earlier item, and combination dependency is their term for symmetrical, mutual effects on both item responses (separately from the trait being measured). Crossed with that distinction, Hoskens and De Boeck also distinguished between *constant* effects (that are independent of θ) and *dimension-dependent* effects that are functions of θ (linear, in their models).

Each of the four combinations of order versus combination dependency with constant versus dimension-dependent effects produces a different set of replacements for the term labeled "interaction?" in Table 6.3; the interested reader is referred to Hoskens and De Boeck (1997) for the fairly involved details. In some cases Hoskens and De Boeck's models require specialized procedures for parameter estimation. However, it is interesting to note that some of their models are algebraically equivalent to redefining the response patterns to a pair of items as a response-pattern testlet and fitting each response pattern as a response category with Bock's (1972, 1997) nominal model as we did in the previous section. Indeed, Hoskens and De Boeck do just that with the data from the "Match" and "Identify" 3 and 4 items described in the previous section, providing a thorough theoretical analysis for a procedure that had been entirely data analytic in origin.

Hoskens and De Boeck generalized their models from the one-parameter logistic to the two-parameter logistic, but the generalized models resist the simple tabulation shown in Table 6.3. Their analysis brings consideration of

Table 6.3. Log Odds of Each Pair of Responses to {0,0}, for One-Parameter Logistic Trace Lines with "Interaction?" Appended for Two of the Response Patterns, to Stand in for Additional Terms That Appear in Models Described by Hoskens and De Boeck (1997)

Response pattern	Log odds of each pair of responses to {0,0}
{0,0}	$\ln\left[\dfrac{T(0,0\|\theta)}{T(0,0\|\theta)}\right] = 0$
{1,0}	$\ln\left[\dfrac{T(1,0\|\theta)}{T(0,0\|\theta)}\right] = (\alpha\theta - \beta_1) + \text{interaction?}$
{0,1}	$\ln\left[\dfrac{T(0,1\|\theta)}{T(0,0\|\theta)}\right] = (\alpha\theta - \beta_2)$
{1,1}	$\ln\left[\dfrac{T(1,1\|\theta)}{T(0,0\|\theta)}\right] = (\alpha\theta - \beta_1) + (\alpha\theta - \beta_2) + \text{interaction?}$

LD in item responses much closer to integration with contemporary cognitive psychology, which is a very promising step for psychometrics.

Approaching the modeling problem from a different perspective, with a different goal, Bradlow, Wainer, and Wang (1999) suggested a modification of the normal ogive IRT model,

$$T(u_{ij}|\theta) = \Phi(z_{ij}), \quad (5)$$

with the addition of a random interaction parameter $\gamma_{id(j)}$ that varies over persons i for each testlet $d_{(j)}$ with which item j is associated, so that the expression for the item response function includes proficiency (θ), slope and discrimination parameters, and the random interaction parameter $\gamma_{id(j)}$:

$$z_{ij} = a_j(\theta_i - b_j - \gamma_{id(j)}) \quad (6)$$

In this model, the parameter $\gamma_{id(j)}$ is a random variable over persons, like θ. $\gamma_{id(j)}$ is defined to have a mean of zero; only its variance (for each testlet) is an estimated parameter. If the variance of $\gamma_{id(j)}$ is zero, there is no LD and the model is for locally independent items. As the variance increases, the model describes increasing LD among the items. This model has subsequently been generalized for graded items and dichotomously scored multiple-choice items (Wainer, Bradlow, & Du, 2000; Wang, Bradlow, & Wainer, 2002).

The main goal Bradlow, Wainer, and Wang (1999) specified for their model was the accurate computation of standard errors in the presence of LD, which can lead to underestimates of standard errors if the LD is ignored (Wainer & Thissen, 1996). However, there are other conceptual advantages associated with this model as well: The Bradlow-Wainer-Wang model is, as a matter of fact, a highly restricted item factor analysis, or multidimensional IRT (MIRT) model. If the expression

$$z_{ij} = a_j(\theta_i - b_j - \gamma_{id(j)}) \quad (7)$$

is expanded by distributing the slope parameter, we obtain

$$z_{ij} = a_j\theta_i - a_jb_j - a_j\gamma_{id(j)}. \quad (8)$$

If we then relabel the random $\gamma_{id(j)}$ parameter $\theta_{d(j)}$, we have a bifactor model with intercept $d_j = a_jb_j$ and additional θs for each testlet $\gamma_{id(j)}$

$$z_{ij} = a_j\theta_{i1} - a_j\theta_{id(j)} - d_j. \quad (9)$$

Table 6.4 shows the constrained bifactor model parameters for 10 hypothetical items in three testlets, showing the Bradlow-Wainer-Wang model expressed as a restricted item factor analysis model, with the variance of the testlet-specific θs (the $\gamma_{id(j)}$'s) estimated. We note that this is a highly restricted MIRT model, with the slope parameter for each item for its testlet-specific factor constrained to be equal to its slope parameter for the general factor. (The negative sign on the testlet-specific slopes is an arbitrary consequence of the arbitrary

Table 6.4. Constrained Bifactor Model Parameters for a Hypothetical 10 Items in Three Testlets, Showing the Bradlow–Wainer–Wang Model Expressed as a Restricted Item Factor Analysis Model, With the Variance of the Testlet-Specific θs (the $\gamma_{id(j)}$s) Estimated

	Slope parameters			Intercepts
a_{11}	$-a_{11}$	0	0	d_1
a_{21}	$-a_{21}$	0	0	d_2
a_{31}	$-a_{31}$	0	0	d_3
a_{41}	$-a_{41}$	0	0	d_4
a_{51}	0	$-a_{51}$	0	d_5
a_{61}	0	$-a_{61}$	0	d_6
a_{71}	0	$-a_{71}$	0	d_7
a_{81}	0	0	$-a_{81}$	d_8
a_{91}	0	0	$-a_{91}$	d_9
a_{101}	0	0	$-a_{101}$	d_{10}

sign of $\gamma_{id(j)}$ in the original parameterization. The combination of the apparently equal factor loadings for the group factors in Table 6.4 with estimated factor variances is actually a set of proportionality constraints [for the factor loadings in a model with all factor variances equal to 1.0] as described by Yung, McLeod, & Thissen, 1999, in their explication of the relationship between the bifactor model and second-order factor analysis. The combination of the algebra previously shown with the proofs provided by Yung et al. show that the Bradlow-Wainer-Wang model is actually reparameterized second-order factor analysis.)

Table 6.5 shows general bifactor model parameters for 10 hypothetical items in three testlets, as might be estimated using the algorithm described by

Table 6.5. General Bifactor Model Parameters for a Hypothetical 10 Items in Three Testlets, as Might Be Estimated Using the Algorithm Described by Gibbons and Hedker (1992) and Implemented in Testfact (Wilson et al., 1998)

	Slope parameters			Intercepts
a_{11}	a_{12}	0	0	d_1
a_{21}	a_{22}	0	0	d_2
a_{31}	a_{32}	0	0	d_3
a_{41}	a_{42}	0	0	d_4
a_{51}	0	a_{53}	0	d_5
a_{61}	0	a_{63}	0	d_6
a_{71}	0	a_{73}	0	d_7
a_{81}	0	0	a_{84}	d_8
a_{91}	0	0	a_{94}	d_9
a_{101}	0	0	a_{104}	d_{10}

Note. In this case, the testlet-specific slopes are estimated and the correlation matrix among the factors is **R** = **I**.

Gibbons and Hedeker (1992) and implemented in Testfact (Wilson, Wood, & Gibbons, 1998). In this case, the testlet-specific slopes are estimated and the correlation matrix among the factors is $\mathbf{R} = \mathbf{I}$. Comparison of Tables 6.4 and 6.5 and reference to the proofs provided by Yung et al. (1999) show that the Bradlow-Wainer-Wang model is hierarchically nested within the more general item bifactor model, indicating that both are mathematical models for the "additional factor" that Lazarsfeld (1950) suggested induces LD.

Multidimensional Models

Full information item factor analysis, or equivalently maximum marginal likelihood estimation for MIRT, was available only in its original exploratory form when Thissen et al. (1989) made use of the technique to examine the degree to which passages induced LD on the reading comprehension test mentioned in the introduction to this chapter. That analysis involved an oblique rotation of a four-factor exploratory solution using item response data for 22 items that were administered in blocks of 7, 4, 3, and 8 following four passages. The factor analytic results suggested correlated factors somewhat aligned with the passage structure, but the correspondence was not perfect.

Gibbons and Hedeker's (1992) algorithm for FIML bifactor analysis has subsequently been added to the computer software Testfact (Wilson, Wood, & Gibbons, 1998). As we showed in the immediately preceding section of this chapter, bifactor analysis is an obvious and straightforwardly interpretable method to investigate the degree of LD within clusters of items. As a concrete illustration, Table 6.6 shows the bifactor three-parameter normal ogive MIRT model slope parameter estimates obtained with FIML for the data obtained with the set of reading comprehension items described by Thissen et al. (1989). The 22 items were administered in blocks of 7, 4, 3, and 8 following four passages; those passage-based groups of items determined the structure of the passage specific factors (Factors 2–5) in the analysis.

Although it is reasonably clear to those familiar with IRT (and MIRT) that many of the slope parameters in Table 6.6 on the passage-specific factors are rather large, the current implementation of the ML estimation algorithm does not provide statistical tests of the null hypotheses that individual loadings on the passage specific factors are zero. (Nonzero loadings on passage specific factors indicate LD. One can obtain an omnibus likelihood ratio test for the null hypothesis that the loadings on the passage specific factors are zero in aggregate, but that is not entirely what is desired.)

Using the alternative Markov chain Monte Carlo (MCMC) approach to estimation for confirmatory item factor analysis, Edwards (2005) implemented Bayesian estimation for a number of models, including the bifactor three-parameter normal ogive MIRT model. Table 6.6 also shows the bifactor three-parameter normal ogive MIRT model slope parameter estimates obtained with MCMC for the same data. Comparing the ML and MCMC entries in Table 6.6, we first note that the two methods (ML and MCMC) yield very similar param-

Table 6.6. Bifactor Three-Parameter Normal Ogive MIRT Model FIML and MCMC Slope Parameter Estimates for Data Obtained With Passage-based Reading Comprehension Items

Passage/ Item	Factor 1 ML	1 MCMC	2 ML	2 MCMC	3 ML	3 MCMC	4 ML	4 MCMC	5 ML	5 MCMC
I / 1	0.52	0.56	0.34	*0.20*						
I / 2	0.31	0.32	0.21	*0.12*						
I / 3	0.66	0.67	0.39	*0.23*						
I / 4	0.77	0.80	0.18	*0.13*						
I / 5	0.39	0.44	0.46	*0.64*						
I / 6	0.46	0.49	0.32	0.45						
I / 7	0.45	0.46	0.19	0.29						
II / 8	0.50	0.51			0.40	0.40				
II / 9	1.08	1.02			1.53	1.41				
II / 10	0.78	0.79			0.58	0.59				
II / 11	0.73	0.75			0.76	0.79				
III / 12	0.76	0.99					0.44	*0.88*		
III / 13	0.85	0.87					0.39	*0.30*		
III / 14	0.46	0.54					0.21	*0.34*		
IV / 15	0.54	0.54							0.15	0.16
IV / 16	0.71	0.71							0.05	*0.09*
IV / 17	0.79	0.77							−.09	*0.04*
IV / 18	0.94	1.00							0.73	0.86
IV / 19	0.48	0.48							0.34	0.36
IV / 20	0.54	0.55							0.31	0.32
IV / 21	0.49	0.50							0.27	0.26
IV / 22	0.76	0.76							0.46	0.48

Note. The 22 items were administered in blocks of 7, 4, 3, and 8 following four passages. MCMC slope estimates printed in italics are within two posterior standard deviations of zero. Slope estimates that are constrained to be zero are omitted from the table. MIRT = multidimensional item response theory; ML = maximum likelihood; MCMC = Markov chain Monte Carlo.

eter estimates.[1] Going beyond that, by its nature MCMC estimation produces a description of the entire Bayesian posterior distribution for each parameter estimate. Slope estimates printed in italics in Table 6.6 are within two posterior standard deviations of zero; using a Bayesian analog of significance testing, we may state that we are not confident that those parameters exceed zero.

---

[1]Edwards's (2005) implementation of MCMC estimation for restricted item factor analysis simultaneously estimates all of the parameters of the three-parameter normal ogive model—the slopes, the intercepts, and the so-called guessing or lower asymptote parameters. The FIML implementation of bifactor analysis in Testfact does not estimate the lower asymptote parameters. To make the comparison between the results in Table 6.6 as direct as possible, the MCMC estimates of the lower asymptote parameters were supplied as fixed values for the ML estimation.

Concluding Comments

Conventional IRT models assume local independence. There are many indicators of LD. Some are specifically designed indices, such as Yen's (1984) Q_3 statistic, Chen and Thissen's (1997) *LD* indices, and some are generic statistics that can be used to detect LD, such as the modification indices provided by SEM software. Others are patterns a skilled data analyst might notice, such as a pair or triplet of items that appear to be more discriminating than an experienced data analyst might expect, and further have content in common. Models designed to parameterize LD may be used in situations in which the design of the test or scale suggests a priori among which items LD may occur.[2] None of these approaches are universally applicable, but sensitivity in data analysis can usually detect LD when it occurs.

There are many solutions to LD that permit IRT analysis of the test or scale. Omission of items, redefining the item responses for use with multicategory models, and explicit models of the dependence are among them.

The presence of LD implies (at some level) another factor, which leads to an interesting question: Is the factor to be measured or considered to be at a lower hierarchical level than the target trait to be measured? In some cases, we have considered it obvious that the LD factors are a nuisance; examples are the following:

- passage factors on reading comprehension tests,
- identification of numerals versus matching numerals,
- "Pushing" and "Hitting," and
- MMPI "use unfair means to gain advantage" and "lie to get ahead."

In other cases, LD may be a clue that there is some interesting factor that deserves measurement but that is represented in some minority amount on the test or questionnaire. For example, as discussed in a previous section of this chapter, on the five-item PedsQL™ Social Functioning Scale, the two items about "do things other kids can do" and "hard to keep up with other kids" exhibited LD. However, subsequent analyses have indicated that those two "performance" items are negatively related to healthiness, whereas the other three items on "getting along with other kids" are positively related with health. Overall, we have indications of two factors of Social Functioning in quality of life and a suggestion to measure both—in this case what appeared at first to be LD has developed into a factor of interest.

The quest for methods to detect or identify LD is by no means over. Future directions for research would certainly include the development of improved LD indices that can be used with larger numbers of items with multiple response categories (as with 5-point Likert-type scales). In addition, explicit modeling of LD, permitting unidimensional scoring on the target dimension with corrected estimates of precision, is in its relative infancy. The Bradlow, Wainer, and Wang

---

[2]There are also procedures intended to detect multidimensionality in test items that are not based on latent variable or IRT models, such as those implemented in the computer software DETECT (Zhang & Stout, 1999a, 1999b) and DIMTEST (Nandakumar & Stout, 1993; Stout, 1987).

(1999) and Gibbons and Hedeker (1992) models do that, but only a range of models is possible. Either FIML or MCMC estimation techniques may provide a basis for parameter estimation and scoring with additional models. Increased use of IRT in the measurement of personality and health outcomes will intensify demand for such techniques. Neither personality measurement nor the measurement of health outcomes has the inexhaustible supply of items that are a matter of principle in, say, the construction of mathematics or reading comprehension tests. As a result, scales comprising a relatively few items must often be modeled and used as they are. Such scales may contain LD, and to use IRT to its fullest potential, that LD must be modeled and accounted for. This chapter has summarized some of 2 decades' efforts toward that end, but there remains work for the future in this aspect of model-based measurement.

References

Barefoot, J. C., Dodge, K. A., Peterson, B. L., Dahlstrom, W. F., & Williams, R. B., Jr. (1989). The Cook-Medley Hostility Scale: Item content and ability to predict survival. *Psychosomatic Medicine, 51,* 46–57.

Bergan, J. R., & Stone, C. A. (1985). Latent class models for knowledge domains. *Psychological Bulletin, 98,* 166–184.

Bock, R. D. (1972). Estimating item parameters and latent ability when responses are scored in two or more latent categories. *Psychometrika, 37,* 29–51.

Bock, R. D. (1997). The nominal categories model. In W. van der Linden & R. K. Hambleton (Eds.), *Handbook of modern item response theory* (pp. 33–50). New York: Springer.

Bradlow, E. T., Wainer, H., & Wang, X. (1999). A Bayesian random effects model for testlets. *Psychometrika, 64,* 153–168.

Chen, W. H., & Thissen, D. (1997). Local dependence indices for item pairs using item response theory. *Journal of Educational and Behavioral Statistics, 22,* 265–289.

Drasgow, F., & Parsons, C. K. (1983). Application of unidimensional item response theory models to multidimensional data. *Applied Psychological Measurement, 7,* 189–199.

Edwards, M. C. (2005). *A Markov chain Monte Carlo approach to confirmatory item factor analysis.* Unpublished doctoral dissertation, University of North Carolina at Chapel Hill.

Gibbons, R. D., & Hedeker, D. R. (1992). Full-information item bi-factor analysis. *Psychometrika, 57,* 423–436.

Harrison, D. A. (1986). Robustness of IRT parameter estimation to violations of the unidimensionality assumption. *Journal of Educational Statistics, 11,* 91–115.

Hill, C. D., Edwards, M. C., Thissen, D., Langer, M. M., Wirth, R. J., Burwinkle, T. M., & Varni, J. W. (2007). Practical issues in the application of item response theory: A demonstration using the Pediatric Quality of Life Inventory (PedsQL) 4.0 Generic Core Scales. *Medical Care, 45,* S39–S47

Hoskens, M., & De Boeck, P. (1997). A parametric model for local dependence among test items. *Psychological Methods, 21,* 261–277.

Jöreskog, K. G., & Sörbom, D. (1996). *Lisrel 8: User's reference guide.* Chicago, IL: Scientific Software International.

Klassen, D., & O'Connor, W. A. (1994). *A model for violence risk assessment: Situational, developmental, and demographic predictors.* Unpublished manuscript.

Lazarsfeld, P. F. (1950). The logical and mathematical foundation of latent structure analysis. In S. A. Stouffer, L. Guttman, E. A. Suchman, P. F. Lazarsfeld, S. A. Star, & J. A. Clausen (Eds.), *Measurement and prediction* (pp. 362–412). New York: Wiley.

Lee, G., Brennan, R. L., & Frisbie, D. A. (2000). Incorporating the testlet concept in test score analyses. *Educational Measurement: Issues and Practice, 19,* 9–15.

Nandakumar, R., & Stout, W. F. (1993). Refinements of Stout's procedure for assessing latent trait multidimensionaltiy. *Journal of Educational Statistics, 18,* 41–68.

Reckase, M. D. (1979). Unifactor latent trait models applied to multifactor tests: Results and implications. *Journal of Educational Statistics, 4,* 207–230.
Samejima, F. (1969). Estimation of latent ability using a response pattern of graded scores. *Psychometrika Monograph Supplement, 34,* 100–114.
Samejima, F. (1997). Graded response model. In W. van der Linden & R. K. Hambleton (Eds.), *Handbook of modern item response theory* (pp. 85–100). New York: Springer.
Sireci, S. G., Thissen, D., & Wainer, H. (1991). On the reliability of testlet-based tests. *Journal of Educational Measurement, 28,* 237–247.
Steinberg, L., & Jorgensen, R. (1996). Assessing the MMPI-based Cook-Medley Hostility scale: The implications of dimensionality. *Journal of Personality and Social Psychology, 70,* 1281–1287.
Steinberg, L., & Thissen, D. (1996). Uses of item response theory and the testlet concept in the measurement of psychopathology, *Psychological Methods, 1,* 81–97.
Stout, W. (1987). A nonparametric approach for assessing latent trait unidimensionality. *Psychometrika, 52,* 589–617.
Thissen, D., & Steinberg, L. (1988). Data analysis using item response theory. *Psychological Bulletin, 104,* 385–395.
Thissen, D., Steinberg, L., & Mooney, J. A. (1989). Trace lines for testlets: A use of multiple-categorical-response models. *Journal of Educational Measurement 26,* 247–260.
Wainer, H., Bradlow, E. T., & Du, Z. (2000). Testlet response theory: An analog for the 3PL model useful in testlet-based adaptive testing. In W. J. van der Linden & C. A. W. Glas (Eds.), *Computerized adaptive testing: Theory and practice* (pp. 245–269). Dordrecht, The Netherlands: Kluwer Academic.
Wainer, H., & Thissen, D. (1996). How is reliability related to the quality of test scores? What is the effect of local dependence on reliability? *Educational Measurement: Issues and Practice, 15,* 22–29.
Wang, X., Bradlow, E. T., & Wainer, H. (2002). A general Bayesian model for testlets: Theory and applications. *Applied Psychological Measurement, 26,* 109–128.
Wilson, D. T., Wood, R., & Gibbons, R. (1998). *Testfact: Test scoring, item statistics, and item factor analysis.* Chicago, IL: Scientific Software International.
Wingersky, M. S., Barton, M., & Lord, F. M. (1982). *LOGIST user's guide.* Princeton, NJ: Educational Testing Service.
Yen, W. M. (1984). Effects of local item dependence on the fit and equating performance of the three-parameter logistic model. *Applied Psychological Measurement, 8,* 125–145.
Yen, W. M. (1993). *Scaling performance assessments: Strategies for managing local item dependence. Journal of Educational Measurement, 30,* 187–214.
Yung, Y. F., McLeod, L. D., & Thissen, D. (1999). On the relationship between the higher-order factor model and the hierarchical factor model. *Psychometrika, 64,* 113–128.
Zhang, J., & Stout, W. F. (1999a). Conditional covariance structure of generalized compensatory multidimensional items. *Psychometrika, 64,* 129–152.
Zhang, J., & Stout, W. F. (1999b). The theoretical Detect index of dimensionality and its application to approximate simple structure. *Psychometrika, 64,* 213–249.

Part III

Model-Based Approaches for Measuring Personality, Psychopathology, and Attitudes From Self-Reports

7

Measuring Psychopathology With Nonstandard Item Response Theory Models: Fitting the Four-Parameter Model to the Minnesota Multiphasic Personality Inventory

Niels G. Waller and Steven P. Reise

Researchers working with psychopathology and personality data[1] are showing increased interest in item response theory (IRT; Bock, 1997; Embretson & Reise, 2000; Hambleton & Swaminathan, 1985) for model-based psychological assessment (Reise, 1999; Reise & Waller, 1990; Reis & Waller, 2001; Steinberg & Thissen, 1995, 1996; Waller, 1999; Waller & Reise, 1989, 1992; Waller, Tellegen, McDonald, & Lykken, 1996). During the past 25 years the one-, two-, and three-parameter logistic models for binary item responses (1PLM; 2PLM; 3PLM; Birnbaum, 1968) have dominated work in this area. More recently, graded response models, nonparametric item response models, and models for multidimensional data (Chernyshenko, Stark, Chan, Drasgow, & Williams, 2001; Ferrando, 2004; Meijer & Baneke, 2004; Junker & Sijtsma, 2001; Santor, Ramsay, & Zuroff, 1994; Wang, Chen, & Cheng, 2004) have also been applied in this domain.

In this chapter we discuss the application of the four-parameter logistic model (4PLM; Barton & Lord, 1981) to psychopathology data. The 4PLM is a relatively old model for binary item responses that has been largely ignored for the past 25 years (although see Hessen, 2004, for a four-parameter, constant discrimination model). An important reason for this neglect is that the original application of the model (Barton & Lord, 1981) to achievement and aptitude data produced disappointing results. Consequently, researchers came to believe that the inclusion of a fourth parameter—a parameter that would allow the

---

Preparation of this paper was supported by the National Institutes of Health (NIH) through the NIH Roadmap for Medical Research Grant (AG015815) and the NIH Roadmap Initiative (P20 RR020750). We thank Dr. Eric Loken for helpful suggestions on estimating the 4PLM via the Gibbs sampler. We also thank Drs. Loken and David Rindskopf for helpful suggestions that improved the clarity of our presentation.

[1] For brevity, in the remainder of this chapter, we use the phrase *psychopathology data* to refer to both psychopathology and personality data.

upper asymptote of the item response function (IRF) to fall below 1.00—was not needed.

Several years ago (Reise & Waller, 2003), in an article that has been credited with reviving interest in the 4PLM (Loken & Rulison, 2006), we suggested that the 4PLM may be uniquely suited for characterizing psychopathology data. In this chapter, we follow up on that idea and show how Bayesian methods using Markov chain Monte Carlo techniques (MCMC; Albert, 1992; Albert & Chib, 1993; Patz & Junker, 1999) can be used to fit the 4PLM to data from the Minnesota Multiphasic Personality Inventory–Adolescent form (MMPI-A; Butcher et al., 1992). The MMPI-A, with its large and heterogeneous pool of item content, is one of the most widely used inventories for psychopathology assessment (Archer & Newsom, 2000; Lees-Haley, Smith, Williams, & Dunn, 1996; Piotrowski & Keller, 1989), and as such it represents an ideal vehicle for investigating the utility of the 4PLM with typical performance data.

We begin the chapter with a brief review of standard IRT models for binary item responses. This material serves as a prelude to our discussion of the 4PLM. Next, we summarize previous attempts to apply IRT to MMPI data and then describe the MMPI-A Low Self-Esteem (LSE) scale (first described in Reise & Waller, 2003) that we use in our illustrations. Using data from 14,843 adolescent boys who completed the LSE while taking the MMPI-A, we next show how nonparametric item response functions can provide suggestive evidence that the 4PLM is needed to characterize psychopathology data. Finally, using a subset of these data, we fit the 4PLM to the LSE scale using MCMC simulations (Albert, 1992; Albert & Chib, 1993; Patz & Junker, 1999). We conclude the chapter by offering some tentative ideas about the interpretation of IRT item parameters in psychopathology data.

Standard Item Response Models for Binary Items

Most readers of this book will be familiar with the models that are described in this section: the one-, two-, and three-parameter logistic models for binary item responses. Persons desiring more information can consult one or more of the excellent introductions to IRT that are available (Embretson & Reise, 2000; Hambleton & Swaminathan, 1985; Hambleton, Swaminathan, & Rogers, 1991; van der Linden & Hambleton, 1997). In this section our modest goal is to briefly review these models to set the stage for our later discussion of the 4PLM.

All models in this chapter assume that a single latent trait underlies performance differences on a psychological scale. Following tradition, we use θ_i to denote the latent trait value for individual i. The one-, two-, and three-parameter logistic models include one-, two-, or three-item parameters to characterize the nonlinear regression of an item response (u) on θ. This nonlinear regression function is called an Item Response Function (IRF). IRFs for the three models can be written as follows:

$$1\text{PLM} \qquad P(u_{ij}=1|\theta_i, b_j) = \frac{1}{1+e^{-D(\theta_i - b_j)}} \qquad (1)$$

$$\text{2PLM} \quad P(u_{ij}=1|\theta_i,a_j,b_j) = \frac{1}{1+e^{-Da_j(\theta_i-b_j)}} \quad (2)$$

$$\text{3PLM} \quad P(u_{ij}=1|\theta_i,a_j,b_j,c_j) = c_j + (1-c_j)\frac{1}{1+e^{-Da_j(\theta_i-b_j)}} \quad (3)$$

The one-parameter model (Rasch, 1960) has one item parameter, b_j, that reflects item difficulty in achievement data or item (symptom) extremity in psychopathology data. As formalized in Equation 1, the 1PLM characterizes the probability of an endorsed response (u) by individual i on item j by a logistic function (with $D = 1.702$ to place the item parameters on the normal ogive metric) of the difference between θ_i and b_j. As illustrated in Panel A of Figure 7.1, the IRFs from the 1PLM have several unique features. Foremost among these are that the IRFs do not cross and each IRF has a lower and upper asymptote of 0 and 1.00, respectively.

The 2PLM (Birnbaum, 1968) adds a second-item parameter that is proportional to the slope of the IRF when $\theta_i = b_j$. This so-called discrimination parameter, a_j, characterizes the degree to which an item discriminates among contiguous latent trait scores. As such, a_j is related to a factor loading when an item-level factor analysis is based on a matrix of tetrachoric correlations (Takane & DeLeeuw, 1987). Panel B of Figure 7.1 displays example IRFs from

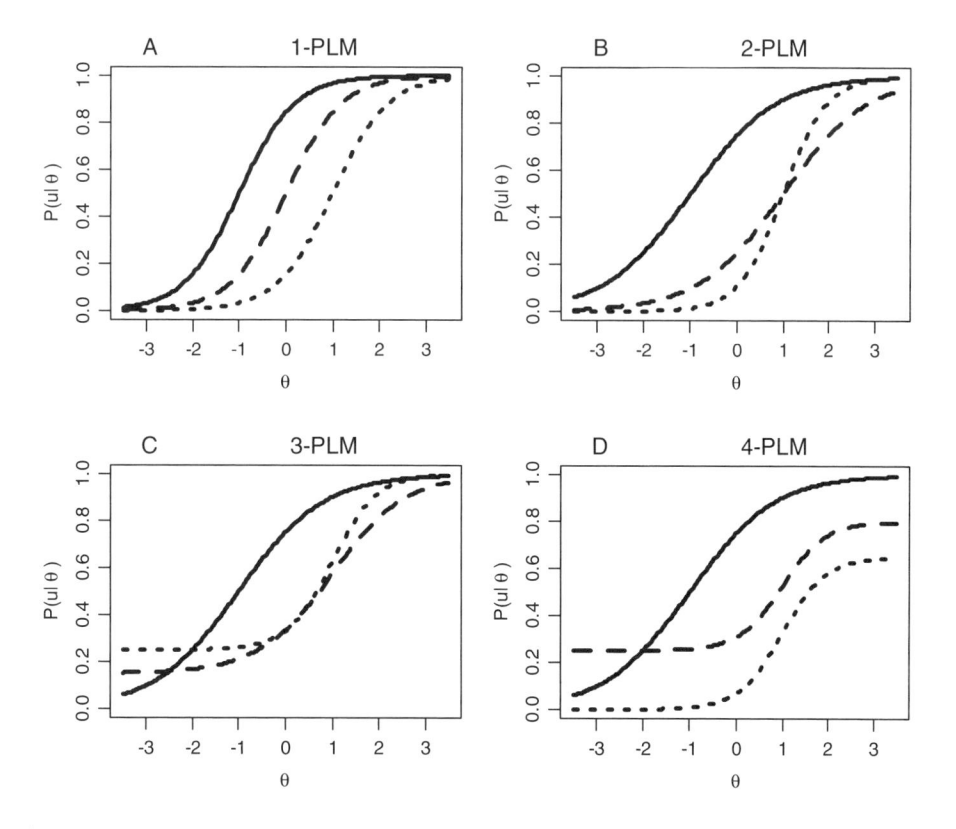

Figure 7.1. Four item response models. PLM = parameter logistic models.

the 2PLM. Although not apparent in the figure, these IRFs—like all IRFs in the 2PLM—have lower and upper asymptotes of 0 and 1.00. In contrast to the 1PLM, the IRFs in the 2PLM can (and frequently do) cross. This seemingly minor difference between the models has engendered considerable controversy in the psychometrics community over the scale properties of IRT trait scores (for opposing views, see Borsboom & Mellenberg, 2004; Michell, 2004; Perline, Wright, & Wainer, 1979).

The 3PLM[2] builds on the previous models by allowing the lower asymptote of an IRF to occur at values other than 0.0. This is accomplished by including a third item parameter, c_j. In aptitude and achievement testing, c_j is often called the *pseudo-guessing parameter* because it allows an IRF to reflect the possibility that on some tests (e.g., multiple choice achievement tests), individuals with infinitely low trait scores can obtain correct responses by chance. In psychopathology data, this interpretation is not feasible because guessing is presumed not to occur. Some researchers suggest that c_j may capture social desirability responding (Roskam, 1985; Rouse, Finger, & Butcher, 1999; Zumbo, Pope, Watson, & Hubley, 1997); however, in a previous publication (Reise & Waller, 2003), we showed that that interpretation is not viable.

Panel C in Figure 7.1 illustrates IRFs from the 3PLM. Notice in this figure that the IRFs in this model can differ in slope (item discrimination), location (item extremity), and lower asymptote.

Modeling MMPI Data With IRT

Earlier we suggested that the MMPI inventories provide an ideal vehicle for studying the application of IRT to psychopathology data. We also noted that in its various forms the MMPI is one of the most widely administered psychological tests (Archer & Newsom, 2000). Given the popularity of these inventories, it is not surprising that researchers have applied IRT models to various MMPI scales (Carter & Wilkinson, 1984; Childs, Dahlstrom, Kemp, & Panter, 2000; Panter, Swygert, Dahlstrom, & Tanaka, 1997; Reise & Waller, 2003; Rouse, Finger, & Butcher, 1999; Waller, Thompson, & Wenk, 1998). Much of this literature is summarized in Waller (1999).

In Reise and Waller (2003), we fit multiple IRT models to MMPI-A data and concluded that the standard (1PLM, 2PLM, and 3PLM) models fail to accurately characterize the functional relations between the item responses and the underlying trait scores. Specifically, our findings suggested that the IRFs of psychopathology data should allow upper asymptotes to be less than 1.00. The 4PLM, which is displayed in Equation 4 and illustrated in the final panel of Figure 7.1, provides a fourth parameter, d_j, that allows variation in the upper asymptotes of the IRF.

$$\text{4PLM} \quad P(u_{ij}=1|\theta_i, a_j, b_j, c_j) = c_j + (d_j - c_j)\frac{1}{1+e^{-Da_j(\theta_i - b_j)}} \quad (4)$$

---

[2]Technically the 3PLM is not a logistic model because the item response function is not a member of the logistic family.

For readers who have not seen our earlier report (Reise & Waller, 2003), we briefly review the findings that encouraged us to explore the 4PLM with psychopathology data. In retrospect, our analyses were deceptively simple. Using one-dimensional factor scales from the MMPI-A, we fit the 3PLM to each scale twice. First, we estimated item parameters after keying the scales to measure psychopathology constructs (i.e., in which higher scores represent increasing levels of maladaptive behavior and cognitions). We called this *3PLM scoring*. We then repeated our analyses after reverse scoring each scale. We called this *3PLMR scoring*. To our surprise, we found support for the three-parameter model in both sets of analyses. In other words, on each scale we found evidence for nonzero lower asymptotes regardless of the direction of scale keying. This finding suggested that the 4PLM would be more appropriate for these data.

Unfortunately, in our earlier work we did not fit the 4PLM to the MMPI-A factor scales. At the time we were unaware of software that could estimate the parameters of this model. We suspect that the 4PLM was not included in commercial IRT programs (e.g., Assessment Systems Corporation, 1997; Zimowski, Muraki, Mislevy, & Bock, 1996) because early applications of the model produced disappointing findings (Barton & Lord, 1981). At this point it may be instructive to review those findings and their subsequent interpretation by the IRT community.

In their original report, Barton and Lord (1981) noted the following:

> Even a high-ability student may make a clerical error in answering an easy item. The introduction of an upper asymptote with a value of *slightly less than* [italics added] 1 should allow a high-ability student to miss an easy item without having his ability estimate drastically lowered. (p. 2)

To test this conjecture, the authors compared the relative performance of the three- and four-parameter models on several data sets collected by Educational Testing Service (i.e., SAT Verbal, SAT Math, GRE Verbal, and AP Calculus). Reviewing their findings, Barton and Lord (1982) concluded the following:

> In view of the failure of the four-parameter model either to consistently improve the likelihood or to significantly change any ability estimates there is no compelling reason to urge the use of this model. The extra computational time required for the more complex derivatives further argues against its use. (p. 6)

This opinion was echoed by Hambleton and Swaminathan (1985), who noted in their influential textbook that the "[4PLM] may be of theoretical interest only because Barton and Lord (1981) were unable to find any practical gains that accrued from the model's use" (pp. 48–49).

Unfortunately, Barton and Lord's negative findings, and the subsequent dissemination of those findings by later textbook authors, effectively stymied research on the 4PLM for a quarter century. Only recently has research on the 4PLM been revived (Linacre, 2004; Loken & Rulison, 2006; Reise & Waller, 2003; Rupp, 2003). It is also unfortunate that in early accounts of this work (e.g., Hambleton & Swaminathan, 1985, pp. 48–49), many authors failed to mention that Barton and Lord never actually estimated the parameters of the 4PLM. Rather, the upper asymptotes in Barton and Lord's study were uniformly constrained to values of 1.00 (representing the 3PLM), 0.99, or 0.98. We suspect that the original authors encountered difficulties when estimating a fourth parameter; in our own labs we were unable to accurately recover the fourth parameter using traditional likelihood methods (e.g., joint maximum likelihood). Our experiences, of course, are not surprising given the well-known difficulty of recovering the third parameter of the 3PLM (Yen, Burket, & Sykes, 1991).

Fitting the 3PLM and 3PLMR to the MMPI-A LSE Scale

In this section, we focus on the psychometric properties of a single MMPI-A scale to more rigorously evaluate the fit of the 4PLM to psychopathology data. To illustrate the 4PLM we chose the 23-item, LSE scale that was first described in Reise and Waller (2003). As noted in our earlier publication, the LSE was derived from factor analyses of tetrachoric correlations (separately) computed on samples of 19,326 adolescent boys and 13,577 adolescent girls. All MMPI-A protocols were completed in one of the following settings: outpatient mental health ($N = 14,843$), inpatient mental health ($N = 1,440$), correctional facilities ($N = 1,001$), drug/alcohol treatment centers ($N = 159$), or medical centers ($N = 219$); all protocols were screened with multiple validity criteria.[3] Given the diversity of the samples, we are relatively confident that the data are representative of the universe of MMPI-A protocols that are obtained in psychopathology research.

In the analyses reported in this chapter, we selected a random sample of 5,000 adolescent boys who completed the LSE in an outpatient mental health setting. We focus on a single setting and a single gender to minimize the effects of differential item functioning. Prior to exploring the fit of the 4PLM to these data, we replicated the analyses (focusing on this data set) that were reported in Reise and Waller (2003). Specifically, we fit the 3PLM and 3PLMR to the LSE item responses using marginal maximum likelihood estimation as implemented in BILOG-MG (Zimowski et al., 1996). In both analyses, we used 41 quadrature points for the theta distribution, a convergence criterion of .0001 for the expectation-maximization (EM) algorithm, and a .10 start value for the lower asymptote parameter. The item parameter estimates from these analyses are reported in Table 7.1.

The findings in Table 7.1 provide alternative and seemingly incompatible views of the psychometric properties of the LSE. At face value, the 3PLM estimates suggest that most items are well characterized by a two-parameter model because virtually all of the $\hat{c}$ parameters are near 0.0. However, the item-level chi-square statistics raise red flags and indicate that all but one item (Item 16) are poorly modeled by the 3PLM. It is interesting that many of these items also have large and significant $\hat{c}_j$ in the 3PLMR results.

---

[3]Protocols were deemed invalid and thus excluded from the analyses if F2 > 18, VRIN ≥ 11, TRIN > 13 or TRIN < 6 for adolescent girls and F2 > 20, VRIN ≥ 13, TRIN > 13, TRIN < 5 for adolescent boys. We thank the University of Minnesota Press for kindly providing us with these data.

Table 7.1. Item Content and IRT Parameter Estimates for the MMPI-A Low Self-Esteem Factor Scale

	3PLM			3PLMR		
Abbreviated item content	a	b	c^a	a	b	c^a
1. Unwillingly did bad things because of friends.	.58	.97	.02	1.01	.15	**.40**
2. Friends convince me to do wrong.	.65	1.12	.01	1.31	.04	**.46**
3. People can easily change my mind.	.75	.90	.01	1.07	−.10	**.32**
4. Avoid doing things because others feel I'm not doing them right.	.68	.91	.02	.77	−.41	**.21**
5. Leave handling of problems to other people.	.73	.80	.03	.72	−.55	.09
6. Often regret things.	.64	−.18	.03	.85	.55	**.13**
7. Don't do something if others don't think its' worth it.	.56	.22	.04	.74	.40	**.20**
8. Lie to get by.	.68	.59	.02	.86	−.05	**.21**
9. My sins should be punished.	.48	1.70	.03	.46	−1.23	.16
10. Want to give up when things aren't going well.	1.02	.38	.01	1.16	−.18	**.09**
11. Feel helpless when facing important decisions.	1.05	.65	.01	1.12	−.46	**.09**
12. Action dictated by others.	.48	.61	.02	1.05	.56	**.38**
13. Even short trips make me nervous.	.55	1.87	.01	.71	−.74	**.43**
14. Jealous of some family members.	.70	1.23	.04	.61	−1.03	.08
15. Often cross street to avoid people.	.64	1.05	.02	.75	−.49	**.23**
16. My sins are unforgivable.	.65	1.74	.03	.56	−1.60	.09
17. Others' success makes me feel a failure.	1.05	.75	.01	1.16	−.54	**.12**
18. Am important.	.60	1.52	.03	.54	−1.34	.06
19. Bothered when nice things are said about me.	.71	1.77	.01	.68	−1.65	.08
20. Can't do anything well.	.93	1.84	.00	1.01	−1.61	.16
21. Give up trying to do things because of lack of confidence.	.99	.39	.01	1.04	−.24	.06
22. Wholly self-confident.	.46	.24	.09	.44	.22	.05
23. Expect to succeed. (False)	.58	1.85	.02	.56	−1.66	.08

Note. IRT = item response theory; MMPI-A = Minnesota Multiphasic Personality Inventory–Adolescent form; PLM = parameter logistic model; 3PLM = three-parameter IRT model when items are keyed in the psychopathology direction; 3PLMR = three-parameter IRT model when items are reverse keyed. Using a $p < .01$ significance level, item level chi-square goodness-of-fit tests indicated that only Item 16 could be adequately modeled by the 3PLM.
^{a}c parameter estimates marked in boldface are significantly different from 0.0.

In contrast to the 3PLM findings, the results of the 3PLMR analysis provide cogent evidence for including a lower asymptote parameter in the model. For instance, relying on the BILOG goodness-of fit index, 57% of the items had lower asymptote estimates that were significantly higher than 0. Considered in aggregate, these findings clearly demonstrate that neither the 2PLM nor the 3PLM is appropriate when the LSE is scored as a psychopathology measure (i.e., when higher scores indicate extreme levels of low self-esteem). For some readers they may also suggest that self-esteem, like IQ, has a natural direction of keying. That is, self-esteem scales—or at least the LSE—should be keyed to measure high self-esteem. Although the notion of unipolar constructs is plausible, it is clearly not the solution to this psychometric conundrum. In some contexts it may be appropriate to measure high self-esteem (e.g., when selecting CEOs of major corporations), whereas in other scenarios it may be more appropriate to measure low self-esteem (e.g., when identifying troubled youth). To allow both possibilities, therefore, we suggest that a better solution is to find a model that fits the data regardless of which pole on the scale is of greater interest.

We used two methods to explore additional models that do not constrain the asymptotes of the item-trait regression functions to occur at 0.0 and 1.00. We believe that the methods complement one another because the first estimates the IRF using a nonparametric method and the second method using a parametric function. The nonparametric method is based on rest score plots (Junker & Sijtsma, 2000); for the parametric method, we fit the 4PLM to the data using a Gibbs sampling technique (Albert, 1992; Albert & Chib, 1993; Baker, 1998; Casella & George, 1992). The results from these analyses are reported in the following sections.

Using Rest-Score Regressions to Explore IRFs

Rest score plots (Junker & Sijtsma, 2000) offer a convenient and informative technique for exploring the general form of an empirical item response function (ERF). A *rest score* is simply a total score in which an item under consideration has been deleted. In simple terms, rest score plots display conditional item response probabilities when the probabilities have been conditioned on rest scores (see Lord, 1980, pp. 18–19). When generated from large N data sets, such ERFs provide information about the function asymptotes. It is important that they can also reveal violations of the monotonicity assumption of logistic IRT models.

Using data from the 14,843 adolescent boys who completed the LSE in an outpatient mental health setting, we created 23 rest score plots for the LSE items. For each item, rest scores were calculated and then divided into 10 equally spaced intervals. For each interval, we calculated item endorsement probabilities and the associated 95% confidence bounds. These conditional probabilities and confidence bounds were then connected by linear interpolation to produce the ERFs.

Unfortunately, due to space limitations, we are unable to reproduce all 23 rest score plots (copies of the plots are available upon request). Nevertheless, several features of these plots warrant comment. For instance, for 22 of the 23 LSE items, the plots revealed that the ERFs were monotonically increasing. The exception to this trend occurred for Item 13, which revealed a monotonicity violation in the last interval. Moreover, in several plots the upper asymptotes of the nonparametric functions were less than 1.00. Across the scale, this was true for 14 of 23 (61%) items. Two items illustrating this feature are represented in Panels A and B in Figure 7.2. Panel A shows the ERF for Item 1. In

A. (Item 1) Unwillingly did bad things because of friends.

B. (Item 12) Action dictated by others.

C. (Item 22) Wholly self-confident. (False)

D. (Item 21) Give up trying to do things because of lack of confidence.

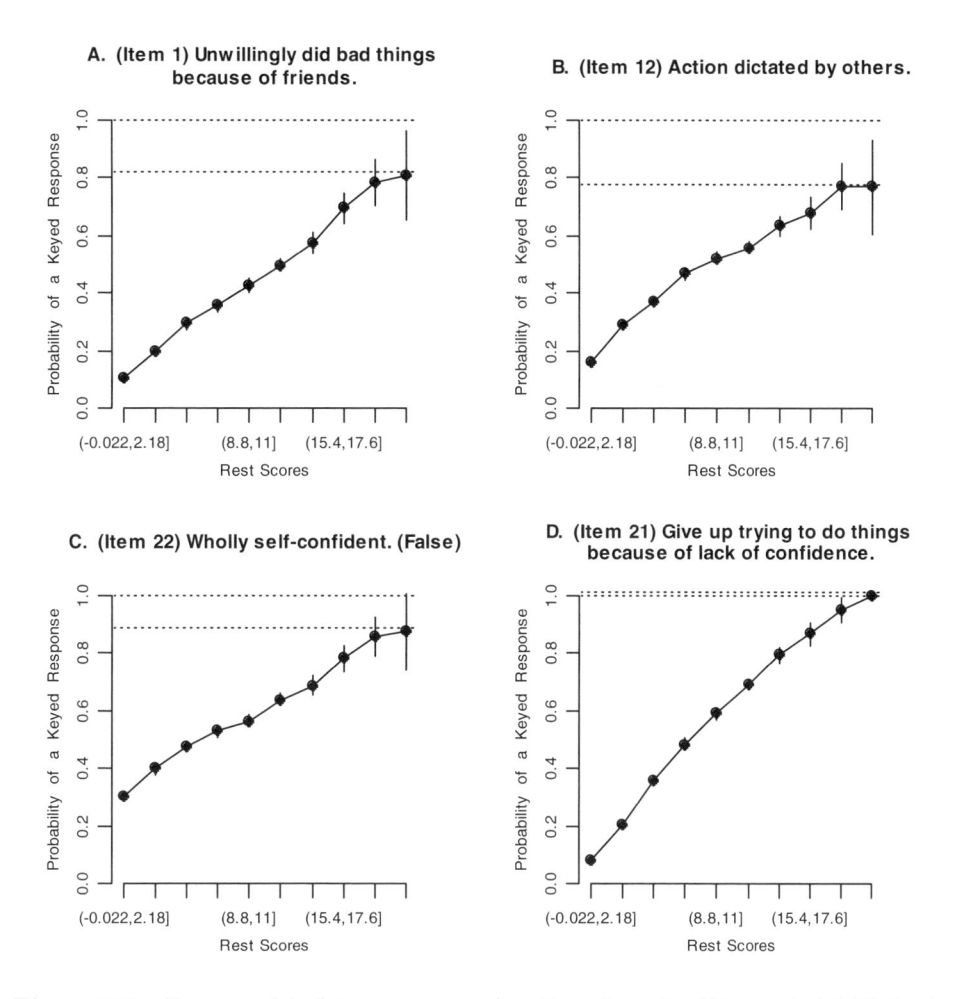

Figure 7.2. Four empirical item response functions from the Minnesota Multiphasic Personality Inventory–Adolescent Low Self-Esteem Factor Scale.

abbreviated form[4] Item 1 reads "Unwillingly did bad things because of friends." Apparently, if the implications of this ERF are to be believed, many adolescent boys with low self-esteem (i.e., high LSE scores) will not act out in the face of peer pressure. The ERF for Item 12 paints a similar picture. Thus, there appears to be a distinct class of boys who will refrain from acting out regardless of their level of low self-esteem. IRT mixture modeling (Mislevy & Verhelst, 1990) could be used to test this conjecture.

The remaining plots in Figure 7.2 suggest that some items of the scale will fit a three-parameter model (e.g., Item 22), whereas for other items (e.g., Item 21) the 2PLM will suffice. The rest score plot for Item 22 is particularly interesting

---

[4]The University of Minnesota Press, copyright holder for the MMPI-A, does not allow publication of the unabbreviated items.

from a clinical standpoint because it suggests that only 1 out of 4 boys (in the current sample) with high self-esteem admits that they are not wholly self-confident. Stated differently, 75% of the boys in our sample with the highest self-esteem scores claimed that they are wholly self-confident. This finding intrigues us because all persons in this sample were receiving outpatient mental health services at the time they completed the MMPI-A. Moreover, clinical experience suggests that individuals who claim to be entirely self-confident are usually narcissistic and self-defensive.

The results from these analyses are in accord with those reported in the previous section. As such, they provide further evidence that a four-parameter model is needed to accurately characterize item response behavior on scales such as the MMPI-A LSE. Later we describe how researchers can estimate the parameters of the 4PLM using general purpose (and freely available) software for Bayesian estimation (Speigelhalter, Thomas, & Best, 2000). Before doing so, we briefly review the so-called Bayesian revolution in statistical computing and discuss why Bayesian methods have begun to dominate contemporary research in IRT.

The Bayesian Revolution in Statistical Computing

During the past 15 years, a not-so-quiet revolution has occurred in the field of statistical computing. This so-called Bayesian revolution has literally transformed the computational landscape of applied statistics (Beaumont & Rannala, 2004; for a review, see Gelman, Carlin, Stern, & Rubin, 2004). Models that were deemed too complex only a decade ago are now routinely estimated via Bayesian methods that rely on Monte Carlo simulations and cheap computer hardware. It would be impossible for us to overstate the importance of these developments. Rupp, Dey, and Zumbo (2004) nicely summarized the situation as follows:

> Bayesian methods have become a viable alternative to traditional maximum likelihood-based estimation techniques and may be the only solution for more complex psychometric structures. Hence, neither the applied nor the theoretical measurement community can afford to neglect the exciting new possibilities that have opened up on the psychometric horizon. (p. 424)

Although there have been many calls to arms (Edwards, Lindman, & Savage, 1963; Novick & Jackson, 1974; Phillips, 1974; Rouanet, 1996), in general, psychologists have been slow to join the Bayesian revolution. It is interesting that psychometricians are a notable exception to this rule. This is especially true for psychometricians who work with IRT.

In the 1980s several researchers described how Bayesian methods could be incorporated into IRT parameter estimation techniques (Swaminathan & Gifford, 1982, 1985, 1986; Tsutakawa & Lin, 1986) to control parameter drift and to improve estimation accuracy in small to moderate sample sizes. Nevertheless, the full power of Bayesian computation for IRT parameter estimation was not realized until the 1990s (Albert, 1992; Albert & Chib, 1993; Baker, 1998; Beguin & Glas, 2001; Fox & Glas, 2001; Johnson & Albert, 1999; Kim, 2001; Patz & Junker, 1999). The primary innovation during this period was the demonstration that IRT parameters could be estimated via MCMC simulations and the Gibbs sampler.

IRT Parameter Estimation Via the Gibbs Sampler

The Gibbs sampler is the workhorse of modern Bayesian computing. Introduced to the statistics community by Gelfand and Smith (1990; for an earlier description of the technique, see Geman & Geman, 1984), the Gibbs sampler is a member of the so-called Metropolis-Hastings family of algorithms (Hastings, 1970; Metropolis, Rosenbluth, Rosenbluth, Teller, & Teller, 1953) that were invented during the development of the atomic bomb. Casella and George (1992) have written a very readable introduction to the Gibbs sampler (see also Congdon, 2001; Gill, 2002; Jackman, 2000, 2004).

In nontechnical terms, the Gibbs sampler simulates a high-dimensional joint distribution of parameter estimates by breaking the problem down into mutually exclusive sets of low-dimensional—read: "easier to simulate"—conditional distributions. This idea is particularly useful in IRT research because IRT models often contain a large number of item and person parameters. For instance, a P-parameter IRT model with K items that is fit to data from N individuals will necessitate the estimation $(P \times K) + N$ parameters. In the example that follows, this translates into 5,092 parameters.

The Gibbs sampler avoids the Herculean task of locating the peak of the likelihood surface in high-dimensional space by taking a radically different approach. Namely, rather than maximize a likelihood function (by setting partial derivatives to zero and then solving), the Gibbs sampler draws simulated values (i.e., estimates) from low-dimensional conditional distributions. The basic idea is to replace complex mathematical analyses with Monte Carlo simulations. If the simulated values are drawn from the appropriate distributions, then in the long run the aggregate values will also define the joint, posterior distribution for the parameters. This latter distribution can then be used to calculate the marginal density for a single parameter or for a combination of multiple parameters. Albert (1992) and Baker (1998) have written informative tutorials of these ideas in the context of IRT. Although the mathematics in these tutorials is not complex, we suspect that implementing these ideas into a workable computer program may present a daunting task for many applied IRT researchers.

Fortunately, it is now possible to estimate IRT models via a Gibbs sampler using general purpose Bayesian engines, such as BUGS (Gilks, Richardson, & Spiegelhalter, 1995), which are both freely available and easily programmed.[5] Several of these engines are included in the R (R Development Core Team, 2006) computing environment (Martin & Quinn, 2006; Thomas, 2006).

In the current study we estimated the 4PLM using a Gibbs sampler as implemented in BRUGS (Thomas, 2006). BRUGS is an open source R package that is based on the OpenBUGS (http://mathstat.helsinki.fi/openbugs/) architecture. Estimation of the model is straightforward in BRUGS and requires little more than the definition of the 4PLM IRF (see Equation 4, supra), the

---

[5]We thank Eric Loken for initial help with the BUGS model.

specification of prior distributions for the model parameters, and code that defines the likelihood function. In our analyses the prior distributions for the item parameters (a, b, c, d) and the latent subject parameter (θ) were defined as follows: $a_j \sim Log-normal(0, 1/11)$, $b_j \sim Normal(0, 1.5)$, $c_j \sim Beta(2, 10)$, $d_j \sim Beta(10, 2)$, and $\theta_i \sim Normal(0, 1)$.

Unfortunately, hardware limitations prohibited us from analyzing the full set of 14,843 response vectors in the male adolescent outpatient sample. To get around these limitations, the analyses were run on a random sample of 5,000 protocols from the larger data set. Program code was written to execute two chains of the Gibbs sampler with 30,000 burn-in draws (i.e., Monte Carlo simulations) followed by an additional 30,000 draws. Although these numbers may appear excessive, previous work in our labs suggested that they are conservative and that smaller numbers may fail to recover the item parameters with sufficient accuracy. During the simulations, we monitored convergence of the Markov chains with the Gelman and Rubin (1992; Brooks & Gelman, 1998) diagnostic, $\sqrt{\hat{R}}$ (for a readable discussion of this index, see Gill, 2002, pp. 399–401). In their original report, the authors stated that $\sqrt{\hat{R}}$ values near 1.00 suggest that the Markov chains have converged to their stationary distributions. In a later publication, Gelman (1996) amended this recommendation and suggested that values less than 1.1 or 1.2 may be adequate for many models.

In the current study the median $\sqrt{\hat{R}}$ for the item parameters was 1.002 with minimum and maximum values of 1.00 and 1.03, respectively. Although these findings are promising, prior work in our lab suggested that Gelman and Rubin's (1992) diagnostics are insufficient arbiters of model-data fit with the four-parameter model. For instance, $\sqrt{\hat{R}}$ values close to 1.00 can be paired with parameter estimates that are clearly outside of the parameter space (e.g., item discrimination values that are greater than 3.00 in the normal metric). We therefore judged the fit of the 4PLM by additional criteria as described in the following section.

The fully Bayesian approach that was implemented in this study yields posterior distributions for all model parameters. These distributions can be summarized by various point estimates or intervals (e.g., means, medians, modes, regions of highest density). To keep matters simple, in Table 7.2 we report the means of the marginal distributions for the item parameters of the LSE scale. Notice in this table that the d_j estimates are uniformly less than 1.00. Moreover, as judged by the 97.5 quantiles of the posterior distributions, we can be highly confident (or as a Bayesian would say: "It is highly probable") that many of the values are significantly less than 1.00.

The previously mentioned rest score plots provide additional support for the notion that the 4PLM is an adequate model for our psychopathology data. In these plots, with few exceptions, the predicted and observed response proportions were highly similar. The worst discrepancy occurred at the low end of Item 9, an item with one of the lowest estimated d values. The low d value, in turn, is likely due to the ambiguity of the item "My sins should be punished." Individuals who do not believe in God and/or the Christian notion of sin may not know how to respond to this item. We can imagine individuals with ele-

Table 7.2. Item Parameters (4-Parameter Model) for the Adolescent Low Self-Esteem Factor Scale

Abbreviated item content	a	b	c	d
1. Unwillingly did bad things because of friends.	1.91	−0.28	0.04	0.52 (.56)
2. Friends convince me to do wrong.	1.95	−0.16	0.02	0.48 (.53)
3. People can easily change my mind.	1.50	0.05	0.02	0.60 (.66)
4. Avoid doing things because others feel I'm not doing them right.	1.12	0.06	0.02	0.63 (.72)
5. Leave handling of problems to other people.	0.89	0.45	0.04	0.82 (.94)
6. Often regret things.	1.08	−0.50	0.06	0.83 (.88)
7. Don't do something if others don't think its' worth it.	1.16	−0.47	0.07	0.71 (.77)
8. Lie to get by.	1.10	0.01	0.04	0.73 (.79)
9. My sins should be punished.	0.78	0.45	0.05	0.57 (.73)
10. Want to give up when things aren't going well.	1.23	0.19	0.01	0.90 (.96)
11. Feel helpless when facing important decisions.	1.34	0.41	0.02	0.85 (.93)
12. Action dictated by others.	1.54	−0.48	0.06	0.59 (.63)
13. Even short trips make me nervous.	1.16	0.18	0.02	0.40 (.49)
14. Jealous of some family members.	0.84	0.72	0.04	0.75 (.91)
15. Often cross street to avoid people.	1.13	0.15	0.03	0.61 (.71)
16. My sins are unforgivable.	0.79	1.19	0.04	0.73 (.94)
17. Others' success makes me feel a failure.	1.27	0.48	0.01	0.84 (.93)
18. Am important.	0.94	1.37	0.09	0.94 (.99)
19. Bothered when nice things are said about me.	0.84	1.44	0.02	0.82 (.97)
20. Can't do anything well.	1.14	1.52	0.00	0.82 (.97)
21. Give up trying to do things because of lack of confidence.	1.10	0.25	0.02	0.93 (.98)
22. Wholly self-confident. (False)	0.72	0.53	0.24	0.95 (.99)
23. Expect to succeed. (False)	0.88	1.56	0.06	0.91 (.99)

Note. Numbers in parentheses are the 97.5 quantiles of the posterior distributions.

vated low self-esteem scores who respond *False* to Item 9 simply because they do not acknowledge a religious contribution to deviant behavior.

To avoid any ambiguity in our own beliefs, we wish to state emphatically that we do not believe that item ambiguity is a general cause of low d values. Other findings in Table 7.2 make that interpretation unsupportable. For instance, 8 of 23 items (Items 1, 2, 3, 4, 9, 12, 13, 15) on the LSE scale had d values that were significantly less than .75 (as judged by the 97.5 quantiles of the posterior distributions), and 3 items (Items 1, 2, & 13) had d values that were significantly less than .60. Nevertheless, most of these items are stated in simple and clear language.

Have We Found a Difference That Makes a Difference?

In this section we consider the important question of whether the added complexity of the 4PLM offers an appreciable difference that makes a difference in the psychometric assessment of low self-esteem. Stated more objectively, we ask: Using our data, would the 3PLM have yielded practically significant differences?

The LSE scale is an MMPI-A factor scale that was designed to identify persons with extreme levels of low self-worth. As a clinical scale, we must consider the consequences of model choice for an individual's diagnostic score. Two ways to do this are to consider the (a) individual trait estimates and (b) the standard errors of those estimates.

We begin by considering the effects of model choice on the estimated trait values. Figure 7.3 shows a scatter plot of the LSE trait estimates for the three- and four-parameter models. The embedded plot in Figure 7.3 focuses on the scores that are greater than 1.00 in the 4PLM scoring. Notice that across the entire range of scores it makes little difference whether a person is scored using the 3PLM or 4PLM: the scores yield highly similar rankings (Spearman's ρ = .99; Pearson's r = .89). However, enlarging our focus on the smaller plot reveals that model choice makes a substantial difference for persons with extreme trait values. The rank order correlation between the scores in the embedded figure is only .45. Moreover, in the smaller plot the 3PLM estimates are generally lower than the 4PLM estimates. Thus, by using the 3PLM with these data a

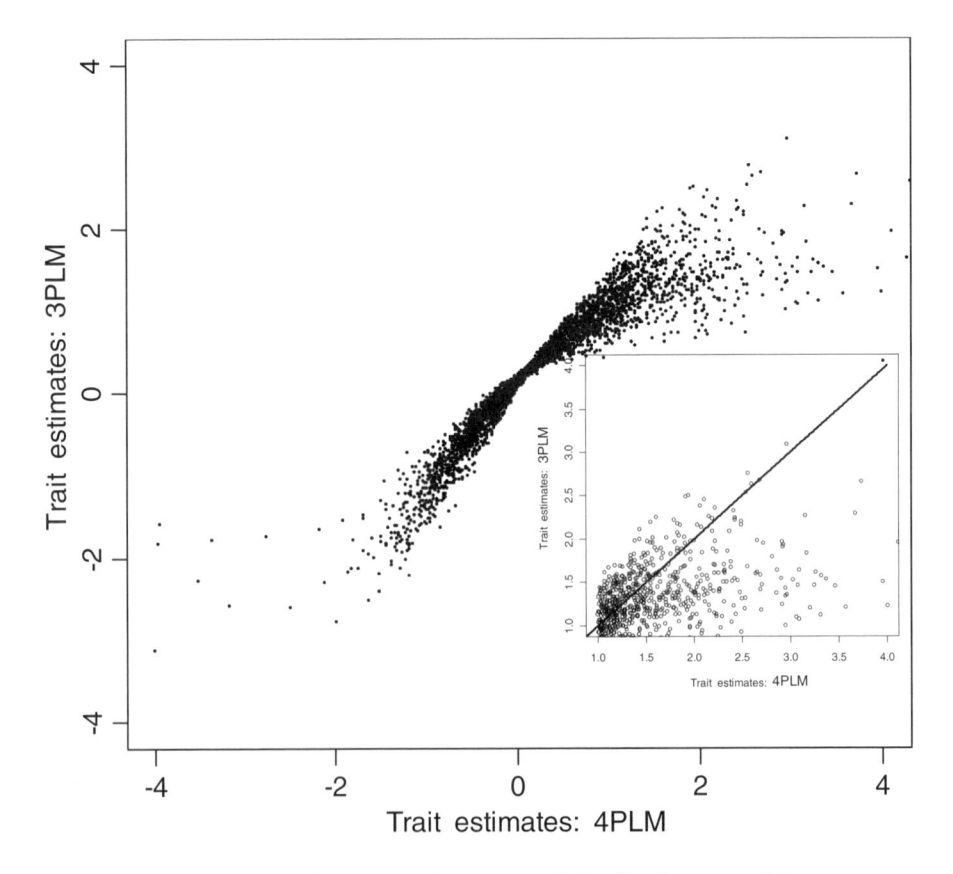

Figure 7.3. Comparison of estimated trait scores in the three- and four-parameter logistic models (PLM).

person runs the risks of underreporting psychopathology for persons of greatest interest to practitioners.

Of course, realizing that the two models yield different trait estimates is only partially interesting unless we understand the causes of those differences. Two of those causes can be gleaned from scatter plots of the item discriminations and item difficulty values from the two models. These plots are shown in Figure 7.4. Even a cursory glance at the plots shows that relative to the 4PLM (a) the estimated item discriminations are smaller in the 3PLM and (b) the estimated item difficulties are larger.

A moment's reflection reveals the logic behind these trends. Consider a three-parameter IRF of a relatively difficult item with poor discrimination. Such an item will not reach its upper asymptote of 1.0 in the range of trait values that are typically encountered in practice ($-4 \leq \hat{\theta} \leq 4$). By implication, the 3PLM must attenuate the item discriminations and inflate the item difficulties to accommodate an IRF from the four-parameter model that has an upper asymptote well below 1.00.

Turning now to the question of score fidelity, we consider how the previous results affect the precision of the estimated trait values. In IRT models score precision is typically indexed by a function of the item parameters known as the expected Test Information Function (TIF; Bradlow, 1996). For the LSE scale, TIFs for the 3PLM and 4PLM are shown in Figure 7.5. Notice in this figure that relative to the 4PLM results, the TIF from the 3PLM (denoted by the dashed line in the figure) provides an overly optimistic assessment of score fidelity for high-scoring individuals. In other words, relative to the 4PLM, the confidence bands for elevated trait estimates would be too small using the 3PLM item parameters. Score fidelity is reported in two metrics in the figure. The left-hand ordinate of Figure 7.6 reports the expected test information using Fisher's information function. The right-hand ordinate reports the conditional score reliability in the (0, 1) range of many familiar reliability coefficients from classical test theory.

Using either metric for the LSE data, the test information in the 4PLM is highly peaked and centered along trait scores that are considerably lower than those of greatest interest to clinicians. The 3PLM findings, on the other hand, suggest that trait precision is relatively high in the clinically significant range. These contradictory findings highlight yet another noteworthy difference between the results of the three- and four-parameter models with our data. It is important that researchers who were guided by these findings to lengthen the LSE would be drawn to items with very different psychometric properties depending upon the model from which they were working.

The TIFs that are displayed in Figure 7.5 were created with the 3PLM and 4PLM results that were reported in Tables 7.1 and 7.2, respectively. As noted previously, the findings in Table 7.2 are simply the means of the 30,000 estimates from the posterior distributions of each parameter. A particularly attractive feature of the fully Bayesian approach to IRT parameter estimation is that the parameter estimates from the posterior distributions are easily combined to produce confidence bands (or probability bands) for various functions of interest to IRT researchers. Two sets of functions for which confidence bands may be particularly informative are IRFs (Thissen & Wainer, 1990) and TIFs.

Figure 7.6 displays 90% probability bands for the 4PLM test information function that was previously displayed in Figure 7.5. The upper and lower limits

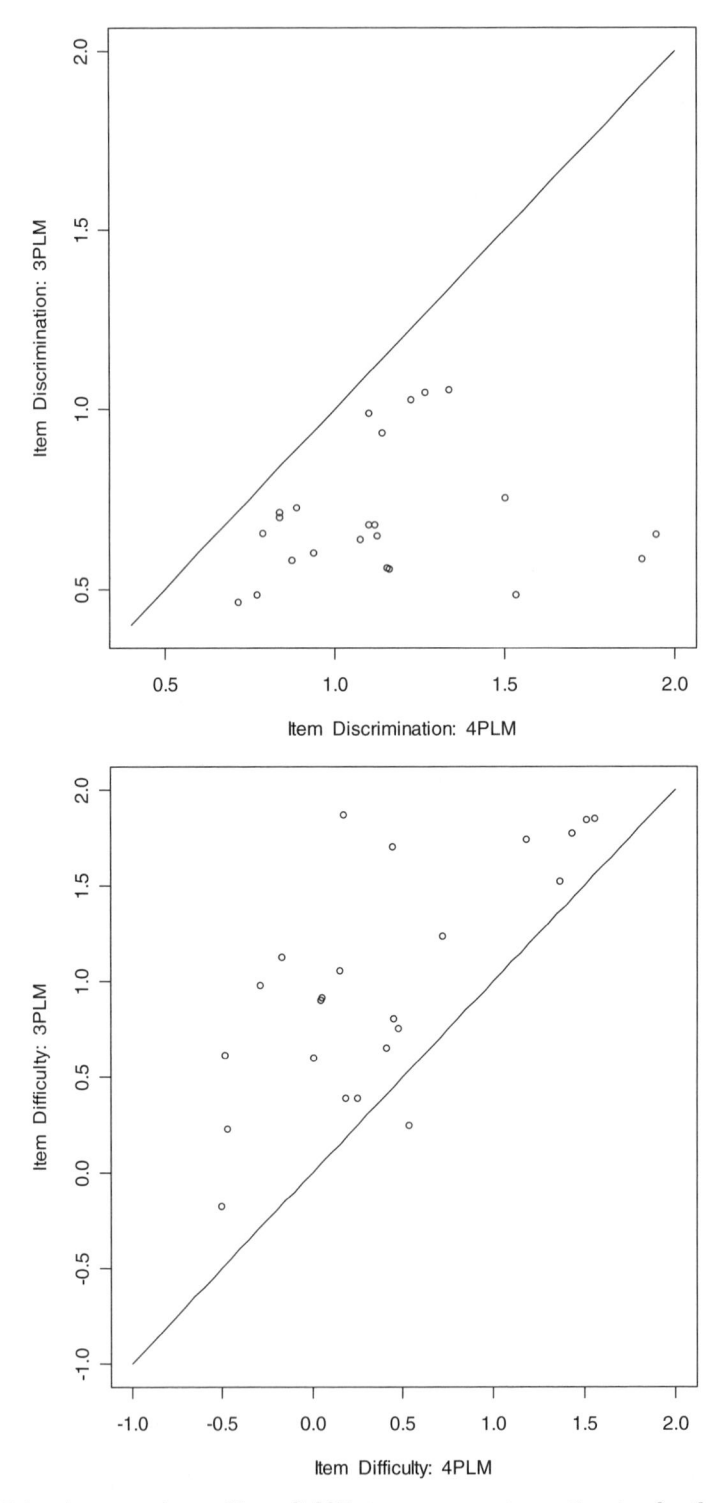

Figure 7.4. A comparison of Low-Self Esteem parameter estimates for the three- and four-parameter logistic models.

Adolescent Low Self Esteem

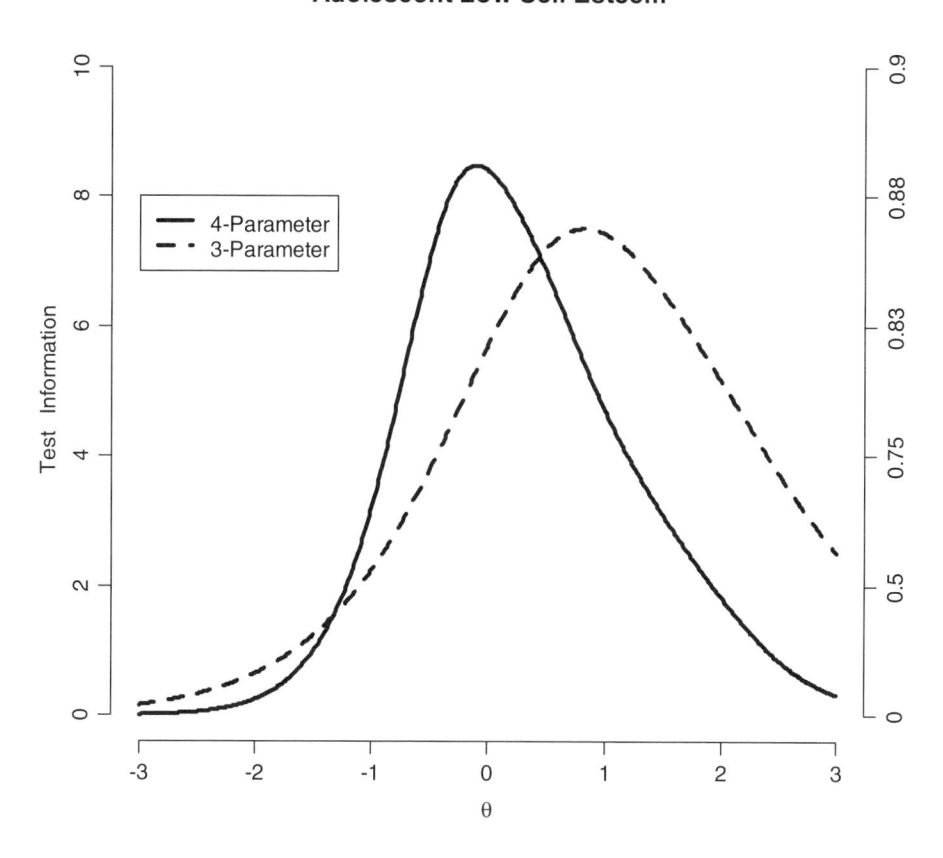

Figure 7.5. Test information functions for the Low Self-Esteem Factor Scale using the three- and four-parameter logistic models.

of these bands were computed by taking the 5th and 95th ranked values of the TIF posterior distribution at regular intervals along the trait range. We contend that these bands tell an important story and that IRT researchers would be well-advised to compute TIF probability bands when assessing the psychometric properties of a test. Notice that with the LSE, the meta-reliability—or the reliability of the reliability estimates—differs across the trait range. At the extremes of the $\hat{\theta}$ range the confidence bands hug the mean TIF values, whereas in the middle of the trait range the bands are more widely spread apart. This indicates that we can be relatively confident that persons with extreme (estimated) trait scores, at either end of the scale, are poorly measured with the LSE scale.

Discussion

IRT models are increasingly being used to solve measurement problems in content areas beyond aptitude and achievement testing. Underlying this trend is the belief that IRT offers practical advantages over classical test theory

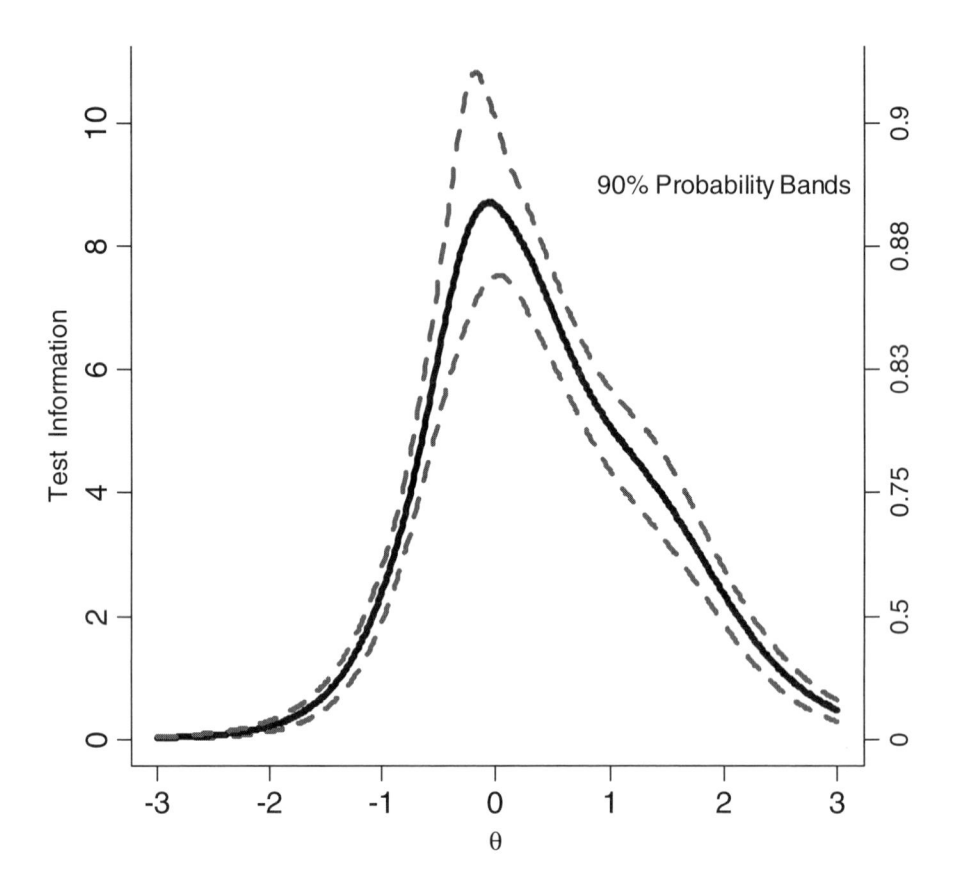

Figure 7.6. Bayesian confidence bands for the test information function: Minnesota Multiphasic Personality Inventory–Adolescent Low Self-Esteem Scale.

(Embretson, 1996). Summarizing these advantages, Reise, Ainsworth, and Haviland (2005, p. 100) recently noted that IRT (a) provides rigorous methods for testing differential item and test functioning in group comparisons; (b) can be used to place individuals from different groups onto a common measurement scale, even when the groups have responded to nonoverlapping item pools; (c) yields test scores with desirable psychometric properties that are well suited for measuring individual change or growth; and (d) provides a methodology for developing individual tailored tests via computerized adaptive testing (Wainer 1990) for more efficient assessment of individual differences. Of course, these desiderata are realized only when IRT models characterize a data set.

In this chapter (cf. Reise & Waller, 2003) we argued that the 4PLM may be needed to characterize psychopathology data, and we illustrated how the Gibbs sampler (Casella & George, 1992) can be used to estimate the parameters of the 4PLM. Specifically, we used a variant of the OpenBUGS computer program (Thomas, 2006) to estimate 4PLM item and person parameters on data from 5,000 adolescent boys who completed the MMPI-A LSE scale in an outpatient mental health setting.

Our original interest in the 4PLM can be traced to earlier work (Reise & Waller, 2003) in which we compared the relative fit of several IRT models with 15 factor analytically derived scales from the MMPI-A (Butcher et al., 1992). That work was motivated by other studies (e.g., Rouse, Finger, & Butcher, 1999) showing that the 3PLM fits MMPI data better than the 2PLM. An important finding from our work is that when MMPI-A factor scales are scored to measure psychopathology, the 3PLM fits better than the 2PLM for approximately 6% of the 316 items on the factor scales. Moreover, several items had unusually large (when judged from the perspective of achievement and ability testing) c parameters. For example, the item "Often talk to strangers" (keyed *False* for Social Discomfort) had an estimated c of .42, and the item "Feel the best ever" (keyed *False* for Depression) had an estimated c of .32. Nevertheless, most items were well characterized by the 2PLM.

While reviewing our findings we realized that when compared with aptitude and achievement data, the direction in which a scale is keyed is less fixed with psychopathology and personality data. After acknowledging this point, it became immediately obvious that had we reversed keyed our scales; items that required a c parameter in our original analyses would now require a d parameter. We found evidence for this view in a series of rest score plots (Junker & Sijtsma, 2000). These points led us to reanalyze our data with the 3PLM after recoding the 15 MMPI-A factor scales to measure the absence of psychopathology.

In these analyses we suggested that $1-c$ could provide an admittedly crude, though nonetheless informative, estimate for d in the reverse-keyed scales. Thus, by analyzing each scale twice, we were essentially fitting a poor man's version of the 4PLM (note, however, that this shortcut for fitting the 4PLM will not give unbiased parameter estimates, and thus we do not recommend it for anything but exploratory analyses). The results from these analyses were intriguing as they bolstered our hunch that the 4PLM was needed to accurately characterize item response behavior on some psychopathology items. By classifying any d (calculated by $1-c$) less than .90 as substantial, we found that more than a third of the 316 items had d parameters that were substantially less than 1.00. Two example items in this category are "Even short trips make me anxious" (keyed *True* for low self-esteem), which had an estimated d of .50, and "Unwillingly did bad things because of friends" (also keyed *True* for low self-esteem), which had an estimated d of .66.

Unfortunately, our enthusiasm for these results was tempered by the fact that our heuristic technique for estimating the 4PLM had not been shown to work in simulated data (because we had yet to carry out the necessary Monte Carlo work). Thus, before embracing the 4PLM as a viable model for psychopathology data, it was critically necessary to estimate the parameters of this model with a psychometrically justifiable method. In this chapter we suggested that the Gibbs sampler offers such a method and that when it is applied to the LSE, there is ample support for the 4PLM with our psychopathology data.

The 4PLM and Low Self-Esteem

Consistent with our earlier findings, the Bayesian results suggest that only 3 of the 23 LSE items have c parameters that are notably higher than 0.00. These items are "Wholly self-confident" (keyed *False*, $c = 0.24$), "Am important" (keyed *False*, $c = 0.09$), and "Don't do something if others don't think it's worth it" (keyed *True*, $c = 0.07$). Apparently, individuals with low LSE scores (i.e., those with high self-esteem) have a nonzero probability of endorsing these items in the keyed direction. Are these findings surprising? We do not believe so. We suspect that these items tap traits in addition to low self-esteem. For instance, the items "Wholly self-confident" or "Am important" may also tap individual differences in humility, modesty, or just plain honesty.

What was surprising, from the standpoint of traditional IRT modeling, was that the Bayesian results also indicated that almost all of the LSE items required a fourth parameter to characterize the upper asymptotes of the IRFs. Several exceptions to this trend were noteworthy by their rarity. For instance, the items "Wholly self confident" (keyed *False*, $d = .95$), "Give up trying to do things because of lack of confidence" (keyed *True*, $d = 0.93$), and "Am important" (keyed *False*, $d = 0.94$) all had d parameters with confidence bounds that included the upper boundary. This suggests that these items—all of which are highly face valid markers of low self esteem—are almost universally endorsed by individuals with high LSE scores.

Turning now to the greater number of items with sizeable d parameters, several LSE items had upper asymptotes as low as .50 or lower. Examples include "Even short trips make me nervous" (keyed *True; $d = 0.40$*), "Friends convince me to do wrong" (keyed *True; $d = 0.48$*), and "Unwillingly did bad things because of friends" (keyed *True; $d = 0.52$*). Psychologically speaking, these findings suggest that less than half of adolescent boys from this population with elevated LSE scores will become agoraphobic or succumb to peer pressures.

Interpreting the c *and* d *Parameters in Psychopathology Scales*

Mathematically speaking, the meanings of the c and d parameters in the 4PLM are unambiguous. When c is greater than zero, the IRF is flat in the lowest trait range; when d is less than 1, the IRF is flat in the highest trait range. In either case the item fails to discriminate among contiguous trait scores in a select trait range. Unfortunately, the psychological meaning of these results is less clear. In earlier work (Reise & Waller, 2003) we offered several interpretations of the c or d parameters in psychopathology assessment. We now expand upon those ideas.

Our work on the 4PLM with MMPI data leads us to believe that there are at least two overlapping reasons why asymptote parameters are needed with psychopathology data: (a) item extremity; and (b) nonsymmetric item ambiguity, which we interpret as a heretofore unrecognized form of item-level multidimensionality.

We first discuss item extremity because it is the easier notion to explain. *Item extremity* refers to symptoms or behaviors with extremely high- or low-base rates. To illustrate this concept, consider the item "Happiest alone," which is keyed *False* on the extraversion factor scale. In a previous report (Reise & Waller 2003) this item had an estimated c parameter of .50 in a very large and heterogeneous sample of persons. This finding suggests that 50% of the least extreme extroverts respond *False* (a keyed response) to the aforementioned item. In other words, being "happiest" when alone is an uncommon attitude among social animals.

Other symptoms with a low-to-moderate base rate may require a d parameter. For instance, in unpublished research (Reise, 2004), we found that the unconditional probability of suicidal ideation in adolescents who are involved in the mental health system is less than .50. It is important that this remained true even for persons high on trait depression. Similar findings are found with other psychopathologies. For instance, Schneider's First Rank symptoms (e.g., auditory hallucinations, thought broadcasting, somatic hallucinations; see Schneider, 1959), which in media accounts are portrayed as pathognomonic for schizophrenia, are actually found in less than 75% of gold standard cases of schizophrenia (O'Grady, 1990). In other words, over 25% of people with schizophrenia do not experience these symptoms. Items that measure these symptoms in diagnostic inventories should have d parameters that are substantially less than 1.00.

We believe that item extremity is a plausible reason, but certainly not the only plausible reason, why c and d parameters are needed in psychopathology models. Indeed, the correlations between the asymptotes and the item difficulty parameters on the 23-item LSE scale were modest to low: $r_{bd} = .51$ (95% CI = .37–.62) and $r_{bc} = .03$ (95% CI = –.18—.20). This suggests that other reasons must account for our findings.

We contend that a second and psychologically more interesting reason for our results is that many psychopathology items are psychometrically ambiguous for individuals at one extreme of the trait continuum, although not ambiguous for individuals at the other extreme. We have called this phenomenon *nonsymmetric, content ambiguity* (Reise & Waller, 2003). In our current thinking, nonsymmetric content ambiguity is a form of item-level multidimensionality.

To illustrate this notion, consider the item "Feel the best ever" (keyed *False* on our Depression factor scale). In our terminology, for highly depressed individuals this item is semantically unambiguous. Individuals in the throes of a depressive episode have (hopefully) felt better at other points in their lives. For a nondepressed individual, however, the meaning of this item is ambiguous. Many nondepressed persons respond *False* (the keyed response) to this item. Presumably these persons are not having the emotional "peak experience" of their lives while completing an omnibus, psychopathology questionnaire with 567 items.

To further illustrate this point, consider the item "Often talks to strangers." Previously, we reported (Reise & Waller, 2003) that this item has a large c parameter when it is keyed *False* on our Social Discomfort factor scale. We also suggested that the item's meaning is clear for socially uncomfortable persons but is less clear for persons who are socially comfortable. Not surprisingly, many individuals who lack social discomfort (i.e., socially comfortable individuals) avoid talking with strangers on buses, trains, and other social settings. A socially comfortable individual may avoid speaking to strangers because, in his or her mind, such behavior is rude or against religious dictate.

Does the 4PLM Offer a Difference That Makes a Difference?

Whether the 4PLM offers a psychometric difference that makes a difference is undoubtedly the central question of this study. We believe that when our results are viewed in aggregate, the answer to this question must be a resounding *yes*.

Previously (e.g., Reise & Waller, 2003), we suggested that for some measurement purposes a 2PLM may suffice even when the data are more accurately modeled by a three- or four-parameter model. Our reasons behind this claim were threefold. First, in our experience with psychopathology data, the relative fit between the models—in absolute terms—is rarely large even when it is statistically significant. (This is not true for the 1PLM which, in our experience, does not fit MMPI data.) Second, trait estimates from the two- and three-parameter models are highly correlated when scores are broadly sampled from the trait continuum. Third, a 2PLM IRF can often approximate a 3PLM or 4PLM IRF with considerable accuracy by simply underestimating the item discrimination parameter.

The above comments notwithstanding, we believe that for many measurement tasks it is critically important to use the most accurate IRT model and that with psychopathology data the best model will sometimes be the 4PLM. Several findings from our work have convinced us of this point. One finding of particular importance to clinical psychologists concerns the relative ordering of trait estimates in the three- and four-parameter models.

It is not surprising that when we considered our aggregate sample of LSE data, we found that the maximum likelihood trait estimates from the three- and four-parameter models were highly correlated. Because correlations are largely determined by scores at the distribution extremes, with heterogeneous samples it makes little difference whether trait estimates are computed by the two-, three- or four-parameter models when comparing score ranks. In each case, the individuals with the highest (or lowest) trait estimates will retain their relative positions regardless of model choice.

Nevertheless, findings that hold for a heterogeneous sample may not generalize to a more homogeneous subsample. For instance, when we restricted our attention to individuals with high LSE scores (i.e., individuals with the lowest levels self-esteem), the rank-order correlation between the 3PLM and 4PLM trait estimates was a modest .45. This finding demonstrates that at the clinically important end of the LSE continuum, model choice is important. As shown earlier in this chapter, the various models also produce strikingly different pictures of measurement precision for this clinical assessment scale. Specifically, the standard errors for the highest scoring subjects on the LSE were considerably larger in the 4PLM than in the 3PLM. Assuming that the 4PLM is the more appropriate model for this scale, our findings suggest that the 3PLM (or 2PLM) provides a false sense of measurement precision for precisely those individuals who are of greatest interest to clinicians.

A few closing remarks concerning the effects of fitting the "wrong" model to psychopathology data deserve mention. We first consider how an item's discrimination parameter can change across models. To keep matters simple, consider a moderately difficult item with a large c parameter. All things considered, the item discrimination for such an item will be higher in the 3PLM than in the

2PLM. Moreover, if the empirical response function has a non-one upper asymptote, then the discrimination parameter will also be higher in the 4PLM relative to the 3PLM. These findings result from a simple geometric fact. Namely, the IRF must rise at a faster rate within a narrower trait range as its asymptotes move inward from 0.0 and 1.0.

Choosing different models will also change item difficulty values. Recall that the difficulty parameter is defined at the inflection point of the IRF. In the 2PLM, the inflection point occurs at the latent trait score that corresponds to a .50 item endorsement probability. In the 3PLM, the inflection point occurs where the response rate is $.5 + \frac{c}{2}$. Thus, for items with nonzero lower asymptotes, the difficulty parameters are shifted upward in the 3PLM relative to the 2PLM. In the 4PLM the inflection point occurs where the response rate equals $\frac{d}{2} + \frac{c}{2}$. Thus, for items with upper asymptotes that are not equal to one, the item difficulties are lower in the 4PLM relative to the 3PLM (because $\frac{d}{2} \leq .5$).

When considered across all items, these location shifts have important consequences for the estimated TIF. Consequently, although the IRF from a 2PLM, 3PLM, or 4PLM may provide similar fits to an empirical item response function, the different item parameter estimates can yield very different pictures of how a test will perform in different samples.

Measurement specialists are beginning to take a second look at the 4PLM (Loken & Rulison, 2006; Reise & Waller, 2003; see also Hessen, 2004). To our knowledge, this chapter describes the first application of the 4PLM to psychopathology data. Naturally, because we are exploring relatively uncharted waters, many questions remain unanswered concerning the usefulness of the 4PLM in other data sets and in other testing domains. In this chapter we applied the 4PLM to a single construct and a single scale. If these results generalize to other constructs and scales, then the 4PLM will become a standard model of IRT.

References

Albert, J. H. (1992). Bayesian estimation of normal ogive item response curves using Gibbs sampling. *Journal of Educational Statistics, 17,* 251–269.

Albert, J. H., & Chib, S. (1993). Bayesian analysis of binary and polychotomous response data. *Journal of the American Statistical Association, 88,* 669–679.

Archer, R. P., & Newsom, C. R. (2000). Psychological test usage with adolescent clients: Survey update. *Assessment, 7,* 227–235.

Assessment Systems Corporation. (1997). *Manual for the XCALIBRE marginal maximum-likelihood estimation program.* St. Paul, MN: Author.

Baker, F. B. (1998). An investigation of the item parameter recovery characteristics of a Gibbs sampling procedure. *Applied Psychological Measurement, 22,* 153–169.

Barton, M. A., & Lord, F. M. (1981). *An upper asymptote for the three-parameter logistic item-response model* (Research Bulletin 81–20). Princeton, NJ: Educational Testing Service.

Bayes, T. (1763). An essay towards solving a problem in the doctrine of chances. *Philosophical Transactions of the Royal Society of London, 53,* 370–418.

Beaumont, M. A., & Rannala, B. (2004). The Bayesian revolution in genetics. *Nature Reviews Genetics, 5,* 251–261.

Beguin, A. A., & Glas, C. A. W. (2001). MCMC estimation and some model-fit analysis of multidimensional IRT models. *Psychometrika, 66,* 541–561.

Birnbaum, A. (1968). Some latent trait models and their use in inferring an examinee's ability. In F. M. Lord & M. R. Novick (Eds.), *Statistical theories of mental test scores.* Reading, MA: Addison-Wesley.

Bock, R. D. (1997). A brief history of item response theory. *Educational Measurement: Issues and Practice, 16,* 21–32.

Borsboom, D., & Mellenberg, G. J. (2004). Why psychometrics is not pathological: A comment on Michell. *Theory and Psychology, 14,* 105–120.

Bradlow, E. T. (1996). Negative information and the three-parameter logistic model. *Journal of Educational and Behavioral Statistics, 21,* 179–185.

Brooks, S. P., & Gelman, A. (1998). Convergence assessment techniques for Markov Chain Monte Carlo. *Statistics and Computing, 8,* 319–335.

Butcher, J. N., Williams, C. L., Graham, J. R., Archer, R., Tellegen, A., Ben-Porath, Y. S., & Kaemmer, B. (1992). *MMPI—A manual for administration, scoring, and interpretation.* Minneapolis: University of Minnesota Press.

Carter, J. E., & Wilkinson, L. (1984). A latent trait analysis of the MMPI. *Multivariate Behavioral Research, 19,* 385–407.

Casella, G., & George, E. I. (1992). Explaining the Gibbs Sampler. *The American Statistician, 46,* 167–174.

Chernyshenko, O. S., Stark, S., Chan, K. Y., Drasgow, F., & Williams, B. (2001). Fitting item response theory models to two personality inventories: Issues and insights. *Multivariate Behavioral Research, 36,* 523–562.

Childs, R. A., Dahlstrom, W. G., Kemp, S. M., & Panter, A. T. (2000). Item response theory in personality assessment: A demonstration using the MMPI-2 Depression Scale. *Assessment, 7,* 37–54.

Congdon, P. (2001). *Bayesian statistical modeling.* New York: Wiley.

Edwards, W., Lindman H., & Savage L. J. (1963). Bayesian statistical inference for psychological research. *Psychological Review, 70,* 193–242.

Embretson, S. E. (1996). The new rules of measurement. *Psychological Assessment, 8,* 341–349.

Embretson, S. E., & Reise, S. P. (2000). *Item response theory for psychologists.* Hillsdale, NJ: Erlbaum.

Ferrando, P. J. (2004). Kernel-smoothing estimation of item characteristic functions for continuous personality items: An empirical comparison with the linear and the continuous-response models. *Applied Psychological Measurement, 28,* 95–109.

Fox, J. P., & Glas, C. A. W. (2001). Bayesian estimation of a multilevel IRT model using Gibbs sampling. *Psychometrika, 66,* 269–286.

Gelfand, A. E., & Smith, A. F. M. (1990). Sampling-based approaches to calculating marginal densities. *Journal of the American Statistical Association, 85,* 398–409.

Gelman, A. (1996). Inference and monitoring convergence. In W. R. Gilks, S. Richardson, & D. J. Spiegelhalter (Eds.), *Markov chain Monte Carlo in practice* (pp. 131–144.). New York: Chapman & Hall.

Gelman, A., Carlin, J. B., Stern, H. S., & Rubin, D. B. (2004). *Bayesian data analysis* (2nd ed.). London: Chapman & Hall.

Gelman, A., & Rubin, D. B. (1992). Inference from iterative simulation using multiple sequences (with discussion). *Statistical Science, 7,* 457–511.

Geman, S., & Geman, D. (1984). Stochastic relaxation, Gibbs distributions, and the Bayesian restoration of images. *IEEE Transactions on Pattern Analysis and Machine Intelligence, 6,* 721–741.

Gilks, W. R., Richardson, S., & Spiegelhalter, D. J. (1995). *Markov chain Monte Carlo in practice.* London: Chapman & Hall.

Gill, J. (2002). *Bayesian methods: A social and behavioral sciences approach.* New York: Chapman & Hall/CRC.

Hambleton, R. K., & Swaminathan, H. (1985). *Item response theory: Principles and applications.* Boston: Kluwer-Nijhoff.

Hambleton, R. K., Swaminathan, H., & Rogers, H. J. (1991). *Fundamentals of item response theory.* Newbury Park, MA: SAGE.

Hastings, W. K. (1970). Monte Carlo sampling methods using Markov chains and their applications. *Biometrika, 57,* 97–109.
Hessen, D. J. (2004). A new class of parametric IRT models for dichotomous item scores. *Journal of Applied Measurement, 5,* 385–397.
Jackman, S. (2000). Estimation and inference: An introduction to Markov chain Monte Carlo. *American Journal of Political Science, 44,* 375–404.
Jackman, S. (2004). Bayesian analysis for political research. *Annual Review of Political Science, 35,* 178–205.
Johnson, V. E., & Albert, J. H. (1999). *Ordinal data modeling.* New York: Springer-Verlag.
Junker, B. W., & Sijtsma, K. (2000). Latent and manifest monotonicity in item response models. *Applied Psychological Measurement, 24,* 65–81.
Junker, B. W., & Sijtsma, K. (2001). Nonparametric item response theory [Special issue]. *Applied Psychological Measurement, 25*(3).
Kim, S. (2001). An evaluation of a Markov chain Monte Carlo method for the Rasch model. *Applied Psychological Measurement, 25,* 163–176.
Lees-Haley, P. R., Smith, H. H., Williams, C. W., & Dunn, J. T. (1996). Forensic neuropsychological test usage: An empirical survey. *Archives of Clinical Neuropsychology, 11,* 45–51.
Linacre, J. M. (2004). Discrimination, guessing and carelessness: Estimating IRT parameters with Rasch. *Rasch Measurement Transactions, 18,* 959–960.
Loken, E., & Rulison, K. L. (2006). *Bayesian estimation of a 4-parameter item response model.* Manuscript submitted for publication.
Lord, F. M. (1980). *Applications of item response theory to practical testing problems.* Hillsdale, NJ: Erlbaum.
Martin, A. D., & Quinn, K. (2006). MCMCpack: Markov chain Monte Carlo (MCMC) Package. R Package Version 0.7-2. Available at http://mcmcpack.wustl.edu
Meijer, R. R., & Baneke, J. J. (2004). Analyzing psychopathology items: A case for nonparametric item response theory modeling. *Psychological Methods, 9,* 354–368.
Metropolis, N., Rosenbluth, A. W., Rosenbluth, M. N., Teller, A. H., & Teller, E. (1953). Equations of state calculations by fast computing machines. *Journal of Chemical Physics, 21,* 1087–1091.
Michell, J. (2004). Item response models, pathological science and the shape of error: Reply to Borsboom and Mellenbergh. *Theory and Psychology, 10,* 121–129.
Mislevy, R., & Bock, R. D. (1998). *BILOG-3; Item analysis and test scoring with binary logistic models* [Computer software]. Mooresville, IN: Scientific Software.
Mislevy, R. J., & Verhelst, N. (1990). Modeling item responses when different subjects employ different solution strategies. *Psychometrika, 55,* 195–215.
Novick, M. R., & Jackson, P. H. (1974). *Statistical methods for educational and psychological research.* New York: McGraw-Hill.
O'Grady, J. C. (1990). The prevalence and diagnostic significance of Schneiderian first-rank symptoms in a random sample of acute psychiatric in-patients. *The British Journal of Psychiatry 156,* 496–500.
Panter, A. T., Swygert, K. A., Dahlstrom, W. G., & Tanaka, J. S. (1997). Factor analytic approaches to personality item-level data. *Journal of Personality Assessment, 68,* 561–589.
Patz, R. J., & Junker, B. W. (1999). A straightforward approach to Markov chain Monte Carlo methods for item response models. *Journal of Educational and Behavioral Statistics, 24,* 146–178.
Perline, R., Wright, B. D., & Wainer, H. (1979). The Rasch model as additive conjoint measurement. *Applied Psychological Measurement, 3,* 237–255.
Phillips, L. D. (1974). *Bayesian statistics for social scientists.* New York: Thomas Y. Crowell.
Piotrowski, C., & Keller, J. W. (1989). Psychological testing in outpatient mental health facilities: A national study. *Professional Psychology: Research and Practice, 20,* 423–425.
R Development Core Team (2009). *R: A language and environment for statistical computing. R Foundation for Statistical Computing.* Vienna, Austria. Available at http://www.R-project.org
Rasch, G. (1960). *Probabilistic models for some intelligence and attainment tests.* Copenhagen: Danish Institute for Educational Research.
Reise, S. P. (2004, July). *Problems in measuring psychopathology constructs with a focus on depression.* Invited talk at the annual meeting of the American Psychological Association, Honolulu, HI.

Reise, S. P. (1999). Personality measurement issues viewed through the eyes of IRT. In S. E. Embretson & S. L. Hershberger (Eds.), *The new rules of measurement: What every psychologist and educator should know* (pp. 219–241). Mahwah, NJ: Erlbaum.

Reise, S. P., & Waller, N. G. (1990). Fitting the two-parameter model to personality data. *Applied Psychological Measurement, 14,* 45–58.

Reise, S. P., & Waller, N. G. (2001). Item response theory for dichotomous assessment data. In F. Drasgow & N. W. Schmitt (Eds.), *Measuring and analyzing behavior in organizations: Advances in measurement and data analysis* (pp. 88–122). San Francisco: Jossey-Bass.

Reise, S. P., & Waller, N. G. (2003). How many IRT parameters does it take to model psychopathology items? *Psychological Methods, 8,* 164–184.

Reise, S. P., Ainsworth, A. T., & Haviland, M. G. (2005). Item response theory: Fundamentals, applications, and promise in psychological research. *Current Directions in Psychological Science, 14,* 95–101.

Roskam, E. E. (1985). Current issues in item response theory. In E. E. Roskam (Ed.), Measurement and personality assessment (pp. 3–20). Amsterdam: North Holland.

Rouanet, H. (1996). Bayesian methods for assessing importance of effects. *Psychological Bulletin, 119,* 149–158.

Rouse, S. V., Finger, M. S., & Butcher, J. N. (1999). Advances in clinical personality measurement: An item response theory analysis of the MMPI-2 PSY-5 scales. *Journal of Personality Assessment, 72,* 282–307.

Rupp, A. A. (2003). Item response theory modeling with BILOG-MG and MULTILOG for Windows. *International Journal of Testing, 3*(4), 365–384.

Rupp, A. A., Dey, D. K., & Zumbo, B. D. (2004). To Bayes or not to Bayes, from whether to when: Applications of Bayesian Methodology to Modeling. *Structural Equation Modeling, 11,* 424–451.

Santor, D. A., Ramsay, J. O., & Zuroff, D. C. (1994). Nonparametric item analyses of the Beck Depression Inventory: Evaluating gender item bias and response option weights. *Psychological Assessment, 6,* 255–270.

Schneider, K. (1959). *Clinical psychopathology.* New York: Grune and Stratton.

Speigelhalter, D., Thomas, A., & Best, N. (2000). WinBUGS Version 1.3 [user's manual]. Cambridge, England: Medical Research Council Biostatistics Unit. Available at http://www.mrc-bsu.cam.ac.uk/bugs)

Steinberg, L., & Thissen, D. (1995). Item response theory in personality research. In P. E. Shrout & S. T. Fiske (Eds.), *Personality research, methods, and theory: A festschrift honoring Donald W. Fiske* (pp. 161–181). Hillsdale, NJ: Erlbaum.

Steinberg, L., & Thissen, D. (1996). Uses of item response theory and the testlet concept in the measurement of psychopathology. *Psychological Methods, 1,* 81–97.

Swaminathan, H., & Gifford, J. A. (1982). Bayesian estimation in the Rasch model. *Journal of Educational Statistics, 7,* 175–191.

Swaminathan, H., & Gifford, J. A. (1985). Bayesian estimation in the two-parameter logistic model. *Psychometrika, 50,* 349–364.

Swaminathan, H., & Gifford, J. A. (1986). Bayesian estimation in the three-parameter logistic model. *Psychometrika, 51,* 589–601.

Takane, Y., & DeLeeuw, J. (1987). On the relationship between item response theory and factor analysis of discretized variables. *Psychometrika, 52,* 393–408.

Thissen, D., & Wainer, H. (1990). Confidence envelopes for item response theory. *Journal of Educational Statistics, 15,* 113–128.

Thomas, A. (2006). BRUGS, Version 0.3-2 [user's manual]. Department of Mathematics and Statistics, University of Helsinki, Finland.

Tsutakawa, R. K., & Lin, H. Y. (1986). Bayesian estimation of item response curves. *Psychometrika, 51,* 251–267.

van der Linden, W. J., & Hambleton, R. K. (Eds.). (1997). *Handbook of modern item response theory.* New York: Springer-Verlag.

Wainer, H. (1990). *Computerized adaptive testing: A primer.* Hillsdale, NJ: Erlbaum.

Waller, N. G. (1999). Searching for structure in the MMPI. In S. Embretson & S. Hershberger (Eds.), *The new rules of measurement: What every psychologist and educator should know* (pp. 185–217). Mahwah, NJ: Erlbaum.

Waller, N. G., & Reise, S. P. (1989). Computerized adaptive personality assessment: An illustration with the Absorption scale. *Journal of Personality and Social Psychology, 57,* 1051–1058.

Waller, N. G., & Reise, S. P. (1992). Genetic and environmental influences on item response pattern scalability. *Behavior Genetics, 22,* 135–152.

Waller, N. G., Tellegen, A., McDonald, R., & Lykken, D. T. (1996). Exploring nonlinear models in personality assessment: Development and preliminary validation of a Negative Emotionality Scale. *Journal of Personality, 64,* 545–576.

Waller, N. G., Thompson, J. S., & Wenk, E. (2000). Black-White differences on the MMPI: Using IRT to separate measurement bias from true group differences. *Psychological Methods, 5,* 125–146.

Wang, W., Chen, P., & Cheng, Y. (2004). Improving measurement precision of test batteries using multidimensional item response models. *Psychological Methods, 9,* 116–136.

Yen, W. M., Burket, G. R., & Sykes, R. C. (1991). Nonunique solutions to the likelihood equation for the three-parameter logistic model. *Psychometrika, 56,* 39–54.

Zimowski, M. F., Muraki, E., Mislevy, R. J., & Bock, R. D. (1996). *BILOG-MG: Multiple group IRT analysis and test maintenance for binary items.* Chicago: Scientific Software International.

Zumbo, B. D., Pope, G. A., Watson, J. E., & Hubley, A. M. (1997). An empirical test of Roskam's conjecture about the interpretation of an ICC parameter in personality inventories. *Educational and Psychological Measurement, 57,* 963–969.

8

MIXUM: An Unfolding Mixture Model to Explore the Latitude of Acceptance Concept in Attitude Measurement

James S. Roberts, Jürgen Rost, and George B. Macready

The latitude of acceptance construct has a long history in the psychology of attitudes and attitude change. The concept can be traced back to attitude studies conducted by Carl Hovland and colleagues during the 1950s, which subsequently spawned the development of social judgment theory (Sherif & Hovland, 1961). Traditional attitude measurement techniques generally attempt to find the location of a given respondent on a unidimensional attitude continuum with poles that represent unfavorableness and favorableness toward the attitude object in question. From this perspective, an attitude is represented by a single point on the latent attitude continuum. In contrast, the latitude of acceptance concept refers to the range of statements that the individual is willing to endorse, and thus, it corresponds to an interval surrounding an individual's location on the attitude continuum.

From a social judgment theory perspective, both the individual's location on the attitude continuum and the individual's latitude of acceptance are important characteristics. For example, two individuals may have identical attitudinal positions on the latent continuum but may differ in their latitudes of acceptance. One of these individuals may be willing to endorse only a narrow range of attitude statements located close to the individual's attitude position, whereas the other person may be willing to endorse a much broader range of statements. Social judgment theory suggests that these latitudes have implications for attitude change (Sherif, Sherif, & Nebergall, 1965). Specifically, the maximum amount of attitude change can be expected when individuals are persuaded to accept statements near the bounds of their latitudes of acceptance. Consequently, a mechanism for estimating an individual's latitude of acceptance should prove useful to researchers interested in attitude change

---

This work was supported by National Science Foundation Grant SES-0133019 and SES0536728, awarded to the first author by the Methodology, Measurement, and Statistics program in the Division of Social and Economic Sciences. The authors are grateful to Chan Dayton and Robert Mislevy for their comments and suggestions throughout the course of this project.

from a social judgment theory perspective. This chapter focuses on the development of a method that can simultaneously estimate an individual's attitude toward a given object and also provide information about the person's latitude of acceptance. The method will combine concepts from both latent class modeling and unfolding item response theory (IRT).

Unfolding Item Response Theory Models

During the last two decades, there has been a substantial amount of research devoted to unfolding IRT models. Both parametric and nonparametric IRT models for unfolding have been proposed for both binary and polytomous responses (see Roberts, Laughlin, & Wedell, 1999, for a list of proposed IRT models for unfolding). The parametric IRT models for unfolding offer the possibility of sample invariant interpretation of item parameters (i.e., item locations and characteristics), item invariant interpretation of person parameters (i.e., attitudes), and the ability to quantify measurement precision at an individual level. These possibilities can lead to improvements in attitude measurement including test equating, item banking, and computerized adaptive testing.

The basic premise underlying unfolding IRT models is that an individual is more likely to endorse a statement to the extent that the sentiment expressed by the statement matches the individual's opinion. Psychometrically, this means that the individual is more likely to endorse a statement to the extent that the statement is located close to the individual on a unidimensional latent attitude continuum. Figure 8.1 illustrates the typical item characteristic curves (ICCs) that are suggested by unfolding IRT models. These curves are different from those found with traditional cumulative IRT models used for testing proficiency. Cumulative models only allow for monotonically increasing item characteristic curves. In the context of attitude measurement, this would imply that one is more likely to endorse a statement to the extent that one's attitude location dominates the location of an item. Several researchers (Andrich, 1996; Roberts, Laughlin, & Wedell, 1999; van Schuur & Kiers, 1994) have suggested that unfolding models are more appropriate than cumulative models when individuals indicate how much they disagree or agree with statements on a typical Likert or Thurstone attitude questionnaire.

Incorporating Latitude of Acceptance Into Unfolding IRT Models

There have been previous efforts to incorporate the latitude of acceptance concept into unfolding IRT models. For example, Luo (1998) developed an IRT model that parameterizes latitude of acceptance. However, this work focused primarily on item-level parameters.[1] Specifically, the characteristic curve for a given item was stretched or shrunk along the latent continuum. In contrast, social

---

[1] Luo (1998) did mention the possibility of parameterizing latitude of acceptance as a person parameter, but this parameterization was never explored.

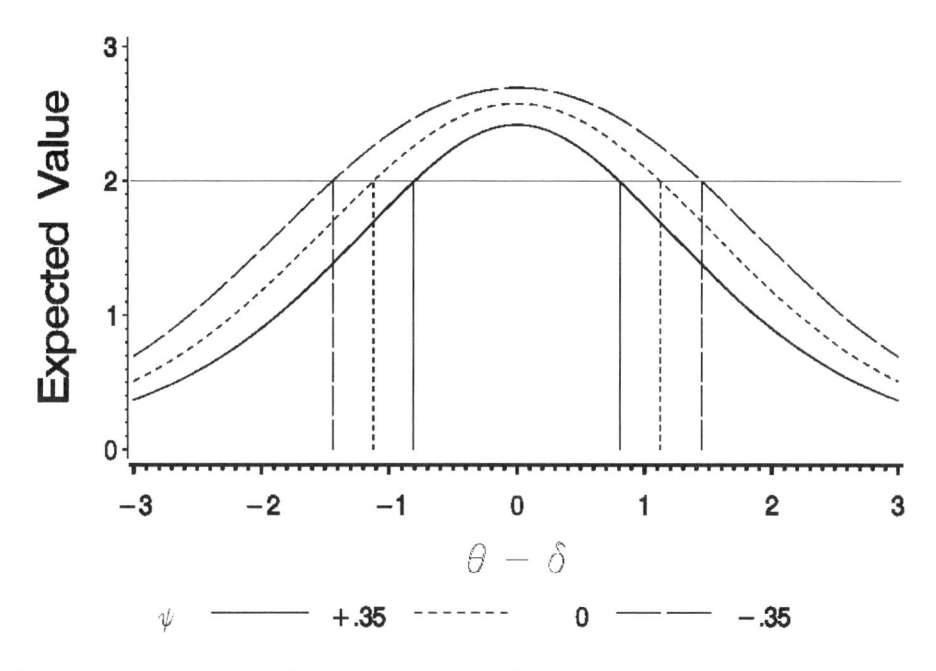

Figure 8.1. Expected value functions under the MIXUM for $\psi_d = +.35$, 0, and $-.35$ in Latent Classes 1 through 3, respectively.

judgment theory depicts the latitude of acceptance concept as a variable that differs among individuals rather than among items. Luo, Andrich, and Styles (1998) came closer to the social judgment perspective when they estimated alternative group latitudes of acceptance for attitudes toward drug testing in the workplace. In their study, a different latitude of acceptance parameter was estimated for each of four groups of students in alternative academic disciplines. In this context, the latitude of acceptance varied across manifest groups of individuals as opposed to items.

The purpose of this article is to illustrate a new way to model the latitude of acceptance construct using an IRT framework that is consonant with social judgment theory. As mentioned above, social judgment theory presumes that latitude of acceptance is a person attribute rather than an item characteristic. An unfolding item response model would ideally include a person-level parameter to reflect latitude of acceptance. Consequently, an unfolding IRT model would need two distinct parameters for every respondent: one parameter that reflects the respondent's position on the latent continuum (i.e., the respondent's attitude) and one that reflects the respondent's latitude of acceptance. Our suspicion, however, is that the degree of parameter estimation difficulty would increase substantially with the addition of a second person parameter to typical unfolding IRT models. We have consequently taken a more cautious approach. Like Luo et al. (1998), we have opted to parameterize the latitude of acceptance in alternative respondent groups. However, our new model is unique in that group membership is itself considered to be a latent variable. The model we propose is therefore a latent mixture of several unfolding models in which item characteristic curves are stretched or shrunk differently along the latent continuum in each of the alternative latent classes (i.e., latent groups). This idea parallels the work of Mislevy and Verhelst (1990), Rost (1990, 1991), and Yamamoto (1989) in the cumulative IRT domain.

A New Model: The Mixed Unfolding Model (MIXUM)

The MIXUM is an adaptation of the graded unfolding model (Roberts & Laughlin, 1996) for polytomous disagree–agree responses. It is appropriate when subjects indicate their level of agreement using either a binary or graded scale. The response scale must be defined so that zero represents the strongest level of disagreement and increasing levels of agreement are indexed by successive integers (e.g., 0 = *strongly disagree,* 1 = *disagree,* 2 = *agree,* and 3 = *strongly agree*). For an individual in latent class d, the model is defined by its response category probability function as follows:

$$P[Z_i = z \mid \theta_j, \psi_d] =$$

$$\frac{\exp\left(z(\theta_j - \delta_i) - z\psi_d - \sum_{k=0}^{z}\tau_k\right) + \exp\left((M-z)(\theta_j - \delta_i) - z\psi_d - \sum_{k=0}^{z}\tau_k\right)}{\sum_{w=0}^{C}\left[\exp\left(w(\theta_j - \delta_i) - w\psi_d - \sum_{k=0}^{w}\tau_k\right) + \exp\left((M-w)(\theta_j - \delta_i) - w\psi_d - \sum_{k=0}^{w}\tau_k\right)\right]}, \quad (1)$$

where

Z_i = an observable response to attitude statement i,
$z = 0, 1, 2, \ldots, C$; $z = 0$ corresponds to the strongest level of disagreement and $z = C$ refers to the strongest level of agreement,
C = the number of observable response categories minus 1,
θ_j = the location of individual j on the attitude continuum,
δ_i = the location of attitude statement i on the attitude continuum,
τ_k = the location of the kth subjective response category threshold on the attitude continuum relative to the location of a given item; $k = 0, \ldots, C$,
ψ_d = the latitude of acceptance parameter for individuals in latent class d; $d = 1, \ldots, D$,
M = the number of subjective response categories minus 1 (note that $M = 2C + 1$).

Note that the value of τ_0 is arbitrarily set to zero, although this choice has no effect on the resulting probabilities. The parameters are constrained to be symmetric about the point $(\theta_j - \delta_i) = 0$, which yields:

$$\tau_{(C+1)} = 0, \quad (2)$$

and

$$\tau_z = -\tau_{(M-z+1)}, \text{ for } z = 1, 2, \ldots C. \quad (3)$$

At a conceptual level, this premise implies that an individual is just as likely to agree with an item located at either −h units or +h units from the individual's position on the attitude continuum. In addition to the traditional location constraint required to achieve identifiability, the following constraint is also needed:

$$\sum_{d=1}^{D} \psi_d = 0. \quad (4)$$

The MIXUM yields symmetric, single-peaked expected value functions that are centered about the $\hat{\theta}_j - \hat{\delta}_i = 0$. The breadth and the maximum of each expected value function are controlled generally across all items by the τ_k parameters. However, the ψ_d parameter essentially adds a constant to each nonzero τ_k parameter within the *dth* latent class. Therefore, the expected value function changes accordingly in each latent class. Figure 1 illustrates the expected value functions obtained with a hypothetical four-category item in each of three latent classes. The hypothetical categories correspond to 0 = *strongly disagree*, 1 = *disagree*, 2 = *agree*, and 3 = *strongly agree*. The vertical lines emanating from the horizontal axis form intervals on the latent continuum in which a given expected value function is greater than two (i.e., in which the function predicts some level of agreement). Conceptually, these intervals correspond to the latitudes of acceptance in the alternative latent classes. The τ_k values for each function are $\tau_0 = 0$, $\tau_1 = -2.4$, $\tau_2 = -1.6$, and $\tau_3 = -.8$. The latitude of acceptance parameter is equal to $\psi_1 = .35$, $\psi_2 = 0$, and $\psi_3 = -.35$ in the three latent classes. This produces the following class-specific thresholds:

Latent Class 1: $\tau_0 = 0$, $\tau_1 = -2.05$, $\tau_2 = -1.25$, and $\tau_3 = -.45$
Latent Class 2: $\tau_0 = 0$, $\tau_1 = -2.40$, $\tau_2 = -1.60$, and $\tau_3 = -.80$
Latent Class 3: $\tau_0 = 0$, $\tau_1 = -2.75$, $\tau_2 = -1.95$, and $\tau_3 = -1.15$.

As shown in Figure 1, adding a positive constant to all nonzero τ_k (as is done in Latent Class 1) causes the associated expected value function to become less spread out across the latent continuum. This yields a more narrow latitude of acceptance. The function also achieves a smaller maximum value in this case. In contrast, when a negative constant is added to all nonzero τ_k (as is done in Latent Class 3), the resulting expected value function becomes more spread out across the latent continuum. This results in a broader latitude of acceptance. The function also achieves a larger maximum value in this case. In summary, positive values of ψ_d are indicative of narrower latitudes, and negative values represent broader latitudes. The ψ_d parameters determine the width of these intervals, although they do not explicitly define their locations on the latent continuum.

Parameter Estimation in the MIXUM

Estimation of MIXUM parameters is accomplished with a two-stage procedure. In the first stage of the procedure, the person parameters, θ_j, are integrated out of the likelihood equation, and the item and latent class parameters are estimated from this marginalized likelihood. Once the item and latent class parameters

The General Logic of the Estimation Algorithm

Estimation of δ_i, τ_k, and ψ_d parameters is accomplished using a marginal maximum likelihood (MML) technique similar to that implemented by Mislevy and Verhelst (1990) and Yamamoto (1989). The technique is based on an expectation-maximization (EM) algorithm in which the estimated proportion of subjects in each latent class (i.e., the estimated mixing proportions) are calculated along with the expected distribution of θ in each class. These values are used to estimate the marginal likelihood function, which is subsequently maximized to find the optimal values of δ_i, τ_k, and ψ_d. The mixing proportions and the empirical distribution of θ in each latent class are obtained as a byproduct of the EM algorithm. Estimation of θ is accomplished using a modified expected a posteriori (EAP) method. Traditionally, an EAP estimate is the mean of the posterior distribution of θ for an individual, given the individual's item responses and the item parameter estimates. In the MIXUM, the item characteristic curves change in each of D latent classes. Therefore, the individual's EAP estimate is calculated D times under the presumption that the individual is a member of each latent class. These D estimates of θ are averaged together using the individual's estimated probabilities of class membership as weights.

The Details of the Estimation Algorithm

Let X_j be one of the N response vectors in the data in which N is the total sample size. Let D be the number of latent groups from which individuals have been sampled. Let x_{ji} refer to the ith element of X_j. Under the assumption of local independence, the conditional probability of observing a particular response vector, X_j, given θ_j and ψ_d is equal to

$$P[X_j | \theta_j, \psi_d] = \prod_{i=1}^{I} P[Z_i = x_{ji} | \theta_j, \psi_d]. \quad (5)$$

If subjects are sampled from D populations, each with a continuous attitude distribution, denoted as $g_d(\theta)$, then the marginal probability of observing one of the N response vectors, X_j, in a given latent group, d, is equal to

$$P_d[X_j] = \int_{-\infty}^{+\infty} \Pr[X_j | \theta_j, \psi_d] g_d(\theta) d\theta. \quad (6)$$

Suppose that the latent group membership was actually observed. The marginal likelihood of the response data could then be written as

$$L = \prod_{d=1}^{D} \prod_{j=1}^{N} \left[P_d(X_j)^{\gamma_{jd}} \right], \quad (7)$$

where γ_{jd} is an indicator variable that is equal to one if the *jth* individual is a member of latent class d and is otherwise equal to zero. The log likelihood would be equal to

$$\ln(L) = \sum_{d=1}^{D}\sum_{j=1}^{N} \gamma_{jd} \ln[P_d(X_j)]. \quad (8)$$

The general form of the first-order partial derivative of the log-likelihood function with respect to δ_i, is given by

$$\frac{\partial \ln(L)}{\partial \delta_i} = \sum_{d=1}^{D}\sum_{j=1}^{N} \frac{\gamma_{jd}}{P_d[X_j]} \frac{\partial P_d[X_j]}{\partial \delta_i}$$

$$= \sum_{d=1}^{D}\sum_{j=1}^{N} \frac{\gamma_{jd}}{P_d[X_j]} \int_{-\infty}^{+\infty} \frac{\partial P[Z_i = x_{ji}|\theta]}{\partial \delta_i} P[X_j|\theta,\psi_d] \frac{g_d(\theta)}{P[Z_i = x_{ji}|\theta,\psi_d]} d\theta. \quad (9)$$

The Equation 9 may be approximated using quadrature based on the rectangle method as follows:

$$\frac{\partial \ln(L)}{\partial \delta_i} = \sum_{d=1}^{D}\sum_{f=1}^{F}\sum_{j=1}^{N} \frac{\gamma_{jd} L_{jd}(V_f) A_d(V_f)}{\tilde{P}_{jd}} \frac{\partial P[Z_i = x_{ji}|V_f,\psi_d]}{\partial \delta_i} \frac{1}{P[Z_i = x_{ji}|V_f,\psi_d]}$$

$$= \sum_{d=1}^{D}\sum_{f=1}^{F}\sum_{z=0}^{C}\sum_{j=1}^{N} \frac{\gamma_{jd} H_{jiz} L_{jd}(V_f) A_d(V_f)}{\tilde{P}_{jd}} \frac{\partial P[Z_i = z|V_f,\psi_d]}{\partial \delta_i} \frac{1}{P[Z_i = z|V_f,\psi_d]}$$

$$= \sum_{d=1}^{D}\sum_{f=1}^{F}\sum_{z=0}^{C} \frac{\bar{r}_{izfd}}{P[Z_i = z|V_f,\psi_d]} \frac{\partial P[Z_i = z|V_f,\psi_d]}{\partial \delta_i} \quad (10)$$

where

$$L_{jd}(V_f) = \prod_{i=1}^{I} P[Z_i = x_{ji}|V_f,\psi_d] \quad (11)$$

$$\tilde{P}_{jd} = \sum_{f=1}^{F} L_{jd}(V_f) A_d(V_f) \quad (12)$$

$$\bar{r}_{izfd} = \sum_{j=1}^{N} \frac{\gamma_{jd} H_{jiz} L_{jd}(V_f) A_d(V_f)}{\tilde{P}_{jd}} \quad (13)$$

and H_{jiz} is a dummy variable that is equal to one when x_{ji} equals z and is equal to zero otherwise. In Equation 10, V_f is a quadrature point, and $A_d(V_f)$ is the rescaled density at V_f for latent group d. These density values constitute the discrete prior distribution of θ. The scale of the $A_d(V_f)$ values is such that

$$\sum_{f=1}^{F} A_d(V_f) = 1. \quad (14)$$

Additionally, $L_{jd}(V_f)$ is the conditional probability of response pattern $\mathbf{X}_j$ at quadrature point V_f in latent group d, $\tilde{P}_{jd}$ is the marginal probability of response pattern $\mathbf{X}_j$ in latent group d, and $\bar{r}_{izfd}$ is the expected frequency of response z for item i at quadrature point V_f in latent group d. Equation 10 includes a derivative of the response category probability function (i.e., $\partial P[Z_i = z|V_f, \psi_d]/\partial \delta_i$) that is thoroughly described in a corresponding technical appendix that may be downloaded from http://www.psychology.gatech.edu/techrep/MIXUM.

The τ_k parameters are constant across items. Therefore, the derivatives of the likelihood function with respect to these parameters are slightly different from those for the δ_i parameters. For a given τ_k, the derivative of the log likelihood is:

$$\frac{\partial \ln(L)}{\partial \tau_k} = \sum_{d=1}^{D} \sum_{j=1}^{N} \frac{\gamma_{jd}}{P_d[\mathbf{X}_j]} \frac{\partial P_d[\mathbf{X}_j]}{\partial \tau_k}$$

$$= \sum_{d=1}^{D} \sum_{j=1}^{N} \frac{\gamma_{jd}}{P_d[\mathbf{X}_j]} \int_{-\infty}^{+\infty} \sum_{i=1}^{I} \left[\frac{\frac{\partial P[Z_i = x_{ji}|\theta, \psi_d]}{\partial \tau_k}}{P[Z_i = x_{ji}|\theta, \psi_d]} \right] P[\mathbf{X}_j|\theta, \psi_d] g_d(\theta) d\theta. \quad (15)$$

Again, this derivative can be approximated using quadrature

$$\frac{\partial \ln(L)}{\partial \tau_k} = \sum_{d=1}^{D} \sum_{f=1}^{F} \sum_{z=0}^{C} \sum_{i=1}^{I} \frac{\bar{r}_{izfd}}{P[Z_i = z|V_f, \psi_d]} \frac{\partial P[Z_i = z|V_f, \psi_d]}{\partial \tau_k}. \quad (16)$$

Equation 16 includes a specific component, $\partial P[Z_i = z|V_f, \psi_d]/\partial \tau_k$, which must be evaluated separately for each τ_k. The derivation of this component is given in the aforementioned technical appendix.

The derivative of the log-likelihood function with regard to a given latent class parameter, ψ_d, is equal to

$$\frac{\partial \ln(L)}{\partial \psi_d} = \sum_{j=1}^{N} \frac{\gamma_{jd}}{P_d[\mathbf{X}_j]} \frac{\partial P_d[\mathbf{X}_j]}{\partial \psi_d}$$

$$= \sum_{j=1}^{N} \frac{\gamma_{jd}}{P_d[\mathbf{X}_j]} \int_{-\infty}^{+\infty} \sum_{i=1}^{I} \left[\frac{\frac{\partial P[Z_i = x_{ji}|\theta, \psi_d]}{\partial \psi_d}}{P[Z_i = x_{ji}|\theta, \psi_d]} \right] P[\mathbf{X}_j|\theta, \psi_d] g_d(\theta) d\theta. \quad (17)$$

Equation 17 can be evaluated with quadrature as follows:

$$\frac{\partial \ln(L)}{\partial \psi_d} = \sum_{f=1}^{F} \sum_{z=0}^{C} \sum_{i=1}^{I} \frac{\bar{r}_{izfd}}{P[Z_i = z|V_f, \psi_d]} \frac{\partial P[Z_i = z|V_f, \psi_d]}{\partial \psi_d} \quad (18)$$

The derivation of $\partial P[Z_i = z|V_f, \psi_d]/\partial \psi_d$ is given in the technical appendix.

An EM algorithm similar to those described by Mislevy and Verhelst (1990) and Yamamato (1989) is used to solve the likelihood equations for δ_i, τ_k, and ψ_d. In the expectation stage of the algorithm, estimates of the $\bar{r}_{izfd}$ quantities are calculated from the observed responses and the provisional item parameter estimates. If the latent group memberships were actually observed, then the γ_{jd} matrix of indicators would be known and the $\bar{r}_{izfd}$ quantities could be calculated using Equation 13. However, the γ_{jd} quantities themselves must be estimated in the expectation step prior to calculating $\bar{r}_{izfd}$ values. Following Mislevy and Verhelst (1990), the posterior expectation of γ_{jd} is given as

$$\bar{\gamma}_{jd} = \frac{\tilde{P}_{jd}\pi_d}{\sum_{v=1}^{D}(\tilde{P}_{jv}\pi_v)}. \qquad (19)$$

Note that π_d and π_v are current estimates of the proportion of individuals in a given latent class. The values of $\bar{\gamma}_{jd}$ can be substituted for γ_{jd} in Equation 13 to calculate $\bar{r}_{izfd}$.

In the maximization stage of the algorithm, the $\bar{r}_{izfd}$ estimates are treated as known constants, and then the likelihood equations are solved. Given that $\bar{r}_{izfd}$ estimates are fixed, it is possible to solve the likelihood equations for each item individually. Similarly, the solution for ψ_d may be derived separately for each latent class. The maximization stage continues until the most likely item parameter and latent group estimates for all items and groups have been computed for a given set of $\bar{r}_{izfd}$ values. The completion of a single expectation stage followed by a single maximization stage constitutes one cycle within the EM algorithm. Additional cycles are conducted until the largest change in any item or latent class parameter estimate, from one cycle to the next, is arbitrarily small (e.g., less than .0005).

The maximization stage of the EM algorithm proceeds in three steps. In the first step, the likelihood equations associated with the ψ_d are solved. The solution is computed using Fisher's method of scoring, and thus, the information for each ψ_d parameter is required. The general formula for information has been derived by Rao (1973), and in this case, it specializes to

$$\tilde{I}_{\psi_d} = \sum_{f=1}^{F}\sum_{i=1}^{I}\bar{N}_{ifd}\sum_{z=0}^{C}\frac{1}{P[Z_i=z|V_f,\psi_d]}\frac{\partial P[Z_i=z|V_f,\psi_d]}{\partial \psi_d}\frac{\partial P[Z_i=z|V_f,\psi_d]}{\partial \psi_d}, \qquad (20)$$

where $\bar{N}_{ifd}$ is the expected number of persons in latent group d at quadrature point V_f who responded to item i

$$\bar{N}_{ifd} = \sum_{z=0}^{C}\bar{r}_{izfd}. \qquad (21)$$

The value of $\bar{N}_{ifd}$ is calculated in the expectation stage of the algorithm and is held constant during the maximization stage. In the method of scoring, the update function used to calculate ψ_d parameters on the qth iteration is given by

$$\psi_{dq} = \psi_{dq-1} + \tilde{I}_{\psi_d}^{-1}\frac{\partial \ln(L)}{\partial \psi_d}. \qquad (22)$$

The ψ_d parameter for a given latent class is updated in an iterative fashion until there is little change from one iteration to the next or until some maximum limit of iterations has been reached (e.g., 30 iterations).

In the second step, the likelihood equations associated with the τ_k parameters are solved. The solution is computed using Fisher's method of scoring, and thus, the information matrix for the τ_k parameters is required. The information matrix is denoted as

$$\tilde{I}_\tau = \begin{bmatrix} \tilde{I}_{\tau_1\tau_1} & \tilde{I}_{\tau_1\tau_2} & \cdots & \tilde{I}_{\tau_1\tau_C} \\ \tilde{I}_{\tau_2\tau_1} & \tilde{I}_{\tau_2\tau_2} & \cdots & \tilde{I}_{\tau_2\tau_C} \\ \vdots & \vdots & \cdots & \vdots \\ \tilde{I}_{\tau_C\tau_1} & \tilde{I}_{\tau_C\tau_2} & \cdots & \tilde{I}_{\tau_C\tau_C} \end{bmatrix}. \quad (23)$$

The elements of the information matrix are derived in Rao (1973) and are equal to

$$\tilde{I}_{\tau_k\tau_{k'}} = \sum_{d=1}^{D}\sum_{f=1}^{F}\sum_{i=1}^{I} \bar{N}_{ifd} \sum_{z=0}^{C} \frac{1}{P[Z_i=z|V_f,\psi_d]} \frac{\partial P[Z_i=z|V_f,\psi_d]}{\partial \tau_k} \\ \frac{\partial P[Z_i=z|V_f,\psi_d]}{\partial \tau_{k'}}. \quad (24)$$

In the method of scoring, the update function used to calculate τ_k parameters on the qth iteration is given by

$$\begin{bmatrix} \tau_1 \\ \tau_2 \\ \cdot \\ \cdot \\ \cdot \\ \tau_C \end{bmatrix}_q = \begin{bmatrix} \tau_1 \\ \tau_2 \\ \cdot \\ \cdot \\ \cdot \\ \tau_C \end{bmatrix}_{q-1} + [\tilde{I}_\tau]^{-1} \begin{bmatrix} \frac{\partial \ln(L)}{\partial \tau_1} \\ \frac{\partial \ln(L)}{\partial \tau_2} \\ \cdot \\ \cdot \\ \cdot \\ \frac{\partial \ln(L)}{\partial \tau_C} \end{bmatrix}. \quad (25)$$

The τ_k parameters for a given item are updated in an iterative fashion until there is little change in parameters from one iteration to the next or until the maximum limit of iterations has been reached.

In the third step of the maximization stage, the likelihood equations for the δ_i parameters are solved for each item individually. The solution is, again, computed using the method of scoring, and the information scalar required in the solution is denoted as $\tilde{I}_{\delta_i}$.

The scalar is derived in Rao (1973) and is equal to

$$\tilde{I}_{\delta_i} = \sum_{d=1}^{D}\sum_{f=1}^{F} \bar{N}_{ifd} \sum_{z=0}^{C} \frac{1}{P[Z_i=z|V_f,\psi_d]} \left(\frac{\partial Pr[Z_i=z|V_f,\psi_d]}{\partial \delta_i}\right)^2. \quad (26)$$

The parameters are updated in an iterative fashion, and the update equation for δ_i on the qth iteration is given by

$$\delta_{iq} = \delta_{iq-1} + \tilde{I}_{\delta_i}^{-1} \frac{\partial \ln(L)}{\partial \delta_i}. \quad (27)$$

Updates continue until there is little change in the δ_i estimate from one iteration to the next or until the maximum limit of iterations has been reached.

The three steps of the maximization stage are performed repeatedly until there is little change in any parameter estimate from one repetition to the next or until 10 repetitions have been performed. The conclusion of the maximization stage constitutes the end of a given EM cycle. The stability of parameter estimates is evaluated at the end of the EM cycle, and additional cycles are performed if needed.

Adjusting Prior Distributions and Updating Mixing Proportion Estimates

Calculation of the $\bar{r}_{izfd}$ quantities in the expectation step of the EM algorithm requires the use of prior distributions for θ in each latent class and estimates of the mixing proportions (i.e., π_d). These quantities are adjusted during the EM algorithm in successive stages. First, the posterior density in each latent class is rescaled so that it integrates to one, and then this density is substituted for the prior density, $A_d(V_f)$, on the next iteration. Specifically, this rescaling is done as follows:

$$A_d(V_f) = \frac{\sum_{i=1}^{I} N_{ifd}}{\sum_{i=1}^{I} \sum_{f=1}^{F} N_{ifd}} \quad (28)$$

Next, the quadrature points in the D classes are rescaled to maintain the location constraint required for model identification. Specifically, this is done by rescaling the quadrature points so that the overall distribution (ignoring latent class structure) has a mean of zero. The constraint required is as follows:

$$\sum_{d=1}^{D} \sum_{f=1}^{F} [A_d(V_f)] V_f = 0 \quad (29)$$

Note that the locations of quadrature points are the same in all latent classes following the implementation of this constraint. Finally, updated estimates of the latent class mixing proportions are substituted for the current estimates one each iteration. Updated estimates are calculated as

$$\pi_d = \frac{\sum_{j}^{N} \bar{\gamma}_{jd}}{N}. \quad (30)$$

All of the foregoing adjustments are implemented after the solution has converged using the initial prior distributions and mixing proportions. Iterations are subsequently continued adjusting both the prior densities and mixing proportions simultaneously until final convergence is achieved.

Developing Initial Item Parameter Values and Empirically Based Prior Distributions

The EM algorithm requires a judicious choice of initial item parameter values in order to avoid local maxima. In practice, these starting values are obtained by estimating item parameters from constrained versions of the MIXUM. For example, the graded unfolding model is used to produce initial δ_i and τ_k estimates under the assumption that all subjects are from a single latent group. (Starting values for the graded unfolding model are given in Roberts & Laughlin, 1996). These estimates are derived using a discrete standard normal prior distribution for θ. Once the estimates for δ_i and τ_k have converged, they are used as initial estimates in the full MIXUM. At this point, empirically based prior distributions for θ in each latent class are used along with empirically derived start-up values for ψ_d. The EM algorithm uses these prior distributions in a static fashion and proceeds until convergence is reached and stable values of δ_i, τ_k, and ψ_d have been achieved. Following this step, the prior distributions of θ in each latent class are adjusted while simultaneously reestimating δ_i, τ_k, and ψ_d parameters. In the final step of the algorithm, the mixing proportions are adjusted along with the corresponding prior distributions of θ while simultaneously estimating the item parameters. This stepwise approach to parameter estimation appears to work well in the limited number of recovery simulations performed to date.

At the beginning of the estimation process for the full MIXUM, a discrete prior distribution for θ must be specified in each latent class. These distributions correspond to the $A_d(V_f)$ values in Equation 10. The social judgment theory literature on latitude of acceptance suggests that latitude is inversely related to (positive or negative) attitude extremity. Therefore, initial prior distributions for θ in each latent class are developed empirically using theory as a guide. This development begins by deriving a rough estimate of each individual's θ_j value. Each of these estimates are calculated by taking a weighted average of preliminary δ_i values corresponding to those items the individual has endorsed to at least some extent. The weights are simply the integer-valued response codes. (Recall that higher levels of agreement are coded with larger integers. Thus, statements that the individual agrees with most strongly receive the most weight when averaging δ_i.) Second, an empirical index of each individual's latitude of acceptance is derived on the basis of the range of preliminary δ_i locations corresponding to items the individual has endorsed. The absolute values of the θ_j estimates along with the empirical estimates of latitude are used to cluster individuals into D groups using a K-means cluster analysis (Hartigan & Wong, 1979). The within-cluster distributions of the signed θ_j estimates are used to develop initial $A_d(V_f)$ values. Specifically, the θ_j estimates within a cluster are assigned to the closest quadrature point, and the proportion of θ_j estimates at each quadrature point is used as the initial value for $A_d(V_f)$. Finally, the initial ψ_d values are calculated by averaging the empirical latitude of acceptance estimates within a given cluster and then rescaling these averages so that they have a mean of zero and a maximum absolute value of 0.2.

Figure 8.2 illustrates a typical prior distribution produced by this empirically based procedure. As shown in the figure, the prior distribution for the first latent class tends to be bimodal in shape with modes at more extreme regions of the continuum. The second latent class tends to have a bimodal shape also, but the modes are generally less extreme than the first. This pattern tends to continue until one considers the final latent class in the series. The final latent class is generally located between the modes of the other distributions and is generally single peaked. The initial ψ_d parameter for the first latent class is usually largest (positive), whereas the parameters for subsequent latent classes become progressively smaller (negative). Consequently, the latitude of acceptance for the first latent class is usually smallest with subsequent classes exhibiting successively broader latitudes of acceptance.

Person Parameter Estimation

The MML estimates of item and latent class parameters are used in conjunction with the observed responses and the individual's estimated probabilities of class membership to derive person parameter estimates. These person parameter estimates constitute the individual attitude estimates. In this study, person

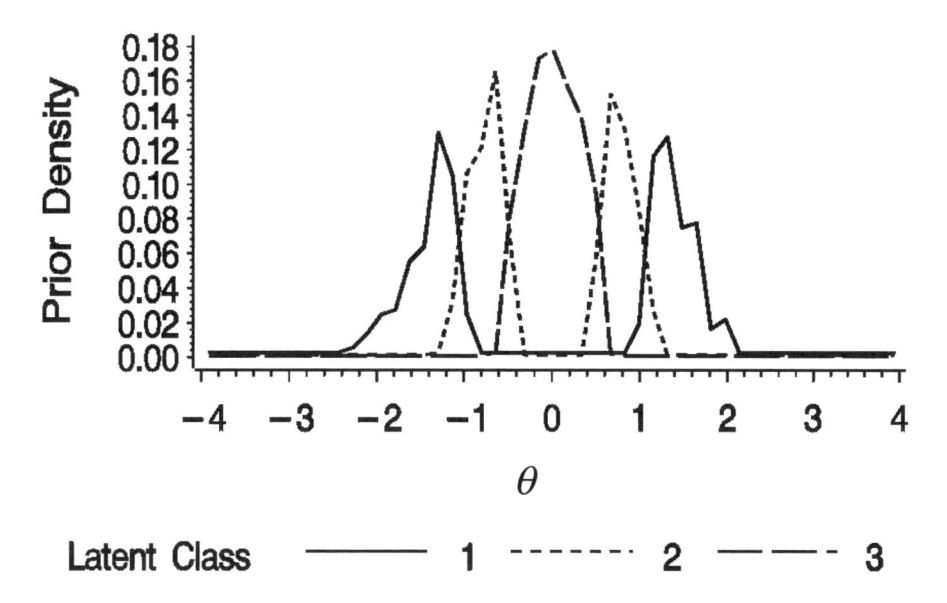

Figure 8.2. A typical set of prior distributions generated by the K-means cluster strategy.

parameter estimates are obtained using a modified EAP procedure in which the estimate for the *jth* individual is calculated as

$$\hat{\theta}_j = \sum_{d=1}^{D} \bar{\gamma}_{jd} \left[\frac{\sum_{f=1}^{F} V_f L_{jd}(V_f) A_d(V_f)}{\sum_{f=1}^{F} L_{jd}(V_f) A_d(V_f)} \right], \quad (31)$$

where $L_{jd}(V_f)$ is the conditional likelihood of observing the *jth* individual's response vector given that the individual is in latent class d and is located at quadrature point V_f. The modified EAP estimate, $\hat{\theta}_j$, is weighted average of D different EAP estimates where each of these EAP estimates are derived by assuming that the individual is a member of the *dth* latent class. The weights for this average are simply the posterior probabilities that the individual belongs to the *dth* latent class. Note that $\bar{\gamma}_{jd}$ and $A_d(V_f)$ in Equation 31 are the adjusted quantities obtained on the last iteration of the MML procedure.

Parameter Recovery

A parameter recovery simulation study was conducted to assess the accuracy of estimates derived with the aforementioned method. The study generated responses from 2,000 simulees to questionnaires of various lengths. The size of the ψ_d was varied along with the true distribution of θ_j and the mixing proportion in each latent class. The details of this study are given in the technical appendix corresponding to this report. The results suggested that MIXUM parameters could be estimated very accurately with long tests (e.g., 60 items with four response categories per item). Shorter tests (e.g., 20 items) could also yield highly accurate estimates when the average absolute difference in ψ_d parameters between adjacent latent classes was .7 or greater.

A Real Data Example

The aforementioned estimation strategy was applied to a large set of responses collected with a questionnaire designed to measure attitude toward abortion. The resulting analysis provided a realistic example of the challenges inherent in the application of the MIXUM. It also illustrated the types of valuable information that the model may provide.

Data and Analysis Strategy

Responses from 750 undergraduate students to 47 items indexing attitudes toward abortion were analyzed in this example. These data were originally reported by Roberts, Donoghue, and Laughlin (2000), who suggested that responses to these 47 statements were unidimensional. The data were originally scored in six response categories (i.e., 0 = *strongly disagree*, 1 = *disagree*,

2 = *slightly disagree,* 3 = *slightly agree,* 4 = *agree,* and 5 = *strongly agree*). However, to induce simplicity in this novel application, Response Categories 1 and 2 were collapsed, as were Response Categories 3 and 4. This yielded four response categories coded as 0 = *strongly disagree,* 1 = *generally disagree,* 2 = *generally agree,* and 3 = *strongly agree.*

Separate solutions were obtained for two, three, four, and five latent classes. Each analysis was performed with a total of 600 quadrature points across all classes in an attempt to balance the number of densities estimated in these analyses. Thus, there were 300 quadrature points for the two-class analysis, 200 quadrature points for the three-class analysis, 150 quadrature points for the four-class analysis, and 120 quadrature points for the five-class analysis. Quadrature points were equally spaced in each group and initially ranged from –4 to +4 prior to adaptation. The convergence criterion was set to .0005.

Results

The optimal number of latent classes for these data was selected using various sources of information, including the interpretability of the solution, the expected number of members in the smallest class, the number of nonredundant parameter estimates,[2] and a variety of information criteria. Table 8.1 gives the number of nonredundant parameter estimates for each model along with the corresponding marginal log likelihood, and the AIC (Akaike's information criterion; Akaike, 1973), BIC (Bayesian information criterion; Schwarz, 1978), and CAIC (consistent Akaike's information criterion; Bozdogan, 1987) information criteria. As shown in the table, the solution with five latent classes had the smallest values for all three information criteria and seemed optimal in that sense. However, the five-class solution had one class with a mere 26.25 expected members (i.e., only 3.5% of the sample). Additionally the five-class solution did not substantially increase the interpretability of the results as compared with the four-class solution. Therefore, it was not considered further. Based on the aforementioned criteria, the four-class solution appeared to provide a reasonable level of model fit, interpretability, and expected number of individuals in each latent class, and it was ultimately selected for further study.

The estimated locations of the 47 abortion attitude statements (i.e., the $\hat{\delta}_i$ values) are shown in Figure 8.3 along with the statement content for prototypical

---

[2] The number of nonredundant parameter estimates is calculated as $I + C + 2*(D - 1) + 600 - D - 1$. This deserves some explanation and cautionary remarks. There are I δ_i parameters and C nonzero τ_k parameters estimated freely in the solution. There are D ψ_d parameters, but they must sum to zero. This summation constraint leads to $D - 1$ free parameters to be estimated. Similarly, there are D π_d parameters, but they must sum to one. This also yields $D - 1$ parameters to be estimated. Finally, there are 600 densities estimated across all latent classes corresponding to the quadrature points in the MML algorithm. However, the densities in each class must sum to one. Additionally, these distributions must have a mean of zero across latent classes. This yields $600 - D - 1$ free density parameters. A word of caution is in order with regard to our inclusion of the $600 - D - 1$ parameters associated with the latent distributions of θ. Although these parameters are free to vary, they do not generally provide nonredundant pieces of information. Nonetheless, we treat them as though they were nonredundant parameters for purposes of model selection.

Table 8.1. Information Criteria for Alternative Latent Class Models

Number of classes	Nonredundant parameters	Marginal ln(L)	AIC	BIC	CAIC
2	649	−36,384.588	74,067.176	77,065.604	77,714.604
3	650	−36,179.995	73,659.991	76,663.038	77,313.038
4	651	−36,073.057	73,448.113	76,455.781	77,106.781
5	652	−35,999.484	73,302.967	76,315.255	76,967.255

Note. AIC = Akaike's information criterion; BIC = Bayesian information criterion; CAIC = consistent Akaike's information criterion.

items. As seen in the figure, the statements were rationally ordered on the latent continuum. The two poles represented extreme prolife and prochoice perspectives, respectively, and statements near these poles reflected this extremity. (Note that the orientation of the poles is arbitrary in symmetric unfolding models.) When moving away from the poles to the more moderate regions of the continuum, the statement content became more moderate in nature but still reflected a somewhat prolife or prochoice opinion depending on which side of the continuum a statement was located. Finally, those statements near the center of the continuum conveyed a more or less neutral sentiment with respect to abortion.

The MIXUM also provided modified EAP estimates of each respondent's location on the latent continuum (i.e., the $\hat{\theta}_j$ values). The relative frequency dis-

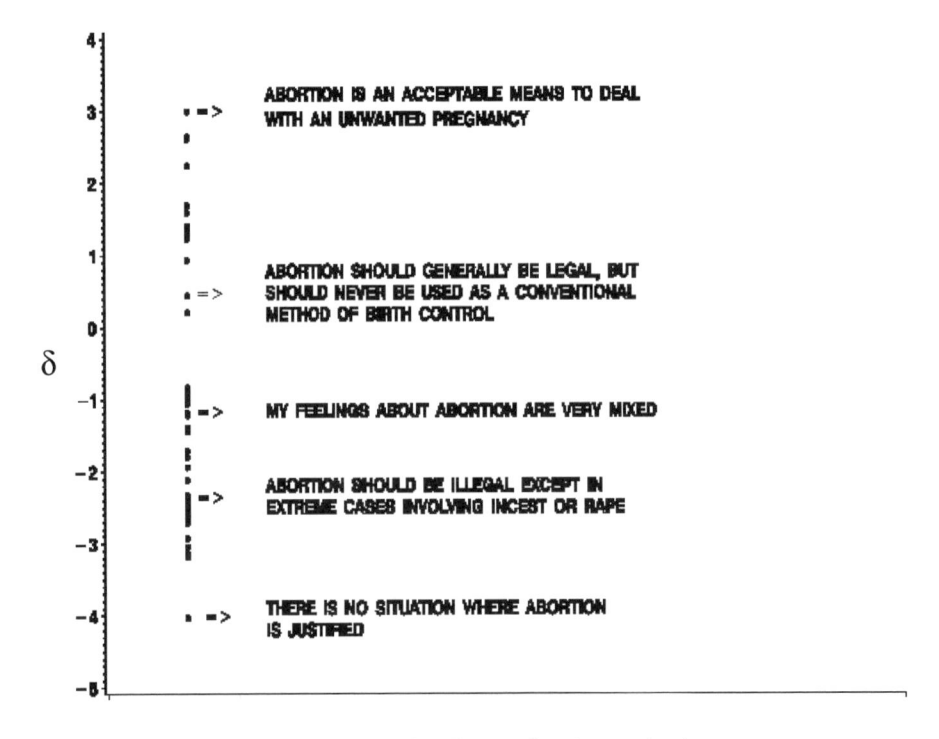

Figure 8.3. MIXUM item locations for the 47 abortion attitude statements.

tribution for these estimates is shown in Figure 8.4. The mean estimate was equal to zero, and the standard deviation of the estimates was equal to 1.555. The median estimate was equal to .424, which fell between the statements "Abortion should be a woman's choice, but should never be used simply due to its convenience" and "Abortion should generally be legal, but should never be used as a conventional method of birth control." These data suggest that the median individual in this sample had a moderately positive orientation toward the practice of abortion.

The mixing proportions associated with the four-class solution were equal to .06, .48, .38 and .08 for Latent Classes 1 through 4, respectively. Thus, each class represented a reasonable number of subjects with the smallest latent class corresponding to an expected frequency of 45 subjects. The estimated τ_k values were equal to $\tau_1 = -3.313$, $\tau_2 = -2.435$, and $\tau_3 = -.925$, and the latitude of acceptance parameters were equal to $\psi_1 = .803$, $\psi_2 = .283$, $\psi_3 = -.205$, and $\psi_4 = -.880$ for the four latent classes, respectively. This led to the four-item expected value functions shown in Figure 8.5. The corresponding latitudes of acceptance are also shown in the figure. The latitudes of acceptance became progressively larger for Latent Classes 1 through 4. Specifically, members of Latent Class 1 had the narrowest latitude. An individual in this class was expected to agree with an attitude statement to some extent if it fell within ± .88 units of the individual's own location on the latent continuum. Members of Latent Classes 2 and 3 exhibited more moderate latitudes of ± 1.35 and ± 1.80, respectively. The

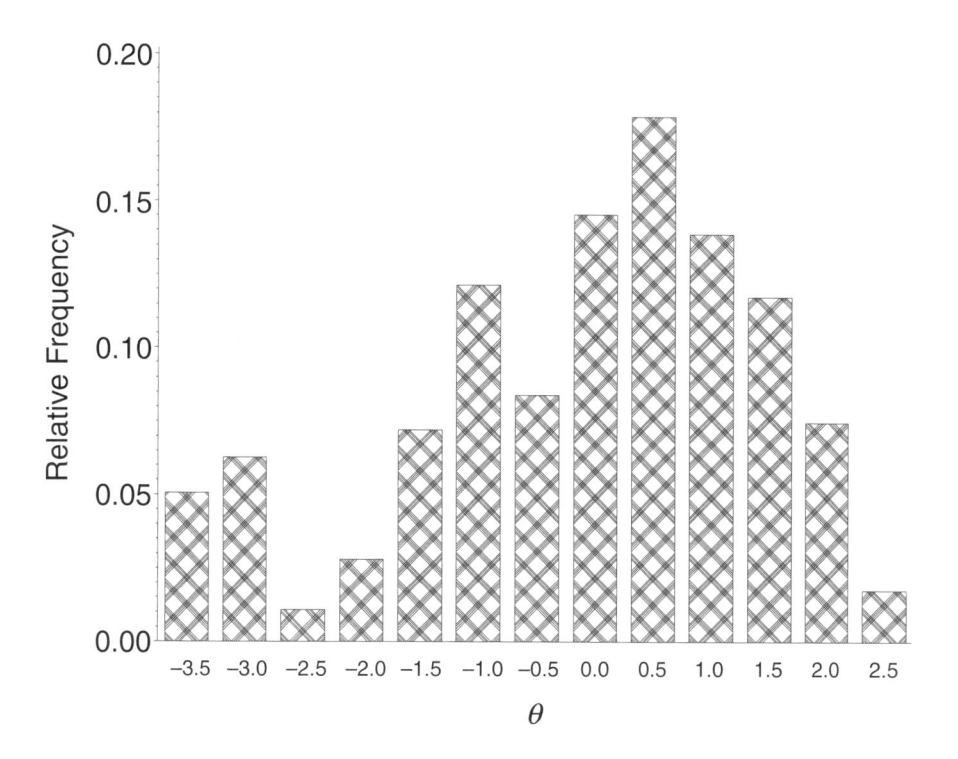

Figure 8.4. Distribution of modified EAP estimates for all 750 respondents.

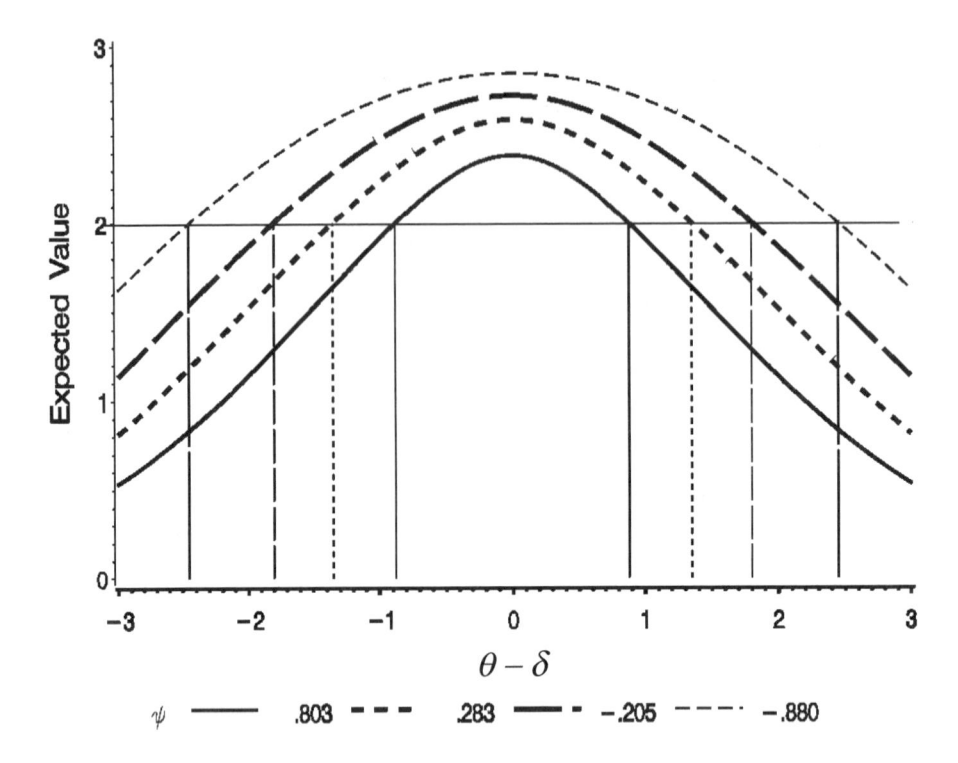

Figure 8.5. MIXUM expected value functions for the four latent classes.

fourth latent class was associated with the largest latitude of acceptance equal to ±2.45. When combined with the values of the mixing proportions listed above, this suggested that the majority of respondents (86%) had moderate latitudes of acceptance. Far fewer individuals had narrow or large latitudes.

The top panel of Figure 8.6 displays the posterior distribution of θ that was estimated with the EM algorithm for the four-class solution. The distributions have been smoothed by summing the posterior densities observed for each set of 10 successive quadrature points within a given latent class. Those individuals with the smallest latitudes of acceptance (i.e., those in Latent Class 1) were primarily located in the extreme prolife and the moderately prochoice regions of the continuum. Those individuals with the broader latitudes of acceptances (i.e., those in Latent Classes 2 and 3) were located primarily in the moderately and extremely prochoice regions of the attitude continuum. Finally, those with the largest latitudes of acceptance (i.e., those in Latent Class 4) were located mostly in the moderately and extremely prochoice regions of the continuum as well.

There are no rigorous model fit statistics for the MIXUM. However, graphical indices of model fit are easily generated. Figure 8.7 provides graphic information about the global fit of the MIXUM to the abortion attitude data. The graph was produced by sorting each person–item pair into homogenous groups of 75 pairs based on $\hat{\theta}_j - \hat{\delta}_i$ values. Within each homogenous group, the average observed response and the average expected value predicated by the MIXUM were calculated and plotted against the average $\hat{\theta}_j - \hat{\delta}_i$ value. As shown in the

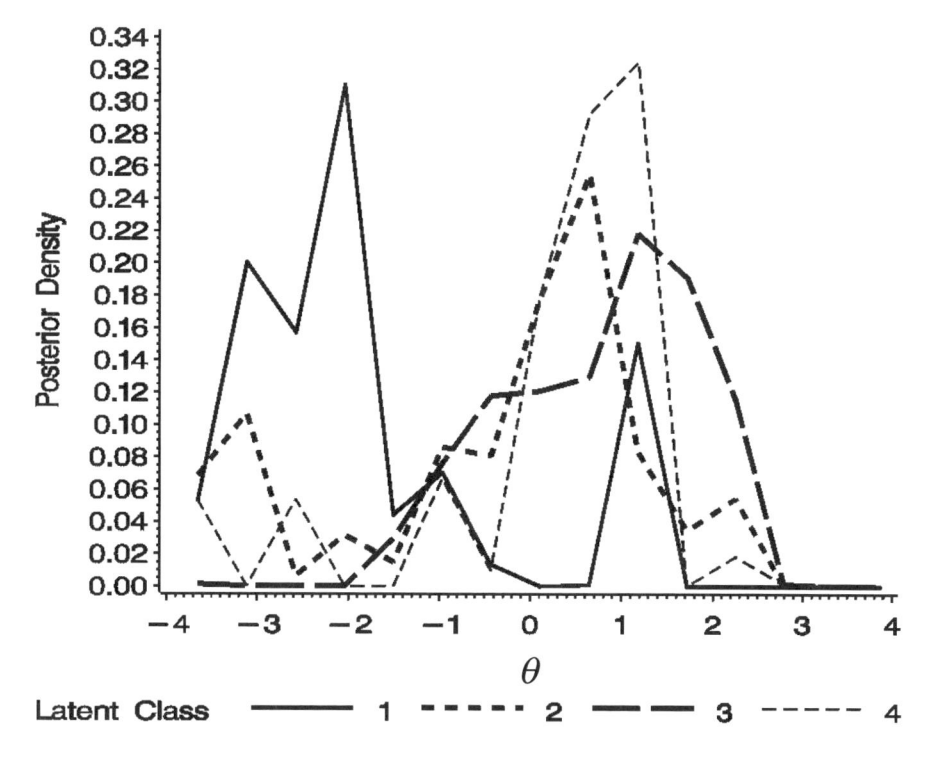

Figure 8.6. Posterior density of θ in each latent class.

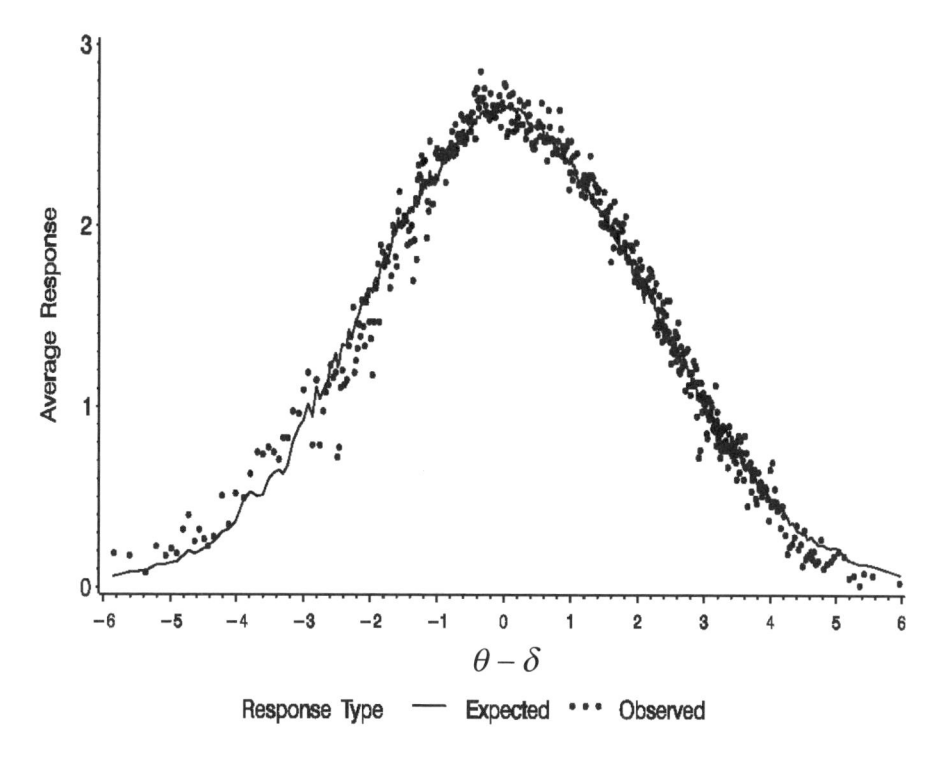

Figure 8.7. Graphical index of global model fit. Average expected values from the MIXUM are given by the solid line, whereas average observed responses are given by the dots.

figure, the MIXUM was able to locate individuals and items on the latent continuum such that more observed agreement was obtained, on average, as $\hat{\theta}_j - \hat{\delta}_i$ approached zero. Moreover, the fit of the average expected value function to the average observed response appeared reasonably good.

Figure 8.8 provides graphical information about item level fit for 10 prototypical items across the attitude continuum. Respondents were first rank ordered on the basis of their $\hat{\theta}_j$ values and then clustered into groups of 30 individuals per group. The average observed item response (dot) and average model expec-

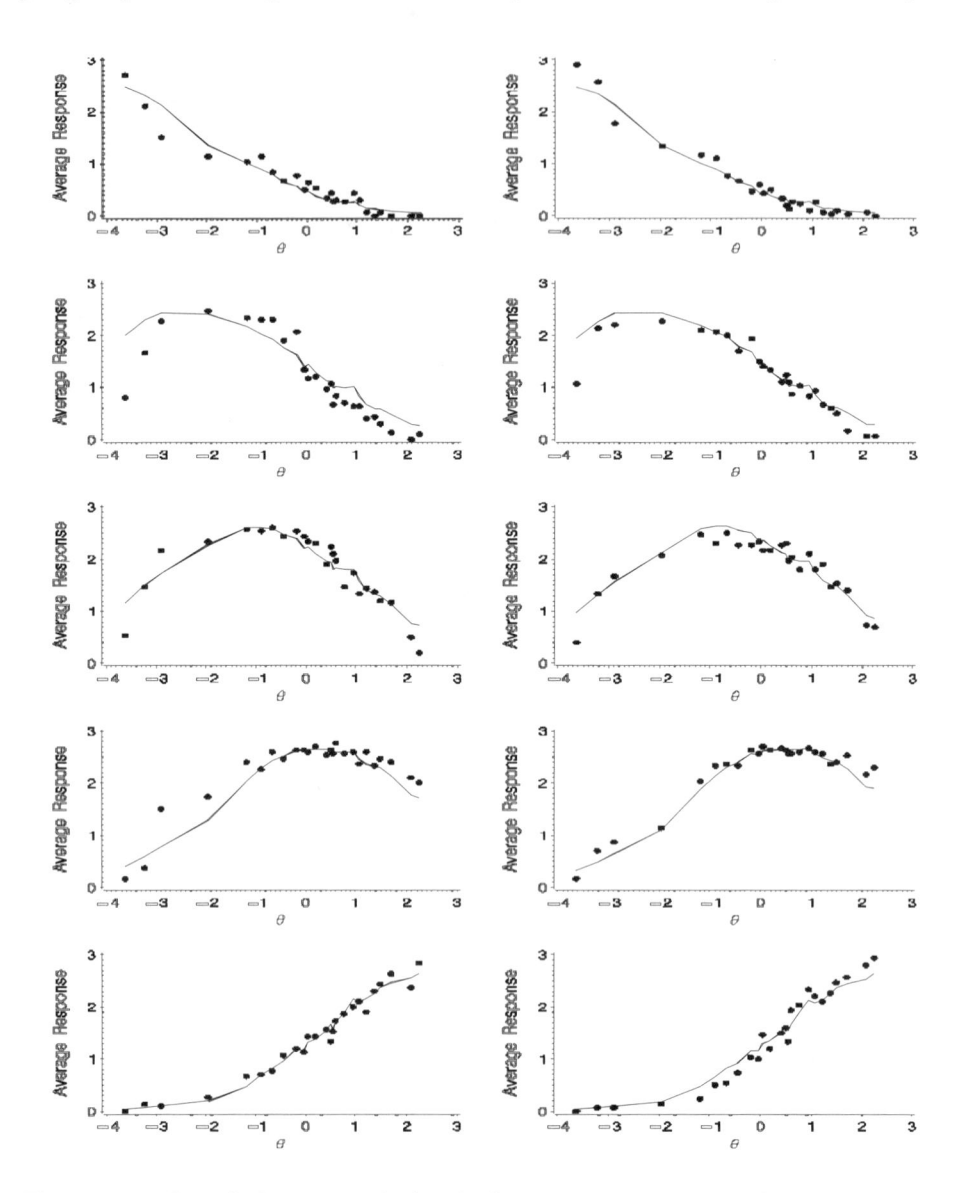

Figure 8.8. Item fit for prototypical attitude statements spanning the entire attitude continuum. The dots represent average observed responses whereas the line represents average model expectations.

tation (solid line) are both plotted as a function of the average $\hat{\theta}_j$ for each respondent group. Most items were fit reasonably well. In those cases in which noticeable misfit occurred, it was usually the case that the model expectations did not fold enough to match the observed responses. (See the second row of panels in Figure 8 for an example.) This suggests that perhaps even more flexibility in the item response function may be warranted. For example, the subjective response category thresholds and/or the discriminating capability could be estimated separately for each item as in the generalized graded unfolding model (Roberts et al., 2000).

Discussion

As shown in the previous example, the MIXUM is able to characterize attitude items, estimate individual attitudes, provide estimates of the latitude of acceptance in alternative latent classes, and estimate the expected proportion of respondents in each class. Additionally, it can estimate the posterior distribution of $\hat{\theta}_j$ in each class. With respect to item characteristics, the attitude statements were ordered on the latent continuum in a logical manner such that those with extremely prolife or prochoice sentiments were located at opposite poles of the continuum (Figure 3). Extremely prolife or prochoice items exhibited item characteristic curves that were, more or less, monotonic in nature (Figure 8). The more moderate prolife or prochoice statements were located at less extreme positions on the continuum and exhibited a marked fold on one side of the corresponding ICCs. The fold emerged because those individuals with attitudes close to the locations of these moderate statements endorsed them the most, whereas respondents with more discrepant attitudes in either direction mitigated their endorsement. Finally, those items that were basically neutral in wording were, indeed, located near the center of the item location distribution and exhibited ICCs that were thoroughly folded on both sides of a single peak. In these cases, individuals with neutral attitudes endorsed the neutral statements the most, and those with moderate or extreme attitudes, in either direction, endorsed the item less and less. The shapes of these ICCs are exactly what one should find when item responses are consistent with an unfolding model.

Although no rigorous indices of model-data fit were offered for the previous example, the graphical indices suggested that the MIXUM fit the responses to these attitude statements reasonably well. The unfolding nature of the responses was evident at both the model and item levels (see Figures 7 and 8). There is still room for improvement, however, and past research has suggested that additional item parameters may be required to provide optimal fit at the item level. Nonetheless, the simple unfolding IRT model embodied in Equation 1 performed adequately when thresholds were modified in alternative latent classes as was done here.

The MIXUM provides the posterior distribution of θ in each class (Figure 6), and these distributions are interesting from a psychological perspective. One might speculate that individuals with more extreme attitudes would have the narrowest latitudes of acceptance, whereas those with more moderate attitudes might be amenable to a broader range of opinions. However, this speculation was only partially confirmed in the previous example. Individuals with the narrowest latitudes of acceptance were primarily located in the extreme prolife region of the continuum, although there was a second cluster of these individuals in the moderately prochoice region as well. In contrast, individuals with the most prochoice orientations were unlikely to possess narrow latitudes. Instead, such individuals were likely to have moderate or even broad latitudes of acceptance. One explanation of these findings is that individuals with more extreme prochoice attitudes are naturally expected to be more tolerant of alternative opinions with regard to abortion. The idea of being prochoice implicitly suggests that one should tolerate other opinions that could lead to broader latitudes of acceptance. In contrast, individuals who hold the most prolife orientations are unlikely to tolerate alternative positions because it would violate the very foundation of their right-to-life opinions.

Individuals with moderately prochoice orientations were represented noticeably in all four latent classes in the previous analysis. Thus, some of these individuals had relatively narrow latitudes of acceptance, whereas others had more moderate or even broad latitudes. This accentuates the point that individuals with nonextreme opinions may be very "ego involved" with their stances and may refuse to endorse statements that deviate much from their moderate positions (Sherif et. al., 1965). Others from this moderate attitude segment may identify less strongly with their attitudes and, consequently, be more accepting of a wider variety of opinions.

Conclusions

The MIXUM appears to be a reasonable method to measure attitudes and quantify the latitude of acceptance simultaneously in large scale attitude measurement situations. MIXUM parameters may be estimated using a flexible MML framework, and initial parameter recovery simulation results suggest that accurate estimates can be obtained in large-scale testing situations. Moreover, the real data analysis reported here suggests that the model can fit responses to a typical attitude questionnaire relatively well.

Although we have focused on quantifying the latitude of acceptance, the general MIXUM strategy is quite flexible and can be used to model other structural features in the context of unfolding IRT models. For example, the MIXUM strategy could be used with a more general IRT model like the generalized graded unfolding model (Roberts et al., 2000). In this case, one or more item parameters could be varied simultaneously in a prespecified number of latent classes. If the concept of latent classes is replaced with a manifest classification variable, then the MIXUM method becomes a multiple group unfolding IRT model similar to those found in the cumulative domain. Finally, if the probability function is allowed to change its parametric form across latent classes, then the method becomes an unfolding analogue of Yamamoto's (1989) hybrid model. These other applications remain for future exploration.

References

Akaike, H. (1973). Information theory and an extension of the maximum likelihood principle. In B. N. Petrov & F. Csake (Eds.), *Second international symposium on information theory* (pp. 267–281). Budapest, Hungary: Akademiai Kiado.

Andrich, D. (1996). A general hyperbolic cosine latent trait model for unfolding polytomous responses: Reconciling Thurstone and Likert methodologies. *British Journal of Mathematical and Statistical Psychology, 49,* 347–365.

Bozdogan, H. (1987). Model-selection and Akaike's information criterion (AIC): The general theory and its analytical extensions. *Psychometrika, 52,* 345–370.

Hartigan, J. A., & Wong, M. A. (1979). Algorithm AS 136: A K-means clustering algorithm. *Applied Statistics, 28,* 100–108.

Luo, G. (1998). A general formulation for unidimensional unfolding and pairwise preference models: Making explicit the latitude of acceptance. *Journal of Mathematical Psychology, 42,* 400–417.

Luo, G., Andrich, D., & Styles, I. (1998). The JML estimation of the generalised unfolding model incorporating the latitude of acceptance parameter. *Australian Journal of Psychology, 50,* 187–198.

Mislevy, R. J., & Verhelst, N. (1990). Modeling item responses when different subjects employ different solution strategies. *Psychometrika, 55,* 195–215.

Rao, C. R. (1973). *Statistical inference and its applications* (2nd. ed.). New York: Wiley.

Roberts, J. S., Donoghue, J. R., & Laughlin, J. E. (2000). A general item response theory mode for unfolding unidimensional polytomous responses. *Applied Psychological Measurement 24,* 3–32.

Roberts, J. S., & Laughlin, J. E. (1996). A unidimensional item response theory model for unfolding responses from a graded disagree-agree response scale. *Applied Psychological Measurement, 20,* 231–255.

Roberts, J. S., Laughlin, J. E., & Wedell, D. H. (1999). Validity issues in the Likert and Thurstone approaches to attitude measurement. *Educational and Psychological Measurement, 59,* 211–233.

Rost, J. (1990). Rasch models in latent classes: An integration of two approaches to item analysis. *Applied Psychological Measurement, 14*(3), 271–282.

Rost, J. (1991). A logistic mixture distribution model for polychotomous item responses. *The British Journal of Mathematical and Statistical Psychology, 44,* 75–92.

Schwarz, G. (1978). Estimating the dimension of a model. *The Annals of Statistics, 6,* 461–464.

Sherif, M., & Hovland, C. I. (1961). *Social judgment: Assimilation and contrast effects in communication and attitude change.* New Haven, CT: Yale University Press.

Sherif, C. W., Sherif, M., & Nebergall, R. E. (1965). *Attitude and attitude change: The social judgment-involvement approach.* Philadelphia: Saunders.

van Schuur, W. H., & Kiers, H. A. L. (1994). Why factor analysis is often the incorrect model for analyzing bipolar concepts, and what model can be used instead. *Applied Psychological Measurement, 18,* 97–110.

Yamamoto, K. (1989). *HYBRID model of IRT and latent class models* (ETS Research Report RR-89-41). Princeton, NJ: Educational Testing Service.

Part IV

Cognitive Psychometric Models for Interactive Item Generation

9

Recent Development and Prospects in Item Generation

Isaac I. Bejar

The perspective taken in this chapter is that item generation should be seen as an opportunity to orchestrate psychometric and psychological considerations with the goal of producing tests that yield scores that have well-founded interpretation for the use to which scores will be put. As we argue throughout, item generation also presents an opportunity for testing psychological theories. Thus, one purpose of this review is to argue that item generation needs to be understood in that larger context. To that effect, we adopt the idea of an item model as the basis for item generation. We define an *item model* as the specifications for authoring an item. The specifications are sufficiently detailed such that items can be instantiated by either algorithmic means or by authors following a set of authoring guidelines. The term has gained some acceptance over the last few years. It was first proposed by LaDuca, Staples, Templeton, and Holzman (1986) and has been adopted by work in item generation. Bejar et al. (2003) defined *item modeling* as

> a construct-driven and validity-enhancing approach because it entails a more thorough understanding of the goals of the assessment and the application of pertinent psychological research to the design of test content than the current mode of item development. That is, item models set the expectation for the behavior of the instances produced by a given model (e.g., difficulty and discrimination) and those expectations can be verified upon administration of a test consisting of those instances, thus providing an opportunity to refine our understanding of the construct and supporting psychological principles. (p. 3)

The language does not stress the mechanism for generation, which could be automated or manual, but rather the implications for validity and the scientific standing of the eventual scores based on items that have withstood theoretical and empirical challenge.

Conceiving item generation as consisting of generation and a prediction about the behavior of the item on the basis of a suitable theory or model is what

---

I am grateful to Randy Bennett, Susan Embretson, and Aurora Graf for their extensive editorial and substantive input, which I believe has improved the document.

Bejar (1993) called a *Popperian mechanism*. Popper (1959/1992) argued that the standing of a scientific theory depended on its falsifiability. That is, producing items based on item models informed by theory presents researchers with the possibility of testing the falsifiability of the theory they have resorted to in building those item models. For example, a theory of what accounts for the psychometric properties of items can be recast as a set of item models. After a test that includes instances of those item models is administered, we are in a position to challenge or corroborate the theory by contrasting the observed and predicted theoretical psychometric attributes of items, such as difficulty, discrimination, and response time. Corroborating the predictions strengthens the item models and the theory behind them. By contrast, inconclusive results, or failing to corroborate the predictions, call for revision to the item models, possibly the theory that led to the formulation of the prediction or the experimental design. Similarly, attempting to account for the psychometric attributes of instances by a competing theory that is construct-irrelevant is informative. Such attempts immunize the assessment development process from the phenomenon of confirmation bias (Nickerson, 1998). If the competing theory fails, researchers have, as a bonus, counterarguments for allegations of construct-irrelevant variance in the eventual scores. By contrast, if the competing theory is confirmed, they have more work to do.

Item models can serve to evaluate a theory while serving pragmatic objectives. For example, tests based on item models could be designed to minimize the possibility of pre-knowledge of test content (Morley, Bridgeman, & Lawless, 2004), an increasing risk under computer-based continuous testing (Davey & Nering, 2002), or to produce a large number of items. However, item models can also be seen as repositories of knowledge for producing items that are aligned with the construct under consideration, which prevents us from inadvertently incorporating into those items the elicitation of construct irrelevant variability in performance. Thus, item models have implications for the validity of an assessment—specifically, the theoretical underpinnings of an assessment, as well as the consequential impact of the assessment. In short, item modeling has implications for implementing the conception of validity described by Messick (1989).

This view of item generation suggests several considerations to keep in mind when evaluating progress in this line of research:

1. One consideration is the theoretical basis, or lack thereof, for an accounting of the variability in the psychometric attributes among instances produced from item models.
2. A second consideration is imputing a psychometric characterization to instances of item models. This requires attention to the statistical means for imputing those psychometric characterizations as well as the means by which we bind the imputed characterization to a specific instance.
3. The third consideration is the mechanism for instantiating items from item models. That is, what forms do item models take in a specific domain?

With respect to the first consideration, Drasgow, Luecht, and Bennett (2006) proposed the distinction between weak and strong theory as a means of distinguishing among approaches to item generation. Operating from strong theory enables the production of items that range in their psychometric attributes in a theoretically predictable manner. By contrast, when researchers operate from weak theory they, in effect, apply case-based reasoning; that is, if they know the psychometric attributes on one item, they should be able to hold constant the psychometric attributes of items like it. At most, they may be able to hold constant the psychometric attributes of instances. Specific approaches to item generation have been associated historically with weak and strong theory, but the association is not essential.

Bejar (2002) discussed a dichotomy for distinguishing between item models designed to produce either isomorphs or variants but did not explicitly associate the distinction with the strength and scope of the theoretical underpinnings behind the item models. (The term *isomorph* has roots in cognitive work [Kotovsky & Simon, 1990] on problem solving concerned with the basis of difficulty in problem solving puzzles like the Tower of Hanoi.) Although item models designed to produce isomorphs can be an instance of case-based reasoning when our theoretical knowledge is limited, such models can also be applied in pursuit of a stronger theory or can even be based on strong theory.

Bejar (2002) also discussed item models that produce variants that range in their psychometric attributes. Examples of such models can be found in the work of Embretson (1998) and Bejar (1990), in which the items are highly figural. The latter case was concerned with mental rotation (Shepard & Metzler, 1971). It is an informative case because a single variable, angular disparity, was the basis for generation and for difficulty modeling, and the difficulty model had strong theoretical backing. In general, however, the variables required for instantiating items and the variables that model the psychometric attributes of the items are not the same (Deane, Graf, Higgins, Futagi, & Lawless, 2006). Angular disparity was such a potent determinant of difficulty in the Bejar (1990) study, as predicted by previous research, that for illustrative purposes it is not necessary to go further. However, a full analysis of the mental rotation test would likely require figure-specific variables for instantiation purposes. Specifically, a megamodel for mental rotation could consist of item models for each possible figure. Within each such model instances of different difficulty could be produced by varying the angular disparity (Hornke, 2002). In short, it appears useful to consider the strength of the theoretical grounding for item generation as an independent facet and distinct from the facets concerning the means for instantiation and imputation of psychometric attributes. We discuss instantiation and imputation of psychometric parameters for each of the domains to be reviewed in the following sections.

The outline for this chapter is as follows. We first discuss the evolution of the concept of validity and connect that evolution with the perspective outlined in this section. We then turn to recent developments in item generation that illustrate the view expressed here and, finally, present some conclusions.

Validity: Item Generation in Context

Although Tyler (1934) did not stress validity in his writing, his careful thinking about the interdependencies among different parts of the assessment design process suggests that he must have thought that the way a measurement instrument was designed had implications for what could be concluded from an analysis of the scores. Those interdependencies and implications for validity are now widely recognized (e.g., Bennett & Bejar, 1998; Embretson, 1983; Haertel, 1985; Kane, 1992; Messick, 1994; Mislevy, Steinberg, & Almond, 2003; Nichols & Sugrue, 1999) but were not emphasized in the Cronbach and Meehl (1955) conception of construct validity. Indeed, Cronbach and Meehl were criticized at the time by Loevinger (1957) for not paying attention to item construction. Although Cronbach and Meehl argued that validation was not different than the scientific process, they paid less attention to the instrumentation or the specifics of the composition of the test, including its content, as they were primarily interested in the nomothetic span of a test, or the relationship of scores of the test in question with those of other tests or with external information. This meant that validation was seen as a process that occurs after the assessment has been completed. They gave as an example the development of the Strong Vocational Inventory Blank (SVIB), which, like many leading instruments at the time, was based on empirical keying. *Empirical keying* refers to scoring responses with reference to the criterion of interest (Mumford & Owens, 1987), but the scoring key is derived empirically and the content of the items is not obviously linked to the construct. For the SVIB, this meant that there was no a priori accounting of the content of each item. The same items were scored with different keys for each possible occupation. Although from a pragmatic point of view the purely empirical approach works very well, in the end there is not an explanation for why it works.

Loevinger (1957) objected to the actuarial determination of scoring keys and argued that "the dangers of pure empiricism" in determining the content and scoring of a test should not be underestimated. She concluded that "the problem is to find a coherent set of operations permitting utilization of content together with empirical considerations" (p. 658). The "coherent set of operations" to which she referred seems to call for the linking of the content and empirical attributes of items. This theme was echoed by Glaser (1963) some years later when he introduced the notion of criterion-referenced testing as a means for understanding the meaning and inferences that could be drawn from a score without the requirement of a norming population. Reflecting on that article years later, Glaser (1994) noted that "systematic techniques needed to be developed to more adequately identify and describe the components of performance, and to determine the relative weighting of these components with respect to a given task" (p. 9).

Embretson (1983) expanded on the importance of the composition of a test; that is, understanding the "components of performance" down to the item level by means of cognitive models of performance. She labeled that aspect of validity *construct representation* and viewed it as complementary to nomothetic span, or the set of relations of scores on the test being validated and scores in other tests or external variables, which was the focus of Cronbach and Meehl's (1955) argument. Whereas Glaser (1963, 1994) and Embretson (1983) were more concerned with the composition of the test, as noted by Messick (1981), Loevinger (1957) advocated, in addition, that items be written so as to challenge the construct; specifically, "the initial item pool is deliberately expanded to include items relevant to competing theories ... as well as items theoretically irrelevant to the construct" (p. 658). In other words, Loevinger advocated attempting not only to base items on a theory but also to falsify the theory behind the content of the items in the process. This, even today, is a very avant-garde idea that is well aligned with specific conceptions of philosophy of science, especially in connection with psychology (Meehl, 1990).[1]

The perspective expressed earlier, that item generation should not be seen as the mass production of items, can now be understood in light of the critical role that the items can play in the validity of scores. That role is enforcing construct representation and, through construct representation, mediating nomothetic span, while providing evidence concerning how well theoretical predictions about items have withstood empirical scrutiny.

Evidence concerning construct representation can be incorporated as part of the validity argument for the assessment as a whole. Kane (1992) and Cronbach (1988) proposed an "argument-based approach" to validity and score interpretation. Kane (2004) specifically advocated the use of an interpretive argument as the mechanism for organizing and structuring the evidence about the interpretations of scores and decisions. Kane (2004) saw the approach as a pragmatic means to organize validity evidence for score interpretation and not as an alternative to construct validation. For example, the emphases in nomological nets as a means of score interpretation (Cronbach & Meehl, 1955) and the idea of construct representation (Embretson, 1983) are some of the raw material for building an argument. Kane (1992) described the general scheme based on argumentation theory (Toulmin, Rieke, & Janik, 1984) as follows:

> One (a) decides on the statements and decisions to be based on the test scores, (b) specifies the inferences and assumptions leading from the test scores to these statements and decisions, (c) identifies potential competing interpretations, and (d) seeks evidence supporting the inferences and assumptions in the proposed interpretive argument and refuting potential counterarguments. (p. 527)

The four-part structure can be thought as the rules of the "validity game" and is not prescriptive about the content of the argument. For example, the argument can be formulated before the assessment is developed or after the assessment is developed. For existing assessments or repurposed assessments, an ad hoc application is all that can be done. However, for new assessments, formulating the argument ahead of time so that it can inform the development is sensible. Evidence-centered design (Mislevy et al., 2003) is also inspired by a Toulmian conception of argument, and, unlike Kane's approach, it is very prescriptive about the timing and sequencing of assessment design activities to ensure that the argument to be made about eventual scores is well supported. There is not

---

[1] In practice, items designed to challenge the construct would be studied outside the operational program.

necessarily a conflict between these two approaches. Kane's perspective is applicable to auditing assessments that are already completed. By contrast, evidence centered design is oriented to improving the chances of passing an eventual audit, so to speak, by, among other things, insuring adequate construct representation. Although every aspect of the design of an assessment relates to construct representation, the principles by which items are produced are especially critical. The challenge for automated item generation work remains how best to incorporate such principles into the assessment design process. The next few sections discuss progress in several domains.

Recent Developments in Item Generation

In this section, we focus on relatively recent literature about item generation in different domains. Within each section, we follow the distinctions drawn earlier concerning the theoretical basis for item modeling, the approach to instantiation, and the psychometric considerations.

Logical Reasoning

Reasoning is clearly an important construct in the assessment of admissions to higher education (Enright & Gitomer, 1989; Powers & Dwyer, 2003; Powers & Enright, 1987) and has been found to be predictive of success in graduate school (Kuncel, Hezlett, & Ones, 2001). Until recently, the Graduate Record Examination (GRE) included a section consisting of two types of reasoning problems, analytical reasoning and logical reasoning, for which there was theoretical and empirical justification (Chalifour & Powers, 1989; Emmerich, Enright, Rock, & Tucker, 1991). One type of reasoning problem can be called deductive, so-called analytic reasoning (AR) problems; the other type of problem consists of inferential reasoning problems, so-called logical reasoning (LR) items. In this section, we review the state of the art for those two item types with respect to item generation.

The LR item type was studied by Yang and Johnson-Laird (2001) with the goal of understanding what accounted for variation in difficulty. A sample GRE LR item is shown in Figure 9.1. Yang and Johnson-Laird (2001) postulated three potential sources of difficulty for this item type: the complexity of the scenario, the nature of the stem, and the nature of the options. Their analysis of difficulty was strongly theoretical in the sense that a specific theoretical perspective, mental model theory (Johnson-Laird, 1983), was the basis of the analysis. They reported no previous relevant psychological literature to model the difficulty of this item type and proposed instead mental model theory (Johnson-Laird & Byrne, 2001) as a means of analyzing the deep structure of LR items. A mental model can be thought of as a representation of a problem. This idea of a mental model is very general because it lends itself to representing a wide variety of situations, ranging from textual to spatial (Johnson-Laird, 1983). The assumed first step in reasoning is to encode or represent the situation, or premise in the case of reasoning. Reasoning about that situation consists of enumerating putative conclusions and attempting to falsify them by means of counter examples

> **Scenario:** Children born blind or deaf and blind begin social smiling on roughly the same schedule as most children, by about three months of' age.
>
> **Stem:** The information above provides evidence to support which of the following hypotheses:
>
> **Distractors:**
> - A. For babies the survival advantage of smiling consists in bonding the caregiver to the infant.
> - B. Babies do not smile when no one else is present.
> - C. The smiling response depends on an inborn unit determining a certain pattern of development.
> - D. Smiling between persons basically signals a mutual lack of aggressive intent.
> - E. When a baby begins smiling its caregivers begin responding to it as they would to a person in conversation.

Figure 9.1. Sample LR item from Yang and Johnson-Laird (2001). From "Mental models and logical reasoning problems in the GRE," by Y. Yang and P. N. Johnson-Laird, 2001, *Journal of Experimental Psychology: Applied, 7,* 308. Copyright by Educational Testing Service, All rights reserved. Reprinted with permission.

until one or more putative conclusions withstand the challenge. For example, a correctly encoded premise of the form

The printer is turned off or broken, or both

can be represented as:

A	the printer is off
B	the printer is broken
A B	the printer is off and broken

Conclusions or inferences, given this premise, can be evaluated. For example, the conclusion

The printer is on and ok

clearly is inconsistent with the text. However,

The printer is on and broken

is somewhat consistent because it refers to a broken printer, albeit it is not a valid conclusion. Thus, according to mental model theory, inferential reasoning is a matter of representing the premises and then testing conclusions against the premise as represented.

Of course, in practice, items are stated in natural language. Therefore, above and beyond the reasoning that these problems require, they also require a reading comprehension process to encode the text of the problem so that reasoning can proceed. This is important for construct representation purposes because a skill besides the one of central interest is required in order to elicit the evidence of central interest, reasoning in this case. It is not surprising that in factor analytic studies that have been carried out on GRE scores, the LR scores load on the verbal factor (Bridgeman & Rock, 1993). The fact that skills other than the central one mediate performance is unavoidable and needs to be handled carefully to avoid reducing construct representation or inadvertently advantaging or disadvantaging some students. Yang and Johnson-Laird (2001) analyzed 120 GRE items and classified them into three categories: inferential problems in which the task requires one to decide "which option is a conclusion the text implies, or which option implies a conclusion in the text"; missing-premise problems, "in which individuals have to determine which option states a missing premise in the text"; and weakness problems "in which individuals have to identify which option states a weakness in an argument in the text" (p. 309).

Mental model theory predicts a difference in difficulty between inferential and missing-premise problems; namely, that identifying a missing premise requires more complex reasoning and therefore should lead to more difficult items, other things being equal. Yang and Johnson-Laird (2001) conducted four experiments and identified three sources of difficulty: (a) the nature of the logical task, confirming that, as predicted by mental model theory, inferential problems are easier than missing-premise problems; (b) the nature of the distractors, confirming that distractors that are consistent with the text would be harder to reject that those that are inconsistent with the text; and (c) the nature of the conclusions, in which the evaluation of valid conclusions was found to be simpler than evaluation of incorrect conclusions.

Rijmen and De Boeck (2001) also examined reasoning, albeit not in a GRE or testing context. The investigation is relevant in light of the results just presented. They contrasted two theoretical perspectives to deductive reasoning: rule theories (e.g., Braine, 1978; Rips & Conrad, 1983) and mental model theory that was applied to the GRE by Yang and Johnson-Laird (2001). Rijmen and De Boeck pointed out that although different rules appear to require different degrees of effort, and therefore contribute differentially to difficulty, the theory itself does not provide the means for estimating a priori what that difficulty is. From a validity perspective, this is not ideal because it still leaves unanswered the question as to why different rules are more difficult (Revuelta & Ponsoda, 1999, p. 247). By contrast, as noted by Rijmen and De Boeck, mental model theory is more amenable to a priori predictions because of how the reasoning process is framed; namely, as requiring to represent situations or premises by enumerating mental models and then falsifying potential deductions. Psychologically, this entails specification of a space of possibilities and a search of that space, and aspects of that process could serve as the basis for theoretical predictions of difficulty a priori.

Research on the LR item type is clearly in its infancy, but it is off to an excellent theoretical start and serves to illustrate how theory can guide item construction. For example, if we were contemplating augmenting the difficulty of logical reasoning tests by means of new item types, it could be possible to evaluate candidates and perhaps rule out some of them purely on the basis of a theoretical analysis. Yang and Johnsoln-Laird (2001) focused, appropriately, on an accounting of psychometric attributes: difficulty. For item modeling purposes, there would have to be attention to how to instantiate items that embody a theory of difficulty. LR items are based on natural language consisting of the scenario, which sets the context, and the stem and corresponding option set. To fully model LR items, a taxonomy of appropriate contexts would be needed. Given such a taxonomy, it may be possible to electronically search text databases for instances of relevant text that would serve as raw material for scenarios. Although the state of the art in text search for item modeling is, itself, nascent, significant progress has been made in the last few years, as discussed in a subsequent section. In the Yang-Johnson-Laird research, the items were "undressed" to uncover their deep logical nature. Whether text search is sufficient to locate scenarios that lend themselves to LR items is an empirical question. Literal search may not be efficient or sufficient to identify candidate scenarios. For example, if we wanted to create isomorphs of the sample problem given in Figure 9.1, it would be ideal to search for text that embodies the following premise: *Animate object of class C1 and animate objects of class C2 exhibit behavior X by the same age.*

If the text database were already encoded in a form that enabled searching it by an abstract query of this type, there may be ways to identify text that might serve as stimulus material. Even then, the located text would have to be evaluated and possibly modified by item authors before it could be used. Nevertheless, it is possible this approach would still result in significant efficiency gains.

Analytical Reasoning

The other (former) component of the GRE analytic section is the AR item type. Whereas the LR item type is thought to measure informal reasoning, the AR item type is viewed as measuring deductive reasoning (Emmerich et al., 1991). A sample item appears Figure 9.2. This item type was the focus of an extensive series of studies at the University of Plymouth (Newstead, Bradon, Evans, & Dennis, 2002; Newstead, Bradon, Handley, Dennis, & Evans, 2006). The overall structure the item sets is the same. A scenario is always an array consisting of at most seven elements (which can be radio segments, floors on a building, tracks on a CD, etc.), and the order in which they are to appear. The stimulus section introduces restrictions or additional information, in this case as to adjacency restrictions between elements of the array. Finally, the stem for an item is presented by stating, in this case, a specific adjacency condition and asking the order in which different segments might be played, given the preceding restrictions. Several items are generated from a given scenario, and stems are classified into (a) possible orders, (b) necessity, (c) impossibility, and (d) impossibility items.

The team's approach to the problem took advantage of their extensive background in the psychology of reasoning (Evans, 1989; Newstead, Pollard, Evans, & Allen, 1992) and the fact that, in addition to developing a model of difficulty, the goal was to generate items as well. They took an admirably ecumenical approach to modeling difficulty. One postulated source of difficulty was the encoding of item text, i.e., effects, which concern the process the text to get to the logical structure, which necessarily would need to be part of any accounting of difficulty, regardless of the theoretical stance. The second source of difficulty they postulated was complexity of rules, which would be theoretically aligned with

> **Scenario**
> An office building has exactly six floors, numbered 1 through 6 from bottom to top. Each of exactly six companies F, G, I, J, K, and M must be assigned an entire floor for office space. The floors must be assigned according to the following conditions:
>
> **Stimulus**
> F must be on a lower floor than G. I must be either on the floor immediately above M's floor or on the floor immediately below M's floor. J can be neither on the floor immediately above M's floor nor on the floor immediately below M's floor. K must be on floor 4.
>
> **Stem**
> If G is on floor 5, which of the following must be true?
>
> **Options**
> (A) F is on floor 1
> (B) F is on floor 3
> (C) I is on floor 1
> (D) J is on floor 6
> (E) M is on floor 2

Figure 9.2. From Table 1 of "Predicting the difficulty of complex logical reasoning problems" by S. E. Newstead, P. Bradon, S. J. Handley, I. Dennis, and J. S. B. T. Evans, 2006, *Thinking & Reasoning, 12*(1), 64. Copyright by Educational Testing Service, All rights reserved. Reprinted with permission.

rule-based approaches to reasoning (e.g., Rips & Conrad, 1983). They also postulated a representational difficulty factor, which would be theoretically aligned with the mental model theory we just discussed in connection with LR items.

The representational emphasis seemed natural, given that think-aloud protocols were examined early in the project (Newstead et al., 2002) and looked like mental models. Moreover, the explicit goal of generating items, not just understanding difficulty, also encouraged an approach that was highly representational. The project was successful in that they were able to effectively predict the difficulty of operationally administered items. They cite correlations ranging from .55 to .76 for the difficulty of items produced by their algorithm and operational difficulty estimates obtained by Educational Testing Service (ETS) based on GRE test takers. (It is important to note that models of difficulty were developed first on a separate set of items and were applied to newly generated items.) Furthermore, the work was theoretically informative with respect to the competing approaches to understanding human reasoning. Referring to the competing models of reasoning, Newstead et al. (2006) concluded that "mental model theorists will take comfort from the finding that semantic informativeness of a rule correlated negatively with difficulty . . . and from a finding that model variability score figured in our difficulty models" (p. 88). That is, the fact that difficulty could be predicted on the basis of an a priori analysis consistent with mental model theory was supportive of mental model theory. However, they concluded that the GRE items are so rich that it is unlikely that a single theoretical accounting of difficulty is feasible.

Unlike the case for LR, in which item generation needs to be assisted by an item writer, it appears possible to generate AR items in an automated fashion. The items generated by the Plymouth project were not ready for use as generated, however, because the language was removed for modeling purposes. Instead, deep or logical structures of items were generated, which then had to be manually fleshed out in natural language. This left the question of how to "dress" such items in an automated fashion once they were generated. Unfortunately, the project did not proceed to that stage. However, an independent effort addressed the problem in a very general form, namely, how to provide a natural language, not necessarily English, facade for such items. Fairon and Williamson (2002) developed a system to generate AR items in French, given a deep structure from the Plymouth project. They labeled their specific approach *finite state templates*. However, any of a number of approaches could serve equally well because natural language generation is a very active area of research (Jurafsky & Martin, 2000).

A full system for AR entails a generation of scenarios from a given context, such as office buildings, CDs, radio segments, seating arrangements, and so on. Given a context, a range of scenarios are feasible that might vary in their difficulty. For the GRE test-taking population, scenarios with six or seven elements (e.g., floors) yield items of an appropriate level of difficulty. However, instantiating such scenarios and wording them appropriately constitutes its own modeling task. A method to model the range of difficulty supported by different scenarios needs to be studied on its own but seems feasible in the Plymouth approach.

What remains to be discussed is the approach to imputing difficulty estimates to the generated items. The approach the Plymouth group took was to define difficulty models on the basis of attributes of the type mentioned earlier—encoding, representational load, and rule difficulty—and develop regression equations for predicting difficulty from those attributes for the different item types mentioned earlier. Recursive tree regression methods (Breiman, Freidman, Olshen, & Stone, 1984), such as those used by Enright and Sheehan (2002), are also applicable and offer several advantages, including the possibility of subsuming under a comprehensive difficulty model several item types. The generation of items with specific difficulty entailed a "search and test" procedure in which the difficulty of potential items was estimated until an item of the desired difficulty was found.

Figural Reasoning

Nomothetic theories of intelligence have long postulated a two-dimensional model of intelligence consisting of fluid and crystallized intelligence (Cattell, 1971; Horn, 1972). The distinction was supported by Carroll (1993) in a meta-analysis of several hundred studies and by an array of nonpsychometric evidence, as well (Horn, 2008). According to Horn (2008), fluid intelligence, or reasoning, "is measured by tasks requiring inductive reasoning ... It indicates capacities for identifying relationships, comprehending implications, and drawing inferences within content that is either novel or equally familiar to all" (Horn, 2008, p. 169). The Raven Progressive Test (Raven, Raven, & Court, 2003) is a quintessential example of a test that aims to measure fluid intelligence. The items in the test consist of a 3×3 matrix containing figures that are related in a way to be discovered by the test taker. Embretson (2002) conducted a major study for this item type.

As noted previously, nomothetic theories of intelligence for the most part do not address, directly, the explicit rules for constructing items and, as a result, are silent regarding the basis for item difficulty and other item attributes (i.e., construct representation). This requires a theory of performance at the item level. According to Embretson (2002),

> A complete theory would specify how each of the underlying processes involved in item solving is influenced by variations in item structures. If variations among the item structures represent the major processes in item solving, stronger prediction of item difficulty should be obtained as compared to variations that are unrelated to the theory. (p. 221)

Embretson relied on a cognitive micromodel of performance on the Raven postulated by cognitive theorists (Carpenter, Just, & Shell, 1990). The Carpenter et al. model assumed one central process, finding correspondences between figures and inducing relationships. In addition, an executive process to manage the process was assumed. The theory was operationalized as two computer programs designed to emulate the performance of average and superior test takers by varying the program's capability on those two postulated skills.

The application of this model work illustrates a strong theory approach to item generation. First, fluid intelligence is well established nomothetically as a high-level construct concerned with individual differences in cognitive functioning. Second, a cognitive microtheory of performance on tests like the Raven was the basis for modeling difficulty. On the basis of the Carpenter et al. (1990) theory, Embretson (2002) formulated several variables to characterize existing items with the intention that these variable serve as predictors of difficulty and also as the basis for instantiating items. Some of the variables were perceptual in nature, which, as we have seen from previous item types, underscores that for the assessment of complex constructs difficulty models may need to incorporate variables beyond the immediate construct of interest. With a difficulty model at hand, the next step was item generation guided by such a difficulty model, which was done by means of item structures.[2] An item structure is the equivalent of an item model designed to instantiate isomorphs. In the case of abstract reasoning, as modeled by Embretson (2002), items consist of a 3×3 matrix, shown in Figure 9.3, in which the last cell of the third row is left blank and the test taker's job is to identify the correct insertion given a series of choices. Given the figural nature of the items, it is feasible to develop algorithms for instantiating items from an item structure that can take the form of a matrix, as shown

---

[2]Item structures, like item models, is a label for a formalism useful for item generation.

$$\begin{pmatrix} a_{f(cir,s),thickness(m)} & a_{f(cir,.5s),thickness(.5m)} & a_{f(cir,.25s),thickness(.25m)} \\ a_{f(tri,s),thickness(m)} & a_{f(tri,.5s),thickness(.5m)} & a_{f(tri,.25s),thickness(.25m)} \\ a_{f(rec,s),thickness(m)} & a_{f(rec,.5s),thickness(.5m)} & a_{f(rec,.25s),thickness(.25m)} \end{pmatrix}$$

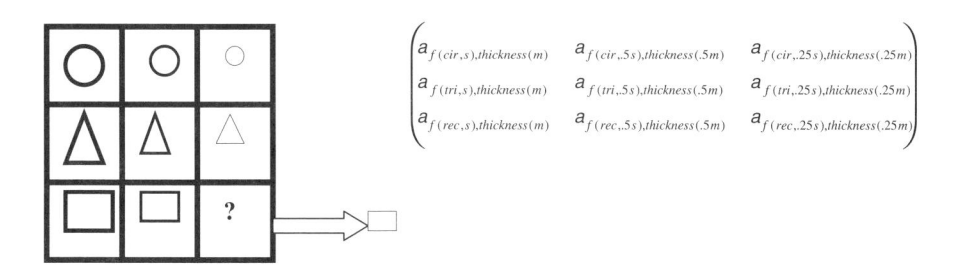

Figure 9.3. A matrix item.

in this example in which the figures (circles, triangles, and rectangles) appear at three sizes and three levels of thickness.

A critical aspect of the work is that the difficulty model was formulated in terms of variables that could be computed directly from the item structure. This makes it possible to impute a difficulty estimate by reference to the item structure that was used to generate it. The exception to this is the perceptual features, which were judged rather than computed. It is important that the difficulty model was tested on newly generated items. To test the model, five items were generated for 30 structures designed to span a range of difficulty. Altogether 150 newly generated items were used to test the theory. The estimated difficulty using one- and two-parameter item response theory (IRT; Lord, 1980) models and the discrimination parameter from the two-parameter logistic (2PL) results were regressed on the item structure, the perceptual features, and the position of the key in the array of possible answers. A multiple correlation of .89 was obtained for each set of difficulty estimates. Embretson (2002) did not explicitly analyze the within-item structure variability, which judging by the plots she presented was not negligible. The ratio of between-item structure variability to within-item structure variability would be an informative statistic for analyses of this type.

Figural abstract reasoning provides an opportunity to implement strong theory approach to item generation and illustrate the potential interplay of psychometric and psychological models. Other examples exist (Arendasy, 2005; Birney, Halford, & Andrews, 2006; Pascual-Leone & Baillargeon, 1994; Primi, Zanarella-Cruz, Muniz-Nascimento, & Petrini, 2006).

Verbal Comprehension

It is possible to envision automatically generating items that assess vocabulary (Scrams, Mislevey, & Sheehan, 2002), listening comprehension (Huang, Liu , & Gao, 2005), verbal analogies (Bejar, Chaffin, & Embretson, 1991; Wesiak, 2003), and sentence-based items (Bejar, 1988; Higgins, 2007; Sheehan & Mislevey, 2001; Sheehan, Kostin, & Futagi, 2005). However, generating reading comprehension items requires a different approach. As was the case for the LR items reviewed previously, a critical component of the reading comprehension items is the passage to be read. The second component, of course, is the questions that assess the comprehension of the text. Thus, modeling reading comprehension items requires modeling of the passage and modeling of the questions asked about the passage. By modeling of the passage, I mean to posit a set of textual attributes that can be used to characterize the text with respect to a specific model reading comprehension. For example, Gorin and Embretson (2006), citing ETS internal manuals, stated that "the difficulty of the reading comprehension items is intended to be based in the passage complexity, not from the difficulty of the question itself" (pp. 395–396). This assertion implies a specific design goal; namely, that the textual attributes of the passage should not figure strongly in the variability difficulty of the items, which is not to say that the level of difficulty should not be based on text of suitable complexity.

The first significant effort to model the assessment of reading comprehension from a cognitive perspective appears to have been by Embretson and Wetzel (1987) and was specifically concerned with item difficulty. They postulated a two-stage process. The first stage, which they called *text representation,* consists of encoding and representing the passage. They proposed a well-known model of reading (Kintsch, 1998) as the basis for this stage of the process. In this model the reader is assumed to iteratively extract a propositional representation of the passage aided by relevant background knowledge at the disposal of the reader. The *propositional density* of a text is assumed to drive difficulty. The second stage, which they called *response decision,* is concerned with answering questions given the passage representation. It too entails constructing a representation of the questions contained in the items. The actual mechanism for answering items is assumed to involve a process to decide the acceptability of each alternative.

At a high level of detail, this formulation is very compatible with those we saw earlier for AR and LR items, especially with respect to the assumption of a means of representing the passage, or premise or scenario in the case of LR and AR item types, respectively. It probably is an idealized characterization of what transpires mentally when taking a reading comprehension test. However, as noted by Rupp, Ferne, and Choi (2006), reading comprehension in a testing context may not be well described by theoretical formulations of the reading process because it is a unique form of reading. Nevertheless, from a theoretical perspective the insufficiency of an off-the-shelf theory to model test behavior is not necessarily fatal. As mentioned earlier, a major advantage of item generation is that it enables fine tuning the theoretical underpinning of items as rounds of data collection are accumulated and theoretical predictions are evaluated.

The study by Gorin and Embretson (2006) is especially informative in that it applied variables from the Embretson and Wetzel (1987) study, developed for the ASVAB (Armed Services Vocational Aptitude Battery) as well as those from the study by Sheehan, Ginther, and Schedl (1999) developed for the TOEFL (Test of English as Foreign Language), to GRE items. In a sense, the Gorin and Embretson study is an attempt to falsify previous models of reading comprehension difficulty on an altogether different test and population. The results suggested that approximately a quarter of the difficulty variance in GRE items was explained by the item attributes from the previous studies (Gorin & Embretson, 2006, p. 404). When difficulty predictors specific to the GRE, passage length and item format, were added, there was a gain of 6%. It is interesting that the textual features, such as propositional density, which had previously been predictors of difficulty, did not emerge as predictors of difficulty for the GRE case. That is, item-level, rather than passage-level, features were the key to accounting for difficulty for GRE items. Although at first sight this is at odds with the assertion to the contrary cited earlier, it need not be. The empirical finding may reflect that GRE text for passages is chosen to be equivalent in complexity, or that the item sets that survive pretesting are homogeneous with respect to textual characteristics, such as propositional density, of the stimulus material.

Fitting models based on different tests is a form of model challenge and is to be applauded. However, it is also the case that the ASVAB and TOEFL have very different purposes and populations. Expanding on Rupp et al.'s (2006) point, not only is the reading process as part of testing a very specialized form of reading, but the reading required by different assessments could well be different, and, therefore, the same models of difficulty perhaps should not be expected to generalize completely. Again, the goal should be to arrive at the appropriate model, drawing as necessary from existing theories and models but also taking into account the specifics of the assessment. Instantiating reading comprehension items is not at the point at which automated generation is feasible. Instead, what is feasible is to assist test designers to author such items with increased efficiency and certainty as to their psychometric attributes. The first step in that process is to be able to locate suitable text for the stimulus. Not surprisingly, the increasing availability of text sources online is the key to that process. In addition, a mechanism is needed to locate potential stimuli in the vast databases of text that are available. The idea for such a system, *SourceFinder,* first emerged in a broader context (Katz & Bauer, 2001) and has since become increasingly optimized for the specific purpose of locating stimuli for reading comprehension item sets (Passonneau, Hemat, Plante, & Sheehan, 2002; Sheehan, Kostin, Futagi, Hemat, & Zuckerman, 2006). Before the system can work, it is necessary to "train" filters that navigate the vast set of possible text. For training passages, a universe of potential passages is first defined as the articles in a collection of journals that are known to have yielded passages in the past. Then articles that are known to be a suitable source and articles that are believed to be unsuitable are gathered, and that designation becomes the dependent variable in an analysis designed to predict suitability of a specific text. Predictors, or independent variables, for such an analysis need to be defined and precomputed so that the resulting prediction equation can be used to quickly locate potentially suitable articles. The success of the system is evaluated in terms of whether more suitable sources are located with the filtering on. Sheehan et al. (2006) concluded that indeed this was the case.

Mathematics

We have left mathematics for last because among efforts to operationalize item generation it has the longest history. The progress in mathematics has been significant on several fronts. In fact, there has been so much research that we can hardly do it justice in the limited space we have. In this section, I discuss in turn theoretical underpinnings, modeling of psychometric attributes, and approaches to instantiation.

The resurgence of cognitive psychology mentioned previously had an effect on the conceptions of problem solving, and specifically K–12 mathematics problem solving. These new conceptions aimed to improve learning through a deeper understanding of the mental problem-solving process or to diagnose underperformance (Brown & Burton, 1978; Hall, Kibler, Wenger, & Truxaw, 1989; Mayer, 1981; Riley, Greeno, & Heller, 1983). The enabling of transfer, for example, was a major objective. These conceptions were general enough to be applicable not just to school problem solving but also to conventional admissions assessments (Bejar, Embretson, & Mayer, 1987).

For example, Riley et al. (1983) presented a detailed analysis of math word problems in elementary grades. At the center of the approach is the idea of a schema (Norman & Rumelhart, 1975). Schemas play a representational role, just like mental models discussed in connection with reasoning item types. Problem solving is seen as reducing a problem statement to its bare essentials—that is, assigning it a schema. They refer to this step as *comprehension*. The next step in the process is to map the conceptual representation to procedures. The last step is to execute those procedures to produce an answer.

The idea of schemas is quite general and more recently has been seen as playing a role in the characterization of expertise in general (Bransford, Brown, & Cocking, 1999). The highest levels of expertise are described as having access to a wider range of schemas to draw from, as well as the ability to use them in ways to solve novel problems. A recent line of research on schema-based transfer instruction (Fuchs, Fuchs, Finelli, Courey, & Hamlett, 2004) has suggested that focusing instruction on schemas appears effective to improve mathematics school achievement, including for students with disabilities. Characterizing a student's schema by means of a sorting task of math problems was studied experimentally for its potential in admissions testing (Bennett & Sebrechts, 1997). Comprehensive discussion of schemas in problem solving and cognition can be found in Marshall (1993), Singley (1995), and Singley and Bennett (2002).

Riley et al. (1983) found that semantic structure was a difficulty factor in the context they studied, elementary mathematics. By *semantic structure,* Riley et al. meant the type of word problem (e.g., change, equalize, combine, compare). These types had different levels of difficulty in the population they studied. Even though detailed models were developed to simulate performance on these problem types, Riley et al. did not propose a theoretical explanation for the ordering of difficulty. Moreover, they pointed out that within each class of problems there was variation in difficulty. Although a descriptive account (Mayer, 1981) is necessarily the first step in building a theoretically based difficulty model, a more satisfying accounting would explain the difficulty among subtypes of problems from variables at a finer grain size than problem type. For example, the schemas the different problem types call for could be inherently more complex because they involve more quantities and more, or more complex, relationships among those quantities. Such an account was subsequently provided by Riley and Greeno (1988).

A further consideration is that measurement constructs are complex. A full accounting of variability in the psychometric attributes of items is likely to require going beyond the construct of immediate interest. For example, the current National Council of Teachers of Mathematics (2006) standards call for communication as part of the definition of mathematics proficiency. The difficulty of items that call for exhibiting communicative ability, such as justifying a solution to a problem, will not be simply a matter of the semantic nature of the problem. More generally, the increased emphasis on more open-ended performance means that the response process is not as structured as is the case of multiple choice items and necessarily (but see Graf, in press) increases the complexity of the target construct.

Embretson (1995) took advantage of the available theorizing on mathematics problem solving to model the difficulty of SAT mathematics word problems. She started with disclosed SAT items as classified into a dichotomy consisting of "rate problems" and "part problems." The rate problems were further subdivided into seven categories and the part problems into three categories. Three "isomorphically equivalent" instances were written for each of the 10 categories and rated on three dimensions: linguistic knowledge (e.g., number of words), schematic knowledge (e.g., number of equations), and strategic knowledge (e.g., determining whether a transformation was necessary). The correlations with difficulty ranged from .14 to .64. Strategic knowledge was the least correlated with difficulty, whereas reading level was the most correlated. Thus, it was possible to establish a link between the postulated difficulty factors and estimated difficulty.

Embretson's (1995) purpose was to assess learning potential rather than item generation per se. By contrast, Enright and Sheehan (2002) conducted an investigation to clarify the constructs assessed by quantitative items on graduate admissions tests. In one study they created items for two content areas: rate and probability. In each content area, they crossed three features at two levels: context (i.e., cost vs. distance-time-rate), complexity (i.e., the number of constraints needed to be kept in mind), and "algebraicness" (i.e., whether the problem required manipulation of variables). The crossing of the three binary features yielded eight item models, and six instances were generated for each, yielding 48 items for each content area. They used regression trees (Breiman et al., 1984) to regress empirical difficulty on the three features and were able to recover the generating principles for the most part. They also analyzed several existing item pools by regressing difficulty on item features. In such pools, the generating principles are not necessarily manipulated, and therefore the results need to be interpreted carefully. For example, a certain feature may not emerge as a difficulty predictor, but that does not mean that it is an unimportant item design principle. We saw, for example, with reading comprehension that propositional density did not emerge as a predictor of difficulty in GRE items, whereas it had been so in other contexts. In general, whenever psychometric attributes of items from existing tests are analyzed, the fact that some content item attributes do not emerge as predictors of psychometric attributes should not be taken to mean that the variable is unimportant for item generation purposes. By the same token, not all the attributes that emerge from the analysis of existing items as predictors of psychometric attributes should necessarily be kept for the generation of future items. For example, careful thought should be given to the appropriate level of verbal knowledge required to mathematics problems.

The absence of a full theoretical accounting of construct representation for all item types does not mean that item generation cannot proceed. An alternative strategy is to use item generation as a means of building a more complete theoretical account from the ground up, one item at a time, so to speak, with the help of item modeling. This strategy would be applicable in the case in which the assessment already exists as well as for new assessments. Recent work with the GRE (Graf, Peterson, Steffen, & Lawless, 2005) is an example of the strategy, which Graf, Peterson, Saldivia, and Wang (2004) called *retrospective*.

The motivation for the work was the increased demand for items needed to preclude preknowledge of test content. By supplementing the existing pool of items with instances produced by item models, the goal was to reduce the exposure of each item. That is, with more items in circulation, each item is seen by relatively fewer students. The approach was very simple: Existing operational items became the basis of creating item models. Each GRE item already in the pool has survived scrutiny and therefore could serve as the basis for generating more items like it. Moreover, each such operational item has been calibrated, meaning that psychometric parameter estimates had been obtained previously as part of the operational-testing program. The goal of this effort was to create an item model that would generate *isomorphs,* that is, items intended to be exchangeable with the source item. The generated items would be calibrated upon generation by inputting the psychometric attributes of the item model, which in this case correspond to the item parameter estimates of the item model, to each instance of the item model. Item models were authored by the Mathematics Test Creation Assistant (Singley & Bennett, 2002). The designer creates a model by imposing constraints on variables that have been created to manipulate the surface realization of items based on the model. Item models were written with the goal of generating as much surface variation as possible while holding difficulty as constant as possible, so that it would be reasonable to impute the psychometric parameters of the source item to every instance.

That is, the "theory" in this case is that experienced test developers can author item models capable of producing isomorphic instances. This is a bottom-up, weak theory approach, in which the goal is to hold the psychometric attributes constant and learn from cases in which this is not the case. (By contrast, in most of the studies we have reviewed the approach is top-down and the goal is to account for variability among classes of item by means of a theoretically stronger approach, such as a cognitively based difficulty model.) To test the theory, several dozen item models based on operational GRE items were written and tested as part of the operational GRE testing program. Specifically, 10 instances of each item model were generated and assigned at random to samples of test takers during several administrations of the GRE. The relative position of the isomorphs was held constant to control position effects (Kingston & Dorans, 1984). The results are presented in Graf et al., 2004, 2005.

The psychometric attributes of model instances based on this design can be compared directly because instances are assigned at random and position effect is controlled for. Although the item models were successful for the most part, a few departed from the expectation. This is an informative outcome because the authors were very experienced test developers. Clearly, even experienced test developers could not anticipate all the sources of difficulty. Hypotheses were formulated for such departures and revised models created to incorporate those hypotheses. Generally, the revised item models yielded instances homogeneous in their psychometric attributes. In effect, with each round stronger theory was applied, illustrating the iterative process of theoretical refinement possible in the context of item generation.

Whereas Graf and her colleagues specifically tested the assumption of isomorphicity, Bejar et al. (2003) took isomorphicity for granted and instead studied the feasibility of substituting first-generation item models for operational items in an experimental GRE adaptive test. On the basis of the results by Graf and her colleagues, it can be assumed that isomorphicity was not completely satisfied. Bejar et al. (2003) referred to this approach as "on the fly" adaptive testing because, in principle, an adaptive system can call on an item model and generate an item on the spot rather than retrieving it from a database. The first-generation item models based on operational GRE items were substituted for a portion of the items in a GRE adaptive test pool and administered to volunteers who had previously taken the GRE with a system that emulated the operational adaptive test in all respects. The design of the study compared the previous operational scores with the score obtained based on the experimental system. Because the pool contained both items and item models and the administration was adaptive, the scores were based on responses to items and instances of item models. For most cases, at least one half of the test consisted of item model instances. The psychometric parameters of the instances were obtained by imputation from the operational item parameters estimates that had served as the basis for the item model, but attenuated by means of expected response functions A key result from the investigation was that the correlation between the operational GRE score and the on-the-fly score was as high as the correlation between GRE scores obtained from students retaking the GRE, suggesting that in practice there was little degradation in precision of measurement due to the use of item models even when it was likely that isomorphicity was not completely satisfied.

Graf et al (2004) also discussed item modeling in a prospective fashion, that is, for assessments that are being developed (Shute, Graf, & Hansen, 2005). The essence of this approach is to carefully model distractors to correspond to prevalent student misconceptions (Graf, 2008). Graf also discussed the possibility of associating instructional feedback with each distracter, as did Morley et al. (2004). These extensions of item models contemplated by Graf have not been extensively tested but are straightforward extensions of item models that could be useful in an instructional context.

The modeling and instantiating infrastructure is, understandably, better developed for mathematics than for content domains. The Mathematics Test Creation Assistant (MTCA) has been in use at ETS for some time (Singley & Bennett, 2002) and continues to be improved through additional flexibility while more powerful systems are being considered (Deane et al., 2006; Deane & Sheehan, 2003). Possible or ongoing extensions of the MTCA include the possibility of providing instance-specific feedback. In addition, it is possible to integrate automated scoring of quantitative responses from generated free response items. In this case, in addition to generating the item, the item model generates an instance-specific scoring key to be applied by the scoring engine. A further area of progress is rendering instances in different languages. A prototype for

Japanese and Spanish has been developed (Higgins, Futagi, & Deane, 2005). Multilingual applications appear to be an area of high interest judging by the several efforts identified as part of this review (Conejo et al., 2004; Strotmann, Ng'ang'a, & Caprotti, 2005).

Conclusions

I hope to have delivered on the promise implied by the chapter's title. However, I also hope to have made clear that item generation is central to the validity argument in support of an assessment. Unless the basis for test specifications, especially content specifications, is explicated in terms of the target construct, for practical purposes the test as implemented defines the construct. For example, verbal ability has at times been defined, by default, as what tests described as verbal measure (Hunt, 1978). This is rather circular and not much different from Boring's (1923) assertion that "intelligence is what the tests test" (p. 5). Construct validation as framed by Messick (1989), but especially demonstrating construct representation (Embretson, 1983), is key to breaking that circularity. Nevertheless, the technical manuals of many assessments address in detail the statistical specifications of such tests but are typically silent about the rationale for content specifications. However, developing an assessment requires a larger investment than in the past, and the assessment can be expected to have a much shorter life span. Therefore, it makes sense to approach the development of an assessment with as complete an explication of the target construct as possible and then approach the development as an iterative design effort. Item generation is a tool in that effort.

The foregoing review has been necessarily selective due to space limitations. However, a reasonable conclusion is that there has been palpable progress in the application of item generation to a wide range of domains. The fact that many of the efforts we examined are closely aligned with developments in validation and assessment design augurs well for the conception of item generation as the production of items in concert with the validity argument we hope to make about scores. The review of psychometric considerations suggests that item modeling does not present insurmountable psychometric problems. Indeed, progress in that area has been significant. This leaves as the central theme for an item-generation research agenda the theoretical basis for item generation, which takes us back to Cronbach and Meehl (1955), who early on stressed the equivalence of validation with the process of scientific theory building and testing. Although they did not emphasize construct representation, I do not think they would have objected to extending their language to be applicable to construct representation. I believe the review suggests that item generation by means of item models, item structures, and similar approaches is a useful tool to ensure construct representation, which as an added bonus can be the means of efficiently producing already calibrated items. That is, item generation needs to be embedded in a larger framework of assessment design, such as evidence-centered design (Mislevy et al., 2003), cognitive design systems (Embretson, 1998), or some other comprehensive assessment design framework (e.g., Wilson, 2005) rather than being treated as an independent process.

One insight from the foregoing review is that no single off-the-shelf theory is likely to be sufficient to model test behavior. The testing situation is unique, and it is unlikely that generic theories would be concerned with the minutiae of test behavior. One implication is that, at best, the designer of the assessment is able to draw from existing theories. However, the designer needs to engage in a significant amount of theorizing as well. (For an example of this process, see Janssen & De Boeck, 1997). That is, for practical purposes, the target construct entails a theory and, like all theories, needs to be tested and refined or discarded. The universe of relevant observables, in the simplest case, is the item models that collectively are intended as the means for eliciting evidence that responses are a function of the postulated construct. The success of a theory cast as a set of item models can be formulated as the extent to which between-item model variability is accounted for and the extent to which within-item model variability is held to a minimum. The within-model variability is relevant theoretically but also psychometrically (Macready & Merwin, 1973; van der Linden & Glas, 2007, p. 821). Sizable within-model variability attenuates the psychometric information that the item model yields. In addition, it suggests that the theoretical accounting is lacking in some respects. By contrast, an accounting of between-item model variability is primarily of theoretical interest. What constitutes an adequate accounting of between-item model variability is evaluated no differently than is any other theory. Is there a more parsimonious accounting? Are there competing accountings that work equally well? Attempting to answer these questions is likely to improve the validity argument for the assessment. However, provided within-item model variability is small, the absence of a full theoretical accounting of between-item model variability is not an impediment to item generation, but, of course, under those circumstances the claim of construct representation would be weakened.

In this review, for the most part, I reported on "ability" testing in which most of the work has taken place relatively recently. For earlier reviews, see Bejar (1993) and Pitoniak (2002) and a book dedicated to item generation (Irvine & Kyllonen, 2002). In an instructional context a relevant means of assessing construct representation is the extent to which improvements in performance can be attributed to relevant instruction (D'Agostino, Welsh, & Corson, 2007). For personality tests (Johnson, 2004), science tests (Solano-Flores, Jovanovic, & Bachman, 1999), or situational tests (Lievens & Sackett, 2007, a somewhat different set of considerations would apply. The "psychometrics of item modeling" has also received attention (for overviews, see Bejar, 2008; Embretson and Yang, 2007).

References

Arendasy, M. (2005). Automatic generation of Rasch-calibrated items: Figural Matrices Test GEOM and Endless-Loops Test EC. *International Journal of Testing, 5,* 197–224.

Bejar, I. I. (1988). A sentence-based automated approach to the assessment of writing: A feasibility study. *Machine-Mediated Learning, 2,* 321–332.

Bejar, I. I. (1990). A generative analysis of a three-dimensional spatial task. *Applied Psychological Measurement, 14,* 237–245.

Bejar, I. I. (1993). A generative approach to psychological and educational measurement. In N. Frederiksen, R. J. Mislevy, & I. I. Bejar (Eds.), *Test theory for a new generation of tests* (pp. 323–359). Hillsdale, NJ: Erlbaum.
Bejar, I. I. (2002). Generative testing: From conception to implementation. In S. H. Irvine & P. C. Kyllonen (Eds.), *Item generation for test development* (pp. 199–218). Mahwah, NJ: Erlbaum.
Bejar, I. I. (2008). *Recent development in item generation* (Research Report RR 09-XX). Princeton, NJ: Educational Testing Service
Bejar, I. I., Chaffin, R., & Embretson, S. E. (1991). *Cognitive and psychometric analysis of analogical problem solving*. New York: Springer-Verlag.
Bejar, I. I., Embretson, S., & Mayer, R. E. (1987). *Cognitive psychology and the SAT: A review of some implications* (Research Report No. RR-87-28). Princeton, NJ: Educational Testing Service.
Bejar, I. I., Lawless, R. R., Morley, M. E., Wagner, M. E., Bennett, R. E., & Revuelta, J. (2003). A feasibility study of on-the-fly item generation in adaptive testing. *Journal of Technology, Learning, and Assessment, 2*(3). Available at http://www.jtla.org
Bennett, R. E., & Bejar, I. I. (1998). Validity and automated scoring: It's not only the scoring. *Educational Measurement: Issues and Practice, 17*(4), 9–16.
Bennett, R. E., & Sebrechts, M. M. (1997). A computer-based task for measuring the representational component of quantitative proficiency. *Journal of Educational Measurement, 34*, 64–77.
Birney, D. P., Halford, G. S., & Andrews, G. (2006). Measuring the influence of complexity on relational reasoning: The development of the Latin Square task. *Educational and Psychological Measurement, 66*(1), 146–171.
Boring, E. G. (1923, June 6). Intelligence as the tests test it. *The New Republic*, 35–37.
Bransford, J. D., Brown, A. I., & Cocking, R. R. (1999). *How people learn*. Washington DC: National Academy Press.
Breiman, L., Freidman, J. H., Olshen, R. A., & Stone, C. J. (1984). *Classification and regression trees*. Belmont, CA: Wadsworth International Group.
Bridgeman, B., & Rock, D. A. (1993). Relationships among multiple-choice and open-ended analytical questions. *Journal of Educational Measurement, 30*, 313–329.
Brown, J. S., & Burton, R. R. (1978). Diagnostic models for procedural bugs in basic mathematics skills. *Cognitive Science, 2*, 155–192.
Carpenter, P. A., Just, M. A., & Shell, P. (1990). What one intelligence test measures: A theoretical account of the processing in the Raven Progressive Matrices Test. *Psychological Review, 97*, 404–431.
Carroll, J. B. (1993). *Human cognitive abilities: A survey of factor analytic studies*. New York: Cambridge University Press.
Cattell, R. B. (1971). *Abilities: Their structure, growth and action*. New York: Houghton Mifflin.
Chalifour, C. L., & Powers, D. E. (1989). The relationship of content characteristics of GRE analytical reasoning items to their difficulties and discriminations. *Journal of Educational Measurement, 26*, 120–132.
Conejo, R., Guzmán, E., Millán, E., Trella, M., Pérez-De-La-Cruz, J. L., & Ríos, A. (2004). SIETTE: A Web-based tool for adaptive testing. *International Journal of Artificial Intelligence in Education, 14*, 29–61.
Cronbach, L. J. (1988). Five perspectives on validity argument. In H. Wainer & H. I. Braun (Eds.), *Test validity* (pp. 3–17). Hillsdale, NJ: Erlbaum.
Cronbach, L. J., & Meehl, P. E. (1955). Construct validity in psychological tests. *Psychological Bulletin, 52*, 281–302.
D'Agostino, J. V., Welsh, M. E., & Corson, N. M. (2007). Instructional sensitivity of a state's standards-based assessment. *Educational Assessment, 12*(1), 1–22.
Davey, T., & Nering, M. (2002). Controlling item exposure and maintaining item security. In C. N. Mills, M. T. Potenza, J. J. Fremer, & W. C. Ward (Eds.), *Computer-based testing: Building the foundation for future assessments*. Mahwah, NJ: Erlbaum.
Deane, P., Graf, E. A., Higgins, D., Futagi, Y., & Lawless, R. (2006). *Model analysis and model creation: Capturing the task-model structure of quantitative domain items* (Research Report No. RR-06-01). Princeton, NJ: Educational Testing Service.
Deane, P., & Sheehan, K. (2003). *Automatic item generation via frame semantics: Natural language generation of math world problems*. Unpublished report. Princeton, NJ.
Drasgow, F., Luecht, R., & Bennett, R. E. (2006). Technology and testing. In R. L. Brennan (Ed.), *Educational measurement* (4th ed., pp. 471–515). Westport, CT: Praeger.

Embretson, S. E. (1983). Construct validity: Construct representation versus nomothetic span. *Psychological Bulletin, 93,* 179–197.

Embretson, S. E. (1995). A measurement model for linking individual learning to processes and knowledge: Application to mathematical reasoning. *Journal of Educational Measurement, 32,* 227–294.

Embretson, S. E. (1998). A cognitive design approach to generating valid tests: Applications to abstract reasoning. *Psychological Methods, 3,* 380–396.

Embretson, S. E. (2002). Generating abstract reasoning items with cognitive theory. In S. H. Irvine & P. C. Kyllonen (Eds.), *Item generation for test development* (pp. 219–250). Mahwah, NJ: Erlbaum.

Embretson, S. E., & Wetzel, D. (1987). Component latent trait models for paragraph comprehension tests. *Applied Psychological Measurement, 11,* 175–193.

Embretson, S. E., & Yang, Y. (2007). Automatic item generation and cognitive psychology. In C. R. Rao & S. Sinharay (Eds.), *Handbook of statistics: Psychometrics* (Vol .26, pp. 747–768). New York: Elsevier.

Emmerich, W., Enright, M. K., Rock, D. A., & Tucker, C. (1991). *The development, investigation, and evaluation of new item types for the GRE analytical measure* (Research Report No. RR- 91-16). Princeton: NJ: Educational Testing Service.

Enright, M. K., & Sheehan, K. M. (2002). Modeling the difficulty of quantitative reasoning items: Implications for item generation. In S. H. Irvine & P. C. Kyllonen (Eds.), *Item generation for test development* (pp. 129–158). Mahwah, NJ: Erlbaum.

Enright, M. R., & Gitomer, D. (1989). *Toward a description of successful graduate students* (Research Report No. RR-89-9). Princeton, NJ: Educational Testing Service.

Fairon, C., & Williamson, D. M. (2002). *Automatic item text generation in educational assessment.* Paper presented at the Traitement Automatique du Langage Naturel (TALN'2002), Nancy, France. Retrieved from http://www.loria.fr/projets/JEP-TALN/actes/TALN/posters/Poster13.pdf

Fuchs, L. S., Fuchs, D., Finelli, R., Courey, S. J., & Hamlett, C. L. (2004). Expanding schema-based transfer instruction to help third graders solve real-life mathematical problems. *American Educational Research Journal, 41,* 419–445.

Glaser, R. (1963). Instructional technology and the measurement of learning outcomes: Some questions. *American Psychologist, 18,* 519–521.

Glaser, R. (1994). Criterion-referenced tests: Part I. Origins. *Educational Measurement: Issues and Practice, 13*(4), 9–11.

Gorin, J. S., & Embretson, S. E. (2006). Item difficulty modeling of paragraph comprehension items. *Applied Psychological Measurement, 30,* 394–411.

Graf, E. A. (2008). *Approaches to the design of diagnostic item models* (Research Report No. RR-08-07). Princeton, NJ: Educational Testing Service.

Graf, E. A. (In press). Defining Mathematics Competency in the Service of Cognitively Based Assessment for Grades 6 Through 8 by Graf Princeton, NJ: ETS.

Graf, E. A., Peterson, S., Saldivia, L., & Wang, S. (2004, October). *Designing and revising quantitative item models.* Paper presented at the Fourth Spearman Conference, Philadelphia, PA.

Graf, E. A., Peterson, S., Steffen, M., Lawless, R. (2005). *Psychometric and cognitive analysis as a basis for the revision of quantitative item models* (Research Report No. RR-05-25). Princeton, NJ: Educational Testing Service.

Haertel, E. (1985). Construct validity and criterion-referenced testing. *Review of Educational Research, 55*(1), 23–46.

Hall, R., Kibler, D., Wenger, E., & Truxaw, C. (1989). Exploring the episodic structure of algebra story problem solving. *Cognition and Instruction, 6,* 223–283.

Higgins, D. (2007). *Item Distiller: Text retrieval for computer-assisted test item creation* (Research Memorandum No. RM-07-05). Princeton, NJ: Educational Testing Service.

Higgins, D., Futagi, Y., & Deane, P. (2005). *Multilingual generalization of the Model Creator software for math item generation* (Research Report No. RR-05-02). Princeton, NJ: Educational Testing Service.

Horn, J. L. (1972). The structure of intellect: Primary abilities. In R. M. Dreger (Ed.), *Multivariate personality research.* Baton Rouge, LA: Claitor.

Horn, J. L. (2008). Spearman's g, expertise, and the nature of human cognitive capability. In P. C. Kyllonen, R. D. Roberts, & L. Stankov (Eds.), *Extending intelligence: Enhancement and new constructs* (pp. 159–194). New York: Rotledge.

Hornke, L. F. (2002). Item generation models for higher cognitive functions. In S. H. Irvine & P. C. Kyllonen (Eds.), *Item generation for test development* (pp. 159–178). Mahwah, NJ: Erlbaum.

Huang, S.-M., Liu, C.-L., & Gao, Z.-M. (2005, July/August). Computer-assisted item generation for listening cloze tests and dictation practice in English. In *Advances in web-based learning— ICWL 2005 4th International Conference, Hong Kong.* Berlin: Springer-Verlag.

Hunt, E. (1978). Mechanics of verbal ability. *Psychological Review, 85,* 109–130.

Irvine, S. H. (2002). The foundations of item generation for mass testing. In S. H. Irvine & P. C. Kyllonen (Eds.), *Item generation for test development* (pp. 3–34). Mahwah, NJ: Erlbaum.

Irvine, S. H., & Kyllonen, P. (Eds.). (2002). Item generation for test development. Mahwah, NJ: Lawrence Erlbaum Associates, Inc.

Janssen, R., & De Boeck, P. (1997). Psychometric modeling of componentially designed synonym tasks. *Applied Psychological Measurement, 21*(1), 1–15.

Johnson, J. A. (2004). The impact of item characteristics on item scale and validity. *Multivariate Behavioral Research, 39,* 273–302.

Johnson-Laird, P. (1983). *Mental models.* Cambridge, MA: Harvard University Press.

Johnson-Laird, P. N., & Byrne, R. M. J. (2001). *Deduction.* Hillsdale, NJ: Erlbaum.

Jurafsky, D., & Martin, J. (2000). *Speech and language processing.* Upper Saddle River, NJ: Prentice Hall.

Kane, M. T. (1992). An argument-based approach to validity. *Psychological Bulletin, 112,* 527–535.

Kane, M. T. (2004). Certification testing as an illustration of argument-based validation. *Measurement: Interdisciplinary Research and Perspectives, 2*(3), 135–170.

Katz, R. K., & Bauer, M. I. (2001). SourceFinder: Course preparation via linguistically targeted web search [Electronic version]. *Educational Technology & Society 4*(3).

Kingston, N. M., & Dorans, N. J. (1984). Item location effects and their implications for IRT equating and adaptive testing. *Applied Psychological Measurement, 8,* 147–154.

Kintsch, W. (1998). *Comprehension: A paradigm for cognition.* Cambridge, England: Cambridge University Press.

Kotovsky, K., & Simon, H. A. (1990). What makes some problems really hard: Explorations in the problem space of difficulty. *Cognitive Psychology, 22,* 143–183.

Kuncel, N. R., Hezlett, S. A., & Ones, D. S. (2001). A comprehensive meta-analysis of the predictive validity of the graduate record examinations: Implications for graduate student selection and performance. *Psychological Bulletin, 127,* 162–181.

LaDuca, A., Staples, W. I., Templeton, B., & Holzman, G. B. (1986). Item modeling procedure for constructing content-equivalent multiple choice questions. *Medical Education, 20*(1), 53–56.

Lievens, F., & Sackett, P. R. (2007). Situational judgment tests in high stakes settings: Issues and strategies with generating alternate forms. *Journal of Applied Psychology, 92,* 1043–1055.

Loevinger, J. (1957). Objective tests as instruments of psychological theory. *Psychological Reports, 3,* 653–694.

Lord, F. M. (1980). *Applications of item response theory to practical testing problems.* Hillsdale, NJ: Erlbaum.

Macready, G. B., & Merwin, J. C. (1973). Homogeneity within item forms in domain referenced testing. *Educational and Psychological Measurement, 33,* 351–360.

Marshall, S. P. (1993). Assessing schema knowledge. In N. Frederiksen, R. J. Mislevy, & I. I. Bejar (Eds.), *Test theory for a new generation of tests* (pp. 155–180). Hillsdale, NJ: Erlbaum.

Mayer, R. E. (1981). Frequency norms and structural analysis of algebra story problems into families, categories and templates. *Instructional Science, 10,* 135–175.

Meehl, P. E. (1990). Appraising and amending theories: The strategy of Lakatosian defense and two principles that warrant it. *Psychological Inquiry, 1*(2), 108.

Messick, S. (1981). Constructs and their vicissitudes in educational and psychological measurement. *Psychological Bulletin, 89,* 575–588.

Messick, S. (1989). Validity. In R. L. Linn (Ed.), *Educational measurement* (3rd ed., pp. 13–103). New York: American Council on Education.

Messick, S. (1994). The interplay of evidence and consequences in the validation of performance assessments. *Educational Researcher, 23*(2), 13–23.

Mislevy, R. J., Bejar, I. I., Bennett, R. E., Haertel, G. D., & Winters, F. I. (In press). Technology supports for assessment design. In G. McGaw, E. Baker, & P. Peterson (Eds.), *International Encyclopedia of Education* (3rd ed.). Oxford, England: Elsevier.

Mislevy, R. J., Steinberg, L. S., & Almond, R. G. (2003). On the structure of educational assessments. *Measurement: Interdisciplinary Research and Perspectives, 1*(1), 3–62.

Morley, M., Bridgeman, B., & Lawless, R. R. (2004). *Transfer between variants of quantitative items* (Research Report No. RR-04-06). Princeton, NJ: Educational Testing Service.

Mumford, M. D., & Owens, W. A. (1987). Methodology review: Principles, procedures, and findings in the application of background data measures. *Applied Psychological Measurement, 11,* 1–31.

National Council of Teachers of Mathematics. (2006). *Curriculum focal points for prekindergarten through grade 8 mathematics: a quest for coherence.* Reston, VA: The National Council of Teachers of Mathematics.

Newstead, S. E., Bradon, P., Handley, S. J., Dennis, I., & Evans, J. S. B. T. (2006). Predicting the difficulty of complex logical reasoning problems. *Thinking & Reasoning, 12*(1), 62–90.

Newstead, S. E., Bradon, P. S. H., Evans, J., & Dennis, I. (2002). Using the psychology of reasoning to predict the difficulty of analytical reasoning problems. In S. H. Irvine & P. C. Kyllonen (Eds.), *Item generation for test development* (pp. 35–51). Mahwah, NJ: Erlbaum.

Newstead, S. E., Pollard, P., Evans, J. S. T., & Allen, J. L. (1992). The source of belief bias effects in syllogistic reasoning. *Cognition, 45,* 257–284.

Nichols, P., & Sugrue, B. (1999). The lack of fidelity between cognitively complex constructs and conventional test development practice. *Educational Measurement: Issues and Practice, 18*(2), 18–29.

Nickerson, R. S. (1998). Confirmation bias: An ubiquitous phenomenon in many guises. *Review of General Psychology, 2,* 175–220.

Pascual-Leone, J., & Baillargeon, R. (1994). Developmental measurement of mental attention. *International Journal of Behavioral Development, 17,* 161–200.

Passonneau, R., Hemat, L., Plante, J., & Sheehan, K. M. (2002). *Electronic sources as input to GRE reading comprehension item development: Sourcefinder prototype evaluation* (Research Report RR-02-120). Princeton, NJ: Educational Testing Service.

Popper, K. R. (1959/1992). *The logic of scientific discovery.* London/New York: Routledge.

Powers, D. E., & Dwyer, C. A. (2003). *Toward specifying a construct of reasoning* (Research Report No. RM-03-01). Princeton, NJ: Educational Testing Service.

Powers, D. E., & Enright, M. K. (1987). Analytical reasoning skills in graduate study: Perceptions of faculty in six fields. *Journal of Higher Education, 58,* 658–682.

Primi, R., Zanarella-Cruz, M. B., Muniz-Nascimento, M., & Petrini, M. C. (2006). Validade de construto de um instrumento informatizado de avalição dinâmica da inteligência fluida. [Construct validity of a computer-based test to evaluate dynamic fluid intelligence] *Psico, 37,* 109–122.

Raven, J., Raven, J. C., & Court, J. H. (2003). *Manual for Raven's progressive matrices and vocabulary scales. Section 1: General overview.* San Antonio, TX: Harcourt Assessment.

Revuelta, J., & Ponsoda, V. (1999). Generación automática de ítems. In J. Olea, V. Ponsoda & G. Prieto (Eds.), *Test informatizados: Fundamentos y aplicaciones.* [Computer-based tests: Foundations and applications] Madrid, Spain: Piramide.

Rijmen, F., & De Boeck, P. (2001). Propositional reasoning: The differential contribution of "rules" to the difficulty of complex reasoning problems. *Memory & Cognition, 29,* 165–175.

Riley, M. S., & Greeno, J. G. (1988). Developmental analysis of understanding language about quantities and of solving problems *Cognition and Instruction, 5*(1), 49–101.

Riley, M. S., Greeno, J. G., & Heller, J. I. (1983). Development of children's problem-solving ability in arithmetic. In H. P. Ginsburg (Ed.), *The development of mathematical thinking* (pp. 153–196). New York: Academic Press.

Rips, L. J., & Conrad, F. G. (1983). Individual differences in deduction. *Cogntion and Brain Theory, 6,* 259–289.

Rupp, A. A., Ferne, T., & Choi, H. (2006). How assessing reading comprehension with multiple-choice questions shapes the construct: A cognitive processing perspective. *Language Testing, 23,* 441–474.

Scrams, D. J., Mislevy, R. J., & Sheehan, K. M. (2002). *An analysis of similarities in item functioning within antonym and analogy variant families* (Research Report No. RR-02-13). Princeton, NJ: Educational Testing Service.

Sheehan, K., & Mislevy, R. J. (2001). *An inquiry into the nature of the sentence-completion task: Implications for item generation* (Research Report No. RR-01-13). Princeton, NJ: Educational Testing Service.

Sheehan, K. M., Ginther, A., & Schedl, M. (1999). Development of a proficiency scale for the TOEFL reading comprehension section Princeton, NJ.

Sheehan, K. M., Kostin, I., & Futagi, Y. (2005). *A semi-automatic approach to assessing the verbal reasoning demands of GRE sentence completion items.* Unpublished report. Princeton, NJ: Educational Testing Service.

Sheehan, K. M., Kostin, I., Futagi, Y., Hemat, R., & Zuckerman, D. (2006). *Inside SourceFinder: Predicting the acceptability status of candidate reading comprehension source documents* (Research Report No. RR-06-24). Princeton, NJ: Educational Testing Service.

Shepard, R. N., & Metzler, J. (1971, February 19). Mental rotation of three-dimensional objects. *Science, 171,* 701–703.

Shute, V. J., Graf, E. A. H., & Hansen, E. (2005). Designing adaptive, diagnostic math assessments for individuals with and without visual disabilities. In L. PytlikZillig, M. Bodvarsson, & R. Bruning (Eds.), *Technology-based education: Bringing researchers and practitioners together* (pp. 169–202). Greenwich, CT: Information Age Publishing.

Singley, M. K. (1995). Promoting transfer through model tracing. In A. McKeough, J. Lupart, & A. Marini (Eds.), *Teaching for transfer: Fostering generalization in learning* (pp. 69–92). Mahwah, NJ: Erlbaum.

Singley, M. K., & Bennett, R. E. (2002). Item generation and beyond: Applications of schema theory to mathematics assessment. In S. Irvine & P. Kyllonen (Eds.), *Item generation for test development*. Mahwah, NJ: Erlbaum.

Solano-Flores, G., Jovanovic, R. J., & Bachman, M. (1999). On the development and evaluation of a shell for generating science performance assessments. *International Journal of Science Education, 29,* 293–315.

Strotmann, A., Ng'ang'a, W., & Caprotti, O. (2005). *Multilingual access to mathematical exercise problems.* Paper presented at the Internet Accessible Mathematical Computation, a Workshop at ISSAC 2005, Beijing, China. Retrieved September 21, 2007, from http://www.symbolicnet.org/conferences/iamc05/iamc05-snc.pdf

Toulmin, S., Rieke, R., & Janik, A. (Eds.). (1984). *An introduction to reasoning* (2nd ed.). New York: Macmillan.

Tyler, R. W. (1934). *Constructing achievement tests.* Columbus, OH: Bureau of Educational Research, Ohio State University.

Van der Linden, W. J., & Glas, C. A. W. (2007). Statistical aspects of adaptive testing. In C. R. Rao & S. Sinharay (Eds.), *Handbook of Statistics: Psychometrics* (Vol. 26, pp. 801–838). New York: Elsevier.

Wesiak, G. (2003). *Ordering inductive reasoning tests for adaptive knowledge assessments: An application of surmise relations between tests.* Graz, Austria: Institut für Psychologie der Universität. Retrieved from http://psydok.sulb.unisaarland.de/volltexte/2004/380/pdf/diss_wesiak.pdf

Wilson, M. (2005). *Constructing measures: An item response modeling approach.* Mahwah, NJ: Erlbaum.

Yang, Y., & Johnson-Laird, P. N. (2001). Mental models and logical reasoning problems in the GRE. *Journal of Experimental Psychology: Applied, 7,* 308–316.

10

Modeling the Effect of Item Designs Within the Rasch Model

Rianne Janssen

In this chapter, a random-effects extension of the linear logistic test model (LLTM; Fischer, 1973, 1983) is proposed that allows modeling the effect of item design matrices within the Rasch model. The item designs can refer to an item groups design or an item features design. The estimation of the resulting crossed random-effects model is discussed, as well as related models within item response theory (IRT). As possible fields of application for models with random-item effects, domain-referenced testing and construct representation research are discussed and illustrated with an example. Another field of application is the domain of automated item generation, which is discussed in other chapters of the present volume.

Nomothetic Span and Construct Representation

In her review of construct validity, Embretson (1983) distinguished two types of construct validation research: nomothetic span and construct representation. *Nomothetic span* is concerned with the relationship of the test with other variables. Studies on nomothetic span are typically offered as the primary data to support construct validity for psychological and educational tests. Depending on the type of relationship, various types of validity can be discerned, such as convergent, differential, and predictive validity. *Construct representation* is concerned with identifying the theoretical mechanisms that underlie item responses, such as information processes, strategies, and knowledge stores. The goal of construct representation research is task decomposition. It is concerned with task variability rather than subject variability.

The two types of construct validation research generally refer to two types of test construction. In a nomothetic span study, the main purpose of the test is to provide a measure of the examinees' proficiency on the underlying variable that the test is designed to measure. From a modeling point of view, the items of such a test are considered to be some representative sample from the tested domain, although the test may be designed according to an item specification table to ensure the content validity of the test. In a construct representation study, the focus is not so much on measuring differences between examinees but on investigating whether the test performance depends on item features that are related to the cognitive processes that are involved. One way to study the cognitive components of a test is to manipulate the item characteristics of the items in the test. Consequently, the item design or test design (Embretson, 1985) becomes a critical part of the test.

It is the purpose of this chapter to present a psychometric model in which the study of the nomothetic span and the construct representation of the tested domain can be combined. The model describes the differences in test performance among the examinees and tests the influence of the factors in the item design on the response behavior. In this model, the explanation of the item responses is complementary to the measurement of individual examinees. The proposed model is not the only possible model that allows for this combined approach. For example, De Boeck and Wilson (2004b) described other psychometric models as well.

Before giving a formal presentation of the model, an example is given to illustrate the approach. The example is analyzed further on in the chapter. After the presentation of the example, two different types of item designs are distinguished.

An Illustrating Example

Vansteelandt (2000) studied individual differences in verbal aggression, making use of a behavioral questionnaire. All the 24 items in the questionnaire referred to verbally aggressive behavior in a frustrating situation. For example, one item is "A bus fails to stop for me. I would curse." The possible responses were "yes," "perhaps," or "no." The data were dichotomized with a 0 for the "no" response and a 1 otherwise.

The questionnaire was constructed according to a specific item design with three item features. The first item feature was the behavior mode. A differentiation was made between two levels: wanting to do (i.e., wanting to curse, wanting to scold, or wanting to shout) and actually doing (i.e., cursing, scolding, or shouting). The reason for the distinction was the possibility of response inhibition in verbally aggressive behavior: One does not always do what one might want to do. The second item feature was the situation type. This factor had two levels as well: situations in which someone else is to blame (e.g., "I miss a train because a clerk gave me faulty information") and situations in which oneself is to blame (e.g., "the grocery story closes just as I am about to enter"). The reason for the inclusion of this factor was the expectation that people display more verbal aggression when someone else is to blame. The final item design factor was the behavior type with the levels *curse, scold,* and *shout*. Summarizing, a $2 \times 2 \times 3$ item features design was used. There were two situations in each cell, leading to 24 items in total. The items were presented to the respondents in random order. Table 10.1 gives an example of the items from an other-to-blame and a self-to-blame situation.

When analyzing this type of questionnaire, one can ask two questions. First, are there systematic individual differences and to which other variables are they related (nomothetic span)? Second, in what way does the response behavior depend on the factors in the item design matrix (construct representation)?

Table 10.1. Items From an Other-to-Blame and a Self-to-Blame Situation From the Verbal Aggression Questionnaire (K. Vansteelandt, 2000) and Their Corresponding Values in the Q-Matrix

Item	Do	Other-to-blame	Curse	Scold	Intercept
I miss a train because a clerk gave me faulty information.					
I would want to curse.	0	1	1	0	1
I would want to scold.	0	1	0	1	1
I would want to shout.	0	1	0	0	1
I would curse.	1	1	1	0	1
I would scold.	1	1	0	1	1
I would curse.	1	1	0	0	1
The grocery store closes just as I am about to enter.					
I would want to curse.	0	0	1	0	1
I would want to scold.	0	0	0	1	1
I would want to shout.	0	0	0	0	1
I would curse.	1	0	1	0	1
I would scold.	1	0	0	1	1
I would curse.	1	0	0	0	1

Note. Data from Vansteelandt (2000).

Two Types of Item Designs

When studying differences among items, two types of item designs can be distinguished: an item groups design and an item features design. The distinction between the two is in line with the distinction between an analysis of variance (ANOVA) design and a regression design. In an item groups design, the items of a test can be partitioned in different subsets, each referring to a different population of items. As an example, consider a test for reading comprehension in French for nonnative students in Grade 8 (Janssen et al., 2005). The test was designed according to the common European framework for languages (Council of Europe, 2001) and measures its first three stages in language learning. For reading comprehension these three levels differ in the type of texts the language learner is able to understand: Level A1 refers to simple sentences, Level A2 to simple texts, and Level B1 to texts concerning daily life. Figure 10.1 presents the distribution of the item difficulty parameters for the three groups of items in the test. When modeling the item groups design of the test, the differences across levels in the distribution of the items are studied.

In an item features design, each item is scored on one or more factors, each of which represents the item's position on an underlying theoretical variable. As an example, the items from a geometric analogy test can differ in encoding complexity and transformation complexity (e.g., Mulholland, Pellegrino, & Glaser, 1980), which are scored as the number of elements in the stimulus and the number of transformations required to convert one stimulus to another stimulus,

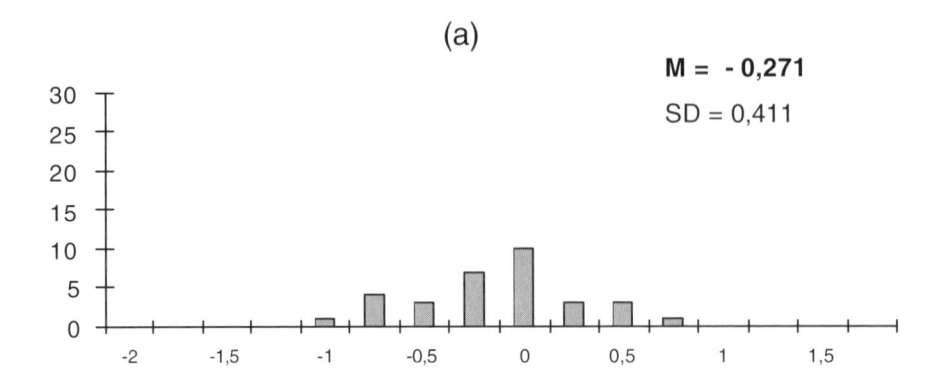

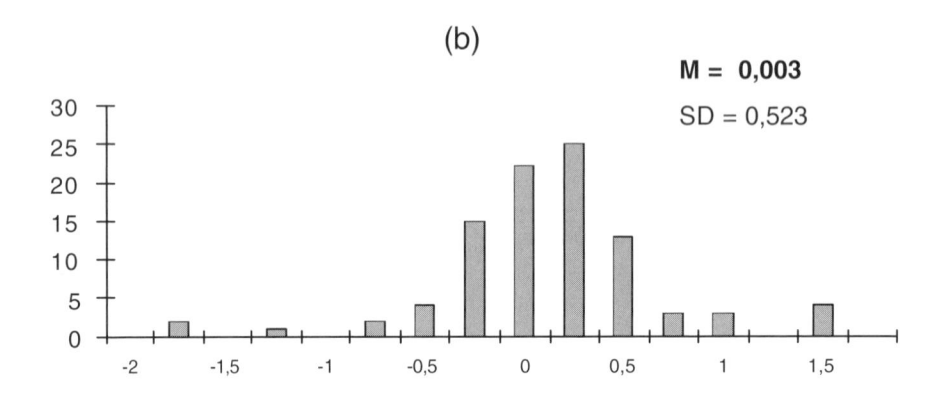

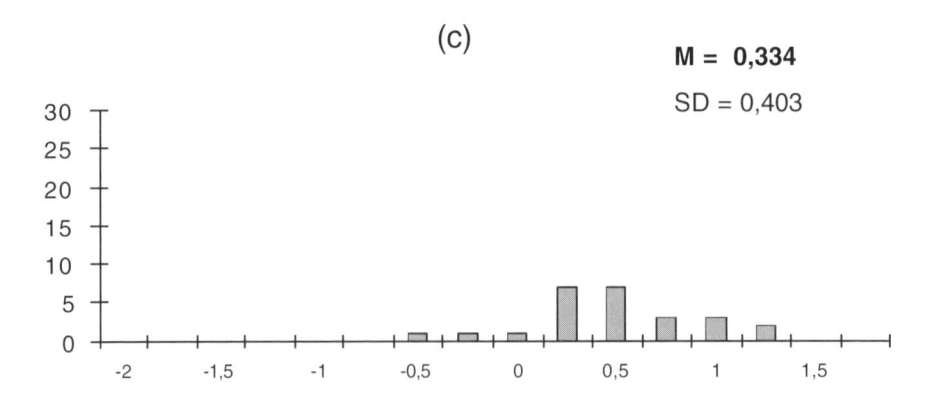

Figure 10.1. Histogram of the item difficulty parameters from a test measuring French reading comprehension for the levels (a) A1, (b) A2, and (c) B1 of the European Framework for Languages.

respectively. One can then study whether a linear combination of these two complexity factors gives good prediction of response accuracy on geometric analogy items. For the verbal aggression questionnaire, the effect of the behavior mode, the situation type, and the behavior type on the inclination to react in a verbally aggressive way can be investigated. The item features of a test can refer to a prior conceptualization of the cognitive structure of the test items, or they can be derived post hoc to describe the characteristics of a given test. Item features can be used for item construction purposes, the exponent of which is automated item generation. Examples of item features in item generation studies can be found in chapters 1 and 9 of this volume.

The distinction between an item groups design and an item features design is merely at a conceptual level. In fact, both designs refer to the same linear model on the item side, as is the case for ANOVA and regression models. Item groups are a special type of item feature. They refer to binary, nonoverlapping item features, which indicate group membership.

In the following pages, a general model is described for modeling item designs within the Rasch model (Janssen, De Boeck, & Schepers, 2003; Janssen, Schepers, & Peres, 2004). The model is based on a random-effects extension of the LLTM, which was developed by Fischer (1973, 1983, 1995). After the presentation of the model, the estimation of the random-effects model and its relationships with other models from IRT are discussed. In the next section, applications of the model are presented. At the end of the chapter, the approach and its advantages are summarized.

The Random-Effects LLTM

The Model

THE RASCH MODEL AS A STARTING POINT. As a starting point, take the Rasch model to model the probability that person i responds correctly to item j. In the Rasch model, both persons and items are assumed to vary along a common, latent scale. A person's position along the latent scale (indicated as θ_i) refers to his or her ability level, an item's position (indicated as β_j) to its difficulty level. The difference between the two positions (i.e., the value of $\theta_i - \beta_j$) determines the probability of success

$$P(X_{ij}=1) = f(\theta_i - \beta_j), \quad (1)$$

where f refers to either the logit or the probit link function. For example, when working with a probit link function, f refers to the cumulative standard normal distribution and the model reads as

$$\Phi(\theta_i - \beta_j) = \int_{-\infty}^{\theta_i - \beta_j} \exp\left(-\frac{1}{2}z^2\right) dz. \quad (2)$$

When $\theta_i = \beta_j$, the success probability is .50. The more θ_i exceeds β_j on the latent scale, the higher the success probability becomes, and vice versa.

Figure 10.2a gives a graphical representation of the Rasch model by means of a directed acyclic graph (see, e.g., Spiegelhalter, Best, Gilks, & Inskip, 1996). In such a graph, circles denote unobserved variables and squares are observed variables. The solid arrows refer to probabilistic relations, whereas the dotted arrows correspond to the deterministic relations in the model. In the Rasch model, there are two real-world components: person and item. The data are modeled in a probabilistic way on the basis of the person ability and item difficulty parameters. Figure 10.2a adds to Equation 1 the assumption that all persons belong to the same population with mean μ_θ and variance σ_θ^2. Although not a necessary part of the Rasch model, the additional assumption is used throughout the present chapter. To identify the origin of the latent scale, μ_θ can be fixed to zero.

THE LLTM. The Rasch model describes the differences in difficulty among the items without taking into account the item design. The LLTM was the first model to add the effect of an item design to the Rasch model. The model starts from an item-by-item predictor matrix Q of size $J \times P$, which describes for each item j its value q_{jp} on item predictor p. The item predictors can refer to an item group (e.g., using a dummy variable) or to an item feature. As an example, Table 10.1 shows an extract from the Q-matrix for the items of two specific situations of the verbal aggression questionnaire. The three item features of the item design were coded into four item predictors, complemented with the constant item predictor (see below). All item features were coded with dummy variables with want, self-to-blame, and shout as the respective reference categories (see Table 10.1). For example, the dummy variable "curse" marks the difference between the behavior "curse" versus the behaviors "scold" and "shout."

The LLTM assumes that the Rasch item difficulty parameters β_j in Equation 1 or 2 can be replaced by a linear combination of the item predictors

$$\beta_j = \sum_{p=1}^{P} q_{jp}\eta_p = q_j\eta, \quad (3)$$

where the η_p are the weight parameters, which are grouped in the vector η of length P. Usually Q contains a constant with $q_{jp} = 1$ for all the items, which acts as the intercept in the linear combination in Equation 3. Figure 10.2b represents the LLTM graphically. In comparison with Figure 10.2a, the effect of item difficulty is replaced with the linear combination of item predictors.

THE LLTM-R. The LLTM is a very stringent model. In practice, likelihood ratio tests of the LLTM against the unconstrained Rasch model almost invariably lead to a significant deviance. Therefore, Janssen et al. (2003) proposed a random-effects version of the LLTM, labeled as LLTM-R (with the "R" referring to "Random"). The LLTM-R adds to the Rasch model that item difficulty is determined only to a certain extent by the linear structure derived from the item design. The "unexplained" part is modeled with a random error term ε_j for each β_j

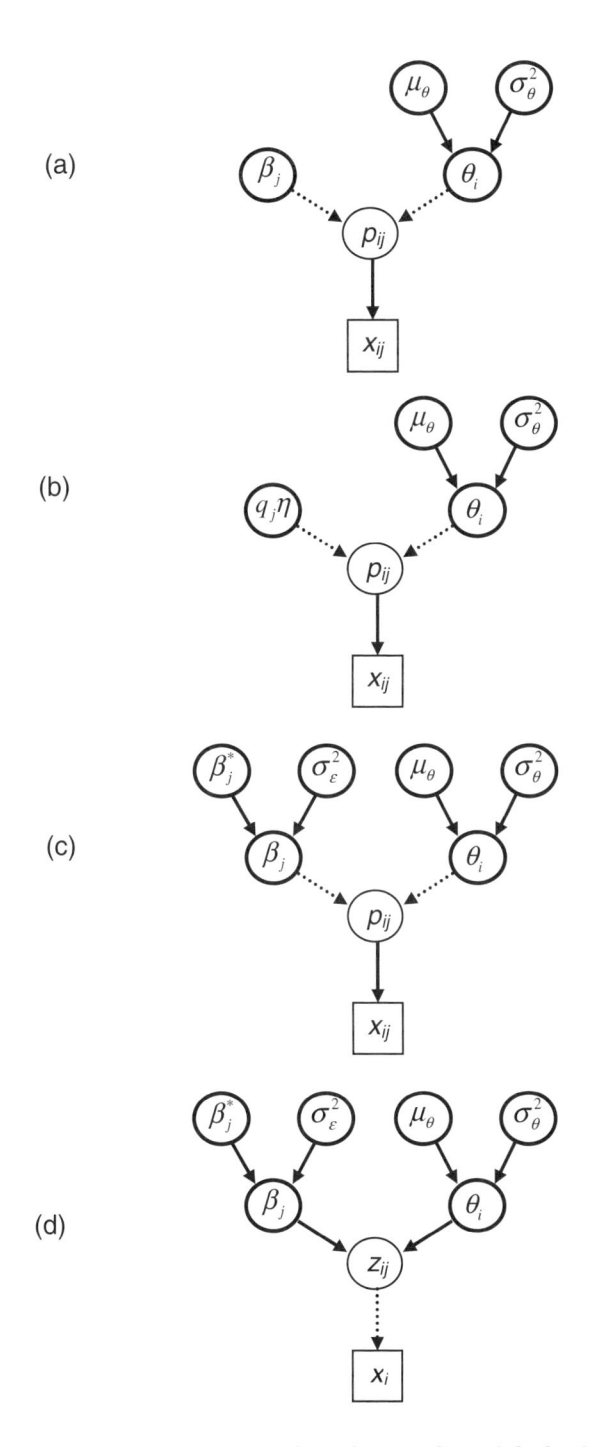

Figure 10.2. Graphical representation of (a) the Rasch model, (b) the linear logistic test model (LLTM), (c) the LLTM-R (R = random), and (d) the LLTM-R with the data augmentation step (J. H. Albert, 1992).

$$\beta_j = q_j\eta + \varepsilon_j = \beta_j^* + \varepsilon_j, \quad (4)$$

where $\varepsilon_j \sim N(0, \sigma_\varepsilon^2)$ with N denoting the normal distribution. β_j^* denotes the difficulty of item j as predicted by the linear structure specified in Q. The model in Equation 4 is formally equivalent with a hierarchical model for the β_j with

$$\beta_j \sim N\left(\beta_j^*, \sigma_\varepsilon^2\right), \quad (5)$$

where β_j^* is defined as in Equation 4. The η and σ_ε^2 are now called the hyperparameters of the LLTM-R, as they specify (together with Q) the mean and variance of the distribution of the β_j.

The LLTM-R can be interpreted in two interrelated ways. The formulation of the model in Equation 4 highlights a random error interpretation of the LLTM-R with σ_ε^2 as the residual variance. The parameters ε_j incorporate random variation in item difficulty for items with the same item design, so that the item design does not need to cover the item difficulties perfectly. The formulation of the model in Equation 5 highlights a random sampling interpretation of the LLTM-R with σ_ε^2 as the within-class variance of the β_j. In this interpretation, the item difficulty parameters of the same item class are considered to be exchangeable members of a population of items defined by the item design vector q_j. The random-effects formulation of the LLTM also allows for a generalization to new items in each cell of the design.

A graphical representation of the LLTM-R is given in Figure 10.2c. It clarifies that the LLTM-R consists of two parts: a model for the data given in Equation 1 or 2 and a model for the item parameters given in Equation 4 or 5. The model for the item parameters specifies that the β_j consist of a linear, structural part β_j^* and a random component ε_j. In contrast with the two previous models, the LLTM-R encompasses three real-world components: person, item, and item population, with the items nested within an item population. In many applications with item features, there is only one item per item population. Because of the item populations, the LLTM-R can be seen as a multilevel model on the item side.

COMPARISON OF THE LLTM-R WITH THE LLTM. Janssen et al. (2003) showed the estimates of η in the LLTM are attenuated in comparison with the corresponding estimates in the LLTM-R. As a general approximation it can be derived (see the Estimation section) that for a given parameter η_p

$$\eta_p^{LLTM} \approx \frac{1}{\sqrt{1+\sigma_\varepsilon^2}} \eta_p^{LLTM-R}. \quad (6)$$

Equation 6 implies that the estimates of the LLTM will be equal to those of the LLTM-R only when $\sigma_\varepsilon^2 = 0$. This is not surprising, as the LLTM is equivalent to the LLTM-R only when the linear combination of item predictors explains item difficulty perfectly. Equation 6 also shows that the larger the unexplained variance, the larger the attenuation effect. The attenuation effect will be less pronounced, the closer η_p is to zero.

Janssen et al. (2003) also showed that within the LLTM the standard errors of the η_p are underestimated. This is a consequence of the fact that the LLTM does not take into account the within-cell variance in the item design matrix. This may lead to a Type I error when rejecting the null hypothesis that a particular η_p equals zero.

Estimation

The LLTM-R is a crossed random-effects model, with a normal distribution at the person mode with $\theta_i \sim N(\mu_\theta, \sigma_\theta^2)$ and at the item mode with $\beta_j \sim N(\beta_j^*, \sigma_\varepsilon^2)$. Estimation of crossed-random effects models for binary responses is a complex statistical problem, for which both likelihood-based and Bayesian solutions exist (Molenberghs & Verbeke, 2004). For the estimation of the LLTM-R, Janssen et al. (2003, 2004) described the pseudo-likelihood approach of Wolfinger and O'Connell (1993) and the Bayesian method of data augmented Gibbs sampling (Albert, 1992; Albert & Chib, 1993). In a sense, both estimation procedures involve the same trick of not modeling the dichotomous response directly, but a related, continuous response instead. In the pseudolikelihood approach, a linear mixed model is iteratively fitted to a pseudoresponse, which is a linearized approximation of the original data based on a Taylor expansion. The pseudolikelihood approach is implemented in the GLIMMIX macro of SAS. The specific commands to estimate the LLTM-R can be found in Janssen et al. (2004). In data-augmented Gibbs sampling, the posterior distribution is augmented with latent data Z_{ij} for each pair of a person and an item. As is shown in Figure 10.2d, the latent data points z_{ij} in a sense replace the success probabilities p_{ij}. Intuitively speaking, one could say that the z_{ij} bring the (dichotomous) data on the same continuous latent scale as the person and items parameters θ_i and β_j.

The data augmentation step is explained in more detail in Figure 10.3. The procedure makes use of the probit link function as presented in Equation 2. This implies that the probability of a correct response is derived from the cumulative standard normal distribution (see Figure 10.3a) and, hence, corresponds to a response surface in the standard normal distribution (see Figure 10.3b). Making use of the properties of a change of variables in a normal distribution, the same response surface can be found in a normal distribution with mean $\theta_i - \beta_j$ and variance of 1, namely, as the probability of a positive value (see Figure 10.3c). The distribution of the Z_{ij} is a zero-truncated normal distribution

$$Z_{ij} \sim N(\theta_i - \beta_j, 1) \text{ with } Z_{ij} \leq 0 \text{ when } x_{ij} = 0, \text{ and } Z_{ij} > 0 \text{ otherwise} \quad (7)$$

The truncation implies that the probability that $Z_{ij} > 0$ equals the probability of a correct response given in Equation 1. Equation 7 shows that the z_{ij} are related in a probabilistic way to the parameters θ_i and β_j, whereas their relationship with the observed response x_{ij} is deterministic (as can be seen from the type of arrows in Figure 10.2d).

Given the data augmentation, the Gibbs conditionals for all model parameters can be derived analytically (see Janssen et al., 2003, 2004). These Gibbs conditionals partition the augmented posterior distribution in a set of conditional

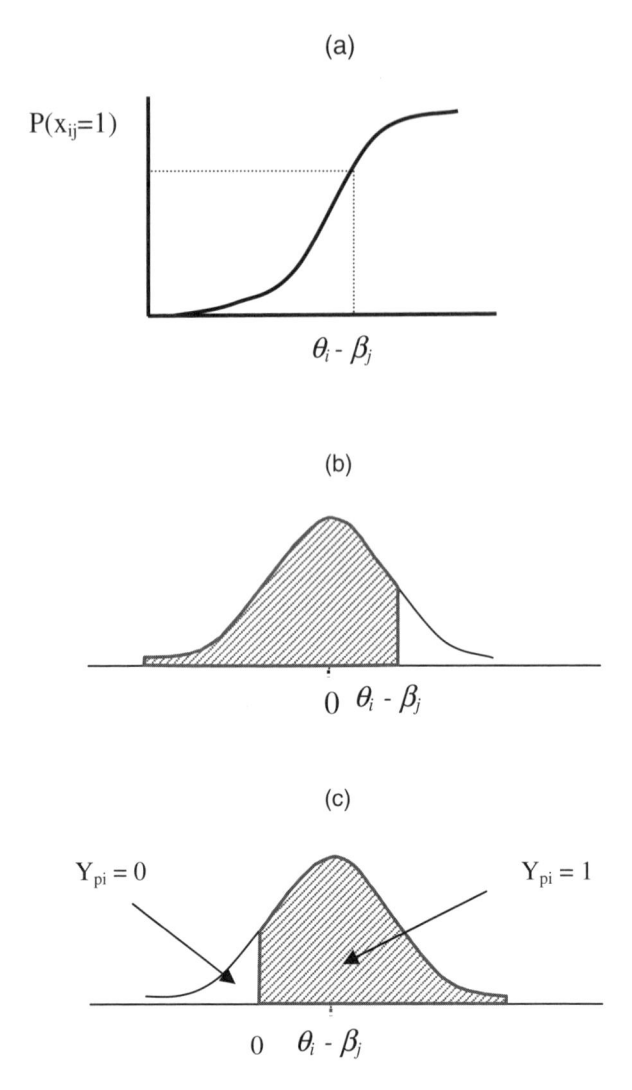

Figure 10.3. The different steps in data augmentation: (a) calculating the success probability with a probit link function, (b) the corresponding response surface in a standard normal distribution, and (c) the equivalent surface in $N(\theta_i - \beta_j, 1)$ and the drawing of the latent data.

distributions for every parameter given the values of the other parameters. This partitioning is used in a Markov chain Monte Carlo procedure or the Gibbs sampling process, in which the augmented posterior distribution is approximated by iteratively drawing samples of parameters from it using the Gibbs conditionals. The Bayesian estimation of a parameter then consists of summarizing the values obtained from the Markov chain by a posterior mean and a posterior standard deviation.

The derivation of the latent data can also be used to explain the attenuation effect in the regression weight η in the LLTM as a scaling effect (De Boeck

& Wilson, 2004a; Snijders & Bosker, 1999). Apart from the variance of θ_i, the latent data are drawn in the LLTM from a scale with a variance of 1. In the LLTM-R, however, the latent data are drawn from a scale with a variance of $1 + \sigma_\varepsilon^2$, as a random effect is added on the item mode. Hence, the latent scales of the two models differ in variance, and, consequently, the values of the LLTM will be smaller than in the LLTM-R. The reduction factor in Equation 6 can be seen as a factor expressing the differences in variance of the latent scales.

Related IRT Models

Mislevy (1988) proposed a random-effects formulation of the LLTM with random variation of the item difficulty parameters with the same generic structure as a means to exploit auxiliary information about the items in the estimation of Rasch item difficulty parameters. However, at that time only a computational approximation based on an empirical Bayes procedure was available for model estimation. A general formulation of the LLTM-R can be found in Albert and Chib (1993). They proposed a hierarchical extension of probit models, in which the weight parameters of a probit regression model are themselves regressed upon other predictor variables.

The LLTM-R can be used to model an item groups design within a Rasch model. Janssen, Tuerlinckx, Meulders, and De Boeck (2000) described a similar, multilevel extension on the item side for the two-parameter IRT model, and Glas and Van der Linden (2003) did the same for the three-parameter model. In these hierarchical models, the items are nested within item groups. Within each item group, the item parameters are modeled as random, whereas the item group parameters are treated as fixed. Whereas the LLTM-R only models the difficulty of the items, the other models also look at the within-group distributions of the item discrimination and the item guessing parameter.

Applications

Overview of Possible Fields of Application

Domain-referenced testing (Janssen et al., 2000), construct representation research (Janssen et al., 2003), and automated item generation (Glas & Van der Linden, 2003) have been studied as fields of application of the IRT models with random effects at the item side. In domain-referenced testing, the principal idea is that the items of a test are a random sample from a domain, which refers to a population of items. Consequently, the item parameters of the test can be seen as random-effect parameters. The domain characteristics can be modeled with the hyperparameters describing the distributions of the random effects. In construct representation research, the effect of the item design on the item parameters is studied. As was shown in Equation 4, in such a situation the item parameters are interpreted as random-effect parameters consisting of a fixed, structural part and a random error part. These two fields of application are illustrated and discussed in the next sections, as examples of modeling an item groups design and an item features design, respectively.

In automated item generation (e.g., Bejar, 2002; Embretson, 1998; 1999), items are seen as clones from a parent. However, the cloning is not perfect, leading to individual item variation. Consequently, each parent characterizes a distribution of items. The expected value of this distribution refers to a typical or "average" item of the family. The variance of the distribution refers to a kind of heredity coefficient, as it indicates how strongly individual items can differ from their parent, or from the typical item. In their multilevel three-parameter model, Glas and Van der Linden (2003) only studied parents as item groups. However, one could also model automatically generated items as items that are generated from a set of item design variables and, hence, according to an item features design (see chap. 1, this volume).

DOMAIN-REFERENCED MEASUREMENT THROUGH MODELING ITEM GROUPS

Domain-referenced measurement. A well-defined behavior domain (Popham, 1978) represents the knowledge and skills required for mastery of a specific content area. The term *domain* refers to a universe of items. A test is supposed to be composed of a random sample from this population of items. A *domain score* reflects the proportion of the domain mastered. An important advantage of the use of domain scores is their ease of interpretation. A domain score is directly linked to the expected performance on a domain of items. It can be seen as an example of criterion-referenced measurement.

IRT-based domain scores. Bock, Thissen, and Zimowski (1997) and Pommerich, Nicewander, and Hanson (1999) showed that IRT models are an indispensable tool for the estimation of domain scores. Both studies start from the assumption that the domain is represented in an item bank. Hence, the performance on any test drawn from that bank (or linked to it by anchor items) can be interpreted in terms of a domain score. Bock et al. (1997) showed that given an estimate of ability based on the performance on a sample of items, the average probability of success on the items of the domain can be calculated. In the case in which the domain consists of several strata, a weighted average is calculated

$$\hat{d}_i = \frac{\sum_{j=1}^{J} w_j p_j(\hat{\theta}_i)}{\sum_{j=1}^{J} w_j}, \qquad (8)$$

where $\hat{d}_i$ refers to the estimated domain score for person i, $p_j(\hat{\theta}_i)$ refers to the probability of success on item j given the estimated ability of person i, and w_j refers to the weight of item j. The sum in Equation 8 is calculated over all J items in the item bank.

Bock et al. (1997) showed that the IRT-based average success probability is a far more accurate predictor for the proportion of mastery of the domain than the classical percentage correct score on the test. Pommerich et al. (1999) extended the use of IRT-based domain scores to estimate a group's average domain score. Schulz, Kolen, and Nicewander (1999) used IRT-based domain scores in a hierarchical test design with domains as item groups. Each domain defines a specific level of achievement on the latent scale and is represented by a pool of items. For each level of achievement, an IRT-based domain score is calculated. Using a .8 criterion to define mastery of a level of achievement, Schulz et al. (1999) showed that Guttmann-consistent patterns of mastery could be inferred from the level scores. Figure 10.4 presents a hierarchical item design for three levels of achievement on the latent scale. The corresponding pattern of mastery is given for the case that the first two levels of achievement are attained.

The hierarchical IRT model. Instead of calculating a domain score as an average probability of success on the items of the domain, a domain score can be estimated by calculating the probability of success on an average item (Janssen, 2002). The average item is defined on the basis of the characteristics of the population distribution of the items of the domain. Consider a test measuring K domains or criteria with $K \geq 1$. Each item j measures a single domain k, hence, the test is compiled according to an item groups design, with each domain referring to an item group. Suppose further that the items are scored dichotomously and that the probability that a person i responds correctly to item j of domain k is modeled according to the Rasch model with ability parameters θ_i and item difficulty parameters β_j (as in Equation 1). It is further assumed that each domain k is characterized by a certain difficulty β_k^* on the latent scale. The difficulty parameters of the items measuring a certain domain are assumed to be located around β_k^* with variance σ_e^2, which is expressed in Equation 5. The variance can be made domain-specific if each domain is measured with a sufficient number of items. When several domains are measured, the hierarchical IRT model assumes that these domains refer to a common latent ability. However, it should be clear that this unidimensionality with respect to the latent continuum does not imply that all domains are equal in difficulty. For example, the ordering of domains may refer to different achievement levels, as in the study by Schultz et al. (1999).

In the hierarchical IRT model, a domain is measured on the same latent continuum as the person ability parameters. Hence, given the values of the

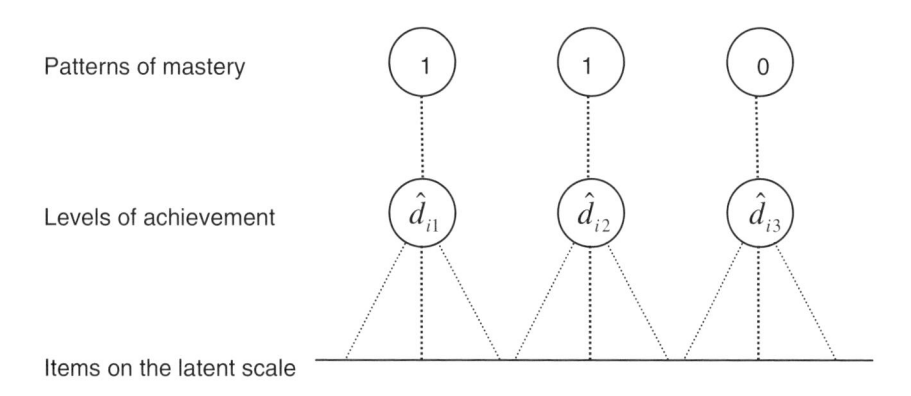

Figure 10.4. Schematic representation of a hierarchical item design (E. M. Schultz, M. J. Kolen, & W. A. Nicewander, 1999).

hyperparameters, one can calculate the probability of mastering domain k for each person i by assuming that the domain acts like an unobserved "super item" Y_{ik} that has to be solved correctly

$$P(Y_{ik} = 1) = f\left(\theta_i - \beta_k^*\right), \quad (9)$$

where f is again the logit or probit link function. The probability in Equation 9 can be seen as an estimate of the domain score.

Using a set of cutoff points on the domain score, respondents can, for example, be classified into three categories with respect to each domain: nonmastery (probability $Pr < 0.5$), transition stage ($0.5 \leq Pr \leq 0.8$), and mastery ($Pr > 0.8$). Passing the .50 probability indicates that the person has a higher probability to solve a randomly selected item from the domain correctly than to solve the item incorrectly. This can be considered as an initial stage of mastery of the domain. Passing the .80 probability indicates that the person's probability of a correct answer is so high that an incorrect response to a randomly selected item from the domain is more likely to be dependent on error fluctuations rather than on a lack of proficiency.

Note that the .50 boundary between nonmastery and the transition stage does not necessarily imply that 50% of the respondents are classified as a nonmaster. A basic property of IRT models is that the estimation of the item parameters (and, hence, of the hyperparameters) is more or less independent of the ability of the persons in the calibration sample. Hence, the percentage of respondents being classified in the nonmastery category can in principle vary between 0 and 100, depending on the location of the respondents on the latent continuum with respect to the location of the domain difficulty.

Domain scores and standard setting. The basic problem of standard setting is to set a minimum level of proficiency to be declared a master in a specific content area and to classify students accordingly on the basis of their test performance. Most standard-setting studies are based on a continuum view of mastery (Meskauskas, 1976). This implies that the test score is assumed to be an index of the progression along a continuously distributed ability dimension. Commonly, an item-centered approach is used to set a cutoff on the continuum. The location of the cutoff score is based on judgments about the expected performance of a minimally competent student on the test items. In this approach, the items of the test are in a sense considered as "fixed" and the discussion is focused on setting a cutoff score on the test score scale.

Domain scores may be used as an alternative approach to standard setting. In domain-referenced measurement, the domain about which mastery classifications are to be made is defined first. In contrast with an item-centered approach to standard setting, test items are considered to be a random sample from this domain. Performance on the test items can be linked to a performance score on the domain. Fixed cut points on the domain scores can then be used for mastery classifications.

Use of domain scores in national assessments. Bock (1996) proposed "public domain scores" as a better way to report assessment results. In his proposal, the item bank is divided into "core items" and θ-items. The core items are domain defining and are chosen on the basis of experts' judgments. They are released to the public, which is not the case for the θ-items. The latter have the primary purpose of estimating the students' ability. Using test equating procedures, the θ-items are linked to the core items. Given the value of θ_i for a student, a domain score can be calculated.

Schulz, Lee, and Mullen (2005) used a domain-level approach to provide criterion-referenced descriptions of growth in achievement for the Grade 8 National Assessment of Educational Progress (NAEP) in mathematics. Growth was conceived of as a sequential mastery of skills. Teachers were able to reliably classify items into one of multiple content domains with an expected order of difficulty. Using expected percentage correct scores on the domains, it was possible to describe each achievement level boundary (basic, proficient, and advanced) on the NAEP scale by patterns of skill that include both mastery and nonmastery. It was shown that higher achievement levels were associated with mastery of more skills, which corresponds to the idea of growth in educational achievement.

Janssen, De Corte, Verschaffel, Knoors, and Colémont (2002) used the hierarchical IRT model of Janssen et al. (2000) to assess how many children in primary education in Flanders reach the attainment targets, which specify the expected basic competencies of children who leave primary education. Using a Bayesian estimation procedure, they estimated the proportion of pupils who had a domain score of at least .50 by counting over Gibbs draws and over students the relative frequency of occurrence of the posterior success probabilities calculated according to the two-parameter version of Equation 9. It was shown that for the attainment targets regarding "Number," the performance on the scales was roughly ordered in terms of the complexity of the mathematical skills involved. The attainment targets of mental arithmetic and written computation were reached by approximately 90% of the children, whereas problem solving and estimation and approximation of numbers were reached by approximately 40%. The ordering may reflect the traditional focus on declarative and lower order procedural skills in Flemish mathematics.

Janssen and Van Nijlen (2003) compared the results of the Bookmark procedure for standard setting (Mitzel, Lewis, Patz, & Green, 2001) with the estimation of domain scores for the 2002 National Assessment of Mathematics in Primary Education in Flanders. Fourteen different scales were involved, covering attainment targets with respect to numbers (four scales), measurement (three scales), geometry (three scales), and strategies and problem solving (four scales). A group of 25 teachers, educational advisors, teacher trainers, members of the inspection, and policymakers set a minimum standard for each scale, indicating the minimum level of performance required to reach the corresponding attainment targets. They gave their judgments in three rounds (individually working, discussing in small groups, and discussing in the large group). The cutoff score was set at the median judgment in the last round. In contrast with the original Bookmark procedure, the judges were provided an item map of each scale. Students were considered masters if they had a probability of at least .50 to answer an item correctly that would be right at the cutoff. Likewise, students were considered to be masters within the hierarchical IRT model of Janssen et al. (2000) if their estimated domain score was at least .50. Figure 10.5 presents a

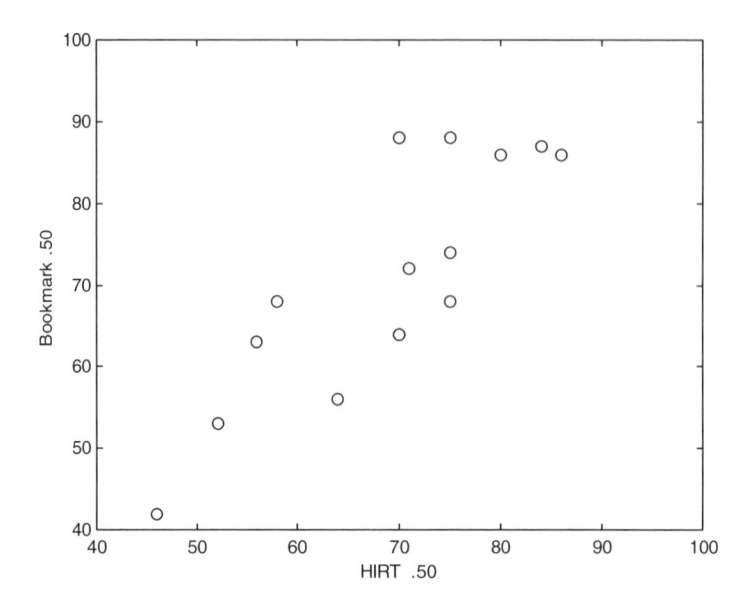

Figure 10.5. Scatter plot of the number of students reaching the attainment targets in mathematics according to the standards from the hierarchical IRT model and from the Bookmark procedure.

scatter plot of the number of students reaching the attainment targets in mathematics according to the Bookmark procedure and according to the domain score procedure. In general, both methods of standard settings gave similar results. This may be seen as an external validation of the use of domain scores in national assessments.

Studying Construct Representation Through Item Feature Designs

The 24 items of the verbal aggression questionnaire of Vansteelandt (2000), which was introduced at the beginning of this chapter, were administered to 316 students of psychology. The resulting data set is one of the example data sets used throughout the volume of De Boeck and Wilson (2004b).

At the person side, trait anger was found to be a significant predictor of the tendency to react in a verbally aggressive way (Wilson & De Boeck, 2004a). The effect of an increase of one standard deviation on the trait anger scale on a .50 probability was to raise that probability to .57. The effect of gender was not statistically significant. Males were not significantly more inclined to verbal aggression than were females.

Janssen et al. (2004) studied the item features design with the LLTM-R. In the present chapter, we redo the analysis with the item features coded with dummy variables. As was shown in Table 10.1, want, self-to-blame, and shout acted as the reference categories of the three design factors. The model was estimated with GLIMMIX. The results of the analysis are presented in Table 10.2.

Table 10.2. Estimated Weights of the Item Predictors With the LLTM-R for the Verbal Aggression Data (Vansteelandt, 2000)

Item predictor	Estimate (SE)
Do (vs. want)	.71 (.17)
Other-to-blame (vs. self-to-blame)	−1.05 (.17)
Curse (vs. scold and shout)	−2.04 (.17)
Scold (vs. curse and shout)	−0.99 (.17)
Intercept	.33 (.17)

Note. LLTM-R = linear logistic test model (R = random); SE = standard error. Data from Vansteelandt (2000).

All estimated effects were significantly different from zero. The effect of behavior mode indicates that when going from wanting to doing, the probability decreases to react verbally. If the probability of wanting were .50, then the probability of doing would be .34. The effect of situation type implies that when others are to blame, verbal aggression is more common than when oneself is to blame. The effect on a probability of .50 for a self-to-blame situation would be to raise it to .74 for an other-to-blame situation. Finally, the effect of behavior type shows that the threshold for cursing is the lowest, followed by scolding and then shouting. If the probability of shouting were .50 in a given situation, the probability of cursing or scolding would rise to .88 and .73, respectively.

Using the empirical Bayes method, the value of the random effects could be calculated, which allows one to compare the values of β_j and their predicted value β_j^*. The correlation between both values over items was .94. Hence, the item features predicted the item thresholds to react in a verbally aggressive way very well. In other words, the item features design taught us something about the construct of self-reported verbally aggressive behavior.

Summary

The present chapter described the random-effects extension of the LLTM, which in itself is an elaboration of the Rasch model. The new model allows one to measure individual differences and at the same time test a theory on the influence of item groups or items features on the response behavior. From the point of view of construct validation research, the model is helpful to study both the nomothetic span of the test (e.g., convergent, differential, and predictive validity) and its construct representation (also called *substantive validity*). An interesting feature of the model is that it shares the advantages of other IRT models, such as the possibility to measure individuals on the same scale while they are taking different subsets of items. One can also investigate the characteristics of a large set of items without the need that one group of examinees has to respond to all of them. It is sufficient to have, for example, different test booklets that are compiled according to an incomplete design with anchor items. The LLTM-R may be applied in different research contexts, both theoretical and practical. The model may be especially promising for automatic item generation studies, as one cannot expect theories to predict item difficulty in a perfect way. Only in the latter case, the LLTM-R is equal to the LLTM. Finally, the LLTM-R gives a model-based assessment of domain scores, which may form an alternative approach to the problem of standard setting.

References

Albert, J. H. (1992). Bayesian estimation of normal ogive item response curves using Gibbs sampling. *Journal of Educational Statistics, 17,* 251–269.
Albert, J. H., & Chib, S. (1993). Bayesian analysis of binary and polytomous response data. *Journal of the American Statistical Association, 88,* 669–679.
Bejar, I. I. (2002). Generative testing: From conception to implementation. In S. H. Irvine & P. C. Kyllonen (Eds.), *Generating items from cognitive tests: Theory and practice* (pp. 199–217). Mahwah, NJ: Erlbaum.
Bock, R. D. (1996). *Public domain scores: A better way to report assessment results.* Unpublished manuscript.
Bock, R. D., Thissen, D., & Zimowski, M. F. (1997). IRT estimation of domain scores. *Journal of Educational Measurement, 34,* 197–211.
Council of Europe (2001). *Common European framework of reference for languages: Learning, teaching, assessment.* Cambridge, England: Cambridge University Press.
De Boeck, P., & Wilson, M. (2004a). A framework for item response models. In P. De Boeck & M Wilson (Eds.), *Explanatory item response models: A generalized linear and nonlinear approach* (pp. 3–41). New York: Springer.
De Boeck, P., & Wilson, M. (Eds.). (2004b). *Explanatory item response models: A generalized linear and nonlinear approach.* New York: Springer.
Embretson, S. E. (1983). Construct validity: Construct representation versus nomothetic span. *Psychological Bulletin, 93,* 179–197.
Embretson, S. E. (1985). Introduction to the problem of test design. In S. E. Embretson (Ed.), *Test design: Developments in psychology and psychometrics* (pp. 3–17). New York: Academic Press.
Embretson, S. E. (1998). A cognitive design system approach to generating valid tests: Application to abstract reasoning. *Psychological Methods, 3,* 380–396.
Embretson, S. E. (1999). Generating items during testing: Psychometric issues and models. *Psychometrika, 64,* 407–433.
Fischer, G. H. (1973). The linear logistic test model as an instrument in educational research. *Acta Psychologica, 37,* 359–374.
Fischer, G. H. (1983). Logistic latent trait models with linear constraints. *Psychometrika, 48,* 3–26.
Fischer, G. H. (1995). The linear logistic test model. In G. H. Fischer & I. W. Molenaar (Eds.), *Rasch models: Foundations, recent developments, and applications* (pp. 131–155). New York: Springer.
Glas, C. A. W., & Van der Linden, W. (2003). Computerized adaptive testing with item cloning. *Applied Psychological Measurement, 27,* 247–261.
Janssen, R. (2002, April). *Model-based classification of students using a hierarchical IRT model for criterion-referenced measurement.* Paper presented at the annual meeting of the National Council on the Measurement in Education, New Orleans, LA
Janssen, R., De Boeck, P., & Schepers, J. (2003). *The random-effects version of the linear logistic test model.* Unpublished manuscript.
Janssen, R., De Corte, E., Verschaffel, L., Knoors, E., & Colémont, A. (2002). National assessment of new standards for mathematics in elementary education in Flanders. *Educational Research and Evaluation, 8,* 197–225.
Janssen, R., Schepers, J., & Peres, D. (2004). Models with item and item group predictors. In P. De Boeck & M. Wilson (Eds.), *Explanatory item response models: A generalized linear and nonlinear approach* (pp. 189–212). New York: Springer.
Janssen, R., Tuerlinckx, F., Meulders, M., & De Boeck, P. (2000). A hierarchical IRT model for criterion-referenced measurement. *Journal of Educational and Behavioral Statistics, 25,* 285–306.

Janssen, R., & Van Nijlen, D. (2003, July). *Judges or models? Comparing the Bookmark procedure with a hierarchical IRT model for standard setting.* Paper presented at the Workshop on Psychometrics and Educational Measurement held at the University of Leuven, Belgium.

Janssen, R., Volckaert, B., Lamote, B., Ceulemans, N., Binon, J., Desmet, P., & Van Damme, J. (2005). *De constructie van een peilinginstrument moderne vreemde talen (Frans) voor de eerst graad secundair onderwijs* [Test development for a national assessment on the curriculum standards of French of Grade 8]. Leuven, Belgium: Leuven Institute for Educational Research, Faculty of Psychology and Educational Sciences, University of Leuven.

Meskauskas, J. A. (1976). Evaluation models for criterion-referenced testing: Views regarding mastery in standard setting. *Review of Educational Research, 45,* 133–158.

Mitzel, H. C., Lewis, D. M., Patz, R. J., & Green, D. R. (2001). The bookmark procedure: psychological perspectives. In G. J. Cizek (Ed.), *Setting performance standards: Concepts, methods, and perspectives* (pp. 249–281). Mahwah, NJ: Erlbaum.

Mislevy, R. J. (1988). Exploiting auxiliary information about items in the estimation of Rasch item difficulty parameters. *Applied Psychological Measurement, 12,* 725–737.

Molenberghs, G., & Verbeke, G. (2004). An introduction to generalized (non)linear mixed models. In P. De Boeck & M. Wilson (Eds.), *Explanatory item response models: A generalized linear and nonlinear approach* (pp. 111–153). New York: Springer.

Mulholland, T., Pellegrino, J. W., & Glaser, R. (1980). Components of a geometric analogy solution. *Cognitive Psychology, 12,* 252–284.

Pommerich, M., Nicewander, W. A., & Hanson, B. A. (1999). Estimating average domain scores. *Journal of Educational Measurement, 36,* 199–216.

Popham, W. J. (1978). *Criterion-referenced measurement.* Englewood Cliffs, NJ: Prentice-Hall.

Schulz, E. M., Kolen, M. J., & Nicewander, W. A. (1999). A rationale for defining achievement levels using IRT-estimated domain scores. *Applied Psychological Measurement, 23,* 347–362.

Schulz, E. M., Lee, W. C., & Mullen, K. (2005). A domain-level approach to describing growth in achievement. *Journal of Educational Measurement, 42,* 1–26.

Snijders, T., & Bosker, R. (1999). *Multilevel analysis.* London: Sage.

Spiegelhalter, D. J., Best, N. G., Gilks, W. R., & Innip, H. (1996). Hepatitis B: A case study in MCMC methods. In W. R. Gilks, S. Richardson, & D. J. Spiegelhalter (Eds.), *Markov chain Monte Carlo in practice* (pp. 21–43). New York: Chapman & Hall.

Vansteelandt, K. (2000). *Formal models for contextualized personality psychology.* Unpublished doctoral dissertation, K. U. Leuven, Belgium.

Wilson, M., & De Boeck, P. (2004). Descriptive and explanatory item response models. In P. De Boeck & M. Wilson (Eds.), *Explanatory item response models: A generalized linear and nonlinear approach* (pp. 44–74). New York: Springer.

Wolfinger, R. D., & O'Connell, M. (1993). Generalized linear mixed models: A pseudo-likelihood approach. *Journal of Statistical Computing and Simulation, 48,* 233–243.

11

Cognitive Design Systems: A Structural Modeling Approach Applied to Developing a Spatial Ability Test

Susan E. Embretson

Traditionally, item and test development have been more an art than a science. Item specifications are usually vague; in fact, sometimes item writers are merely instructed to develop new items to be similar to those on an existing test. Thus, empirical item tryout is essential to ensure item quality. This process is not only expensive but also creates substantial delays in the test development process. In 1970, Cronbach (p. 508) noted that the design and construction of test items had received little scholarly attention and essentially was viewed as an art form (e.g., Wesman, 1971, p. 81). Although some progress has been made in explicating content domains for achievement tests (Schmeiser & Welch, 2006), current item development practice falls far short of the theoretical process envisioned by Bormuth (1970), especially for ability tests. Yet, substantial research from cognitive psychology is available on the theoretical mechanisms underlying many types of test items (see chap. 9, this volume).

Spatial ability tests are no exception to this description, even though the underlying processes in performing spatial tasks often have been studied by cognitive psychologists (e.g., Just & Carpenter, 1985). The Assembling Objects (AO) test, for example, was developed as part of the U.S. Army's Project A (Peterson et al., 1990). In Project A, tests were developed and evaluated for possible inclusion on the Armed Services Vocational Aptitude Battery (ASVAB) to increase the prediction of job performance (Campbell, 1990). The goal was to measure the spatial rotation component of spatial ability. In the AO task (see Figure 11.1), pieces of an object are presented, and the examinee selects from four alternatives to identify the object that results from assembling the pieces. No details on item construction are given in Peterson et al., however. Thus, traditional item development procedures probably were applied, perhaps with the item writers instructed to model the AO items after a similar test (e.g., Tinker, 1944). Since the initial development of the AO test in Project A, a consideration basis for a scientific approach to developing AO items has emerged from cognitive psychology research (e.g., Just & Carpenter, 1985; Mumaw & Pellegrino, 1984).

This chapter describes a system of test development that is based on a scientific approach to designing and calibrating item psychometric properties. The

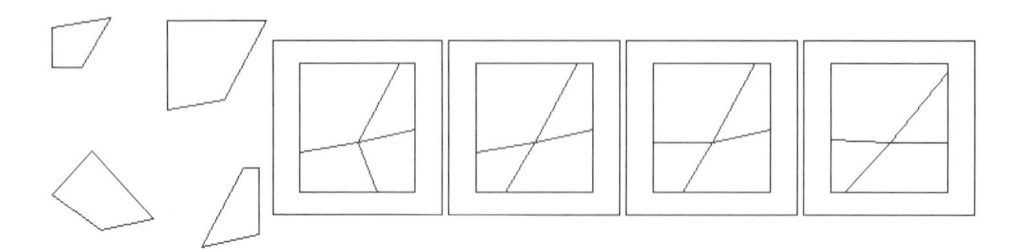

Figure 11.1. An AO item from item generator.

cognitive design system approach (Embretson, 1998) can also lead to automatic item generation. Bejar (2002) classified it as a structural modeling approach (Bejar et al., 2003) to item generation because the underlying structures that produce item difficulty and other psychometric properties are identified. In some cases, item structures based on the cognitive model can be embedded in a computer program to automatically generate items to target levels and sources of difficulty.

In this chapter, an overview of the cognitive design system approach and appropriate psychometric models are given. Then, the results from a project on the AO test are described in detail to illustrate the various properties.

The Cognitive Design System Approach

The research effort in the cognitive design system approach contrasts sharply with traditional test development methods in the balance of research effort. In the traditional test development approach, little effort is invested in studying the impact of the stimulus features of items that may impact performance. Thus, the major research effort occurs with the requirement of empirical tryouts for all new items. In contrast, the cognitive design system approach involves prior research effort to understand the sources of item complexity, and then much less effort in item tryout and the further development of the item bank. Thus, it is important to describe the stages of test development and the relative advantages of the structural model approach.

Steps in the Cognitive Design System Approach

In this section, the steps that are involved in implementing the cognitive design system approach will be briefly described. The approach requires relatively more effort than traditional item development; however, this effort leads to advantages in item quality and efficient item production which are also noted in this section.

DEVELOPMENT OF THE THEORETICAL FRAMEWORK. In the cognitive design system approach, as in traditional test development, the process begins with specifying the goals of measurement. In the traditional approach, the primary specified goals often concern the external relationship of test scores; for example, one stated goal for the Scholastic Aptitude Test has been to measure the abilities that predict 1st-year college grades. However, in the cognitive design system approach, specifying the construct representation of the test in terms of the processes, components, and knowledge to be involved in test performance (see Embretson, 1983, 1998) also has major importance. Specifying the construct representation for the test facilitates distinguishing between construct-relevant versus construct-irrelevant processes in items.

The next step is identifying both general and specific features of items. Item type and item format are general features, whereas the stimulus content that varies between items within a certain type and format are item-specific features. Traditional item development is concerned primarily with specifying general features. However, the cognitive design system approach also involves giving substantial attention to the specific features.

Next, a cognitive theory is developed to relate the item features to cognitive processes and item difficulty. Most ability and achievement test items are complex, requiring multiple stages of information processing to arrive at a solution, each of which is influenced by one or more specific item features. This step in the cognitive design system approach most likely will include a review of research on similar and related tasks that have been studied by cognitive psychology methods. For example, the difficulty of paragraph comprehension items is impacted by both vocabulary level and syntax, which influence the difficulty of encoding text meaning (Gorin, 2005). Other features influence the difficulty of different stages, such as text mapping and decision difficulty. This step in test development often involves research to further examine the impact of some specific features on item complexity. The end result is a postulated cognitive model that represents the sources of cognitive complexity in the items.

RESEARCH ON THE THEORETICAL FRAMEWORK. The postulated cognitive model must be evaluated for empirical plausibility. Item performance is modeled from variables that represent the sources of cognitive complexity in the model. The dependent variable is item performance, which includes item response accuracy and response time, as well as item response theory (IRT) parameters, such as item difficulty and item discrimination. The independent variables are the scored features of items that represent sources of processing difficulty as determined in the preceding step. The plausibility of the cognitive model is evaluated by the overall predictability of item performance and by the specific impact of the various sources of cognitive complexity in the items, as indicated by the estimated weights of the cognitive variables. These weights can be used not only to explain current item performance, but also to provide predictions of the properties of new items. Thus, to summarize this stage, the following relationship is developed:

$$\text{Stimulus features} \rightarrow \text{Process difficulty} \rightarrow \text{Item properties}.$$

To test the model, ideally a cognitive IRT model is applied to item response data that were collected on a large set of items administered to an appropriate sample. Cognitive IRT models include interpretable parameters for the cognitive model variables, as well as associated indices to evaluate overall fit of the data to the model. Further, the parameters in the cognitive IRT models are useful for item banking. Unfortunately, raw item responses often cannot be made available for operational tests. Although regression modeling can be applied by using item difficulty and discrimination estimates obtained from traditional IRT models as the dependent variables, there are some disadvantages. Because the number of observations equals the number of items in the regression modeling approach, the standard errors for the cognitive model variables are often relatively large.

Next, the plausibility of the cognitive model as a basis for item generation is tested by systematically varying the sources of cognitive complexity. Appropriate studies may vary items on only a single feature of the model or simultaneously vary several sources of cognitive complexity. If raw item response data are available, cognitive psychometric models (see the next section) may be applied to estimate the impact of the cognitive model variables on item properties.

ITEM DESIGN, ITEM GENERATION, AND ITEM BANKING. If the preceding stages are successful, the properties can then be used for item generation and for item banking. Test specifications can be based on the cognitive model variables to include only those sources of complexity that are consistent with the purposes of measurement. Further, items can be banked by the levels and sources of cognitive complexity using the predicted difficulties from the cognitive psychometric model. Finally, for some types of items, automatic item generators can be developed by incorporating the various combinations of sources of complexity into structures that produce items and estimate expected item properties.

Advantages of the Cognitive Design System Approach

Developing items with the cognitive design system has several advantages. First, construct validity is explicated at the item level. The relative weights of the underlying sources of cognitive complexity represent what the item measures. Messick (1995) described this type of item decomposition as supporting the substantive aspect of construct validity. Second, a plausible cognitive model provides a basis for producing items algorithmically. Items with different sources of cognitive complexity can be generated by varying aspects of the cognitive model. These variables also have potential to be embedded in a computer program to generate large numbers of items with predictable psychometric properties. Third, test design for ability tests can be based on features that have been supported as predicting cognitive complexity and item psychometric properties. That is, the test blueprint can be based on stimulus features of items that have empirical support. Fourth, the empirical tryout of items can be more efficiently targeted. Typically, item banks have shortages of certain levels of difficulty. By predicting item properties such as item difficulty, only those items that correspond to the target levels can be selected for tryout. Furthermore, items with construct-irrelevant sources of difficulty can be excluded from tryout. Fifth, predictable psychometric properties can reduce the requisite sample size for those items that are included in an empirical tryout (Mislevy, Sheehan, & Wingersky,

1993). The predictions set prior distributions for the item parameters, which consequently reduce the need for sample information. Under some circumstances, predicted item parameters function nearly as well as actually calibrated parameters (Bejar et al., 2003; Embretson, 1999). Sixth, a successful series of studies for the cognitive design system approach can provide the basis for adaptive item generation. That is, rather than selecting the optimally informative item for an examinee, instead the item is generated anew based on its predicted psychometric properties, as demonstrated by Bejar et al (2003). Finally, score interpretations can be linked to expectations about an examinee's performance on specific types of items (e.g., Embretson & Reise, 2000, p. 27). Because item psychometric properties and ability are measured on a common scale, expectations that the examinee solves items with particular psychometric properties can be given. However, the cognitive design system approach extends this linkage because the item solving probabilities are related to various sources of cognitive complexity in the items. Stout (2007) views this linkage as extending continuous IRT models to cognitive diagnosis, in the case of certain IRT models. Some of these models are presented in the next section.

Overview of Cognitive Psychometric Models

In cognitive psychometric models, substantive features of items are linked to item difficulty and other item parameters. These models include the linear logistic test model (LLTM; Fischer, 1973), the two-parameter logistic constrained model (2PL-Constrained, Embretson, 1999), and the random effects linear logistic test model (LLTM-R; Janssen, Schepers, & Peres, 2004). The hierarchical IRT model (Glas & van der Linden, 2003) is included as a cognitive model in this section because it includes parameters for item families, which are groups of related items. The hierarchical IRT model becomes a cognitive model when the item family consists of variants of an existing item that have differing surface features but the same underlying structure. The models are reviewed and compared with their counterparts in traditional IRT models.

The least complex of the traditional IRT models is the Rasch model because items differ only in difficulty. If b_i is the difficulty of item i and θ_j is the ability of person j, then the probability that the person j passes item i, $P(X_{ij} = 1)$, is given by the Rasch model as follows:

$$P(X_{ij} = 1 | \theta_j, b_i) = \frac{\exp(\theta_j - b_i)}{1 + \exp(\theta_j - b_i)}. \quad (1)$$

Thus, the difference between the person's ability and the item's difficulty determines the probability of solving a particular item. If the ability exceeds the item difficulty, then the probability that the item is solved is greater than .50, and the probability becomes increasingly larger the more the ability exceeds item difficulty. If the item difficulty is greater than ability, then Equation 1 yields probabilities smaller than .50. In applications of the model, item difficulties are estimated for each item. These values are then used for test equating and to estimate the abilities for examinees on a common scale.

The LLTM (Fischer, 1973) is a generalization of the Rasch model in which item difficulty is replaced with a model of item difficulty. The probability that person j passes item i, $P(X_{ij}=1)$ depends on q_{ik}, the score of item i on stimulus feature k in the cognitive complexity of items, and η_k is the weight of stimulus feature k in item difficulty. Thus, LLTM may be written as follows:

$$P(X_{ij}=1|\theta_i,\mathbf{q}_j,\mathbf{\eta}) = \frac{\exp\left(\theta_i - \sum_{k=1}^{K} q_{jk}\eta_k\right)}{1+\exp\left(\theta_i - \sum_{k=1}^{K} q_{jk}\eta_k\right)}. \quad (2)$$

In Equation 2, q_{i1} is unity and η_1 is an intercept. Compared with Equation 1, item difficulty is replaced by a prediction from a weighted combination of stimulus features that represent the cognitive complexity of the item. Janssen, Schepers, and Peres (2004) added a random error term to the LLTM, so that the variance in item difficulty that is not accounted for by the model may be estimated.

Another traditional IRT model is the 2PL model. In contrast to the Rasch model in Equation 1, the 2PL model includes a term, a_i, to represent the discrimination of item i on the latent trait. The probability that person j passes item i in the 2PL is written as follows, where b_k and θ_i are defined as in Equation 1:

$$P(X_{ij}=1|\theta_j,b_i,a_i) = \frac{\exp(a_i(\theta_j - b_i))}{1+\exp(a_i(\theta_j - b_i))}. \quad (3)$$

A cognitive model version of the 2PL model, the 2PL-Constrained model (Embretson, 1999), includes cognitive complexity models for both item difficulty and item discrimination. In this model, q_{ik} and q_{im} are scores on stimulus features k and m in item i. Then, η_k is the weight of stimulus factor k in the difficulty of item i, τ_m is the weight of stimulus factor m in the discrimination of item I, and θ_j is defined as in Equation 3. The 2PL-Constrained model gives the probability that person j passes item i as follows:

$$P(X_{ij}=1|\theta_j,\mathbf{q},\mathbf{\eta},\mathbf{\tau}) = \frac{\exp\left(\sum_{m=1}^{M} q_{im}\tau_m \left(\theta_j - \sum_{k=1}^{K} q_{ik}\eta_k\right)\right)}{1+\exp\left(\sum_{m=1}^{M} q_{im}\tau_m \left(\theta_j - \sum_{k=1}^{K} q_{ik}\eta_k\right)\right)} \quad (4)$$

where q_{i1} is unity for all items and so τ_1 and η_1 are intercepts. Compared with Equation 3, in Equation 4 both the item difficulty parameter b_i and the item discrimination parameter a_i are replaced with cognitive models.

The hierarchical IRT model (Glas & van der Linden, 2003) is similar to the 3PL IRT model because it includes item parameters for difficulty, discrimination, and guessing. In the 3PL model, the probability that person j passes item i is given as follows:

$$P(X_{ij}=1|\theta_j,b_i,a_i,c_i) = c_i + (1-c_i)\frac{\exp(a_i(\theta_j - b_i))}{1+\exp(a_i(\theta_j - b_i))}. \quad (5)$$

where a_i, b_i, and θ_j are defined as in the 2PL model in Equation 3 and c_i represents a lower asymptote, which is often considered to represent guessing effects.

In the hierarchical IRT model (Glas & van der Linden, 2003), the parameters represent a common value for a family of items rather than individual items. The family could represent items with the same underlying sources of difficulty but varying in surface features. For example, in mathematical word problems, the same essential problem can be presented with different numbers, actors, objects, and so forth.

In the hierarchical model, the probability is given for person j passing item i from family p, and the item parameters are given for the item family, as follows:

$$P(X_{ijp} = 1 | \theta_j, a_{ip}, b_{ip}, c_{ip}) = c_{ip} + (1 - c_{ip}) \frac{\exp(a_{ip}(\theta_j - b_{ip}))}{1 + \exp(a_{ip}(\theta_j - b_{ip}))}. \quad (6)$$

where a_{ip} is item slope or discrimination of item family p, b_{ip} is the item difficulty of item family p, c_{ip} is lower asymptote of item family p, and θ_j is ability. The model also includes parameters to estimate variability of the parameters within families.

A Cognitive Design System Approach to Measuring Spatial Ability

In this section, the steps involved in applying the cognitive design system approach to test development are illustrated with an application to a test of spatial ability. A project to identify the substantive aspects of construct validity and to develop an item generator was undertaken for the AO test on the ASVAB. Some results from that project (Embretson, 2000) are described.

Development of the Theoretical Framework

This section describes how a theoretical framework for AO items was developed. This stage involved both literature reviews and an examination of previous research findings.

GOALS OF MEASUREMENT. The first step is to identify the goals of measurement underlying the construction of the AO test. The AO test was developed in Project A (Peterson et al., 1990), which had the general goal of increasing the predictability of job performance over the existing ASVAB subtests. More specifically, the AO test was constructed to measure spatial visualization ability, particularly the mental rotation aspect, which was not represented directly in the other ASVAB subtests. That is, the AO test was intended to measure a person's ability to mentally rotate objects and anticipate their appearance in a new orientation. Lohman's (2000) review indicated that tasks similar to the AO items measure a general spatial visualization ability, which factor analytic studies often find as indistinguishable from general fluid intelligence (i.e., non-verbal reasoning). According to Lohman (2000), rotation is best distinguished by highly speeded two-dimensional rotation tasks or by three-dimensional rotation tasks. The AO task as shown in Figure 11.1 is more complex than two-dimensional rotation tasks because it involves many figures or pieces that vary in several other features as well as in spatial orientation. Further, AO items are not administered as a speeded test. Thus, it seems plausible that AO items may measure aspects of intelligence beyond the rotation component of spatial ability.

TASK FEATURES. Next, the general and the specific features of the AO task were identified. The general features of an AO task consist of (a) a two-dimensional representation of assembled objects and pieces, (b) a stem that consists of pieces that can be assembled into an object, (c) a drawing of the object that can be assembled from the pieces, (d) three drawings of objects that cannot be assembled from the pieces (i.e., the distractors), (e) a multiple-choice decision format, and (f) responses that are displayed linearly to right of the stem. One important implication of the general task features is that processes to represent decisions about response alternatives are needed because the objects are presented in a multiple-choice format. Another implication is that the distance of the key from the stem may vary substantially, which could be an important source of between-item differences. Finally, item size should be constant regardless of test presentation mode (i.e., paper and pencil, computerized) because object comparisons are involved. The perception of the object differences is influenced by object display size.

Specific features in the stems of AO items include the number of pieces and the regularity of the piece shapes, as well as the dispersion and orientation of the pieces in the stem compared with the assembled object. Specific features of the response alternatives include the distance of the correct response from the stem as well as the similarity of the distractors to correct response. Specific features potentially have importance for a cognitive model of the task to predict differences in item difficulty and response time.

LITERATURE SEARCH. The next step is to review the literature for relevant cognitive research. Many studies are available on the impact of differences in object orientation in making comparisons (e.g., Just & Carpenter, 1985; Shepard & Feng, 1971). Mental models theory has been found applicable to explain performance on spatial tasks (Byrne & Johnson-Laird, 1989; Glasgow & Malton, 1999) as contrasted with a rule-based or inferential approach. However, complex spatial tasks often can be solved by more than one strategy. Specific to object assembly, it has been found that instructions can determine whether verbal or spatial processes are applied to the Minnesota Paper Form Board (Johnson, Paivio, & Clark, 1990). Another relevant literature from cognitive psychology concerns visual search tasks (Duncan & Humphreys, 1989). This literature provides information about visual display features that make visual search tasks more difficult, such as position displacement, figure orientation, and context.

The most directly relevant background literature was a series of studies (Mumaw & Pellegrino, 1984; Pellegrino, Mumaw, & Shute, 1985; Pellegrino & Glaser, 1982) in which a cognitive model for AO tasks was developed. The postulated cognitive model consisted of five processes: encoding, search, rotation, comparison, and response. Using a verification version of the AO task (i.e., true/false item format), strong support for the process theory was found. Processing difficulties were explicitly linked to stimulus features that varied between items to represent the postulated processes. Both item response time and error rates were modeled from item differences in the stimulus features. Strong empirical support for the cognitive model was obtained by mathematically modeling item response time and error rates at both the group and individual level.

THE COGNITIVE MODEL. Embretson and Gorin (2001) generalized Mumaw and Pellegrino's (1984) cognitive process model to accommodate AO test items. The Mumaw and Pellegrino cognitive model required generalization because it was developed for a verification format rather than the multiple-choice format of AO test items. Thus, Embretson and Gorin (2001) added a two-stage decision process to the processing model. In a two-stage decision task, the examinee first attempts to falsify response alternatives by a fast, holistic process. Then, the nonfalsified alternatives are processed more extensively in an attempt to confirm the required features for the assembled object. Support for two-stage models has been found for other ability task items, such as inductive reasoning tasks (Pellegrino, 1982) and paragraph comprehension items (Embretson & Wetzel, 1987).

Figure 11.2 presents the postulated model for AO items. This model is similar to Embretson and Gorin's (2001) model, although the details of processing differ somewhat, especially for the confirmation process. Like Mumaw and Pellegrino (1984), the postulated cognitive model combines elements of visual search with spatial manipulation. The first stage is encoding of the stem elements. Encoding difficulty is postulated to be influenced by the number and the complexity of the pieces in the stem. Piece complexity, in turn, is influenced by

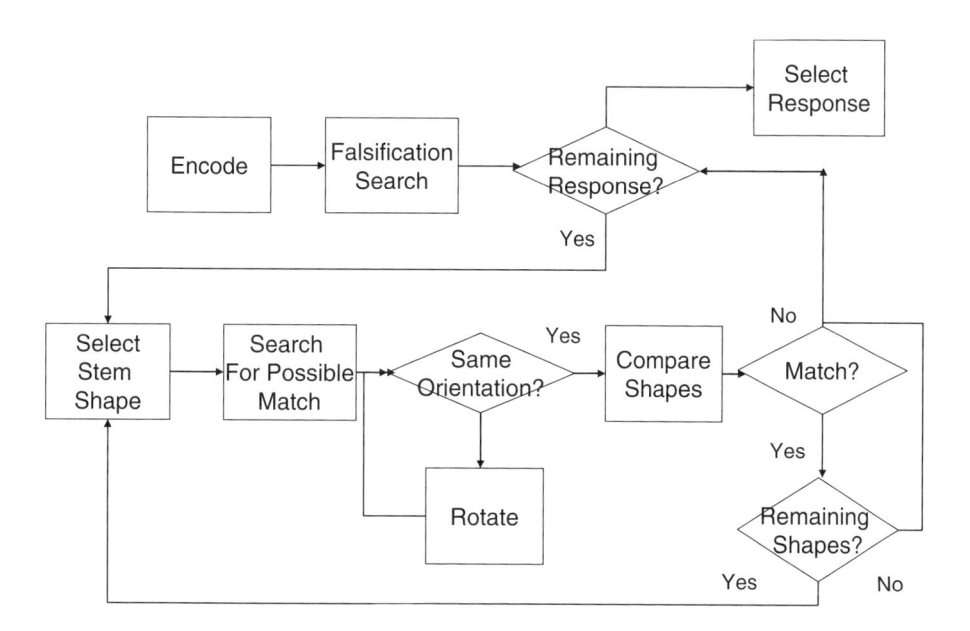

Figure 11.2. The cognitive model.

the number of edges and curves, as well as by the availability of verbal labels to describe the piece (i.e., circle, triangle, etc.). The second stage is falsification, in which the examinee is postulated to search for response alternatives with grossly inappropriate features, such as the wrong number of pieces and obviously mismatched pieces compared with the stem. This stage involves a visual search process, and it is hypothesized to be relatively easiest as the dissimilarity between the stem and the distractor pieces increases (Duncan & Humphreys, 1989). The falsification process is hypothesized to be self-terminating within alternatives, such that processing of a response alternative ceases when a mismatch is detected. It is also postulated that falsification processing is exhaustive between alternatives, such that all response alternatives are checked.

The last stage in Figure 11.2 is the confirmation process, which is hypothesized to be applied only to the nonfalsified alternatives. This stage involves searching, rotating, and comparing shapes between the stem and the response alternative. The difficulty of the search process is generally determined by the similarity of the target to the pieces in the response field (Duncan & Humphreys, 1989). Therefore, the difficulty of the search depends on the displacement and orientation of the piece in the alternative relative to its position in the stem. Further, the difficulty of comparing shapes depends on the angular disparity between corresponding but mismatching pieces. Thus, difficulty is determined by the number of displaced pieces, the number of rotated pieces, and the number of pieces mismatched by small angular disparities. The difficulty of confirming the pieces in the correct response is hypothesized to increase as the distance of the stem from the correct response increases. With increasing distance, separate eye fixations are required to compare objects as presented on computer monitors and thus increasing the role of mental imagery or other representational processes. Finally, the difficulty of the search and comparison processes for distractors also increases with the expected number of comparisons to detect a mismatched piece. That is, item difficulty and response time are hypothesized to increase with the number of comparisons. The confirmation process is postulated to be applied exhaustively to the nonfalsified response alternatives, including the case in which the correct response is the only remaining nonfalsified alternative.

Research on the Theoretical Framework

The following sections present a description of the methods underlying the reanalysis of the Embretson and Gorin (2001) data.

PLAUSIBILITY OF THE COGNITIVE MODEL FOR AO ITEMS ON THE ASVAB. Embretson and Gorin (2001) presented results that supported many aspects of a model similar to Figure 11.2. Item response time and item difficulty were modeled by variables that represented the complexity of the various processing stages using hierarchical regression. However, the final hierarchical regression models did not support two major variables that were postulated to represent spatial processes in the confirmation stage, the number of displaced pieces, and the number of rotated pieces. Although the variables had significant correlations with both item difficulty and mean item response time, they did not have significant weights in the final regression model. Embretson and Gorin (2001) attributed these results to the incidental correlations of the number of displaced pieces and the number of rotated pieces with other cognitive model variables. Intercorrelation among independent variables in a cognitive model is an inherent limitation of modeling existing tests because they are not designed to isolate the independent effects of design variables. Other limitations involved in modeling existing tests include smaller variances of the stimulus features and, frequently, the availability of only item statistics for modeling, which decreases the power to find effects.

In the study reported in the following section, two data sets with different items were available. This design permits the plausibility of the cognitive model to be assessed on each data set individually and jointly and hence may counteract some of the disadvantages of modeling items from a single existing test. Three dependent variables were examined: item difficulty, item discrimination, and mean item response time. These dependent variables have different sources of importance for the model. First, item difficulty is a major dependent variable both cognitively and psychometrically. Cognitive complexity in the various processing stages is hypothesized to increase the likelihood of errors and hence impact item difficulty. Second, item discrimination is an important psychometric variable that indicates the strength of relationship of item responses to the latent trait. Sources of cognitive complexity in items associated with decreased item discrimination lead to increased measurement error for the latent trait. Third, mean item response time has two sources of importance: establishing the cognitive processing model and providing psychometrically relevant information for test equating. The plausibility of the model variables as influencing processes is supported if the variables contribute to predicting response time. That is, if a process occurs, then stimulus features that impact its difficulty will also impact response time. Psychometrically, mean item response time provides some important auxiliary information for test equating including equating adaptive tests. Tests are usually constrained so that the number of items and the maximum testing time is constant across examinees. Despite careful equating for psychometric properties based on modeling item response accuracy, administering too many items that are associated with longer response times can lead to insufficient testing time and consequently lowered scores on a particular test form.

Method
Tests and item bank. All items were from the AO item bank on the ASVAB. Several different outer shapes are found in the item bank, including squares, circles, rectangles, hexagons, and triangles, as well as distorted versions of these shapes (i.e., ovals, flat hexagons, etc.). All items that were available for this study had been administered by computer.

Design. Although raw item response data were not available, item parameter estimates for the 3PL model and mean item response times were available for two different data sets. The 3PL-model parameter estimates for the new items had been through common items. The mean response times were not explicitly linked. However, they can be regarded as randomly equivalent because items (or whole tests) were randomly assigned to examinees in both data sets.

For the Fixed Content Test data set, examinees were administered one of four forms following an operational administration of the ASVAB. Each test form consisted of 25 unique items and 8 linking items that were repeated on at least one other form, for a total of 115 items. For the Seeded data set, which had been modeled previously by Embretson and Gorin (2001), individual items were administered in the context of an adaptive AO test from the ASVAB tests. A total of 149 items were seeded randomly within operational adaptive tests based on the calibrated item bank. Item parameters for the Seeded data set were linked to the item parameters for the operational AO items. Thus, data for a total of 264 items were available for the cognitive models.

Participants. The participants were military recruits who were taking the ASVAB. The Fixed Content Test was administered to 9,321 examinees, who were randomly assigned to one of the four test forms. The participants were told that their scores would not count. For the Seeded data set, the item calibrations were based on approximately 1,500 examinees per item. Thus, for each item, very stable estimates of item parameters and response times were available. Although participants were told that some items would not count, no information was given about which items were seeded.

Cognitive model variables. The cognitive model variables were scored for every item in both data sets. The difficulty of encoding the item stem was modeled by four variables as follows: (a) number of pieces—the number of shapes; (b) number of edges—the total number of edges in all pieces; (c) verbal labels—the number of pieces with verbal labels (i.e., circles, right triangles, hexagons, pyramids, etc.); and (d) curved pieces—the number of pieces with curved edges. The difficulty of falsification was represented by a single variable: falsifiable distractors—the number of distractors falisified by gross mismatch (i.e., number of pieces, piece size, number of edges in the shapes). The difficulty of the confirmation process was represented by the following five variables: (a) displaced pieces—the number of pieces differing in position from the stem to the correct response, (b) rotated pieces—the number of pieces differing in orientation between the stem and the correct response, (c) target distance—the distance of the correct response from the stem, (d) small angles—a binary variable indicating small angular disparities in the mismatch of pieces in the distractor to the pieces in the stem, and (e) number of cycles—the expected number of comparison cycles to disconfirm the closest nonfalsifiable distractor. The latter variable was scored from the number of pieces in the closest distractor that are mismatched to the stem. If all pieces are mismatched, then only one comparison is required to reject the distractor. If only one piece is mismatched, then more comparison cycles are expected, depending on the number of pieces. Thus, the expected number of comparison cycles E[c] required to detect a mismatched piece was estimated by the following mathematical model:

$$E[c] = \Gamma x [b/(p-x)][1 - c^{x-1} P_{c=x}]$$

where p is number of pieces, b is the number of mismatched pieces, x is the number of cycles, and $P_{c=x}$ is the probability that the number of cycles equals x. Compared with Embretson and Gorin's (2001) analysis of AO items, all variables were identical except target distance, which was added to reflect spatial processing difficulty in comparing the correct response to the stem.

Results

Descriptive statistics. Because both data sets were from empirical tryouts, items with discriminations less than .80 were trimmed to avoid modeling poor quality items. Thus, the models are based on 104 and 128 items, respectively, for the Fixed Content Test and the Seeded items. The means were compared between tests with a multivariate analysis of variance. For the dependent variables, item difficulty, item discrimination, and response time, the means differed significantly overall between tests (Wilk's $\Lambda = .202$), $F(3, 228) = 300.845, p < .001$, with a large effect size ($\eta^2 = .798$). The univariate tests indicated that the means for item difficulty, $F(1, 230) = 14.046, p < .001$, and item discrimination, $F(1, 230) = 11.975, p = .001$, were significantly higher on the Fixed Content Test, although the effect sizes were small ($\eta^2 < .058$). The mean for response time, $F(1, 230) = 323.333, p < .001$, was higher on the Seeded items and the effect size was large ($\eta^2 = .584$).

The means of the cognitive model variables also differed between tests (Wilk's $\Lambda = .814$), $F(10, 220) = 5.035, p < .001$, with a small effect size ($\eta^2 = .186$). The univariate tests indicated that the means for curved pieces, $F(1, 229) = 8.247, p = .004$, and mismatched angles, $F(1, 229) = 8.344, p = .004$, were greater on the Fixed Content Test, whereas the mean for rotated pieces, $F(1, 229) = 5.706, p = .018$, was greater on the Seeded items. All effect sizes were small ($\eta^2 < .035$). The Box M test indicated that the covariances between the independent variables also varied significantly across tests ($p < .001$). Thus, the tests did not represent the AO design variables equivalently.

Item difficulty was significantly correlated with most independent variables in both data sets. It had significant positive correlations with number of pieces, number of edges, displaced pieces, target distance, number of cycles, and small angles, and significant negative correlations with the verbal labels and falsifiable distractors. Additionally, item difficulty had a significant positive correlation with rotated pieces in the Seeded items. In contrast, item discrimination was not highly correlated with the independent variables. No significant correlations were observed with any independent variable in the Fixed Content Test, but significant negative correlations were observed with curved edges and small angles in the Seeded items. In both data sets, response time had significant positive correlations with number of pieces, angles, and number of cycles, and significant negative correlations with verbal labels and falsifiable distractors. Further, response time had significant positive correlations with rotated pieces and displaced pieces for the Seeded items, but not for the Fixed Content Test.

Cognitive models. The three dependent variables—item difficulty, item discrimination, and mean item response time—were modeled separately for both data sets using hierarchical regression. Then, the data sets were modeled jointly using structural equation modeling.

For the hierarchical regression analyses, the independent variables were ordered by the postulated temporal ordering of the stages of encoding, falsification, and confirmation. Item difficulty had strong and similar patterns of predictability by processing stage for both the Fixed Content Test ($R = .70, p < .01$) and the Seeded test items ($R = .68; p < .01$), and each stage significantly increased prediction for both tests. However, the details of the model, the regression coefficients that represent unique impact for each variable, differed across data sets. The only independent variable that was consistently significant across data sets was target distance, which had a positive regression coefficient. Only number of pieces, rotated pieces, displaced pieces, and target distance had significant regression coefficients ($p < .05$) for the Fixed Content Test items, and only target distance, small angles, and number of cycles had significant regression coefficients for the Seeded items.

Item discrimination was not highly predictable in either data set. The cognitive model did not significantly predict item discrimination for the Fixed Content Test items, although statistical significance was achieved for the Seeded items ($R = .41, p < .05$). The only variable in the model with a significant regression coefficient was curved pieces, with a significant negative weight, whereas small angles had a marginally significant weight.

For mean item response time, moderate prediction from the cognitive model variables in the Fixed Content Test items ($R = .62, p < .05$) and stronger prediction in the Seeded items ($R = .74, p < .01$) was observed. As for the item difficulty model, each processing stage had a significant increment to prediction, thus supporting the necessity of each stage. Also similar to item difficulty, the details of the model varied across data sets. Significant regression coefficients were obtained for falsifiable distractors, rotated pieces, displaced pieces, and target distance for the Fixed Content Test and for the number of pieces, number of edges, verbal labels, and number of cycles for the Seeded items.

Structural equation modeling was applied to further understand the differences between the two tests. The covariance matrices differed significantly ($\chi^2 = 253.883, df = 91; p < .001$). However, because the overall test reflects both differences in variances and covariances between tests, a merged regression model may fit adequately if the tests differ primarily in the variances rather than in the independent to dependent variable regressions. Thus, a multiple group structural equation model was specified to build a common regression model for the three dependent variables across the two data sets. The variances and covariances between the independent variables were freely estimated within tests, but the regression coefficients for the cognitive model variables were constrained to be equal across tests. Although the model did not fit statistically ($\chi^2 = 71.877, df = 30; p < .001$), the comparative fit index (CFI) exceeded the recommended minimum level of .95 (CFI = .959) and the root mean square residual (RMR) was smaller than the recommended level of less than .05 (RMR = .046). Thus, good fit was obtained for the common regression weights.

Table 11.1 presents the common regression weights for each dependent variable. For item difficulty, the cognitive model variables with significant coefficients were in the expected direction. That is, significant positive regression coefficients were found for number of pieces, rotated pieces, displaced pieces, and target distance, although significant negative regression coefficients were found

Table 11.1. Regression Coefficients for Cognitive Model Constrained Across Samples

	Difficulty		Response time		Discrimination	
Variable	B	SE_B	B	SE_B	B	SE_B
Number of pieces	.171**	.040	.514†	.275	.053	.032
Number of edges	.000	.005	.160**	.036	.000	.004
Curved pieces	−.014	.013	−.092	.091	−.033**	.011
Verbal labels	−.079**	.018	−.456**	.118	−.007	.014
Falsifiable distractors	−.106**	.040	−.126	.261	−.012	.031
Rotated pieces	.113**	.033	.553*	.229	−.009	.027
Displaced pieces	.040*	.016	.319*	.129	−.018	.015
Target distance	.082**	.018	.187	.121	.010	.014
Small angles	.077	.064	.172	.423	−.086†	.050
Number of cycles	.051	.047	.684**	.289	−.030	.034

†$p < .10$. *$p < .05$. **$p < .01$.

for verbal labels and falsifiable distractors. Number of edges, curved edges, small angles, and number of cycles did not have significant unique relationships with item difficulty. For mean item response time, the significant coefficients for the model variables were also in the expected direction. Significant positive regression coefficients were found for number of pieces, number of edges, rotated pieces, displaced pieces, and number of cycles, whereas a significant negative regression coefficient was found for verbal labels. Falsifiable distractors, target distance, curved pieces, and small angles did not have significant unique correlations with item response time. Finally, for item discrimination, the only significant predictor variable was curved pieces, which had a negative weight. Also, small angles had a marginally significant negative weight.

Discussion

The results from the two data sets strongly support the plausibility of the cognitive model for the AO items. Moderate to strong prediction was obtained for item difficulty and mean item response time in the full cognitive model. Approximately 50% of the variance in the dependent variables was explained by the model. This level of prediction for item difficulty provides a sound basis for item generation. Simulation studies have shown that prediction of item parameters at this level leads to only modest increases in measurement error if predicted item parameters are substituted for calibrated parameters (Embretson, 1999; Mislevy, Sheehan, & Wingersky, 1993). Further, all three global processing stages in the cognitive model—encoding, falsification, and confirmation—were supported. That is, significant incremental contributions to prediction were found for the variables that represent cognitive complexity of the three stages in the hierarchical regression analysis in both data sets. Thus, at a general level, as in Embretson and Gorin (2001), the plausibility of the cognitive model is supported.

However, as a basis for item design, it is also important to understand the impact of the specific sources of complexity in each processing stage. These variables can potentially be varied to create new items with target levels and sources of difficulty. Embretson and Gorin's (2001) analysis did not provide clear support for the role of specific variables within processing stages. Similar findings were obtained in this study from the separate models for the two data sets. However, the merged cognitive models across data sets supported the expected role for most independent variables for item difficulty and mean item response time. These results contrast sharply with Embretson and Gorin's (2001) analysis, in which significant unique impact was not found for some major variables (e.g., rotated pieces, displaced pieces). The most plausible explanation is the increased power of the current study, which results from both the increased number of observations and the method of analysis that was more robust across the incidental correlations among the independent variables.

For the encoding stage, the number of pieces in the stem was significantly associated with both increased item difficulty and mean item response time, as expected. Also as expected, pieces in the stem that were easily labeled verbally were associated with significantly less difficulty and response time. The number of edges in the pieces, on the other hand, was associated with significantly increased response time but not with increased item difficulty.

For the falsification stage, the number of falsifiable distractors was significantly related to decreased item difficulty but not to significantly decreased item response time. These results are only partially expected from the cognitive model presented in Figure 11.2. Both decreased item difficulty and item response time were expected from the model in which falsification is hypothesized to result in the elimination of some distractors from further processing and the continued processing of nonfalsifiable distractors.

For the confirmation stage, the two variables that represent spatial processing, the number of displaced pieces and rotated pieces, had significant positive weights in the models for both item difficulty and mean item response time. Further, the distance of the correct answer from the stem was a significant predictor of item difficulty, as expected. These results support the hypothesis that increased spatial and imagery processing is required as the pieces cannot be viewed in a single eye fixation. Finally, the expected number of comparison cycles to reject the closest distractor significantly increased processing time, as expected.

In summary, all but two cognitive model variables had significant impact for either item difficulty or item response time. Thus, the role of most variables in the cognitive model was strongly supported, which supports their potential to be varied in generating items to target sources and levels of complexity. It is interesting that the two independent variables that were not related to item difficulty or item response time were related to item discrimination. That is, the number of curved pieces in the stem and the number of distractor pieces with small angular disparities compared with the stem were related to decreased item discrimination.

PLAUSIBILITY OF THE COGNITIVE MODEL FOR ALGORITHMICALLY GENERATED ITEMS. The cognitive models in the preceding studies support the possibility of developing item specifications for AO items that are based on cognitive processing characteristics. The overall processing model provided moderately strong prediction of item difficulty and mean item response time. The impact of all three processing stages was supported. Therefore, in the current study, item specifications based on all three stages were developed to generate a new set of AO items. To the extent that the empirical properties of the new items are predictable from the cognitive model, support would be obtained for generating items with target levels and sources of processing complexity.

In this study, a large number of AO items were generated by crossing the sources of processing difficulty, encoding, falsification, and confirmation. One goal of this study was to evaluate the cognitive model as a basis for generating AO items. Another goal was to examine the independent impact of the cognitive model variables in an experimental design. In contrast, the cognitive model was examined in the preceding study on existing items in which the variables had incidental correlations, which can lead to confounded effects.

A final goal was to estimate the weights for the cognitive model with a statistically more appropriate modeling approach than was used in the preceding study. Model-based IRT approaches, such as the cognitive IRT models that were reviewed previously, have several advantages compared with the hierarchical regression modeling that was applied in the preceding study. First, the results interface with contemporary item banking because IRT parameters are estimated. IRT parameters are useful for test equating and computerized adaptive testing. Second, the standard errors for the estimated cognitive model parameters generally will be smaller. The standard errors in LLTM and the 2PL-constrained model are based on the full data set (i.e., raw item responses), whereas in the hierarchical regression analysis the standard errors depend on the number of items. Third, the estimated weights for the cognitive variables are statistically more justifiable when they depend on the amount of available data. In typical item tryouts, some items and combinations of independent variables have more data available than other combinations. The hierarchical regression estimates used in the preceding study were obtained without regard to the number of cases on which the item difficulties were estimated. In contrast, model-based IRT parameter estimates depend on the amount of available data. In the current study, a full information model-based IRT approach was possible because raw item response data were obtained.

Method

Item development. Because a very large number of items can be generated by crossing the levels of the variables in a cognitive model, a restricted set of features was specified in the current study. First, only three frame shapes for the assembled objects were specified: squares, circles and triangles. Second, for all items, three or more lines (i.e., radiants) were drawn from a single centerpoint to each side. To define reference points for drawing the objects, a 3×3 grid, spanning the height and the width of each object frame, was overlaid on each object frame. The location of the centerpoint in terms of the grid was counterbalanced across items. Third, each radiant was projected to a different side unless the number of radiants exceeded the number of sides. In the latter case, two radiants must be projected to the same side. With this set of drawing constraints, the number of pieces equals the number of radiants. Fourth, two types of distractors were constructed. In comparison with the correct response, either the centerpoint was moved or the attachment point of one radiant was moved. This variable was counterbalanced across items.

Variables from all three stages, as defined in the preceding study, were manipulated to design the source of cognitive complexity in the items. A total of 48 unique item structures were specified by crossing Encoding (3) × Falsification (4) × Rotation (2) × Displacement (2). For encoding, the three levels were defined by the number of pieces, ranging from three to five. For falsification, the four levels consisted of the number of falsifiable distractors, ranging from zero to three. For both rotation and displacement, the two levels were present versus absent. Items were generated for all 48 structures using circles and rectangles, for a total of 96 items. However, to maintain perceptual quality, triangles were not used in the full set of structures. That is, triangle items with five pieces were confusing perceptually, so the triangles were used with only the 32 structures that had three or four pieces. Thus, 128 items were generated from the item structures. An additional 14 items were constructed to represent special combinations of design features involving salient verbal labels.

Cognitive model variables. Scores for the cognitive model variables were obtained from the item specifications and drawing constraints, as follows: (a) number of pieces was scored as the number of radiants in a shape, (b) falsifiable distractors was scored by the number of distractors with large changes as described previously, (c) verbal labels was scored directly from the number of pieces and frame type (i.e., because of the drawing constraints, the only shapes with labels were triangles and wedges), (d) rotated pieces was scored as a binary variable defined by the item design as described previously, (e) displaced pieces was scored as a binary variable defined from the item design, (f) target distance was scored as the position of the key, (g) small angles was scored as the proportion of shapes in the closest distractor that were mismatched by small angular disparities (1.00 for small centerpoint changes; 2/[the number of pieces], for small radiant changes; 0, otherwise), and (h) number of cycles was computed from the number of mismatched pieces in closest nonfalsifiable distractor (0, if all distractors are falsifiable; 2, for radiant attachment changes; the number of pieces for centerpoint changes).

Two cognitive model variables were not included in the current study. Curved pieces were not included because the only curves permitted under the drawing constraints were the edges of circle shapes. Thus, curved pieces were entirely dependent on stem shape. Number of edges, on the other hand, depended completely on stem shape and the number of pieces, because interior shapes were not permitted. Thus, these variables have limited meaning, given the drawing constraints. Furthermore, neither variable had a significant weight in the merged model of item difficulty in the preceding study.

Participants. The participants were 321 undergraduates at a large midwestern university. They were participating to fulfill a course requirement. Approximately equal numbers of men and women were tested.

Test design. To allow each participant to complete the items within a half-hour session, test forms with 45 or 46 items each were constructed. Each test form contained 32 common items, which represented a counterbalanced version of the design conditions. Each test form also contained 13 or 14 unique items. Thus, the full sample data is available for 32 items, whereas the remaining items were administered to subsets of the sample. A total of eight test forms were constructed to administer all the items.

Procedure. Participants were randomly assigned to a test form. All test forms were administered by computer in a laboratory of five computer stations. Items were administered without time limits and both item responses and item response times were recorded. Testing was completed within a half hour for all participants.

Results

Psychometric characteristics. Because this study is the first empirical tryout of the algorithmically generated items, psychometric quality was assessed. Of the 142 items in the study, 90.6% had biserial correlations greater than .25, which indicates that the new items were generally performing well against internal criteria. The items with low biserial correlations were eliminated from further analysis, as well as the 14 items that represented special combinations of design features. For the remaining 111 items, the mean biserial correlation was moderately high (M = 0.56, SD = 0.17), indicating that the items were sufficiently discriminating. The mean p value was also high (M = .76, SD = .14), indicating that the test was relatively easy for the sample of college students.

Descriptive statistics. The means for the independent variables were compared with the means in the preceding study using a standardized effect size (d). The means and standard deviations in the preceding study were averaged to serve as the comparison set. The means for the dependent variables were not compared because of differences in anchoring the IRT estimates as well as differences in the testing populations.

For the encoding variables, number of pieces ($d = .36$) and verbal labels ($d = .35$) were all smaller in the current study. The mean of falsifiable distractors was also substantially smaller ($d = -.78$) in the current study. For the confirmation variables, target distance ($d = -.03$) and small angles ($d = .10$) were approximately equal between the two studies. However, displaced pieces ($d = .67$) and number of cycles ($d = .27$) were greater in the current study, whereas rotated pieces was substantially less in the current study ($d = -1.08$). Thus, the experimental design of the items in the current study led to different levels on several cognitive model variables. The direction of some differences, based on the correlations in the preceding study, could be expected to increase item difficulty (i.e., verbal labels, falsifiable distractors, displaced pieces, and number of cycles), whereas other differences could be expected to decrease item difficulty (number of pieces and rotated pieces). These differences also could impact the levels of prediction of item properties that are obtained.

Correlations between the variables were then examined. Item difficulty and item response time were moderately intercorrelated ($r = .46$). For the encoding process variables, the number of pieces had significant positive correlations with both item difficulty and mean item response time. Compared with the preceding study, the magnitudes are somewhat smaller. The correlations of verbal labels with item difficulty and mean item response time were not significant. In contrast, in the preceding study, verbal labels had significant negative correlations with both item difficulty and mean item response time. Falsifiable distractors had significant negative correlations with both item difficulty and response time, which was somewhat smaller than the correlations in the preceding study. For confirmation, rotated pieces, target distance, and number of cycles had significant positive correlations with both item difficulty and item response time, whereas displaced pieces had a significant positive correlation only with item difficulty, which was consistent with the preceding study. The positive correlations of rotated pieces with item difficulty and item response time were also consistent with the preceding study, although somewhat higher in the magnitude. Finally, small angles had a significant negative correlation with item difficulty, which is inconsistent with the previous study because the correlations had been positive. Thus, with one exception, the correlations of the cognitive model variables were generally consistent between the newly generated items and the items in the preceding study, although somewhat different in magnitude.

Cognitive models. Full information models were applied to estimate the impact of the cognitive model variables on both item difficulty and item response time. A set of comparison models were included to examine fit.

For item difficulty, the impact of the cognitive model variables was estimated by fitting the LLTM and the 2PL-Constrained model to the data. Estimates for the model parameters were obtained using a nonlinear mixed modeling procedure with random effects (i.e., the SAS NLMIXED program) on the common items. The measurement scale was identified by specifying a standard normal distribution of ability ($\theta \sim N(0,1)$). Three comparison models were also estimated with the nonlinear mixed modeling procedure: (a) the Rasch model, in which separate difficulties are estimated for each item; (b) the 2PL model, in which difficulty and discrimination are estimated for each item; and (c) a null model, in which all items are equally difficult and discriminating.

Several indices of fit were examined including a χ^2 test of model differences, the Akaike Information Criterion (AIC) index, and an incremental fit index. The χ^2 test is obtained from the difference in –2 times the log likelihood between alternative models. This difference indicates whether or not the models differ statistically in explaining the data. The difference in the number of parameter estimates is the degrees of freedom. In contrast, the AIC index gives credit for parsimony, as its magnitude depends on both the likelihood of the data and the number of parameters in the model. Accordingly, the model with the smallest AIC is the best model. The incremental fit index ($\Delta^{1/2}$; Embretson, 1997) is based on the log likelihoods of alternative models. The index compares the improvement of fit for a model over a null model with relative to a saturated model. The index is similar in magnitude to a multiple correlation.

The chi-square tests and the AIC index were inconsistent in indicating whether item discrimination parameters were needed to model the data. The AIC was lowest for the Rasch model, indicating that it was the best overall model. Because the Rasch model does not include parameters to represent item differences in discrimination, it would seem that these parameters are not needed. However, the chi-square tests indicated that including item discrimination parameters led to significantly better fit. That is, the 2PL model fit the data significantly better than did the Rasch model (χ^2/df = 2.40, df = 31; p < .001), and the 2PL-constrained model fit the data significantly better than did LLTM (χ^2/df = 10.50, df = 8; p < .001). Because the results were not consistent, cognitive models both with and without varying item discrimination parameters are presented.

For the models without varying item discrimination parameters, the comparison of LLTM with the null model (χ^2/df = 141.87, df = 8; p < .001) was highly significant, indicating that the cognitive model significantly predicts item difficulty. LLTM did not perfectly predict item difficulty, as indicated by a statistically significant difference from the Rasch model (χ^2/df = 17.39, df = 22; p < .001). However, the incremental fit index ($\Delta^{1/2}$ = .850) indicated that substantial prediction was obtained.

For the model with varying item discriminations, the 2PL-constrained model, the comparisons were based on the 2PL model as the saturated model. The comparison of the 2PL-constrained model with the null model (χ^2/df = 141.87, df = 16; p < .001) was highly significant, indicating that the cognitive model significantly predicted item difficulty. The 2PL-constrained model did not perfectly predict item difficulty and item discrimination, as indicated by a statistically significant difference from the 2PL model (χ^2/df = 9.086, df = 46, p < .001). However, the fit index ($\Delta^{1/2}$ = .849) indicated that substantial prediction was obtained.

Table 11.2 presents the prediction weights for the cognitive model for both LLTM and the 2PL-constrained model. For LLTM, all cognitive model variables were significant predictors of item difficulty except small angles. All weights were in the predicted direction. For the 2PL-constrained model, all cognitive model variables except verbal labels and number of cycles were significant predictors of item difficulty. All weights were in the expected direction except the

Table 11.2. Parameter Estimates for the LLTM and the 2PL-Constrained Model on Algorithmically Generated AO Items

| | LLTM | | | 2PL-constrained | | | | | |
| | | | | Item difficulty | | | Item discrimination | | |
Item predictor	η	se	t	η	se	t	τ	se	t
Constant	−3.693	.175		−4.204	.353		2.083	.600	
Pieces	.118**	.041	2.87	.477**	.069	6.91	.611**	.108	5.67
Labels	.141**	.025	5.74	−.064	.041	−1.56	−.348**	.057	−6.11
Falsifiable	−.198**	.040	−4.96	−.207**	.050	−4.10	.099	.107	0.93
Rotation	.634**	.054	11.74	.486**	.076	6.37	−.358**	.136	−2.64
Displacement	.274**	.055	4.96	.424**	.081	5.22	.438**	.148	2.95
Target distance	.379**	.023	16.26	.316**	.033	9.64	−.077	.057	−1.34
Angles	.187	.101	1.85	−.305*	.146	−2.08	−.816**	.287	−2.84
Cycles	.395**	.060	6.61	.101	.066	1.53	−.725**	.198	−3.66

Note. LLTM = linear logistic test model; 2PL = two-parameter logistic; AO = Assembling Objects.
*p < .05. **p < .01

weight for small angles, which was negative rather than positive. Item discrimination was significantly predicted by several variables; number of pieces and displaced pieces had significant positive weights, whereas verbal labels, rotated pieces, small angles, and number of cycles had significant negative weights.

Response time was modeled by an analogous procedure, using a mixed-modeling procedure for continuous variables on the full set of items. Three models were estimated: (a) a null model, in which all items had the same mean response time; (b) a cognitive model, with the eight cognitive variables used to predict item difficulty; and (c) a saturated model, in which separate parameters are estimated for each item. Examinees were specified as random variables, and the predictors from three models were specified as fixed variables. To meet normality assumptions, response times were converted to logarithms. The comparison of the cognitive model with the null model ($\chi^2/df = 27.25$, $df = 8$, $p < .001$) was highly significant, indicating that the cognitive model significantly predicted mean log item response. The cognitive model did not perfectly predict item response time, as indicated by a statistically significant difference from the saturated model ($\chi^2/df = 4.87$, $df = 103$, $p < .001$). However, a fit index based on the log likelihoods ($\Delta^{1/2} = .883$) indicated that substantial prediction was obtained.

Table 11.3 presents the parameter estimates for the cognitive model, along with standard errors and significance tests. It can be seen that the weights for all model variables were significant except small angles and number of cycles. Number of pieces, rotated pieces, displaced pieces, and target distance were associated with significantly increased log response time, whereas verbal label and falsifiable distractors were associated with significantly decreased log response time. These results are mostly consistent with the merged analysis in the preceding study in which number of pieces, verbal labels, rotated pieces, and displaced pieces had significant or marginally significant weights. However, falsifiable distractors was not a significant predictor in the preceding study, whereas the number of cycles was a significant predictor.

Discussion. The results strongly support the validity of the cognitive model as a basis for item generation. More than 90% of the new items had acceptable psychometric properties. Further, both item difficulty and item response time

Table 11.3. Estimates, Standard Errors, and Significance Tests for the Cognitive Model of Mean Log Response Time on Algorithmically Generated Assembly Object Items

Parameter	Estimate	SE	df	t	Sig.
Intercept	2.130311	.040070	5354.282	53.165	.000
Number of pieces	0.129167	0.009959	4618.368	12.970	.000
Verbal labels	−0.041761	.006219	4513.820	−6.716	.000
Falsifiable distractors	−0.079431	.009903	5171.030	−8.021	.000
Rotated pieces	0.214757	.012889	8453.402	16.662	.000
Displaced pieces	0.097440	.012699	9461.323	7.673	.000
Target distance	0.030900	.005596	6670.048	5.522	.000
Small angles	−0.020860	.017960	4006.186	−1.161	.246
Number of cycles	0.011930	.017289	3570.885	.690	.490

were predicted from the variables of the cognitive model, which were directly manipulated. Both LLTM and the 2PL-constrained model were used to estimate the cognitive model parameters for item difficulty, whereas an analogous mixed-modeling procedure was applied to model item response item. The fit indices for the cognitive models were high, comparable to multiple correlations in the middle to high .80s, indicating that more than 70% of the differences between items in difficulty and response time were explained by the cognitive model. Thus, strong support for the cognitive models were obtained, consistent with Embretson and Gorin's (2001) research, as well as with earlier research on a verification version of AO (Mumaw & Pellegrino, 1984; Pellegrino et al., 1985; Pellegrino & Glaser, 1982).

This study had a more powerful design to isolate the impact of the model variables than the preceding study because the variables were manipulated or counterbalanced to avoid confounded effects. Further, full information IRT-based models were used to estimate the effects. It is interesting that most results on the impact of the individual variables in the cognitive model were consistent with the merged analysis of the two item banks in the preceding study.

For the encoding stage, the number of pieces was associated with increased item difficulty and response time, as expected from the cognitive model. These results are also consistent with the findings of the preceding study. The presence of item pieces with verbal labels, however, had unexpected effects. Although the verbal labels variable was associated with decreased item response time, as expected, it was associated with increased item difficulty, rather than the expected decreased item difficulty as obtained in the preceding study. These results may be due to the scoring of the verbal labels variable in the current study. In the preceding study, verbal labels scores were obtained from human raters; in the current study, the scores were based on the drawing constraints. The results suggest that further research is needed to clarify how formal features of items relate to human judgments of whether or not the pieces in AO have verbal labels that aid item solving.

For the falsification stage, item difficulty and item response time decreased when the items had pieces with readily falsifiable distractors. These results were expected from the cognitive model, as falsifiable distractors have salient features that differ from the key, such as the wrong number of pieces and obviously incongruent shapes. In the preceding study, both item difficulty and response time decreased with the number of falsifiable alternatives, although the latter relationship was not statistically significant, which did not fully support the cognitive model in Figure 11.2. However, the results from the current study, with a more powerful design, support the model.

For the confirmation stage, item difficulty and item response time increased as the number of rotated pieces, displaced pieces, and target distance (i.e., of the key to stem) increased, as expected from the cognitive model. In general, the variables from the confirmation stage of processing had greater impact than did the variables from the other stages. Similar results were obtained from the preceding study. These effects are consistent with increased involvement of spatial visualization in item solving. The impact of the other confirmation variables, small angular disparities and the number of comparison cycles, differed across models in the current study. Neither of these variables was significant in the preceding study. Research is needed on the degrees of angular disparity that are readily judged as different between pieces, so as to produce more valid scoring of AO items on this variable.

The impact of the cognitive model on item discrimination was estimated in the 2PL-constrained model. Item discrimination increased with the number of pieces and the number of displaced pieces, whereas item discrimination decreased with small angular disparities, number of cycles, number of rotated pieces, and verbal labels. Apparently the design and modeling procedures in the current study led to a more powerful test of effects compared with the preceding study in which only small angular disparities had a significant weight in the merged model.

The results have some interesting implications for what is measured by the AO items that were studied here. The original goal in developing a test with AO items in Project A (Peterson et al., 1990) was to measure the rotation component of spatial visualization. However, the cognitive model that was supported by the current study and the preceding study includes several more sources of item complexity than rotation. That is, the confirmation stage is a visual search process in which corresponding objects are identified, rotated, and compared. Displacement of pieces, target distance, and possibly other stimulus factors increase the load of spatial visualization but not the rotation component. Further, support for a falsification stage in processing the multiple choice format of the AO items was obtained. That is, the examinee may implement a strategy of eliminating distractors that have clearly discrepant pieces from the assembled object. Finally, the number of rotated pieces in the current study was associated with decreased item discrimination, whereas the number of pieces and the number of displaced pieces were associated with increased discrimination. These results are also inconsistent with the AO test measuring the rotation component of spatial visualization. Taken together, these results suggest that AO items do not uniquely measure spatial rotation. As indicated by Lohman's (2000) review, they may be more saturated with fluid intelligence or general spatial visualization processes than spatial rotation. The results also have implications for test design. Whether AO items measure primarily spatial visualization, rotation, or fluid intelligence can be changed by the test design specifications based on the cognitive model variables. That is, the role of rotation can be increased by decreasing emphasis on falsifiable distractors, displaced pieces, and target distance. Or, conversely, the role of visual search can be emphasized by increasing piece displacement and target distance. The role of fluid intelligence would be increased by making the items more amendable to strategies to handle complexity, such as increasing the number of falsifiable distractors. Which one of these traits to emphasize depends on the purpose of testing. If the goal is to increase incremental validity, as in the military, research is needed to determine which sources of item difficulty are more important in producing the incremental validity of the AO test over the other ASVAB subtests.

The next stage in the cognitive design system approach is implementing an item design strategy, generating items, and banking items by their structural parameters. An item generator for AO items has been developed (a beta version is described in Embretson, 2000). Embretson and McIntyre (2008) described results from an initial tryout of 56 items, emphasizing the rotation and displacement aspects of the cognitive model. The item difficulties were moderately well predicted using the weights for the LLTM on Table 11.2. The next step is to increase the scope of items produced by the generator and then produce a large bank of new items.

General Discussion

This chapter described a cognitive design system approach to test development. In this approach, items may be generated to predictable levels and sources of difficulty using model-based estimates of how item stimulus features impact performance. Unlike traditional test development, the cognitive design system approach provides test design principles that can lead to generating items with target levels and sources of item complexity. The cognitive design system approach is most effectively implemented when the parameters of a cognitive IRT model can be estimated. These parameters not only have implications for the substantive aspect of validity but also can be used to guide test and item design.

The cognitive design system approach was illustrated with an application to the measurement of spatial ability. Results from a research project on the AO test on the ASVAB were presented. A cognitive model to explain the sources of item complexity was presented, and two studies on the model were discussed. The cognitive model was strongly supported for explaining empirical item properties on existing AO items and new AO items that were produced by manipulating the cognitive model variables. Thus, the cognitive model is adequate to guide item and test design.

A final stage in the cognitive design system approach is to develop an automatic item generator to produce items. Such a generator has been developed for AO items, based on the research presented in this chapter. The initial results are promising (Embretson & McIntyre, 2008); item difficulties were predictable directly using the LLTM weights in the studies reported in this chapter. More research is clearly needed, but the results are promising for developing items to target levels and sources of cognitive complexity. Automatic item generation is an active research area. The interested reader should consult chapter 9 of this volume for a comprehensive review of item generation.

References

Bejar, I. I. (2002). Generative testing: From conception to implementation. In S. H. Irvine & P. C. Kyllonen (Eds.), *Item generation for test development* (pp. 199–218). Mahwah, NJ: Erlbaum.

Bejar, I. (2008). Model based item generation: A review of recent research. In S. E. Embretson (Ed.), *New directions in measuring psychological constructs with model-based approaches*. Washington, DC: American Psychological Association Books.

Bejar, I., Lawless, R., Morley, M., Wagner, R., Bennett, R., & Revuelta, J. (2003). A feasibility study of on-the-fly item generation in adaptive testing. *Journal of Technology, Learning, and Assessment, 2*(3).

Bormuth, J. R. (1970). *On the theory of achievement test items.* Chicago, IL: University of Chicago Press.
Byrne, R. M., & Johnson-Laird, P. N. (1989). Spatial reasoning. *Journal of Memory and Language, 28,* 564–575.
Campbell, J. P. (1990). The Army selection and classification project (Project A). *Personnel Psychology, 43,* 231–239.
Cronbach, L. J. (1970). Review of "On the theory of achievement test items" by J. R. Bormuth. *Psychometrika, 35,* 509–511.
Duncan, J., & Humphreys, G. (1989). Visual search and stimulus similarity. *Psychological Review, 96,* 433–458.
Embretson, S. E. (1997). Multicomponent latent trait models. In W. van der Linden & R. Hambleton (Eds.), *Handbook of modern item response theory* (pp. 305–322). New York: Springer-Verlag.
Embretson, S. E. (1983). Construct validity: Construct representation versus nomothetic span. *Psychological Bulletin, 93,* 179–197.
Embretson, S. E. (1998). A cognitive design system approach to generating valid tests: Application to abstract reasoning. *Psychological Methods, 3,* 300–396.
Embretson, S. E. (1999). Generating items during testing: Psychometric issues and models. *Psychometrika, 64,* 407–433.
Embretson, S. E. (2000). *Generating assembling objects items from cognitive specifications* (Final Report Subcontract No. SubPR98-11). Alexandria, VA: HumRRO.
Embretson, S. E., & Gorin, J. (2001). Improving construct validity with cognitive psychology principles. *Journal of Educational Measurement, 38,* 343–368.
Embretson, S. E., & McIntyre, H. (2008). Automatic item generation: A new method for test development. In M. Williams and P. Vogt (Eds.), *The SAGE handbook of methodological innovation.* London: SAGE.
Embretson, S. E., & Reise, S. (2000). *Item response theory for psychologists.* Mahwah, NJ: Erlbaum.
Embretson, S. E., & Wetzel, D. (1987). Component latent trait models for paragraph comprehension tests. *Applied Psychological Measurement, 11,* 175–193.
Fischer, G. H. (1973). Linear logistic test model as an instrument in educational research. *Acta Psychologica, 37,* 359–374.
Glas, C. A. W., & Van der Linden, W. (2003). Computerized adaptive testing with item cloning. *Applied Psychological Measurement, 27,* 247–261.
Glasgow, J., & Malton, A. (1999). A semantics for model-based spatial reasoning. In G. Rickheit & C. Habel (Eds.), *Mental models in discourse processing and reasoning: Advances in psychology.* Amsterdam: North-Holland/Elsevier.
Gorin, J. (2005). Manipulating processing difficulty of reading comprehension questions: The feasibility of verbal item generation. *Journal of Educational Measurement, 42,* 351–373.
Janssen, R., Schepers, J., & Peres, D. (2004). Models with item and item group predictors. In P. De Boeck & M. Wilson (Eds.), *Explanatory item response models.* New York: Springer.
Johnson, C. J., Paivio, A. U., & Clark, J. M. (1990). Spatial and verbal abilities in children's cross-modal recognition: A dual coding approach. *Canadian Journal of Psychology, 43,* 397–412.
Just, M., & Carpenter, P. (1985). Cognitive coordinate systems: Accounts of mental rotation and individual differences in spatial ability. *Psychological Review, 92,* 137–172.
Mislevy, R. J., Sheehan, K. M., & Wingersky, M. (1993). How to equate tests with little or no data. *Journal of Educational Measurement, 30,* 55–76.
Lohman, D. F. (2000). Complex information processing and intelligence. In R. J. Sternberg (Ed.), *Handbook of intelligence.* Cambridge, England: Cambridge University Press.
Messick, S. (1995). Validity of psychological assessment. *American Psychologist, 50,* 741–749.
Mumaw, R. J., & Pellegrino, J. W. (1984). Individual differences in complex spatial processing. *Journal of Educational Psychology, 76,* 920–939.
Pellegrino, J. W. & Glaser, R. (1982). Inductive reasoning. In R. J. Sternberg (Ed.), *Analyzing aptitudes for learning: Inductive reasoning.* Hillsdale, NJ: Erlbaum.
Pellegrino, J. W., Mumaw, R., & Shute, V. (1985). Analyses of spatial aptitude and expertise. In S. Embretson (Ed.), *Test design: Developments in psychology and psychometrics.* New York: Academic Press.
Peterson, N. G., Hough, L. M., Dunnette, M. D., Rosse, R. L., Houston, J. S., Toquam, J. L. & Wing, H. (1990). Project A: Specification of the predictor domain and development of new selection/classification tests. *Personnel Psychology, 43,* 247–276.

Schmeiser, C. B., & Welch, C. J. (2006). Test development. In R. L. Brennan (Ed.), *Educational measurement* (4th ed., pp. 307–353). Westport, CT: Praeger.

Shepard, R. N., & Feng, C. (1971). A chronometric study of mental paper folding. *Cognitive Psychology, 3,* 228–243.

Stout, W. (2007). Skill diagnosis using IRT-based continuous latent trait models. *Journal of Educational Measurement, 44,* 313–324.

Tinker, M. A. (1944). Speed, power, and level in the Revised Minnesota Paper Form Board Test. *Journal of Genetic Psychology, 64,* 93–97.

Wesman, A. G. (1971). Writing the test item. In R. L. Thorndike (Ed.), *Educational measurement.* Washington, DC: American Council on Education.

Index

Åberg-Bengtsson, L., 112–114
Ability model, 40–41
Abortion attitudes study, 188–196
Academic psychology, 84
Acceptance concept, 175–178, 188–196
Achievement tests, 247
Adaptive item generation, 219, 251
Aggen, S. H., 25
Aggression, verbal. *See* Verbal aggression
Ainsworth, A. T., 164
Akaike Information Criterion (AIC) index, 189, 266
Albert, J. H., 157
Alcoholics, 76–77
Analysis of variance (ANOVA) design, 229
Analytical reasoning
    on Graduate Record Exam, 206
    item generation for, 209–211
Andrich, D., 177
Anger, 242–243
Angular disparity, 203
ANOVA (analysis of variance) design, 229
AO test. *See* Assembling Objects test
Argumentation theory, 205
Armed Services Vocational Aptitude Battery (ASVAB), 112, 214, 215, 247, 253, 256–258
Arpeggio software, 53
Assembling Objects (AO) test, 247, 248, 253–271
Assessments, diagnostic. *See* Diagnostic assessments
Assessment triangles, 37
ASVAB. *See* Armed Services Vocational Aptitude Battery
Attenuation effect, 234
Attitude measurement, 175–176, 188–196
Autocorrelations, 44
Automata theory, 85
Automatic item generation, 211, 237–238, 248, 250, 271

Baker, F. B., 157
Balke, G., 106
Bamber, D., 71
Barton, M. A., 151
Batchelder, W. H., 71, 73, 75, 80–83, 90
Bayesian approaches
    to estimation, 18, 45, 62–63, 241
    to Rasch-binary multinomial processing trees, 90–91
    to statistical computing, 156–158

Bayesian information criterion (BIC), 189
Bejar, I. I., 2, 202, 203, 219, 248
Bennett, R. E., 203
Beta-binary multinomial processing trees (beta-BMPTs), 90
Bias, 21, 76
BIC (Bayesian information criterion), 189
Binary multinomial processing tree (BMPT) models, 78–82, 86, 89–90
Birenbaum, M., 38
Bock, R. D., 238, 240–241
Bollen, K. A., 101–103
Bookmark procedure, 241–242
Boring, E. G., 84, 220
Boston Naming Test, 83
Bradlow, E. T., 138
Brain damage, 76
Braun, H., 2
Broad visual perception, 111
BRUGS, 157
BUGS, 157
Burt, C., 98

Calibration, of items, 2
Carlstedt, B., 117
Carpenter, P. A., 212
Carroll, J. B., 111
Carstensen, C. H., 30
Casella, G., 157
Cattell, R. B., 111
Chain plots, 44
Choi, H., 214
Chosak-Reiter, J., 83
Class dependency, 25–26
Classical test theory (CTT), 3, 19
Class memberships, 23, 26
Clustering, 73–76
Coan, R. W., 98
Cognitive complexity, 250, 257
Cognitive design systems approach, 247–271
    advantages of, 250–251
    cognitive psychometric models, 251–253
    to measuring spatial ability, 253–271
    steps in, 248–250
Cognitive modeling, 83–89. *See also* Multinomial processing tree models
    and history of psychology, 84–85
    item response theory vs., 85–89
Cognitive psychometric models, 251–253
Cognitive psychometrics, 71

Colémont, A., 241
College Board, 48, 58
Combination dependencies, 137
Compensatory multiple classification latent class models, 42
Compensatory skill interaction, 50
Complexity
　cognitive, 250, 257
　item, 248
Comprehension, 216
Computational rules, 79
Computerized Adaptive Testing (H. Wainer), 1
Confirmation, 256, 258, 260–263, 266, 269–270
Confirmation bias, 76
Confusion matrices, 72
Congeneric test theory, 107
Conjunctive multiple classification latent class models (MCLCMs), 42
Conjunctive skill interaction, 50
Consortium to Establish a Registry for Alzheimer's Disease, 83
Construct representation, 204, 227–228, 242–243
Construct validation research, 227
Construct validity, 102, 204
Content validity, 102
Convergence checking, 43–44, 63
Cook-Medley Hostility Scale of MMPI, 126–127
Correlational disciplines, 1
Criterion validity, 102
Cronbach, L. J., 3, 4, 204, 205, 220, 247
Crystallized intelligence, 111, 211
CTT. *See* Classical test theory
Cureton, E. E., 100–101

Darwin, Charles, 84
Data analysis models, 71
De Boeck, P., 4, 27, 136, 137, 208, 228, 237
De Corte, E., 241
Densities, normal, 16–18
Design matrices, 27–28
Developmental processes, 26
Dey, D. K., 156
Diagnostic and Statistical Manual of Mental Disorders (DSM–IV–TR), 60
Diagnostic assessments, 35–67
　attributes in, 38–39
　development/analysis of tasks in, 39–40
　educational measurement example, 49–60
　estimation of model parameters in, 42–43
　evaluation of results from, 43–46
　and evidence-centered design paradigm, 37
　psychological assessment example, 60–66
　psychometric model for, 40–42
　purpose of, 37–38
　systems for scoring/reporting of, 47–48
　terminology of, 36
Diagnostic models, 27–28
Diagrams, Tables, and Maps (DTM) test, 112–114
DiBello, L. V., 28, 45
Dick, M. B., 83
Differential validity, 26
Difficulty models, 212–213
Dimension-dependent effects, 137
DINA model, 42, 43, 62
DINO model, 42, 43, 62, 65, 66
Disagree-agree responses, 178
Disjunctive multiple classification latent class models, 42
Domain-referenced testing, 237–242
Donoghue, J. R., 188
Draney, K., 26
Drasgow, F., 131, 203
Drug testing, 177
DTM (Diagrams, Tables, and Maps) test, 112–114
Dyslexia, 83

EAP (expected a posteriori) score, 135
ECD. *See* Evidence-centered design
Educational measurement, 49–60
Educational Measurement, 98
Educational Testing Service (ETS), 45, 49, 151, 210, 219
ELL (LanguEdge English Language Learning) assessment, 49
EM algorithm. *See* Expectation-maximization algorithm
Embretson, S. E., 204–205, 212–214, 217, 227, 255–257, 270–271
Empirical item response functions (ERFs), 154
Empirical keying, 204
EMstats, 46
Encoding, 214, 255, 258, 260–265, 269
End of test factor, 113–116
Engelhard, G., 1
English psychology, 84–85
Enright, M. K., 217
Equating, 47
ERFs (empirical item response functions), 154
Estes, W. K., 87
Estimated posterior distribution, 44
Estimation
　in educational measurement example, 53–58
　in MIXUM, 180–188

of model parameters in diagnostic
    assessments, 42–43
of normal mixture models, 18
point and interval parameter, 81, 82
in psychological assessment example, 63
with random-effects linear logistic test
    model, 235–237
of skill masteries using subscore, 48
ETS. *See* Educational Testing Service
Everson, H. T., 26
Evidence-centered design (ECD), 37, 205
Evolution, 84
Examinees, 36, 46
Expectation–maximization (EM) algorithm,
    18, 43–44, 81–82, 180–186, 192
Expected a posteriori (EAP) score, 135
Expected value functions, 177
Experimental disciplines, 1
Explanatory Item Response Models
    (P. De Boeck and M. Wilson), 2
*The Expression of Emotions in Man and
    Animals* (Charles Darwin), 84
External validity
    defined, 36
    in psychological assessment example,
        65–66
Eyewitness memory, 76

Factor analysis, 100–101
Factorial perception experiments, 88
Fairon, C., 211
Falsification, 256, 258, 260–264, 269, 270
Feasel, K., 60
Fern, T., 214
Figural abstract reasoning, 213
Figural reasoning, 211–213
FIML estimation. *See* Full-information
    maximum likelihood estimation
Finite state templates, 211
Fischer, G. H., 1
Fisher, Roland, 85
Fisher information matrix, 81
FLMP (fuzzy logic model of perception), 88–89
Fluid intelligence, 111, 211–212, 270
Foot-length measures example, 12–15
Formann, A. K., 25, 30
Four-parameter logistic (4PLM) model
    application of, 147
    and Gibbs Sampler, 157–159
    and modeling MMPI data, 150–151
    in psychometric assessment of low self-
        esteem, 159–169
    psychometric differences with, 168–169
Fredericksen, N. A., 2
Free-recall memory, 73–76
Full-information maximum likelihood
    (FIML) estimation, 126, 128, 140

Fusion model system, 52
Fuzzy logic model of perception (FLMP),
    88–89

G^2 LD index, 128
Galton, Sir Francis, 84–85
Gambling, 60–66
Gambling Research Instrument (GRI), 60, 65
Game theory, 85
GDM (general diagnostic model), 28–30
Gelman, 44
Gender differences, in test performance, 113
General Condorcet model, 90
General diagnostic model (GDM), 28–30
General DTM factor, 113–116
Genetics, 72
George, E. I., 157
German experimental psychology, 84, 85
Gibbons, R. D., 140
Gibbs Sampler, 157–159, 164, 235, 236
Glas, C. A. W., 237, 238
Glaser, R., 204–205
GLIMMIX macro, 235, 242
Goodness-of-fit, 81, 82
Gorin, J., 255–257
Gorin, J. S., 214
Gorsuch, R. L., 105
Gosset, William, 85
Graduate Record Examination (GRE),
    206–209, 211, 214–215, 217–219
Graduate school, 206
Graf, E. A., 219
GRI. *See* Gambling Research Instrument
Gustafsson, J. E., 106, 108, 109, 111–112,
    117, 119

Haberman, S. J., 25, 28, 30
Hambleton, R. K., 151
Hanson, B. A., 238
Harrison, D. A., 131
Haviland, M. G., 164
Hedeker, D. R., 140
Henson, R. A., 45, 48, 60, 62, 63, 65
Heterogeneous instruments, 98, 108
Hidden structure, 15
Hierarchical factor model, 106
Hierarchical item response theory model,
    239–240, 251–253
Hierarchical modeling approaches, 104–110
Hierarchical regression, 256, 260
Higher education, 206
Higher order (HO) model, 104–107
Hill, C. D., 129–131
Hindsight bias, 76
Holzman, G. B., 201
HO (higher order) model, 104–107
Homogeneous tests, 108, 109

Horn, J. L., 111, 211–212
Hoskens, M., 136, 137
Hu, X., 73, 80, 81, 90
Humphreys, L. G., 97
HYBRID model, 26
Hypothesis testing, 81

IMstats, 46, 57
Independent and identically distributed (i.i.d.) observations, 78
Indicator matrices, 39–40
Individual differences
    in aggregated data, 87
    in correlational discipline, 1
    in history of psychology, 85
    in memory study, 77–78
    in verbal aggression, 228
Inferential reasoning, 206
Information pooling, 76
Information sciences, 85
Information theory, 85
Intelligence, 97, 108, 111, 211–212, 270
Internal consistency, 3, 107
Internal validity
    defined, 46
    in educational measurement example, 57, 58
IRFs. *See* Item response functions
IRT. *See* Item response theory
IRT models. *See* Item response theory models
Isomorphs, 203, 218
Item banking, 241, 250
Item complexity, 248
Item design, 227–231, 250
Item extremity, 166–167
Item generation, 201–221, 250
    for analytical reasoning, 209–211
    evaluating progress in, 202–203
    for figural reasoning, 211–213
    for logical reasoning, 206–209
    for mathematics, 215–220
    as Popperian mechanism, 202
    structural modeling approach to, 247–248
    validity in, 204–206
    for verbal comprehension, 213–215
Item master, 36
Item modeling, 201–202
Item performance, 249
Item response data, 19–22
Item response functions (IRFs)
    and diagnostic assessments, 36, 40–42
    for standard item response models, 148–149
Item response probabilities, 2–3
Item response theory (IRT). *See also* Mixture distribution item response theory
    cognitive memory modeling vs., 85–89
    development of, 1
    and diagnostic assessments, 35
    for disentangling constructs, 123, 126, 130–136, 138, 142–143
    multidimensional, 27–28
    and research on psychological constructs, 2
Item response theory-based parametric latent class models, 36, 47, 48, 60
Item response theory (IRT) models, 25–30, 147–169
    advantages of, 163–165
    applications, 26–27
    cognitive psychometric models, 251–253, 263
    and diagnostic models, 27–28
    differences with 4PLM model, 168–169
    difficulty with, 213
    for estimation of domain scores, 238–239
    with interaction parameters, 136–140
    mixture general diagnostic model, 28–30
    and MMPI–A LSE Scale, 152–154, 159–167
    modeling MMPI data with, 150–152
    psychometric models, 72
    rest score regressions in, 154–156
    standard item response models, 148–150
    unfolding, 176–178
    use of Gibbs Sampler in, 157–159
Item response theory parameters, 249–250

Jang, E. E., 49, 50, 53, 55–58
Janssen, R., 234, 235, 237, 241
Johnson-Laird, P. N., 206, 208
Jones, L., 60
Jorgensen, R., 128
Journal of Mathematical Psychology, 84
Junker, B., 36
Junker, B. W., 28

Kane, M. T., 205, 206
Karabatsos, G., 90
Kelderman, H., 12, 25
Klauer, K. C., 90
Klein, M., 38
Knapp, B. R., 71
Knoors, E., 241
Knowledge factor (Knowl), 115–117
Kolen, M. J., 238–239
Kubarych, T. S., 25

LaDuca, A., 201
Lag, 75
Language testing, 29
LanguEdge English Language Learning (ELL) assessment, 49

Latent class analysis (LCA)
    in mixtures of distribution for discrete
        observed variables, 22–24
    in skills diagnosis, 41
Latent parameters, 78
Latent structure analysis, 124
Latent trait theory, 124
Latent variables, 19, 123–124
Laughlin, J. E., 188
Lazarsfeld, P. F., 123–124, 126, 140
LCA. *See* Latent class analysis
LD. *See* Local dependence
LD indices, 128
Lee, W. C., 241
Letter identification, 76
Likert-type response scales, 128, 129
Linear logistic test model (LLTM). *See also*
        Random-effects linear logistics test
        model
    as diagnostic model, 28
    estimation with, 266–267, 269
    and item design, 232
    item difficulty in, 252
    random-effects linear logistic test model
        vs., 234–237
    standard errors in, 263
Lisrel 8, 129
LLTM. *See* Linear logistic test model
LLTM-R. *See* Random-effects linear logistic
        test model
Local dependence (LD), 125–143
    detection of, 126–132
    examples, 142
    modeling tests with, 132
    multidimensional models for, 140–141
    parametric models for, 136–140
    and redefining item responses, 132–136
Local independence, 23, 125
Located latent class models, 24–25
Loevinger, J., 204, 205
Logical reasoning, 206–209
LOGIST, 132
Lohman, D. F., 253
Lord, F. M., 151
Lucke, J. F., 98, 107
Luecht, R., 203
Luo, G., 176, 177

Macready, G. B., 12, 25
Manifold, V., 71
Marginal maximum likelihood (MML), 25,
    187
Marginal maximum likelihood estimation
    (MMLE), 43
Markov chain Monte Carlo (MCMC) methods,
    18, 43, 44, 56, 63, 65, 140, 141, 157, 236
Mastery, 47, 55, 57, 240, 241

Mathematical word problems, 253
Mathematics
    item generation for, 215–220
    skills diagnoses of, 41–42
Mathematics Test Creation Assistant
    (MTCA), 218, 219
Maximum likelihood estimates (MLEs), 76
McDonald, R. P., 107, 110
McIntyre, H., 270–271
MCLCMs (multiple classification latent
    class models), 42
MCMC methods. *See* Markov chain Monte
    Carlo methods
Mdltm, 29
Meehl, P. E., 204, 220
Mehta, P. D., 25
Memory
    in cognitive modeling, 85–89
    free-recall, 73–76
    recall, 82–83
Mental model theory, 208, 254
Mental rotation tests, 203
Messick, S., 118, 250
Meulders, M., 237
Minnesota Multiphasic Personality Inventory
    (MMPI), 126–127, 150–152
Minnesota Multiphasic Personality
    Inventory—Adolescent (MMPI–A),
    152–156, 159–167
Minnesota Paper Form Board, 254
MIRT. *See* Multidimensional item response
    theory
MIs (modification indices), 128–129
Mislevy, R. J., 2, 12, 25, 237
Mixed number subtraction, 11
Mixed Unfolding Model (MIXUM), 177–196
    attitudes toward abortion example,
        188–196
    elements in, 178–179
    expected value functions under, 177
    flexibility of, 196
    parameter estimation, 179–188
Mixture distribution item response theory,
    11–30
    foot length example, 12–15
    mixtures of continuous random
        variables, 15–18
    mixtures of distributions for discrete
        observed variables, 18–25
    models, 25–30
Mixture general diagnostic model, 28–30
Mixtures of continuous random variables,
    15–18
Mixtures of distributions for discrete
    observed variables, 18–25
    item response data, 19–22
    latent class analysis, 22–24
    located latent class models, 24–25

MLEs (maximum likelihood estimates), 76
MML. *See* Marginal maximum likelihood
MMPI. *See* Minnesota Multiphasic Personality Inventory
MMPI–A. *See* Minnesota Multiphasic Personality Inventory—Adolescent
Modeling
  cognitive, 83–89
  item, 201–202
  psychometric, 84–91
  regression, 250
  structural, 248
Modification indices (MIs), 128–129
Molenaar, I. V., 1
Monotonicity, 21, 24
Mooney, J. A., 126
Morley, M., 219
MPT models. *See* Multinomial processing tree models
MTCA (Mathematics Test Creation Assistant), 218, 219
Mullen, K., 241
Multidimensional item response theory (MIRT), 27–28, 138, 140–141
Multidimensional models, 140–141
Multilingual tests, 220
Multinomial processing tree (MPT) models, 71–83
  for clustering in free-recall memory, 73–76
  for psychological assessment, 82–83
  psychometric modeling concepts in, 89–91
  for special populations, 76–78
  structure of, 72–73
  terminology, 78–82
Multiple-choice tasks, 5
Multiple classification latent class models (MCLCMs), 42
Multiple regression analysis, 97–98
Multiple-skill tasks, 39

National Assessment of Educational Progress (NAEP), 30, 241
National Assessment of Mathematics in Primary Education, 241
National assessments, 240–242
National Council of Teachers of Mathematics, 217
Neale, M. C., 25
Nested factor (NF) model, 106–107, 109, 110, 115, 117
Newstead, S. E., 210
Nicewander, W. A., 238–239
NIDA model, 42
Nomological nets, 205
Nomothetic span, 204, 227–228
Nomothetic theories of intelligence, 211
Nonsymmetric content ambiguity, 167

Objective Measurement: Theory Into Practice (M. Wilson and G. Engelhard), 3
Object perception, 76
Observable categories, 78
Omission, of items, 132
One-parameter logistic model (1PLM), 148–150
Operations research, 85
Order dependencies, 137
Orthogonal factors, 106

Pair-clustering model, 74–76
Paired comparison model, 88
Paired-comparison scaling models, 71–72
Parameter estimation, 179–188
Parameter recovery, 188
Parameters
  and diagnostic assessments, 42–45
  item response theory, 249–250
  latent, 78
  of memory models, 87
Parametric models, 136–140
Parametric stochastic models, 86
Parsons, C. K., 131
Pathological gambling, 60–66
Pearson, K., 14, 85
PedsQL™ Physical Functioning Scale, 130–132
PedsQL™ Social Functioning Scale, 129
Person parameter estimation, 187–188
Phillips, G. A., 90
Plymouth project, 211
Pommerich, M., 238
Popper, K. R., 202
Popperian mechanisms, 202
Population information, 18
Posterior predictive model (PPM), 45
Posterior probability of mastery (ppom), 52
Preliminary SAT/National Merit Scholarship Qualifying Test (PSAT/NMSQT), 48, 58
Proactive interference, 76
Probability of pathological gambling (PPG), 63, 66
Process dissociation procedure, 76
Proficiency scaling, 47
Project A (U.S. Army), 247
Propositional density, 214
Propositional reasoning, 76
PSAT/NMSQT (Preliminary SAT/National Merit Scholarship Qualifying Test), 3, 48
Psychological assessment, 60–66, 82–83
Psychological measurement, 97–119
  in correlational discipline, 1
  hierarchical modeling approaches to, 104–110

historical perspective on, 99–101
psychometric concepts in, 101–104
Swedish Scholastic Aptitude Test
     example, 110–118
unidimensionality in, 97–99
Psychology
  academic, 84
  history of, 84–85
Psychometric concepts, 101–104
Psychometric model
  for diagnostic assessments, 40–42
  in educational measurement example, 52
  in psychological assessment example, 62
Psychometric modeling
  and history of psychology, 84–85
  item response theory in, 85–89
  for measurement, 1
  in multinomial processing tree models, 89–91
Psychometrics, 71, 85
Psychometric Society, 83–84
Psychometrika, 84
Public domain scores, 240–241

Q_3 statistic, 128
Q-matrices, 27–29, 40, 44–45, 50, 51, 55, 61
Quantitative factor (Quant), 113–117

Random-effects linear logistic test model (LLTM-R), 231–244
  applications of, 237–243
  and construction representation, 242–243
  estimation in, 235–237
  interpretation of, 234
  Rasch model in, 231–232
  related models, 237
Rasch-binary multinomial processing trees, 90
Rasch model
  estimation with, 266–267
  probability in, 20–22, 251
  in random-effects linear logistic test model, 231–233
  and Saltus model, 26–27
  two-parameter, 88, 89
Rasch Models (G. H. Fischer and I. V. Molenaar), 1
Raven Progressive Test, 119, 212
Reading comprehension, 229–230
Reading skills, 111
Reasoning
  analytical, 206, 209–211
  figural, 211–213
  inferential, 206
  logical, 206–209
  propositional, 76
Reasoning skills, 111

Recent Victimization Scale, 126, 134
Reckase, M. D., 131
Recursive tree regression methods, 211
Referent generality, 98, 104, 108
Regression analysis, 97–98
Regression design, 229
Regression modeling, 250
Reise, S. P., 164
Reliability
  in congeneric test theory, 107
  estimation of, 45–46, 56, 57
  measures of, 109–110
  as psychometric concept, 101–103
Reparameterized unified model (RUM), 42, 43, 47, 49, 52
Reporting, 47–48
Residual-based statistics, 128
Response decision, 214
Response inhibition, 228
Response probabilities, 23
Rest score regressions, 154–156
Retrieval (memory), 76–77, 82–83
Retroactive interference, 76
Retrofitting, 38
Retrospective strategy, 218
Riefer, D. M., 71, 73, 75–77, 82
Rijmen, F., 27, 208
Riley, M. S., 216
Roberts, J. S., 188
Roberts, R. D., 112
Rost, J., 12, 25, 26–27, 30
Rotation tasks, 253–254
Roussos, L. A., 28, 45, 47
Rubin, 44
Rule space approach, 27
Rule theories, 208
RUM. *See* Reparameterized unified model
Rupp, A. A., 156, 214

Saltus model, 26
Schiz, 167
Schizophrenia, 76–77, 83
Schmid and Leiman transformation, 105, 107
Schmitt, J. E., 25, 30
Schneider's First Rank symptoms, 167
Scholastic Aptitude Test, 217, 249
Schulz, E. M., 238–239, 241
Score interpretations, 251
Score Report Plus (College Board), 48
Score reports, 48, 58, 66
Scoring, 47–48
SEB (Swedish Enlistment Battery), 117, 118
Self-esteem, 153–159, 163–166
Semantic structure (in math problems), 216
Seminonparametric estimation, 25
SEM (structural equation modeling) software, 128

Shankle, W. R., 83
Sheehan, K. M., 217
Signal detection models, 71
Sijtsma, K., 28
Sinharay, S., 45
Skill profiles, 36
Skills diagnosis, 35–48
    assessment purpose in, 37–38
    description of attribute space in, 38–39
    development/analysis of tasks in, 39–40
    specification of psychometric model in, 40–42
Skill variables, 22
Smith, Jared, 90
Social cognition, 76
Social judgment theory, 175–177
Social networks, 76
Society for Mathematical Psychology, 83–84
Software
    for analyzing MPT models, 82
    Arpeggio, 53
    for structural equation modeling, 128
SOGS (South Oaks Gambling Screen), 60
SourceFinder, 215
Source of information, 76
South Oaks Gambling Screen (SOGS), 60, 65
Spatial ability, 253–271
Spearman, Charles, 85, 91
Special populations, 76–78
Speech perception, 76
Stahl, C., 90
Standard setting, 47, 240, 241
Standiford, S., 38
Staples, W. I., 201
State testing programs, 37
Statistical genetics, 72
Statistical inference, 81
Statistical theory, 85
Statistics, 85
Steinberg, L., 125, 126, 128, 132, 134, 135
Stochastic processes, 85, 86
Storage (memory), 76–77, 82–83
Stout, W., 28, 45
Strong Vocational Inventory Blank (SVIB), 204
Structural equation modeling (SEM) software, 128
Structural modeling, 248
Styles, I., 177
Substantive validity, 243
Sufficiency, 21
Suicidal ideation, 167
SVIB (Strong Vocational Inventory Blank), 204
Swaminathan, H., 151
Swedish Enlistment Battery (SEB), 117, 118

Swedish Scholastic Aptitude Test (SweSAT), 110–119
    combination of, with other tests, 117–118
    development of, 110–111
    research on, 111–112
    sources of variance in diagrams, tables, and maps test, 112–114
    sources of variance in scores, 114–116
Systematic bias, 21

Tatsuoka, K. K., 12, 38, 46, 48
Tatsuoka, M. M., 46
Taylor expansion, 235
Templeton, B., 201
Templin, J. L., 45, 47, 48, 60, 62, 63, 65
Testable assumptions, 22
Test design, 22
Testfact, 127, 140
Test Information Function (TIF), 161
Testlet-based analysis, 133–135
Test of English as a Foreign Language (TOEFL), 45, 214, 215
Test-taking training, 25
Test Theory for a New Generation of Tests (N. A. Fredericksen, R. J. Mislevy, and I. I. Bejar), 2
Test Validity (H. Wainer and H. Braun), 2
Text representation, 214
Theoretical framework, 248–250, 253–271
Thissen, D., 125, 126, 128, 132, 134, 135, 140, 238
Thorndike, R. L., 99–101, 119
Three-parameter logistic model (3PLM), 149–154, 161–162, 168–169, 252, 257
Three-stratum model, 111
Thurstone, L. L., 104
TIF (Test Information Function), 161
TOEFL. *See* Test of English as a Foreign Language
Training, test-taking, 25
Transfer, 216
Tree architecture, 78–79
Tuerlinckx, F., 237
Two-parameter logistic-constrained model, 252, 266, 269, 270
Two-parameter logistic model (2PLM), 149–150, 168, 169, 252, 263, 266–267
Two-parameter Rasch model, 88
Tyler, R. W., 204

Unidimensionality, 97–99
U.S. Army, 247

Validity
    differential, 26
    estimation of, 46, 57, 58
    external, 36, 65–66

    in item generation, 204–206
    measures of, 109–110
    as psychometric concept, 102–103
    substantive, 243
    types of, 227
    and variance in test scores, 100
Van der Linden, W., 237, 238
Van Nijlen, D., 241
Vansteelandt, K., 228
Variance, 99–102, 108, 110, 112–116
Verbal aggression, 228–229, 242–243
Verbal comprehension, 213–215
Verhelst, N. D., 12, 25
Vermunt, J. K., 30
Verschaffel, L., 241
Violence, 134
Visual perception, 111
Visual search tasks, 254
Vocabulary, 111
von Davier, M., 12, 26–30, 45

Wainer, H., 1, 2, 138
Wang, X., 138
Wedman, I., 111–112
Weschler test series, 97
Westerlund, A., 111–112
Wetzel, D., 214
Williamson, D. M., 211
Wilson, M., 1, 2, 26, 228
Wolfe, J. H., 17
Wundt, Wilhelm, 84

Xu, X., 29, 30

Yamamoto, K., 26, 28, 30
Yang, Y., 206, 208
Yen, W. M., 131
Yung, Y. F., 139

Zimowski, M. F., 238
Zumbo, B. D., 156

About the Editor

Susan E. Embretson, PhD, is a professor of psychology at the Georgia Institute of Technology in Atlanta. She received her doctoral degree in psychology from the University of Minnesota in 1973 and was a professor at the University of Kansas from 1974 until 2004. Dr. Embretson's research focuses on modern psychometric methods, particularly on the integration of cognitive theory into psychometric models and test design. Most recently, she has been exploring how test items can be automatically generated by artificial intelligence to target levels and cognitive sources of difficulty to optimally measure each individual examinee during testing; the measurement areas have included fluid reasoning, spatial ability, mathematical reasoning, and verbal comprehension. Dr. Embretson was awarded the Distinguished Scientific Contribution Award from the American Psychological Association's (APA's) Division of Evaluation, Measurement, and Statistics in 2001, and the Technical and Scientific Contribution Award from the National Council on Measurement in Education during 1994 to 1996. She also received the Palmer O. Johnson Award (with Ken Doyle) from the American Educational Research Association in 1976. She has served as president of APA's Division of Evaluation, Measurement, and Statistics (1990–1991), the Society for Multivariate Experimental Psychology (1997–1998), and the Psychometric Society (1998–1999).